Frommer's®

SO-AHI-811

Edinburgh & Glasgow
2nd Edition

by Barry Shelby

Here's what the critics say about Frommer's:

"Amazingly easy to use. Very portable, very complete."

—Booklist

"Detailed, accurate, and easy-to-read information for all price ranges."
—Glamour Magazine

"Hotel information is close to encyclopedic."

—Des Moines Sunday Register

"Frommer's Guides have a way of giving you a real feel for a place."
—Knight Ridder Newspapers

Wiley Publishing, Inc.

About the Author

Barry Shelby was born in 1960 in Berkeley, California, and he graduated from the University of California in 1982. He later received a master's degree in journalism from Northwestern University in Illinois. For 13 years, he was an editor at *World Press Review* magazine in Manhattan. Since moving to Scotland in 1997, he has been a castle caretaker on the Clyde Coast, a "temp" with the national railway company, and a freelance contributor to newspapers and magazines, including the *Guardian*, the *Glasgow Herald*, and *The List*. He is married to a Scot and lives in Glasgow's East End.

Published by:

Wiley Publishing, Inc.

111 River St.
Hoboken, NJ 07030-5774

ISBN: 978-0-470-05531-1

Editor: Marc Nadeau
Production Editor: Suzanna R. Thompson
Cartographer: Anton Crane
Photo Editor: Richard Fox
Anniversary Logo Design: Richard Pacifico
Production by Wiley Indianapolis Composition Services

Front cover photo: Diners seated at outdoor cafe along Edinburgh's Miracle Mile
Back cover photo: Edinburgh shop window

For information on our other products and services or to obtain technical support, please contact our Customer Care Department within the U.S. at 800/762-2974, outside the U.S. at 317/572-3993 or fax 317/572-4002.

Wiley also publishes its books in a variety of electronic formats. Some content that appears in print may not be available in electronic formats.

Manufactured in the United States of America

5   4   3   2   1

Contents

List of Maps   vii

What's New in Edinburgh & Glasgow   1

1   The Best of Edinburgh & Glasgow   3

1 Frommer's Favorite Edinburgh &
Glasgow Experiences 3

2 Best Castle & Palace 5

3 Best Cathedral & Churches 5

4 Best Galleries & Museums 6

5 Best in Great Glasgow
Architecture .7

6 Best Accommodations 7

7 Best Dining Bets 8

8 The Best Bars & Pubs 9

2   Planning Your Trip to Edinburgh & Glasgow   10

1 Visitor Information 10

Pre-Departure Checklist 11

2 Entry Requirements & Customs 14

3 Money 15

4 When to Go 17

*Edinburgh & Glasgow Calendar
of Events* 18

5 Travel Insurance 20

6 Health & Safety 21

7 Specialized Travel Resources 23

8 Planning Your Trip Online 25

9 The 21st-Century Traveler 26

10 Getting There 27

11 Packages for the Independent
Traveler 30

Ask Before You Go 30

12 Escorted General-Interest Tours 31

13 Tips on Accommodations 31

14 Recommended Books & Films 33

3   Suggested Edinburgh & Glasgow Itineraries   35

1 Edinburgh in 3 Days 35

2 Glasgow in 3 Days 37

3 Edinburgh & Side Trips in 1 Week 37

4 Glasgow & Side Trips in 1 Week 39

4   Getting to Know Edinburgh   42

1 Essentials 43

*Edinburgh Neighborhoods
in Brief* 48

Finding an Address 49

2 Getting Around 49

Fast Facts: Edinburgh 51

5 Where to Stay in Edinburgh   54

1 New Town .55
    Family-Friendly Hotels 60
2 Old Town .60

3 West End .63
4 Southside .64
5 Leith & North of New Town 65

6 Where to Dine in Edinburgh   67

1 Restaurants by Cuisine 68
2 New Town & West End 69
    Family-Friendly Fare 74
3 Old Town .75

4 Southside .77
5 Leith 78
6 Picnic Fare 80

7 Exploring Edinburgh   81

    Suggested intineraries 81
1 Some Top Attractions 84
    Frommer's Favorite Edinburgh
    Experiences 85
2 Additional Attractions 91
    The Father of Dr. Jekyll &
    Mr. Hyde .92

    Britannia: The Royal Yacht 93
3 Gardens & Parks 95
4 Organized Tours 96
5 Special Events & Festivals 96
6 Sports & Outdoor Activities 97

8 Edinburgh Strolls   99

    Walking Tour 1: The Royal Mile 99
    Walking Tour 2: South of the
    Royal Mile 104

    Walking Tour 3: New Town 107
    Walking tour 4: Leith 112

9 Edinburgh Shopping   116

1 The Shopping Scene 116
2 Shopping A to Z 117

    Tracing Your Ancestral Roots 122

10 Edinburgh After Dark   124

1 The Performing Arts 124
2 The Club & Music Scene 128
3 Pubs & Bars 129

4 Gay & Lesbian Edinburgh 132
5 Cinema .132

11 Side Trips from Edinburgh   134

1 Linlithgow & West Lothian 134

2 North Berwick & East Lothian 137

*Guided Minitours
from Edinburgh* 140

3 South of the City & the Borders . . .140

*Sir Walter Scott: Inventor
of Historical Novels* 142

4 North of Edinburgh to Fife 143

Hitting the Links 145

12 Getting to Know Glasgow   149

1 Essentials 150

*Glasgow Neighborhoods
in Brief* 156

2 Getting Around 158

Fast Facts: Glasgow 160

13 Where to Stay in Glasgow   163

1 Merchant City & East End 163

2 Commercial Center 167

3 The West End 169

Family-Friendly Hotels 171

14 Where to Dine in Glasgow   174

1 Restaurants by Cuisine 175

2 Merchant City 178

3 Glasgow Commercial Center 180

Family-Friendly Fare 180

Tea for Two 184

4 The West End 184

5 The Southside 187

6 Picnic Fare 188

15 Exploring Glasgow   189

Suggested Itineraries 192

1 Some Top Attractions 192

*Frommer's Favorite Glasgow
Experiences* 193

2 Additional Attractions 197

*Ahead of His Time: Charles
Rennie Mackintosh* 198

*Unappreciated Genius: Alexander
"Greek" Thomson* 200

3 Gardens & Parks 200

4 Organized Tours 201

5 Some Special Events 202

6 Sports & Outdoor Activities 203

16 Glasgow City Strolls   205

*Walking Tour 1: The Merchant
City & the East End* 205

*Walking Tour 2: The Commercial
Center* 209

Walking Tour 3: The West End 213

Walking Tour 4 : The Southside . . .217

17 Glasgow Shopping   221

1 The Shopping Scene 221   **2** Shopping A to Z 224

18 Glasgow After Dark   229

1 The Performing Arts 229   **4** Gay & Lesbian Glasgow 238

2 The Club & Music Scene 234   **5** Cinema 239

3 Bars & Pubs 236

19 Side Trips from Glasgow   240

1 Ayrshire & "Burns Country" 240   **4** West Coast Highlights 249

Burns: Poet, Humanitarian &
Skirt Chaser 245

2 Culzean 246

Arran: "Scotland in Miniature" 247

3 Golfing Heavens: Troon &
Turnberry .247

Gigha: The "Good Isle" 251

5 Loch Lomond 252

Hiking the West Highland Way 253

6 Stirling & The Trossachs 254

7 The Clyde Valley 255

Appendix: Edinburgh & Glasgow in Depth   257

1 History 101 257   **2** A Portrait of the Scots 261

Index   263

List of Maps

Scotland   12

Edinburgh in 3 Days   36

Glasgow in 3 Days   38

Edinburgh & Side Trips in 1 Week   39

Glasgow & Side Trips in 1 Week   40

Greater Edinburgh   43

Edinburgh Neighborhoods   46

Edinburgh Accommodations   56

Edinburgh Dining   70

Edinburgh Attractions   82

Walking Tour: Old Town & The Royal Mile   101

Walking Tour: South of the Royal Mile   105

Walking Tour: New Town   109

Walking Tour: Leith   113

Edinburgh Shopping   118

Edinburgh After Dark   126

Side Trips From Edinburgh   135

Greater Glasgow   151

Glasgow Neighborhoods   154

Glasgow Underground   159

Glasgow Accommodations   164

Glasgow Dining   176

Glasgow Attractions   190

Walking Tour: The Merchant City & the East End   207

Walking Tour: The Commercial Center   211

Walking Tour: The West End   215

Walking Tour: The Southside   219

Glasgow Shopping   222

Glasgow After Dark   230

Side Trips from Glasgow   241

An Invitation to the Reader

In researching this book, we discovered many wonderful places—hotels, restaurants, shops, and more. We're sure you'll find others. Please tell us about them, so we can share the information with your fellow travelers in upcoming editions. If you were disappointed with a recommendation, we'd love to know that, too. Please write to:

Frommer's Edinburgh & Glasgow, 2nd Edition
Wiley Publishing, Inc. • 111 River St. • Hoboken, NJ 07030-5774

An Additional Note

Please be advised that travel information is subject to change at any time—and this is especially true of prices. We therefore suggest that you write or call ahead for confirmation when making your travel plans. The authors, editors, and publisher cannot be held responsible for the experiences of readers while traveling. Your safety is important to us, however, so we encourage you to stay alert and be aware of your surroundings. Keep a close eye on cameras, purses, and wallets, all favorite targets of thieves and pickpockets.

Other Great Guides for Your Trip:

Frommer's Scotland

Scotland For Dummies

Frommer's Great Britain

Frommer's Britain's Best-Loved Driving Tours

Frommer's European Cruises & Ports of Call

Frommer's Star Ratings, Icons & Abbreviations

Every hotel, restaurant, and attraction listing in this guide has been ranked for quality, value, service, amenities, and special features using a **star-rating system.** In country, state, and regional guides, we also rate towns and regions to help you narrow down your choices and budget your time accordingly. Hotels and restaurants are rated on a scale of zero (recommended) to three stars (exceptional). Attractions, shopping, nightlife, towns, and regions are rated according to the following scale: zero stars (recommended), one star (highly recommended), two stars (very highly recommended), and three stars (must-see).

In addition to the star-rating system, we also use **seven feature icons** that point you to the great deals, in-the-know advice, and unique experiences that separate travelers from tourists. Throughout the book, look for:

Finds	Special finds—those places only insiders know about
Fun Fact	Fun facts—details that make travelers more informed and their trips more fun
Kids	Best bets for kids and advice for the whole family
Moments	Special moments—those experiences that memories are made of
Overrated	Places or experiences not worth your time or money
Tips	Insider tips—great ways to save time and money
Value	Great values—where to get the best deals

The following **abbreviations** are used for credit cards:

AE	American Express	DISC	Discover	V	Visa
DC	Diners Club	MC	MasterCard		

Frommers.com

Now that you have this guidebook to help you plan a great trip, visit our website at **www.frommers.com** for additional travel information on more than 3,500 destinations. We update features regularly to give you instant access to the most current trip-planning information available. At Frommers.com, you'll find scoops on the best airfares, lodging rates, and car rental bargains. You can even book your travel online through our reliable travel booking partners. Other popular features include:

- Online updates of our most popular guidebooks
- Vacation sweepstakes and contest giveaways
- Newsletters highlighting the hottest travel trends
- Online travel message boards with featured travel discussions

What's New in Edinburgh & Glasgow

Edinburgh and Glasgow are reasonably energetic cities, certainly the most dynamic in Scotland, and among the most lively and sophisticated outside of London in the entire U.K. Many Britons are impressed by how both Edinburgh and Glasgow feel less provincial than bigger cities in England.

Politically, the country of Scotland is still adjusting to having its own parliament, set up in the new buildings near the Palace of Holyroodhouse in Edinburgh. Although the Parliament is often criticized in the tabloid mass-circulation press (or by devoted Unionists who disagree in principal with a separate legislative body in Scotland), public opinion polls tell a different tale. Scots appear to be more interested in their local Scottish parliamentarians (known as MSPs) than those who represent them at Westminster in London (aka MPs). The 2007 elections may throw up some surprises and will, no doubt, revive debate as to whether Scotland should be fully independent.

Alas, the controversial **Parliament** building itself suffered another embarrassment in 2006, when a 3.7m (12-ft.) oak beam along the ceiling of its main debating chamber came loose. No one was hurt, but that part of the building was closed temporarily, and MSPs were forced to cram into a committee room too small for their numbers. However attractively modern, the edifice does seem a bit jinxed. See p. 88.

Here are some of the other latest developments in Edinburgh and Glasgow to consider.

PLANNING YOUR TRIP England appears to be a hotbed of some Islamic fundamentalism, and allegations of terrorist plotting have become more commonplace. A scare in August 2006 effectively shut down airports in London—severely disrupting flights to and from both Edinburgh and Glasgow airports. In most cases, internal U.K. flights were simply cancelled, and people had to wait or make alternative plans, such as taking the train. Flying directly to Glasgow or Edinburgh from outside of the U.K. may be a safer bet than coming via busy Heathrow, which is bound to be a perceived terrorist target.

SMOKING IN PUBLIC Since April 2006, Scottish law has banned smoking in all enclosed public spaces, which includes all pubs, bars, cafes, bistros, and restaurants. Some venues have established outdoor areas where customers can smoke.

ACCOMMODATIONS In Edinburgh, the **George** hotel, 19–21 George St. (© **0131/225-1215**), has had its public rooms, in-house bar, and restaurant completely updated in 2006. See p. 58. Opening in the summer of 2006 at the other end of George Street is **Tigerlily**, 125 George St. (© **0131/225-5005**), a new boutique hotel, with designer bar and restaurant. At the top end of the capital's accommodations, the luxurious serviced apartments of the **Chester Residence,** 9 Chester St. (© **0131/226-2075**), are drawing some rave reviews. See p. 63. In Glasgow, the same can be said of **Glasgow Loft Apartments,** 134 Renfrew St. (© **0141/419-1915**). See p. 167.

DINING In Edinburgh, the boom in Thai restaurants seems to never end. One of the best new restaurants is **Time 4 Thai,** 45 N. Castle St. (© **0131/225-8822**). See p. 74. Another recent welcomed addition is **Calistoga,** 93 St. Leonard St. (© **0131/668-4207**), which, as its name suggests, offers California-style cuisine and Napa Valley wines. See p. 78. In Glasgow, **Michael Caines @ ABode,** 129 Bath St. © 0141/572-6011) is the most significant recent development on the dining scene in the city center. See p. 181. Also worth noting is a branch of the London-based Japanese noodle bar, **Wagamama,** 97–103 W. George St. (© **0141/229-1468**), which helps to confirm Glasgow's cosmopolitan, big city credentials. See p. 183. On the city's

Southside, **Urban Grill,** 61 Kilmarnock Rd. (© **0141/649-2745**), has made an impressive debut. See p. 188. (Watch for the same team to open a similar operation called **Urban Bar and Brasserie** in Glasgow's Commercial Center on St. Vincent Place.)

ATTRACTIONS The biggest news by far is in Glasgow: The long-anticipated and truly well-received reopening of the **Kelvingrove Art Gallery and Museum,** Argyle Street (© **0141/276-9599**). After its 3-year renovation, the home of the city's core art and artifact collection drew some quarter-million visitors in just its first 2 weeks. See p. 195. Less impressive, but still welcomed in Edinburgh, is the refurbished **Scottish Storytelling Centre** and **John Knox House,** 43 High St. (© **0131/556-9579**). See p. 87. Next to come to the capital is dedicated exhibition space for the **Scottish National Photography Centre,** which may open in the old Royal High School on Calton Hill in 2008. Meanwhile, Glasgow anticipates a new, dashingly modern **Museum of Transport** on the south banks of the River Clyde.

1

The Best of
Edinburgh & Glasgow

Given the contrasting reputations of Edinburgh and Glasgow, any traveler who hasn't examined a map of Scotland might be forgiven for thinking that they are separated by hundreds of miles. In fact, Scotland's two primary cities are only about 72km (45 miles) apart, but almost everyone who visits them will be struck by their differences.

And although there is a good deal of competition (and some envy, too) between the two cities—like The Beatles' Lennon and McCartney—they are strongest as a pair, each bringing value to the partnership.

Both cities contribute mightily—and equally—to the cultural vibrancy of the nation. With this in mind, the country would do well to improve the public transportation links between the two cities, especially in the wee small hours.

To the east, the capital, Edinburgh, has an almost fairy-tale setting, with its imposing castle high on one hill. Built on ancient volcanoes and first established because of its secure and defensible position, it has become a crossroads. Practically everyone who comes to Scotland today spends some time in Edinburgh. And its midsummer international Festival is one of the biggest in the world. Edinburgh is the second most popular tourist destination in Great Britain following London, and it's not hard to see why. Compact and tidy, it is more of a big town than a small city.

In the west, Glasgow, on the other hand, is not a place that anyone might call precious. In comparison to Edinburgh, Glasgow was settled much earlier because it was an ideal place to ford the River Clyde, which later gained a reputation for shipbuilding and industry. Today Glasgow resembles nothing but a modern city. It has overcome its 20th-century associations with grime, grit, and gangsters—and now it is arguably more vibrant than Edinburgh, with a vigorous indigenous music and art scene. Without a picturesque castle or twee palace, it exemplifies urban Scotland: historic, dynamic, increasingly cosmopolitan, and attuned to the world. In 1990, it was named European Culture Capital and in 1999, U.K. City of Architecture and Design.

Edinburgh and Glasgow have a lot to offer individually, and taken as a duo, they are more impressive still. Both cities are among Europe's most dynamic centers. Edinburgh is the seat of Scottish royalty and government, and urban Glasgow boasts lively culture and Victorian splendor.

1 Frommer's Favorite Edinburgh & Glasgow Experiences

- **Visiting a Pub:** In Edinburgh, there are a good number of more traditional pubs, many of which serve hand-pulled, cask-conditioned ales made in Scotland and England. Glasgow's scene is more modern, with several so-called "style" bars as well as the more traditional pubs. As the evening wanes and you've established common ground with the locals, you'll realize you're having one of your most authentic Scottish experiences. We list our favorite pubs in chapters 10 and 18.

- **Experiencing Edinburgh's Famous Festival:** The Edinburgh Festival has become one of world's most prestigious annual cultural events. In fact, it encompasses several "festivals" at once. While the International Festival is primarily devoted to classical music and dance, it's the Fringe that really draws people. There are hundreds of stages with music, drama, comedians, and other entertainers. Plus book, film, and jazz festivals take place between the end of July and the first of September. If you're planning to sample the many offerings, make your hotel and flight reservations early. See p. 96.

- **Savoring the Cuisine:** No, we're not joking. Fresh fish and seafood harvested from Scotland's icy lochs and seas is world-class. Then there is lamb and Aberdeen Angus beef. If you think the food in Scotland is rotten, you've not been there in some time. Scotland, like Britain as a whole, has made leaps and bounds in improving the reputation of its cuisine. We review some of the best restaurants in chapters 6 and 14.

- **Enjoying Art in Galleries & Museums:** Edinburgh is the home to the Scottish National Gallery, and the country's collection ranges from Renaissance painting to pop art sculptures. Glasgow has one of the best municipally owned collections of art in the U.K. and possibly Europe. The crowning glory for many critics is the Burrell Collection, which was bequeathed to the city by an industrialist, but the now restored Kelvingrove is the soul of the city's collection. For

the rundown on galleries and museums in both cities, see chapters 7 and 15.

- **Playing Golf:** Yes, most people think of St. Andrews, Gleneagles, Troon, or Turnberry. But both Edinburgh and Glasgow have fine courses. The birthplace of the sport's rules is Edinburgh. While the historic Leith Links are no longer playable, the short course Bruntsfield Links, closer to the city center, can be played—and all you need is a ball, pitching wedge, and putter.

- **Strolling in Parks or Gardens:** In the capital, you have the option of the Meadows, the splendid Royal Botanic Gardens, Holyrood Park, Arthur's Seat, or Calton Hill. Glasgow (which many believe means "Dear Green Place") has a host of options from Glasgow Green along the River Clyde to Kelvingrove Park in the salubrious West End. See chapters 7 and 15.

- **Shopping:** Glasgow has become the second biggest retail playground in Britain after London. And, as no self-respecting city likes to be upstaged, Edinburgh is giving chase. There is a combination of posh department stores, such as Harvey Nichols; old favorites, such as the House of Fraser or Jenners; and plenty of trendy designer shops. For more details on shopping, see chapters 9 and 17.

- **Discovering Ancient Edinburgh:** Just take a stroll off one of the many narrow lanes from the Royal Mile in the city's Old Town to get a sense of what ancient Edinburgh was like. Although not as well preserved as some continental examples of medieval Europe, it is not too bad. In addition to exploring on your own, walking tours will help to heighten the experience. See chapter 7.

- **Admiring Victorian Glasgow:** Glasgow's city fathers contemplated tearing down its Victorian-built heritage after World War II. It was perceived as old fashioned and not projecting the progressive image that they wanted. Thank goodness, someone talked some sense into them. Though a lot of buildings have been (and continue to be knocked down), much remains to indicate that the Victorian builders were to the U.K. what ancient Romans were to Italy: masters of the craft. For walking tours that highlight Glasgow's best architecture, see chapter 16.

2 Best Castle & Palace

- **Edinburgh Castle:** It is a landmark that symbolizes this city in the way that the Eiffel Tower represents Paris or the Empire State Building exemplifies Manhattan. Begun around A.D. 1000 at the highest point of a narrow ridge, it is a natural fortress, with only one easy approach. The castle has witnessed some of the bloodiest and most treacherous events in Scottish history. Today it is home to the crown jewels and the famous stone of Scone on which ancient Scottish royalty was crowned. See p. 84.

- **Palace of Holyroodhouse:** At the opposite end of Edinburgh's Royal Mile from the Castle, Holyrood has housed an assortment of monarchs involved in traumatic events. Highlights of the palace are the oldest surviving section, King James Tower, where Mary Queen of Scots lived on the second floor. The building's present form largely dates from the late 1600s, when it was rebuilt in a dignified neo-Palladian style, and the pile remains an official residence for British royalty. See p. 88.

3 Best Cathedral & Churches

- **Glasgow Cathedral:** In the 7th century, St. Mungo (or St. Kentigern) is believed to have built a wooden structure here, intending it as his headquarters and eventual tomb. It burned down, but a stone cathedral was begun in the 1300s. This is mainland Scotland's only complete medieval cathedral, the finest example of its type. In the 1600s, the Protestant reformers stripped it of anything hinting at Roman Catholic idolatry, although Mungo still apparently rests here. See p. 193.

- **St. Giles:** In Edinburgh's Old Town, the auld kirk of St. Giles was perhaps a victim of over-enthusiastic Victorian renovation, but it is still an imposing piece of ecclesiastical architecture. Here is where John Knox, Scotland's Martin Luther, preached his sermons on the Reformation. See p. 86.

- **St. Vincent Street Church:** Access is limited as the Free Church of Scotland is still using this kirk in Glasgow, but the landmark is a beautiful example of the work of Alexander "Greek" Thomson, Glasgow's largely unknown genius of the Victorian era. The clock tower is decorated in all manner of exotic yet sympathetic Egyptian, Assyrian, and even Indian-looking motifs and designs. See p. 194.

4 Best Galleries & Museums

EDINBURGH

- **National Gallery of Scotland:** This is not one gallery but rather a set of museums. The flagship, on the Mound in the middle of the Princes Street Gardens, offers a small but choice collection that includes works by such great and diverse artists as Velázquez and Cézanne, plus Scottish master works. Other branches include the Gallery of Modern Art and the associated Dean near the Water of Leith, as well as the National Portrait Gallery on Queen Street. See p. 90 and 91.

- **Museum of Scotland:** In 1998, the collections of the Royal Museum of Scotland and the National Museum of Antiquities were united into a coherent whole. Here you'll find practically everything you ever wanted to know about Scotland from prehistory to the Industrial Age, from Pictish artifacts to a milk bottle carried by Sean Connery when he was a milkman. See p. 89.

GLASGOW

- **Burrell Collection:** The contents of this collection were accumulated through the exclusive efforts of one Sir William Burrell (1861–1958), who basically spent his fortune on collecting art and artifacts—then ensured it all went to the city of Glasgow. Now on display in a postmodern building on Glasgow's Pollok Country Park, it's one of Scotland's most admired museums, with a strong focus on medieval art, 19th-century French paintings, and Chinese ceramics. See p. 196.

- **Hunterian Art Gallery:** This museum owns much of the artistic estate of James McNeill Whistler, as well as housing a re-creation of the home of Scotland's most famous architect and designer, Charles Rennie Mackintosh. On display are grand oils by Whistler, Reubens, and Rembrandt as well as one of the country's best collections of 19th-century Scottish paintings. See p. 195.

- **Kelvingrove Art Gallery and Museum:** Reopened in 2006, this diverse collection of art and antiquaries is in the second most visited gallery and museum in the U.K. outside of London. See p. 195.

Highlights of Historic Edinburgh

Gladstone's Land, now run by the National Trust for Scotland, is a 17th-century merchant's house and worth a visit to get the impression of how confined living conditions were some 400 years ago on the Royal Mile. On the second floor, in the front room that Gladstone added, you can see the original facade with its classical friezes of columns and arches. Here, as well, is the sensitively restored timber ceiling. See p. 85. Across town, the **Georgian House** is in Charlotte Square, which was designed by the great Robert Adam. This town house is set out and decorated in the manner of the 18th century. See p. 91.

5 Best in Great Glasgow Architecture

- **Glasgow School of Art:** Architect Charles Rennie Mackintosh's global reputation rests in large part on his magnificent Glasgow School of Art, which is still in use. It's a highlight of the Mackintosh trail, which legions of his fans follow through the city every year. Nearby is his ground-breaking facade for the Willow Tea Rooms. See p. 194.

- **Holmwood House:** On the city's Southside, this villa is probably the best example of Alexander "Greek" Thomson's innovative style as applied to stately Victorian homes. Magnificently original, its restoration (which is ongoing) has revealed that the architect was concerned with almost every element of the house's design. See p. 196.

6 Best Accommodations

EDINBURGH

- **Best Boutique Hotel:** In an upscale neighborhood, **The Bonham,** 35 Drumsheugh Gardens (✆ **0131/226-6050**), offers some of the most alluring accommodations in a city filled with fine hotels. Alternatively, the same company offers **The Howard,** 34 Great King St. (✆ **0131/557-3500**). See p. 63 and 55.

- **Best Traditional Hotel:** With a Michelin-star restaurant, doormen in kilts, and a romantic pile to rival any others, the **Balmoral,** 1 Princes St. (✆ **0131/556-2414**), is legendary, and its location is smack in the heart of the capital. See p. 55.

- **Best Rooms near the Castle:** As its list of celebrity guests testifies, the **Witchery,** Castlehill (✆ **0131/225-5613**), offers opulence and individuality in a manner not seen anywhere else in the Old Town. See p. 61.

- **Best Hotel in Leith:** At the port of Leith, **Malmaison,** 1 Tower Place (✆ **0131/555-6868**), is about a 15-minute ride north of Edinburgh's center. Named after Joséphine's mansion outside Paris, it celebrates the Auld Alliance of France and Scotland and was created from a 1900s Victorian building. Malmaison once housed indigent seamen but today is an oasis of chic. See p. 65.

- **Best Hotel Health Spa:** Near the city's conference center, the **Sheraton Grand,** 1 Festival Sq. (✆ **0131/229-9131**), has wonderful facilities in an adjoining building, highlighted by a roof-top indoor/outdoor pool. See p. 63.

GLASGOW

- **Best Boutique Hotel:** In a West End neighborhood filled with similar sandstone-fronted town houses, **One Devonshire Gardens,** 1 Devonshire Gardens (✆ **0141/339-2001**), still stands out. It's a re-creation of a high-bourgeois, very proper Scottish home from the early 1900s, boasting antique furnishings and discreetly concealed modern comforts. See p. 169.

- **Best Hip Hotel:** With only some 18 rooms, the **Brunswick Hotel,** 106–108 Brunswick St. (✆ **0141/552-0001**), exudes cool in the city's Merchant City. The design is modern and minimalist but with character and class. See p. 166.

- **Best in the Commercial Center:** Linked to the hotel with the same name in Edinburgh (see above), this **Malmaison,** 278 W. George St. (✆ **0141/572-1000**), is in a building that dates from the 1800s. It welcomes visitors with Scottish hospitality and houses them with quite a bit of style. See p. 168.

- **Best Moderately Priced Hotel:** In the leafy West End, **The Town House,** Hughenden Terrace (© **0141/357-** 0862), is a fine small hotel with charm, individual touches, and competitive rates. See p. 172.

7 Best Dining Bets

EDINBURGH

- **Best Fine-Dining Restaurant:** With one of the city's precious Michelin stars and its most talented chef/ owners, **Restaurant Martin Wishart,** 54 The Shore, Leith (© **0131/553-3557**), is where the leading out-of-town chefs want to dine when they visit Edinburgh. See p. 78.
- **Best Cafe:** In the heart of Old Town, **Spoon,** 15 Blackfriars St. (© **0131/556-6922**), forks out some the best salads and sandwiches in Edinburgh—and the freshly made soups are even better. See p. 77.
- **Best Vegetarian Restaurant:** Near the Royal Mile, **David Bann's Vegetarian Restaurant,** 56–58 St. Mary's St. (© **0131/556-5888**), continually sets the highest standards for meat-free dining. See p. 75.
- **Best Modern Scottish Restaurant:** Owned by Andrew and Lisa Radford, **Atrium,** 10 Cambridge St. (© **0131/228-8882**), offers dishes prepared with flair and imagination but without excessive amounts of fuss or overly fancy presentation. See p. 69.
- **Best Restaurant Views:** It's a dead heat between **Oloroso,** 33 Castle St. (© **0131/226-7614**), and **Forth Floor,** Harvey Nichols, 30–34 St. Andrew Sq. (© **0131/524-8350**). Both offer wonderful cooking of fresh Scottish produce to go with those scenic vistas. See p. 72 and 69.
- **Best on a Budget:** Nothing fancy, but the **Kebab Mahal,** 7 Nicolson Sq. (© **0131/667-5214**) serves up good, hearty Indian food at budget prices. See p. 78.

GLASGOW

- **Best Seafood Restaurant:** One of the consistently best restaurants in the entire city, **Gamba,** 225a W. George St. (© **0141/572-0899**), specializes in superb seafood, showing off some of Scotland's best natural produce. See p. 181.
- **Best Indian Restaurant:** The competition is stiff, but the nod goes to **The Dhabba,** 44 Candleriggs (© **0141/ 221-1663**), in the Merchant City for its North Indian specialties and contemporary interiors. See p. 179.
- **Best City Centre Fine-Dining Restaurant:** Newly opened in late 2005, **Michael Caines @ ABode** (© **0141/572-6011**), is the one to watch in the commercial center with stylish and exceptional cooking. See p. 181.
- **Best Cafe:** Perhaps more of a bistro than cafe, **Café Gandolfi,** 64 Albion St. (© **0141/552-6813**), offers straightforward and delicious dishes, whether a bowl of Cullen *skink* (smoked haddock chowder) or a sirloin steak sandwich. See p. 179.
- **Best in 'Burbs:** It may be the best in greater Glasgow: **The Wild Bergamot,** 1 Hillhead St., Milngavie (© **0141/956-6515**), is tiny, but its reputation is increasingly large. See p. 185.
- **Best on a Budget:** A brief stroll from the shopping precincts of Sauchiehall Street, the **Wee Curry Shop,** 7 Buccleuch St. off Cambridge St. (© **0141/ 353-0777**), is a tiny gem of a restaurant, serving freshly prepared Indian cuisine at bargain prices. See p. 183.

8 The Best Bars & Pubs

EDINBURGH

- **Best in New Town:** In a city famous for its pubs, the **Café Royal Circle Bar,** 17 W. Register St. (*© 0131/556-1884*), stands out. This longtime favorite, boasting lots of atmosphere and Victorian trappings, attracts a sea of drinkers—locals as well as visitors. See p. 130.
- **Best in Stockbridge:** At the heart of the village of Stockbridge, **The Bailie Bar,** 2 St. Stephen St. (*© 0131/225-4673*), usually has plenty of banter between the regulars and the staff, and no music ever drowns out the conversation here. See p. 130.
- **Best in Old Town:** Just below the castle, the **Bow Bar,** 80 W. Bow (*© 0131/226-7667*), pours some of the best ales in town in a traditional and comfortable pub with a good whisky selection, too. See p. 131.
- **Best in Leith: The Shore,** 3–4 The Shore (*© 0131/553-5080*), fits seamlessly into the seaside port ambience, without resorting to a lot of the usual decorations of cork and netting. Excellent food, too. See p. 132.
- **Best for Folk Music:** It is a tossup between **Sandy Bell's,** 25 Forrest Rd. (*© 0131/225-2751*), and the **Royal Oak,** 1 Infirmary St. (*© 0131/557-2967*), when it comes to spontaneous Scottish folk and poetry. Try both if this is your bag. See p. 128.

GLASGOW

- **Best in the Commercial Center:** With its long, horseshoe-shaped bar and central location, the **Horse Shoe,** 17 Drury St. between Renfield & W. Nile sts. (*© 0141/229-5711*), is a throwback to the days of so-called Palace Pubs in Scotland. See p. 237.
- **Best in the Merchant City:** Unless you are looking for a style bar (of which there are plenty), the **Babbity Bowster,** 16 Blackfriars St. (*© 0141/552-5055*), is ideal for a drink and some conversation, although live folk music jams take over on Saturday afternoons. See p. 237.
- **Best in the West End:** The competition is furious and the selection is vast, but we'll give the nod to **Brel,** 39–43 Ashton Lane (*© 0141/342-4966*), for its combination of good ambience, excellent location, and decent Belgian-inspired grub. See p. 238.
- **Best for Whisky:** With a selection of single malts that numbers easily into the hundreds, the **Pot Still,** 154 Hope St. (*© 0141/333-0980*), is the place to go for a wee dram. See p. 237.
- **Best for Rock Music:** It is a tossup between the near legendary **King Tut's Wah-Wah Hut,** 272 St. Vincent St. (*© 0141/221-5279*), or **Nice 'n' Sleazy,** 421 Sauchiehall St. (*© 0141/333-9637*), and both draw the best in local indie band talent. See p. 235.

2

Planning Your Trip to Edinburgh & Glasgow

Edinburgh and Glasgow, separated by less than 80km (50 miles), are the primary cities of Scotland and significant metropolises in the United Kingdom, as well. Each has an increasingly busy international airport and a city center railway terminal that regularly receives trains traveling north from London, other cities in England, and from places elsewhere in Scotland.

Although Scotland likes to think of itself as a separate country, the central United Kingdom government in London regulates all issues regarding international visitors and immigrants, and the same rules apply to travel to Scotland as to traveling in any part of England, Wales, and Northern Ireland.

This chapter is devoted to the when, where, and how of your trip—as well as the advanced planning required to get your traveling act together and take it, literally, on the road. For city-specific planning information, see "Fast Facts" in chapters 4 and 12.

1 Visitor Information

Before you go, you can get information from offices of the **British Tourist Authority**—now rebranded in this Internet age as **VisitBritain** (www.visitbritain.com or www.visitscotland.com).

In the **United States:** 551 Fifth Ave., Suite 701, New York, NY 10176-0799 (© **800/462-2748,** or 212/986-2200 in New York; fax 212/986-1188); 625 N. Michigan Ave., Suite 1001, Chicago, IL, 60611-1977 (© **800/462-2748**); 10880 Wilshire Blvd., Suite 570, Los Angeles, CA, 90024 (© **310/470-2782**). In **Canada:** 5915 Airport Rd., Suite 120, Mississauga, ON L4V 1T1 (© **888/VISIT-UK** in Canada; fax 905/405-1835 in Toronto). In **Australia:** Level 2, 15 Blue St., North Sydney NSW 2060 (© **02/9021-4400;** fax 02/9377-4499).

In **New Zealand:** c/o British Consulate General Office, Level 17, IAG House, 151 Queen St., Auckland 1 (© **09/303-1446;** fax 09/309-1899).

If you're in London, you can visit the Scottish Tourist Board—rebranded **VisitScotland,** 19 Cockspur St., London SW1 Y5BL (© **0207/930-8661**); it's near Trafalgar Square, open May to September on Monday through Friday from 9:30am to 6:30pm and Saturday from 10am to 5pm. October to April the hours are Monday through Friday 10am to 6pm and Saturday noon to 4pm.

Once in Edinburgh or Glasgow, you will find the Tourist Information Centres more useful. In the capital, the main office is the **Edinburgh Information Centre,** atop the Princes Mall near

Pre-Departure Checklist

- Did you find out your daily ATM withdrawal limit in dollars, keeping in mind the pound's recently strong exchange rate?
- To check in at the airport with an e-ticket, do you have the credit card you bought your ticket with or a frequent-flier card?
- If you purchased traveler's checks, have you recorded the check numbers, and stored the documentation separately from the checks?
- Did you make sure your favorite attraction is open? Call ahead for opening and closing times, especially for travel off-season.
- Do any hotel, theater, restaurant, or other arrangements need to be booked in advance—especially if you're going to Edinburgh in August?

Waverley Station (© **0131/473-3800** or 0845/225-5121; fax 0131/473-3881; www.edinburgh.org). It can give you sightseeing information and also arrange lodgings. The center sells bus tours, theater tickets, and souvenirs of Edinburgh. It also has racks and racks of free brochures. It's open year-round, though hours vary from month to month. The summer hours are slightly longer and winter times shorter, but typically you'll find the office open Monday through Saturday from 9am to 7pm and Sunday from 10am to 7pm. There is an information desk at Edinburgh International Airport, open typically Monday through Sunday 7am to 6:30pm.

In Glasgow, the **Greater Glasgow and Clyde Valley Tourist Board,** 11 George Sq. (© **0141/204-4400;** www.seeglasgow. com) is in the heart of the city. In addition to piles of brochures, there is a small book shop, *bureau de change,* and hotel reservation service. During peak season, it is open Monday to Saturday from 9am to 7pm and Sunday from 10am to 6pm. Hours are more limited during winter months.

WHAT'S ON THE WEB?

There are naturally a host of websites that vary in usefulness. The Great Britain tourist board's **www.travelbritain.org** has the overall U.K. picture.

But for information on Scotland, it is probably easier and better to go directly to **www.visitscotland.com** or **www.to scotland.com**, both of which have detailed information, offer brochures online, provide trip-planning hints, and even provide prompt answers for e-mail queries. A slightly more corporate view is at **www. scotexchange.net**. The other useful and official tourism websites for Edinburgh and Glasgow are, as already noted, **www. edinburgh.org** and **www.seeglasgow. com**.

The two organizations that operate most of Scotland's historical sites have websites as well: **www.historic-scotland.gov.uk** for Historic Scotland and **www.nts.org.uk** for the National Trust of Scotland.

For an independent view, though it is not clear how often they are updated, try **www.scotland-info.co.uk**, **www. undiscoveredscotland.co.uk**, or **www. rampantscotland.com**.

Scotland

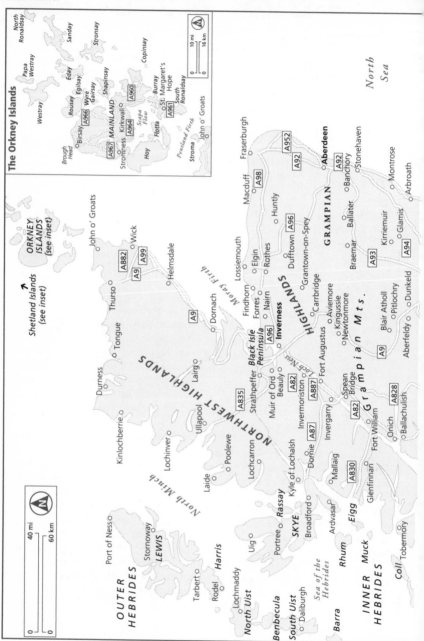

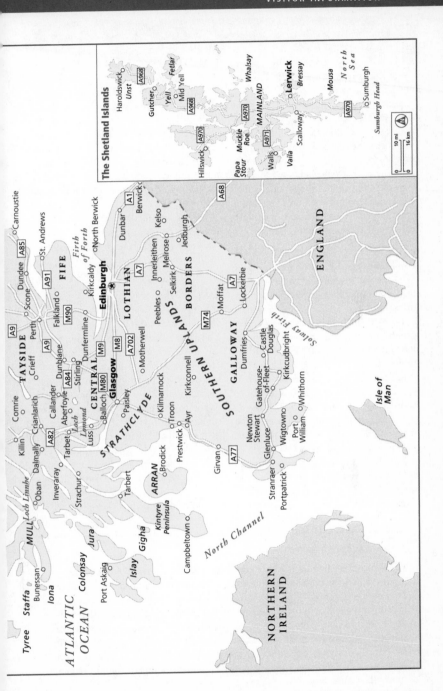

2 Entry Requirements & Customs

ENTRY REQUIREMENTS

All U.S. citizens, Canadians, Australians, New Zealanders, and South Africans must have a valid passport. No visa is required. An immigration officer may also want proof of your intention to return to your point of origin (usually a round-trip ticket) and visible means of support while you're in Scotland. If you're planning to fly from the United States or Canada to the United Kingdom and then on to a country that requires a visa (India, for example), you should secure that visa before you arrive in Britain.

OBTAINING A PASSPORT

For Residents of the United States: Whether you're applying in person or by mail, you can download passport applications from the U.S. State Department website at **http://travel.state.gov**. For general information, call the **National Passport Agency** (© **202/647-0518**). To find your regional passport office, either check the U.S. State Department website or call the **National Passport Information Center** (© **900/225-5674**); the fee is 55¢ per minute for automated information and $1.50 per minute for operator-assisted calls.

For Residents of Canada: Passport applications are available at travel agencies throughout Canada or from the central **Passport Office,** Department of Foreign Affairs and International Trade, Ottawa, ON K1A 0G3 (© **800/567-6868;** www.dfait-maeci.gc.ca).

For Residents of Ireland: You can apply for a 10-year passport at the **Passport Office,** Setanta Centre, Molesworth Street, Dublin 2 (© **01/671-1633;** www.irlgov.ie/iveagh). Those under age 18 and over 65 must apply for a €12 3-year passport. You can also apply at 1A South Mall, Cork (© **021/272-525**) or at most main post offices.

For an up-to-date country-by-country listing of passport requirements around the world, go the "Foreign Entry Requirement" web page of the U.S. State Department at http://travel.state.gov.

CUSTOMS

WHAT YOU CAN BRING INTO SCOTLAND

The same rules for travel to any part of the U.K. apply to travel to Scotland. From outside the European Union, you can bring in for your own use without paying tax or duty: 200 cigarettes, 100 cigarillos, 50 cigars, or 250 grams of smoking tobacco; 60cc of perfume; 2 liters of still table wine; 250cc eau de toilette; 1 liter of spirits or strong liqueurs or 2 liters of fortified wine; £145 worth of all other goods, including gifts and souvenirs. Any amounts over these limits should be declared.

(Tips Passport Savvy

Allow plenty of time before your trip if applying for a new passport or renewing an old one; processing normally takes 3 weeks but can take longer during busy periods (especially spring). And keep in mind that if you need a passport in a hurry, you'll pay a higher processing fee. When traveling in Scotland, you don't need to carry your passport with you. If you do, safeguard it in an inconspicuous, inaccessible place such as a money belt and keep a copy of the critical pages with your passport number in a separate place. If you lose your passport, visit the nearest consulate of your native country as soon as possible for a replacement.

If you bring in goods from a European Union member country on which tax has been paid in that country, no tax or duty is due (as long as they are for your own personal use.) Some special rules may apply, however, for tobacco from some E.U. countries.

For up to date information on customs, go to **www.hmrc.gov.uk** and search for "information for travelers."

WHAT YOU CAN TAKE HOME FROM SCOTLAND
U.S. Citizens

For specifics on what you can bring back and the corresponding fees, download the invaluable free pamphlet *Know Before You Go* online at **www.cbp.gov.** (Click on "Travel," and then click on "Know Before You Go! Online Brochure.") Or contact the **U.S. Customs & Border Protection (CBP),** 1300 Pennsylvania Ave. NW, Washington, DC 20229 (*©* **877/287-8667**), and request the pamphlet.

Canadian Citizens

For a clear summary of Canadian rules, write for the booklet *I Declare,* issued by the **Canada Border Services Agency** (*©* **800/461-9999** in Canada, or 204/983-3500; www.cbsa-asfc.gc.ca).

Australian Citizens

A helpful brochure available from Australian consulates or Customs offices is *Know Before You Go.* For more information, call the **Australian Customs Service** at *©* **1300/363-263,** or log on to www. customs.gov.au.

New Zealand Citizens

Most questions are answered in a free pamphlet available at New Zealand consulates and Customs offices: *New Zealand Customs Guide for Travellers, Notice no. 4.* For more information, contact **New Zealand Customs,** The Customhouse, 17–21 Whitmore St., Box 2218, Wellington (*©* **04/473-6099** or 0800/428-786; www. customs.govt.nz).

3 Money

It's a good idea to exchange at least some money—at least enough to cover airport incidentals and transportation to your hotel—before you leave home, so you can avoid lines at airport ATMs. You can exchange money at your local American Express or Thomas Cook office or your bank. If you're far away from a bank with currency-exchange services, American Express offers travelers checks and foreign currency, though with a $15 order fee and additional shipping costs, at www. americanexpress.com or *©* **800/807-6233.**

POUNDS & PENCE

Britain's decimal monetary system is based on the pound sterling (£), which is made up of 100 pence (written as "p"). "Quid" is similar to "buck" in the U.S.: British slang for a pound. Scotland issues its own currency, but English and Scottish money are interchangeable (although using Scottish notes in England can sometimes be problematic). There are £1 and £2 coins, as well as coins of 50p, 20p, 10p, 5p, 2p, and 1p. Banknotes come in denominations of £5, £10, £20, and £50.

Regarding the U.S. Dollar, the British Pound & the Euro

Europe's primary currency, the euro, is not officially used in Scotland, as Great Britain steadfastly refuses to give up the British pound. As a result, all prices in this book are noted only in pounds and dollars at a rate of £1 = $1.85. However, some euro-friendly businesses in central Edinburgh and Glasgow will accept euro coins and notes.

Unlike in England, Scots still use £1 notes, as well.

As a general guideline, the price conversions in this book have been computed at the rate of **£1 = US$1.85.** Bear in mind, however, that exchange rates fluctuate constantly, and, in recent years, quite dramatically. In any given month, it has been not usual for the pound's worth to vary by as much as 15¢. For more exact ratios between these and other currencies, check an up-to-date source before you arrive in Scotland, such as **www.xe.com/ucc**.

Prices in Scotland will make it seem like an expensive destination, on a par with visiting major U.S. cities, for example, rather than central European countries. That is particularly true with hotels, dining out and drinking in pubs. In general, goods and services are priced in the same amount as they would be in U.S. dollars, but that means they really cost almost twice as much. For example, a £200 iPod is selling for nearly $400. Exceptions to this rule are theater and cinema tickets, which are about the same and sometimes cheaper given the exchange rate.

In Edinburgh and Glasgow, as well as in most towns around these cities, there are as many ATMs (or Cash Points, as they are called) as you would find in any major city. The most prevalent network is Cirrus.

ATMs

The easiest and best way to get cash away from home is from an ATM, sometimes referred to as a "cash machine," or a "cash point." The **Cirrus** (© **800/424-7787;** www.mastercard.com) and **PLUS** (© **800/ 843-7587;** www.visa.com) networks span the globe; look at the back of your bank card to see which network you're on, then call or check online for ATM locations at your destination. Be sure you know your personal identification number (PIN) and daily withdrawal limit before you depart. **Note:** Remember that many banks impose a fee every time you use a card at another bank's ATM, and that fee can be higher for international transactions (up to $5 or more) than for domestic ones (where they're rarely more than $2). In addition, the bank from which you withdraw cash may charge its own fee. For international withdrawal fees, ask your bank.

CREDIT CARDS

Credit cards are another safe way to carry money. They also provide a convenient record of all your expenses, and they generally offer relatively good exchange rates. You can withdraw cash advances from your credit cards at banks or ATMs, provided you know your PIN. Keep in mind that you'll pay interest from the moment of your withdrawal, even if you pay your monthly bills on time. Also, note that many banks now assess a 1% to 3% "transaction fee" on **all** charges you incur abroad (whether you're using the local currency or your native currency).

Credit cards universally accepted are MasterCard and Visa, with American Express allowed less frequently. In the past few years, Scotland has imposed a "Chip and Pin" system, which means that all credit cards issued have a computer chip imbedded in them and users must know their PIN numbers. In effect, the PIN has replaced the signature on credit card purchases. Many businesses can over-ride the "Chip and Pin" requirement, although it often depends on staff's knowledge of the equipment that the business uses.

TRAVELER'S CHECKS

Traveler's checks are becoming something of an anachronism. These days, traveler's checks are less necessary because 24-hour ATMs allow you to withdraw small amounts of cash as needed. You can buy traveler's checks at most banks. They are offered in denominations of $20, $50, $100, $500, and sometimes $1,000. Generally, you'll pay a service charge ranging from 1% to 4%.

The most popular traveler's checks are offered by **American Express** (© 800/807-6233 or 800/221-7282 for card holders—this number accepts collect calls,

offers service in several foreign languages, and exempts Amex gold and platinum cardholders from the 1% fee); **Visa** (© 800/732-1322)—AAA members can obtain Visa checks for a $9.95 fee (for checks up to $1,500) at most AAA offices or by calling © 866/339-3378; and **MasterCard** (© 800/223-9920).

American Express (see "Fast Facts" in chapters 4 and 12 for addresses), **Thomas Cook, Visa,** and **MasterCard** offer **foreign currency traveler's checks,** which are useful if you're traveling to one country, or to the Euro zone; they're accepted at locations where dollar checks may not be.

If you carry traveler's checks, keep a record of their serial numbers separate from your checks in the event that they are stolen or lost. You'll get a refund faster if you know the numbers.

4 When to Go

WEATHER

If dry and sunny weather is a vital concern, the climate in Scotland can seriously affect your travel plans. The Lowlands usually have a moderate year-round temperature. In spring, the average temperature is 53°F (12°C), rising to about 65°F (18°C) in summer. By the time the crisp autumn has arrived, the temperatures have dropped to

spring levels. In winter, the average temperature is 43°F (6°C). Temperatures in the north of Scotland are lower, especially in winter, and you should dress accordingly. It rains a lot in Scotland, but perhaps not as much as age-old myths would have it: The rainfall in Edinburgh is exactly the same as that in London. September can be the sunniest month.

Average Temperature & Rainfall in Edinburgh & Glasgow

	Jan	Feb	Mar	Apr	May	June	July	Aug	Sept	Oct	Nov	Dec
Temp. (°F)	38	38	42	44	50	55	59	58	54	48	43	40
Temp. (°C)	3	3	6	7	10	13	15	14	12	9	6	4
Rainfall (in.)	2.2	1.6	1.9	1.5	2.0	2.0	2.5	2.7	2.5	2.4	2.5	2.4

WHEN YOU FIND BARGAINS

The cheapest time to travel to Scotland is off season: **November** through **Easter** (excluding Christmas and New Year's). Airlines have been offering cut-rate fares during these periods. And weekday flights are always cheaper than weekend

fares, often by at least 10%. Most tourist attractions in Edinburgh and Glasgow are open year-round, but outside these cities many are not.

Rates for hotels hit their peak in the high season from **June** through **September,** and also from **mid-December** to the first week of **January.** Mid-July and August are when most Britons take their holidays, so besides the higher prices, you'll have to deal with crowds and limited availability of accommodations.

Spring offers the countryside at its greenest, autumn brings on steely skies, and summer's warmth gives rise to the music and theater festivals. But winter offers savings across the board and a chance to see Scots going about their everyday lives largely unhindered by tourist invasions.

HOLIDAYS

The following holidays are celebrated in Scotland: New Year's Day (Jan 1–2), Good Friday and Easter Monday, May Day (May 1), spring bank holiday (last Mon in May), summer bank holiday (first Mon in Aug), Christmas Day (Dec 25), and Boxing Day (Dec 26).

EDINBURGH & GLASGOW CALENDAR OF EVENTS

January

Celtic Connections, Glasgow. This celebration of folk and traditional music is one of the largest of its kind in the world, drawing musicians from throughout Scotland, Wales, and Ireland, as well as the Basque country and North America. Call ☎ **0141/353-8000.** Throughout January.

Burns Night. Naturally, during the celebrations to honor Robert Burns, there's much toasting with whisky and the eating of haggis, the arrival of which is announced by a bagpipe. January 25.

February

New Territories, Glasgow. An international festival of performance arts, especially contemporary dance and theater. Early February to mid-March.

March

Whuppity Scourie, Lanark. Residents in this town south of Glasgow get so

tired of winter that they stage this traditional ceremony to chase it away. March 1.

Glasgow Comedy Festival. Inaugurated in 2003, this festival brings a diverse range of funny men and women to stages around the city. Call ☎ **0141/552-2070.** Mid-March.

Ceilidh Culture, Edinburgh. A showcase of traditional Scottish arts, whether song, storytelling, or dance. Held in 30 venues across the city. Call ☎ **0131/228-1155.** Late March to mid-April.

April

Glasgow Art Fair. Galleries from across the U.K. set up stalls in big tents on George Square. First weekend in April.

Glasgow International. A fortnight-long celebration of contemporary visual art at a host of local galleries, which present a range of exhibitions. Last 2 weeks of April.

Triptych. As the name implies, this is a contemporary and avant-garde music festival that takes place in three cities: Edinburgh, Glasgow, and Aberdeen. Last weekend in April.

Beltane Fire Festival, Edinburgh. This one celebrates paganism and the alleged arrival of summer on Calton Hill with primal drums and dancing. A bit of nudity is almost guaranteed. April 30.

May

Big Big Country, Glasgow. A festival of "Americana" with country, folk, roots, and bluegrass music from U.S. and U.K. artists. Mid-May.

Burns and A' That, Ayr, south of Glasgow. A celebration of the life of Robert Burns with contemporary artists and performers—mainly in music. For details, call ☎ **0129/229-0300.** Late May.

June

Royal Highland Show, at the Ingliston Showground, outskirts of Edinburgh. This show is devoted to agriculture and commerce. For details, call ✆ **0131/335-6200.** Mid- to late June.

Pride, Edinburgh and Glasgow. Scotland's annual gay celebration alternates between Edinburgh and Glasgow. You'll see a quirky, boisterous parade through the heart of Glasgow or along Princes Street in Edinburgh. Sometime in June.

West End Festival, Glasgow. The city's most vibrant neighborhoods throw a party that includes live music concerts, a street parade, and other events. Throughout most of June.

Glasgow International Jazz Festival. Jazz musicians from all over the world come together to perform at various venues around the city. End of June.

July

Scottish Open, Loch Lomond, northwest of Glasgow. Traditionally played on the weekend before the Open tournament in Britain, drawing many of the stars of international golf. Mid-July.

Glasgow River Festival. A 2-day event with exhibitions, sailings and other festivities on the River Clyde. Mid-July.

Edinburgh International Jazz & Blues Festival. Of the various events that dominate the Edinburgh social calendar in summer, this one is the first to kick off. End of July into August.

August

Edinburgh Festival. Scotland's best-known event is actually various festivals—Jazz, Book, International, and Fringe—taking place concurrently in the Scottish capital. The Fringe alone encompasses some 1,800 performances. An arts bonanza, it draws major talent from around the world. Log onto www.edinburghfestivals.co.uk. Throughout August.

Edinburgh Military Tattoo. A spectacular every evening at Edinburgh Castle Esplanade, featuring precision marching and army bands from across the globe. Call ✆ **0870/755-5118.** Throughout August.

Piping Live!, Glasgow. Bagpipe players and bagpipe bands from around the world gather in the city for a week long festival that culminates with the **World Pipe Band Championships**—a virtual orgy of bagpiping, as up to 1,000 kilted participants strut their stuff. Call ✆ **0141/241-4400.** Mid-August.

September

Doors Open Day, Edinburgh and Glasgow. One weekend in the month, the public is given unique access to landmark buildings that are normally off limits.

October

BLOCK, Glasgow. A weeklong architectural festival organized by the Lighthouse, with exhibits, walks, and talks. Call ✆ **0141/204-4400.** First week of October.

Darvel Music Festival, Ayrshire, south of Glasgow. A recent addition to the Strathclyde cultural calendar with an eclectic array of musicians, focusing on folk and up-and-coming talent. First week of October.

Glasgay!, Glasgow. One of the U.K.'s largest festivals of gay, lesbian, and transgender culture, with club nights, music, performance art. Mid-October through mid-November.

International Story Telling Festival, Edinburgh. Events at various venues in the capital help to celebrate the oral tradition of Scotland and other nations. Call ✆ **0131/556-9579.** Last 2 weeks in October.

November

Edinburgh Christmas. The capital gets an early start on the holiday season with outdoors markets and fairground rides. Late November through Christmas.

Glasgow on Ice. An outdoor ice skating rink is set up in George Square, along with carnival rides and gift booths. Late November to Christmas Eve.

December

Hogmanay, Edinburgh and Glasgow. New Year's Eve—Hogmanay—is traditionally bigger for the Scots than Christmas. Events in the capital include a torchlight procession, a fire festival along Princes Street, a carnival, and a street theater spectacular. Both cities stage outdoor concerts on Hogmanay. The celebration in Edinburgh begins in the last week of December and continues past New Year's Day.

5 Travel Insurance

Because Scotland is far from home, and a number of things could go wrong—lost luggage, trip cancellation, a medical emergency—strongly consider travel insurance. Check your existing policies and credit card coverage before you buy travel insurance. You may already be covered for lost luggage, cancelled tickets, or medical expenses.

The cost of travel insurance varies widely, depending on the cost and length of your trip, your age and health, and the type of trip you're taking, but expect to pay between 5% and 8% of the vacation itself. You can get estimates from various providers through InsureMyTrip.com. Enter your trip cost and dates, your age, and other information, for prices from more than a dozen companies.

TRIP-CANCELLATION INSURANCE

Trip-cancellation insurance will help retrieve your money if you have to back out of a trip or depart early, or if your travel supplier goes bankrupt. Permissible reasons for trip cancellation can range from sickness to natural disasters to the State Department declaring a destination unsafe for travel.

For more information, contact one of the following recommended insurers: **Access America** (© 866/807-3982; www.accessamerica.com); **Travel Guard International** (© 800/826-4919; www.travelguard.com); **Travel Insured International** (© 800/243-3174; www.travelinsured.com); and **Travelex Insurance Services** (© 888/457-4602; www.travelex-insurance.com).

MEDICAL INSURANCE

Scotland has the U.K.-wide National Health Service, which provides residents with free care. Visitors needing emergency treatment will be admitted into hospital wards without questions or evidence of

Travel in the Age of Bankruptcy

Airlines go bankrupt, so protect yourself by **buying your tickets with a credit card.** The Fair Credit Billing Act guarantees that you can get your money back from the credit card company if a travel supplier goes under (and if you request the refund within 60 days of the bankruptcy). **Travel insurance** can also help, but make sure it covers against "carrier default" for your specific travel provider. And be aware that if a U.S. airline goes bust mid-trip, a 2001 federal law requires other carriers to take you to your destination (albeit on a space-available basis) for a fee of no more than $25, provided you rebook within 60 days of the cancellation.

ability to pay. Extended treatment in a hospital may result in a bill, however.

For travel overseas, most U.S. health plans (including Medicare and Medicaid) do not provide coverage, and the ones that do often require you to pay for services upfront and reimburse you only after you return home. As a safety net, you may want to buy travel medical insurance, particularly if you're traveling to a remote or high-risk area where emergency evacuation might be necessary. If you require additional medical insurance, try **MEDEX Assistance** (✆ 410/453-6300; www.medexassist.com) or **Travel Assistance International** (✆ 800/821-2828; www.travelassistance.com; for general information on services, call the company's Worldwide Assistance Services, Inc., at ✆ **800/777-8710**).

LOST-LUGGAGE INSURANCE
On flights within the U.S., checked baggage is covered up to $2,500 per ticketed passenger. On international flights (including U.S. portions of international trips), baggage coverage is limited to approximately $9.07 per pound, up to approximately $635 per checked bag. If you plan to check items more valuable than what's covered by the standard liability, see if your homeowner's policy covers your valuables, get baggage insurance as part of your comprehensive travel-insurance package, or buy Travel Guard's "BagTrak" product.

If your luggage is lost, immediately file a lost-luggage claim at the airport, detailing the luggage contents. Most airlines require that you report delayed, damaged, or lost baggage within 4 hours of arrival. The airlines are required to deliver luggage, once found, directly to your house or destination free of charge.

6 Health & Safety

STAYING HEALTHY
Scotland poses no particular health concerns. The crisis over so-called mad-cow disease has passed and in fact it apparently never affected cattle in Scotland. Restrictions have been lifted, but it has been suggested that it's safer to eat beef cut from the bone instead of served on the bone. Avian flu remains a concern here as almost everywhere, but the country is not particularly vulnerable.

In general, contact the **International Association for Medical Assistance to Travelers** (IAMAT; ✆ 716/754-4883, or 416/652-0137 in Canada; www.iamat.org) for tips on travel and health concerns in the countries you're visiting, and for lists of local, English-speaking doctors. The United States **Centers for Disease Control and Prevention** (✆ 800/311-3435; www.cdc.gov) provides up-to-date information on health hazards by region or country and offers tips on food safety. The website www.tripprep.com, sponsored by a consortium of travel medicine practitioners, may also offer helpful advice on traveling abroad. You can find listings of reliable clinics overseas at the **International Society of Travel Medicine** (www.istm.org).

WHAT TO DO IF YOU GET SICK AWAY FROM HOME
If you need a doctor, your hotel can recommend one, or you can contact your embassy or consulate. If you need an ambulance, dial **999.** *Remember:* U.S. visitors are eligible for free emergency care. For follow-up care, you should expect to be asked to pay. We list **hospitals** and **emergency numbers** under "Fast Facts," p. 51 and p. 160.

If you suffer from a chronic illness, consult your doctor before your departure. Pack **prescription medications** in

Avoiding "Economy Class Syndrome"

Deep vein thrombosis, or as it's know in the world of flying, "economy-class syndrome," is a blood clot that develops in a deep vein. It's a potentially deadly condition that can be caused by sitting in cramped conditions—such as an airplane cabin—for too long. During a flight (especially a long-haul flight), get up, walk around, and stretch your legs every 60 to 90 minutes to keep your blood flowing. Other preventative measures include frequent flexing of the legs while sitting, drinking lots of water, and avoiding alcohol and sleeping pills. If you have a history of deep vein thrombosis, heart disease, or another condition that puts you at high risk, some experts recommend wearing compression stockings or taking anticoagulants when you fly; always ask your physician about the best course for you. Symptoms of deep vein thrombosis include leg pain or swelling, or even shortness of breath.

your carry-on luggage, and carry them in their original containers, with pharmacy labels—otherwise they might not make it through airport security. Carry the generic name of prescription medicines, in case a local pharmacist is unfamiliar with the brand name.

STAYING SAFE

Like most big cities in the Western world, Edinburgh and Glasgow have their share of crime. Handguns are banned by law, however, and shootings are exceedingly rare. Knives present a problem but one largely confined to youth gangs. Fights can flare up unexpectedly in either city, but in Glasgow, particularly, during heated soccer matches; exercise caution if any are being played during your stay. Marches of the Orange Order in June and July can also be scenes of random aggression.

In general, however, compared to most large cities of Europe, Edinburgh and Glasgow are equally safe, and violent crime against visitors is extremely rare. The same precautions prevail in these larger cities as they do elsewhere in the world. Tourists are typically prey to incidents of pickpocketing; mugging; "snatch and grab" theft of mobile phones, watches, and jewelry; and theft of unattended bags, especially late at night, in poorly lit areas of the city. Also

avoid visiting ATMs if it is late and not many people are around.

Visitors should take steps to ensure the safety of their passports. In Scotland, you are not expected to produce photo identity to police authorities, and passports may be more secure in locked hotel rooms or safes.

DEALING WITH DISCRIMINATION

Both Edinburgh and Glasgow are progressive cities and, in Scotland, discrimination is punishable by law. Racial flare-ups have occurred in housing projects on the cities' outskirts where asylum seekers have been sent. Travelers should not experience any discrimination, although gay and lesbian tourists do occasionally report cool receptions at smaller hotels and B&Bs.

ECOTOURISM

Scotland has begun to capitalize on "Green Tourism" but, as such, it doesn't apply to visits to Edinburgh and Glasgow.

You can find ecofriendly travel tips, statistics, and touring companies and associations—listed by destination under "Travel Choice"—at the TIES website, www. ecotourism.org. **Ecotravel.com** is part online magazine and part ecodirectory that lets you search for touring companies in several categories (water-based, land-based, spiritually oriented, and so on). Also check out **Conservation International** (www.conservation.org)—which, with *National Geographic Traveler*, annually presents **World Legacy Awards** (www.wlaward.org) to those travel tour operators, businesses, organizations, and places that have made a significant contribution to sustainable tourism.

7 Specialized Travel Resources

TRAVELERS WITH DISABILITIES

Most disabilities shouldn't stop anyone from traveling. There are more options and resources out there than ever before.

Many Scottish hotels, museums, restaurants, and sightseeing attractions have wheelchair ramps and toilets for disabled people. Recent changes in Scottish law have also put the onus on all new premises to have wheelchair accessibility. At historical sites, however, and in older buildings, access can be limited. Not all public transport is accessible for travelers with disabilities.

Many travel agencies offer customized tours and itineraries for travelers with disabilities. Among them are **Flying Wheels Travel** (✆ 507/451-5005; www.flyingwheelstravel.com), **Access-Able Travel Source** (✆ 303/232-2979; www.access-able.com), and **Accessible Journeys** (✆ 800/846-4537 or 610/521-0339; www.disabilitytravel.com). **Avis Rent a Car** has an "Avis Access" program that offers such services as a dedicated 24-hour toll-free number (✆ 888/879-4273) for customers with special travel needs; special car features such as swivel seats, spinner knobs, and hand controls; and accessible bus service.

Organizations that offer assistance to disabled travelers include **MossRehab** (www.mossresourcenet.org), the **American Foundation for the Blind (AFB;** ✆ 800/232-5463; www.afb.org), and **SATH (Society for Accessible Travel & Hospitality;** ✆ 212/447-7284; www.sath.org). **AirAmbulanceCard.com** is now partnered with SATH and allows you to preselect top-notch hospitals in case of an emergency.

The community website **iCan** (www.icanonline.net/channels/travel) has destination guides and several regular columns on accessible travel. Also check out the quarterly magazine *Emerging Horizons* (www.emerginghorizons.com), and *Open World* magazine, published by SATH.

GAY & LESBIAN TRAVELERS

Bars, clubs, and hotels catering exclusively to gay and lesbian travelers do exist in Edinburgh and Glasgow. For advice and information on local events, call the **Lothian Gay and Lesbian Switchboard** (✆ 0131/556-4049) or the **Strathclyde Gay and Lesbian Switchboard** (✆ 0141/847-0447). Scotland allows for civil partnerships, but gay-bashing does occasionally happen.

The **International Gay and Lesbian Travel Association (IGLTA;** ✆ 800/448-8550 or 954/776-2626; www.iglta.org) is the trade association for the gay and lesbian travel industry, and offers an online directory of gay- and lesbian-friendly travel businesses; go to their website and click on "Members."

Many agencies offer tours and travel itineraries specifically for gay and lesbian travelers. Among them are **Above and Beyond Tours** (✆ 800/397-2681; www.abovebeyondtours.com), **Now, Voyager** (✆ 800/255-6951; www.nowvoyager.com), and **Olivia Cruises & Resorts** (✆ 800/631-6277; www.olivia.com).

Gay.com Travel (✆ 800/929-2268 or 415/644-8044; www.gay.com/travel or www.outandabout.com), is an excellent online successor to the popular *Out & About* print magazine. It provides regularly updated information about gay-owned, gay-oriented, and gay-friendly lodging, dining, sightseeing, nightlife, and shopping establishments in every important destination worldwide.

The following travel guides are available at many bookstores, or you can order them from any online bookseller: *Frommer's Gay & Lesbian Europe* (www.frommers. com), an excellent travel resource to the top European cities and resorts; *Spartacus International Gay Guide* (Bruno Gmünder Verlag; www.spartacusworld.com/gay guide) and *Odysseus: The International Gay Travel Planner* (Odysseus Enterprises Ltd.); and the *Damron* guides (www.damron.com), with separate, annual books for gay men and lesbians.

SENIOR TRAVEL

Many discounts are available to seniors. Even if discounts aren't posted, ask if they're available. Seniors should always exercise caution in historic sites, where the ground can be uneven, and on cobbled streets in Edinburgh.

Members of **AARP** (formerly known as the American Association of Retired Persons), 601 E St. NW, Washington, DC 20049 (© **888/687-2277**; www.aarp. org), get discounts on hotels, airfares, and car rentals. AARP offers members a wide range of benefits, including *AARP: The Magazine* and a monthly newsletter. Anyone over 50 can join.

Many reliable agencies and organizations target the 50-plus market. **Elderhostel** (© **877/426-8056**; www.elderhostel. org) arranges study programs for adults 55 and up. **ElderTreks** (© **800/741-7956**; www.eldertreks.com) offers small-group tours to off-the-beaten-path or adventure-travel locations, restricted to travelers 50 and older. **INTRAV** (© **800/456-8100**; www.intrav.com) is a high-end tour operator that caters to the mature, discerning traveler (not specifically seniors), with trips around the world that include guided safaris, polar expeditions, private-jet adventures, and small-boat cruises down jungle rivers.

Recommended publications offering travel resources and discounts for seniors include: the quarterly magazine *Travel 50 & Beyond* (www.travel50andbeyond. com); *Travel Unlimited: Uncommon Adventures for the Mature Traveler* (Avalon); *101 Tips for Mature Travelers,* available from Grand Circle Travel (© **800/221-2610** or 617/350-7500; www.gct.com); and *Unbelievably Good Deals and Great Adventures That You Absolutely Can't Get Unless You're Over 50* (McGraw-Hill), by Joann Rattner Heilman.

FAMILY TRAVEL

When booking overnight rooms, ask whether family suites are available. Historical attractions in Edinburgh and Glasgow often offer family tickets. Finally, look for our "Kids" icon, indicating attractions, restaurants, and hotels that are especially family-friendly.

Familyhostel (© **800/733-9753;** www.learn.unh.edu) takes the whole family, including kids 8 to 15, on moderately priced U.S. and international learning vacations. Lectures, field trips, and sightseeing are guided by a team of academics.

Recommended family travel websites include **Family Travel Forum** (www. familytravelforum.com), **Family Travel Network** (www.familytravelnetwork.com), **Traveling Internationally with Your Kids** (www.travelwithyourkids.com), and **Family Travel Files** (www.thefamilytravel files.com),

STUDENT TRAVEL

If you're traveling internationally, you'd be wise to arm yourself with an **International Student Identity Card (ISIC),** which offers substantial savings on rail passes, plane tickets, and entrance fees. It

Should They Stay or Should They Go?

Psychologically speaking, Scotland is a politically conflicted place. In 1999, its Parliament was restored after being dissolved for nearly 300 years following the union between England and Scotland in 1707. Most Scots have a fierce pride in their country, which is every bit as old as its larger and more dominant neighbor to the south. But whether that self-belief will ever translate into complete self-government is open to debate.

The traditional political parties—Labour, Conservative, and Liberal Democrat—remain staunchly in favor of the current union, while the leading independence group, the Scottish National Party, has seen its percentage of the vote drop in 21st-century elections. But SNP members are not the only ones who advocate Scottish independence: New parties with growing electoral success, such as the Greens and Scottish Socialists, also back full autonomy from rule in London.

also provides you with basic health and life insurance and a 24-hour help line. The card is available from **STA Travel** (© **800/781-4040** in North America; www.sta.com or www.statravel.com; or www.statravel.co.uk in the U.K.), the biggest student travel agency in the world. If you're no longer a student but are still under 26, you can get an **International Youth Travel Card (IYTC)** from the same people; this entitles you to some discounts (but not on museum admissions). **Travel CUTS** (© **800/667-2887** or 416/614-2887; www.travelcuts.com) offers similar services for both Canadians and U.S. residents. Irish students may prefer to turn to **USIT** (© **01/602-1600;** www.usitnow.ie), an Ireland-based specialist in student, youth, and independent travel.

8 Planning Your Trip Online

SURFING FOR AIRFARE

The most popular online travel agencies are **Travelocity** (www.travelocity.com, or www.travelocity.co.uk), **Expedia** (www.expedia.com, www.expedia.co.uk, or www.expedia.ca), and **Orbitz** (www.orbitz.com).

In addition, most airlines now offer online-only fares that even their phone agents know nothing about. For the websites of airlines that fly to and from your destination, go to "Getting There," p. 27.

SURFING FOR HOTELS

In addition to **Travelocity, Expedia, Orbitz, Priceline,** and **Hotwire** (see above), the following websites will help you with booking hotel rooms online:

- www.hotels.com
- www.travelaxe.net
- www.tripadvisor.com

It's a good idea to **get a confirmation number** and **make a printout** of any online booking transaction.

SURFING FOR RENTAL CARS

For booking rental cars online, the best deals are usually found at rental-car company websites, although all the major online travel agencies also offer rental-car reservations services.

9 The 21st-Century Traveler

INTERNET ACCESS AWAY FROM HOME

WITHOUT YOUR OWN COMPUTER

To find cybercafes in your destination check www.cybercaptive.com and www.cybercafe.com. There are a host of Internet cafes in both Edinburgh and Glasgow, increasing numbers of bars where there is wireless access to the Internet, and plenty of public libraries with computer terminals.

Aside from formal cybercafes, most youth hostels and public libraries have Internet access. Avoid hotel business centers unless you're willing to pay exorbitant rates.

WITH YOUR OWN COMPUTER

More and more hotels, cafes, and retailers are signing on as Wi-Fi (wireless fidelity) "hotspots." Mac owners have their own networking technology: Apple AirPort. Boingo (www.boingo.com) and Wayport (www.wayport.com) have set up networks in airports and high-class hotel lobbies. IPass providers (see below) also give you access to a few hundred wireless hotel lobby setups. To locate other hotspots that provide free wireless networks in cities around the world, go to www.personaltelco.net/index.cgi/WirelessCommunities.

For dial-up access, most business-class hotels throughout the world offer dataports for laptop modems, and a few thousand hotels in the U.S. and Europe now offer free high-speed Internet access. In addition, major Internet Service Providers (ISPs) have local access numbers around the world, allowing you to go online by placing a local call. The iPass network also has dial-up numbers around the world. You'll have to sign up with an iPass provider, who will then tell you how to set up your computer for your destination(s).

For a list of iPass providers, go to www.ipass.com and click on "Individuals Buy Now." One solid provider is i2roam (© 866/811-6209 or 920/235-0475; www.i2roam.com).

Wherever you go, bring a connection kit of the right power and phone adapters, a spare phone cord, and a spare Ethernet network cable—or find out whether your hotel supplies them to guests.

CELLPHONE USE

The three letters that define much of the world's wireless capabilities are GSM (Global System for Mobiles), a big, seamless network that makes for easy cross-border cellphone use throughout Europe and dozens of other countries worldwide. In the U.S., T-Mobile, AT&T Wireless, and Cingular use this quasi-universal system; in Canada, Microcell and some Rogers customers are GSM, and all Europeans and most Australians use GSM. If your cellphone is on a GSM system, and you have a world-capable multiband phone, such as many Sony Ericsson, Motorola, or Samsung models, you can make and receive calls across civilized areas around much of the globe. Just call your wireless operator and ask for "international roaming" to be activated on your account. Unfortunately, per-minute charges can be high—usually $1 to $1.50 in Western Europe and up to $5 in places such as Russia and Indonesia.

For many, renting a phone is a good idea. (Even worldphone owners will have to rent new phones if they're traveling to non-GSM regions, such as Japan or Korea.) While you can rent a phone from any number of overseas sites, including kiosks at airports and at car-rental agencies, we suggest renting the phone before you leave home. North Americans can rent one before leaving home from

InTouch USA (℃ 800/872-7626; www. intouchglobal.com) or **RoadPost** (℃ 888/290-1606 or 905/272-5665; www.roadpost.com). InTouch will also, for free, advise you on whether your existing phone will work overseas; simply call ℃ 703/222-7161 between 9am and 4pm EST, or go to **http://intouchglobal.com/travel.htm**.

Buying a phone can be economically attractive, as many nations have cheap prepaid phone systems. Once you arrive at your destination, stop by a local cellphone shop and get the cheapest package; you'll probably pay less than $100 for a phone and a starter calling card. Local calls may be as low as 10¢ per minute, and in many countries incoming calls are free.

Wilderness adventurers, or those heading to less-developed countries, might consider renting a **satellite phone ("satphone")**. It's different from a cellphone in that it connects to satellites and works where there's no cellular signal or ground-based tower. You can rent satellite phones from RoadPost (see above). InTouch USA (see above) offers a wider range of satphones but at higher rates. Per-minute call charges can be even cheaper than roaming charges with a regular cellphone, but the phone itself is more expensive. As of this writing, satphones were outrageously expensive to buy, so don't even think about it.

10 Getting There

BY PLANE

Carriers that fly directly to Edinburgh and Glasgow from the U.S. have changed over the past few years. For example, in 2006, American Airlines unexpectedly announced it would terminate its summer service from Chicago to Glasgow. Most long-haul flights arrive and depart from Glasgow's airport. See "Essentials" in chapter 12.

But London accepts flights from all corners of the globe, of course. Internally, **British Airways** (℃ 800/247-9297, or 0870/850-9850 in the U.K.; www.ba.com) offers frequent nonstop flights daily from London's Heathrow Airport to both Edinburgh and Glasgow. **BMI** (formerly British Midland; ℃ 0870/607-0555; www.flybmi.com) also flies from Heathrow to both Edinburgh and Glasgow. It is a member of the international "Star Alliance" which includes carriers such as Air Canada, Air New Zealand, United, and US Airways. **Ryanair** (℃ 0871/246-0000; www.ryanair.com) is a budget airline that flies from Stansted outside London to Prestwick south of Glasgow.

GETTING INTO TOWN FROM THE AIRPORT

Getting from the airports to Edinburgh or Glasgow is easy and relatively quick. See "Essentials" in chapters 4 and 12.

FLYING FOR LESS: TIPS FOR GETTING THE BEST AIRFARE

- Passengers who can book their ticket either **long in advance or at the last minute,** or who **fly midweek** or at **less-trafficked hours** may pay a fraction of the full fare. If your schedule is flexible, say so, and ask if you can secure a cheaper fare by changing your flight plans.
- Search **the Internet** for cheap fares (see "Planning Your Trip Online," above).
- Keep an eye on local newspapers for **promotional specials** or **fare wars,** when airlines lower prices on their most popular routes. You rarely see fare wars offered for peak travel times, but if you can travel in the off-months, you may snag a bargain.
- Try to book a ticket **in its country of origin.** If you're planning a one-way

flight from Johannesburg to Bombay, a South Africa–based travel agent will probably have the lowest fares. For multileg trips, book in the country of the first leg; for example, book New York–London–Amsterdam–Rome–New York in the U.S.

- **Consolidators,** also known as bucket shops, are great sources for international tickets, although they usually can't beat Internet fares within North America. Start by looking in Sunday newspaper travel sections; U.S. travelers should focus on the *New York Times, Los Angeles Times,* and *Miami Herald.* U.K. travelers should search in the *Independent, The Guardian,* or *The Observer.* For less-developed destinations, small travel agents who cater to immigrant communities in large cities often have the best deals. *Beware:* Bucket shop tickets are usually nonrefundable or rigged with stiff cancellation penalties, often as high as 50% to 75% of the ticket price, and some put you on charter airlines, which may leave at inconvenient times and experience delays. Several reliable consolidators are worldwide and available online. **STA Travel** has been the world's lead consolidator for students since purchasing Council Travel, but their fares are competitive for travelers of all ages. **ELTExpress (Flights.com; ☎ 800/TRAV-800;** www.eltexpress.com) has excellent fares worldwide, particularly to Europe. They also have "local" websites in 12 countries. **FlyCheap** (☎ **800/FLY-CHEAP;** www.1800flycheap.com), owned by package-holiday megalith MyTravel, has especially good fares to sunny destinations. **Air Tickets Direct** (☎ **800/778-3447;** www.airticketsdirect.com) is based in Montreal and leverages the currently weak Canadian dollar for low fares; they also book trips to places that

U.S. travel agents won't touch, such as Cuba.

- Join **frequent-flier clubs.** Frequent-flier membership doesn't cost a cent, but it does entitle you to better seats, faster response to phone inquiries, and prompter service if your luggage is stolen or your flight is canceled or delayed, or if you want to change your seat. And you don't have to fly to earn points; **frequent-flier credit cards** can earn you thousands of miles for doing your everyday shopping. With more than 70 mileage awards programs on the market, consumers have never had more options. Investigate the program details of your favorite airlines before you sink points into any one. Consider which airlines have hubs in the airport nearest you, and, of those carriers, which have the most advantageous alliances, given your most common routes. To play the frequent-flier game to your best advantage, consult Randy Petersen's **Inside Flyer** (www.insideflyer.com). Petersen and friends review all the programs in detail and post regular updates on changes in policies and trends.

LONG-HAUL FLIGHTS: HOW TO STAY COMFORTABLE

- Your choice of airline and airplane will definitely affect your leg room. Find more details about U.S. airlines at **www.seatguru.com.** For international airlines, the research firm Skytrax has posted a list of average seat pitches at **www.airlinequality.com.**
- Emergency exit seats and bulkhead seats typically have the most legroom. Emergency exit seats are usually left unassigned until the day of a flight (to ensure that someone able-bodied fills the seats); it's worth getting to the ticket counter early to snag one of these spots for a long flight. Many

Jetlag is a pitfall of traveling across time zones. If you're flying north–south and you feel sluggish when you touch down, your symptoms will be the result of dehydration and the general stress of air travel. When you travel east–west or vice-versa, however, your body becomes thoroughly confused about what time it is, and everything from your digestive system to your brain is knocked for a loop. Traveling east, say from Chicago to Paris, is more difficult on your internal clock than traveling west, say from London to Hawaii, because most peoples' bodies are more inclined to stay up late than fall asleep early.

Here are some tips for combating jet lag:

- **Reset your watch** to your destination time before you board the plane.
- **Drink lots of water** before, during, and after your flight. Avoid alcohol.
- **Exercise and sleep well** for a few days before your trip.
- If you have trouble sleeping on planes, **fly eastward on morning flights.**
- **Daylight** is the key to resetting your body clock. At the website for **Outside In** (www.bodyclock.com), you can get a customized plan of when to seek and avoid light.

passengers find that bulkhead seating (the row facing the wall at the front of the cabin) offers more legroom, but keep in mind that bulkheads are where airlines often put baby bassinets, so you may be sitting next to an infant.

- To have two seats for yourself in a three-seat row, try for an aisle seat in a center section toward the back of coach. If you're traveling with a companion, book an aisle and a window seat. Middle seats are usually booked last, so chances are good you'll end up with three seats to yourselves.
- Ask about entertainment options. Many airlines offer seatback video systems where you get to choose your movies or play video games—but only on some of their planes. (Boeing 777s are your best bet.)
- To sleep, avoid the last row of any section or the row in front of an emergency exit, as these seats are the least likely to recline. Avoid seats near highly trafficked lavatory areas. Avoid seats in the back of many jets—these can be narrower than those in the rest of coach. You also may want to

reserve a window seat so you can rest your head and avoid being bumped in the aisle.

- Get up, walk around, and stretch every 60 to 90 minutes to keep your blood flowing. See "Avoiding 'Economy Class Syndrome'" on p. 22.
- Drink water before, during, and after your flight to combat the lack of humidity in airplane cabins. Avoid alcohol, which will dehydrate you.
- If you're flying with kids, don't forget to carry on toys, books, pacifiers, and chewing gum to help them relieve ear pressure buildup during ascent and descent.

BY CAR

If you're driving north to Scotland from England, it's fastest to take the **M1 motorway** north from London. You can reach M1 by driving to the ring road from any point in the British capital. Southeast of Leeds, you'll need to connect with **A1** (not a motorway), which you take north to Scotch Corner. Here **M1** resumes, ending south of Newcastle-upon-Tyne. Then you can take **A696,** which becomes **A68,** for its final run north into Edinburgh.

If you're in the west of England, go north along **M5,** which begins at Exeter (Devon). Eventually this will merge with **M6.** Continue north on M6 until you reach a point north of Carlisle. From Carlisle, cross into Scotland near Gretna Green. Continue north along **A74** via Moffat. The A74 soon becomes the **M74** heading toward Glasgow. If your goal is Edinburgh, not Glasgow, various roads will take you east to the Scottish capital, including **M8,** which goes part of the way, as do **A702, A70,** and **A71** (all these routes are well signposted). See "Essentials" in chapters 4 and 12.

BY TRAIN OR BUS

From England, two main rail lines link London to Scotland. The most popular and fastest route is **King's Cross Station** in London to Edinburgh, going by way of Newcastle. Trains cross from England into Scotland at Berwick-upon-Tweed. If you're going via the west coast, trains leave **Euston Station** in London for Glasgow, by way of Carlisle. Most of these trains take at least 5 hours to reach Glasgow. See "Essentials" in chapters 4 and 12.

The journey from London to Glasgow and Edinburgh by bus can take up to 12 hours although direct buses can make the trip in less than 10 hours. Nevertheless, it'll get you there for about £45 ($83) standard round-trip fare. **National Express** (© **0870/580-8080;** www. nationalexpress.com) runs buses daily (typically 9:30am, noon, and 11pm for direct service) from London's Victoria Coach Station to Edinburgh's Bus Station near St. Andrew Square; while direct buses for Glasgow's **Buchanan Street Bus Station,** about 2 blocks north of the Queen Street Station on North Hanover Street (© **0870-608-2608**), leave London's Victoria Coach Station at 9am and 11:30pm. Scottish **CityLink** (© **0870/ 550-5050** or www.citylink.co.uk) also has frequent bus service to and from Edinburgh, with a standard one-way ticket costing £5 ($9.25).

11 Packages for the Independent Traveler

Package tours are simply a way to buy the airfare, accommodations, and other elements of your trip (such as car rentals, airport transfers, and sometimes even activities) at the same time and often at discounted prices.

Tips Ask before You Go

Before you invest in a package deal or an escorted tour:

- Always ask about the **cancellation policy.** Can you get your money back? Is there a deposit required?
- Ask about the **accommodations choices and prices** for each. Then look up the hotels' reviews in a Frommer's guide and check their rates online for your specific dates of travel. Also find out what types of rooms are offered.
- Request a complete **schedule** (escorted tours only).
- Ask about the **size** and demographics of the group (escorted tours only).
- Discuss what is included in the **price** (transportation, meals, tips, airport transfers, and such; escorted tours only).
- Finally, look for **hidden expenses.** Ask whether airport departure fees and taxes, for example, are included in the total cost—they rarely are.

One good source of package deals is the airlines themselves. Most major airlines offer air/land packages, including **American Airlines Vacations** (© 800/321-2121; www.aavacations.com), **Delta Vacations** (© 800/221-6666; www.deltavacations.com), **Continental Airlines Vacations** (© 800/301-3800; www.covacations.com), and **United Vacations** (© 888/854-3899; www.unitedvacations.com). Several big **online travel agencies** —Expedia, Travelocity, Orbitz, Site59, and Lastminute.com—also do a brisk business in packages.

Travel packages are also listed in the travel section of your local Sunday newspaper. Or check ads in the national travel magazines such as *Arthur Frommer's Budget Travel Magazine, Travel + Leisure, National Geographic Traveler,* and *Condé Nast Traveler.*

12 Escorted General-Interest Tours

Escorted tours are structured group tours, with a group leader. The price usually includes everything from airfare to hotels, meals, tours, admission costs, and local transportation.

Despite the fact that escorted tours require big deposits and predetermine hotels, restaurants, and itineraries, many people derive security and peace of mind from the structure they offer. Escorted tours—whether they're navigated by bus, motor coach, train, or boat—let travelers sit back and enjoy the trip without having to drive or worry about details. They take you to the maximum number of sights in the minimum amount of time with the least amount of hassle. They're particularly convenient for people with limited mobility and they can be a great way to make new friends.

On the downside, you'll have little opportunity for serendipitous interactions with locals. The tours can be jam-packed with activities, leaving little room for individual sightseeing, whim, or adventure—plus they often focus on the heavily touristed sites, so you miss out on many a lesser-known gem.

13 Tips on Accommodations

EDINBURGH

Edinburgh offers an awful lot of accommodations for visitors, from the super posh and ridiculously pricey five-star hotels to down-and-dirty bunkhouses and youth hostels. It is a city that anticipates bundles of tourists and travelers, whether backpackers, families, or business types in the Scottish capital on commercial or governmental matters. But be warned, however. During the 3- to 4-week period of the Edinburgh Festival every summer, the hotels fill up. If you're planning a visit at that time, be sure to reserve your accommodation as far in advance as possible. Otherwise you'll end up in a town or village as much as 40km (55 miles) from the city center. And don't be surprised if the rates in Edinburgh are higher during August, particularly at guesthouses and smaller hotels.

The **Edinburgh Information Centre,** near Waverley Station, atop the Princes Mall shopping center, 3 Princes St. (© **0131/473-3800** or 0845/225-5121; fax 0131/473-3881; www.edinburgh.org; bus: 3, 8, 22, 25, or 31), compiles a lengthy list of small hotels, guesthouses, and private homes providing a bed-and-breakfast for as little as £20 ($37) per person. A £3 ($5.50) booking fee is charged and a 10% deposit is expected. Allow about 4 weeks' notice, especially during summer. It's open year-round; typically the hours are Monday through Saturday from 9am to 7pm and Sunday from 10am to

7pm, though it is open later during the Festival and closes earlier in the winter months.

GLASGOW

The tourist trade in Glasgow is less seasonal than in Edinburgh with fewer visitors in general coming to Scotland's largest city. However, it has become a popular spot for business conferences while the increase in budget-airline flights from the European continent seems to have increased the overall number of visitors. So if, for example, an international association of dentists is in town, finding accommodation can be difficult.

Until recently, many tourism industry observers said Glasgow suffered from a shortage of hotel rooms, but new places such as the Radisson SAS have changed the equation. Whenever you're coming, it's recommended that you reserve a room in advance. Some rates are predictably high (especially so if the pound remains strong), but many business-oriented hotels offer bargains on weekends and the number of budget options is increasing.

The Glasgow and Clyde Valley tourism office (www.visitscotland.com) offers an **Information & Booking Hot Line** (© **0845/225-5121** from within the U.K., or 01506/832-121 from outside the U.K.). Lines are open (local time) Monday to Friday from 8am to 8pm, Saturday from 9am to 5:50pm, and Sunday from 10am to 4pm. The fax number is 01506/832-222. The fee for this booking service is £3 ($5.50).

TOURIST BOARD RANKINGS

The Scottish Tourist Board does rank the accommodations at hundreds of hotels, guesthouses, B&Bs, and self-catering apartments. While helpful, these stars are largely based upon available amenities, such as 24-hour room service, ironing boards or spas, which may not be relevant for each and every traveler. Also, not all hotels and guesthouses are part of the scheme, although they may be no less attractive.

SAVING ON YOUR HOTEL ROOM

The **rack rate** is the maximum rate that a hotel charges for a room. Hardly anybody pays this price, however, except in high season or on holidays. To lower the cost of your room:

- **Ask about special rates or other discounts.** You may qualify for corporate, student, military, senior, frequent flyer, trade union, or other discounts.
- **Dial direct.** When booking a room in a chain hotel, you'll often get a better deal by calling the individual hotel's reservation desk rather than the chain's main number.
- **Book online.** Many hotels offer Internet-only discounts, or supply rooms to Priceline, Hotwire, or Expedia at rates much lower than the ones you can get through the hotel itself.
- **Remember the law of supply and demand.** Resort hotels are most crowded and therefore most expensive on weekends, so discounts are usually available for midweek stays. Business hotels in downtown locations are busiest during the week, so you can expect big discounts over the weekend. Many hotels have high-season and low-season prices, and booking even 1 day after high season ends can mean big discounts.
- **Look into group or long-stay discounts.** If you come as part of a large group, you should be able to negotiate a bargain rate. Likewise, if you're planning a long stay (at least 5 days), you might qualify for a discount. As a general rule, expect 1 night free after a 7-night stay.
- **Avoid excess charges and hidden costs.** When you book a room, ask

whether the hotel charges for parking. Use your own cell phone, pay phones, or prepaid phone cards instead of dialing direct from hotel phones, which usually have exorbitant rates. Finally, ask about local taxes and service charges, which can increase the cost of a room by 15% or more.

- **Book an efficiency.** A room with a kitchenette allows you to shop for groceries and cook your own meals. This is a big money saver, especially for families on long stays.

- **Consider enrolling in hotel "frequent-stay" programs,** which are upping the ante lately to win the loyalty of repeat customers. Frequent guests can now accumulate points or credits to earn free hotel nights, airline miles, in-room amenities, merchandise, tickets to concerts and events, discounts on sporting facilities—and even credit toward stock in the participating hotel, in the case of the Jameson Inn hotel group.

LANDING THE BEST ROOM

Somebody has to get the best room in the house. It might as well be you. You can start by joining the hotel's frequent-guest program, which may make you eligible for upgrades. A hotel-branded credit card usually gives its owner "silver" or "gold" status in frequent-guest programs for free. Always ask about a corner room. They're often larger and quieter, with more windows and light, and they often cost the same as standard rooms.

When you make your reservation, ask if the hotel is renovating; if it is, request a room away from the construction. Ask about nonsmoking rooms, rooms with views, rooms with twin, queen- or king-size beds. If you're a light sleeper, request a quiet room away from vending machines, elevators, restaurants, bars, and discos. Ask for a room that has been most recently renovated or redecorated.

If you aren't happy with your room when you arrive, ask for another one. Most lodgings will be willing to accommodate you.

14 Recommended Books & Films

BOOKS
BIOGRAPHY

The Life of Robert Burns, by Catherine Carswell (Canongate Classics, 1998), is the groundbreaking look at the life of Scotland's national poet first published in the 1930s. So frank was Carswell's assessment—particularly regarding the poet's romantic and sexual liaisons—that Burns Clubs took offense. But it is such honesty that makes her version indispensable. *Robert Louis Stevenson: A Biography,* by Claire Harman (Harper Collins, 2005), is the latest and eminently readable tome on the frail Edinburgh-born author and adventurer, who was arguably Scotland's greatest writer.

FICTION

Set in 18th-century Edinburgh, Sir Walter Scott's *The Heart of Midlothian* (Penguin Classics) was declared a masterpiece in 1818, and it remains his seminal piece of fiction, influencing the later works of authors such as Balzac, Hawthorne, and Dickens. *Kidnapped,* by Robert Louis Stevenson (Penguin Classics), follows the adventures of young David Balfour after he is spirited out of Edinburgh and ends up on the wrong side of the law in the Western Highlands. It is as entertaining today as it was upon publication in 1886.

First published in 1981, *Lanark: A Life in Four Books* by Alasdair Gray (Canongate, 2002) is perhaps the most important novel to be published in Scotland in the last century. Despite some fantastical detours, it gets to the core of urban Scotland.

Black & Blue by Ian Rankin (St. Martin's Press, 1999) is one of several crime novels that turn on the life of Rankin's troubled antihero Inspector Rebus. In this volume, Rebus moves back and forth between his home in Edinburgh and Glasgow. Another master of the modern crime genre is Glasgow's Denise Mina, who has published *Garnethill* and *Exile.*

The Prime of Miss Jean Brodie by Muriel Spark and *Trainspotting* by Irving Welsh are both better known for their cinematic adaptations, but in their own very different ways, they manage to capture elements of Edinburgh life.

HISTORY

Although histories of Britain generally neglect Scotland, good recently published historical overviews of Scotland include *The Scottish Nation: 1700–2000* by academic Tom Devine (Penguin, 2001). *Stone Voices: The Search for Scotland,* by Neal Ascherson (Hill & Wang, 2003), is a quest for the national character of Scotland, although the Edinburgh-born author and veteran foreign correspondent finds it a tad hard to pin down. American historian Arthur Herman's *The Scottish Enlightenment: The Scot's Invention of the Modern World* (Crown, 2001) offers a clear and extremely readable explanation of the impact that Scottish thinkers—predominantly based in Edinburgh and Glasgow—have had on the world and the United States in particular.

FILMS

My Name Is Joe (1998) paints a grim if accurate picture of contemporary Glaswegians struggling with their addictions and inner demons, although the film's not lacking humor or romance.

Better known is *Trainspotting* (1996), which stars Ewan McGregor in a gritty and often hilarious account of a group of unrepentant drug-addled characters in Edinburgh. Finally, *Gregory's Girl* (1981) offers a simple story of an awkward high school student (John Gordon-Sinclair) in a modern (and hideous) 1960s "New Town" development near Glasgow. Quirky but loveable.

Suggested Edinburgh & Glasgow Itineraries

Few travelers have unlimited time, and you may find a few suggested itineraries for 3-day and weeklong visits to Edinburgh and Glasgow, and the areas around them, helpful. These itineraries build on the information found in chapters 7 and 15, and also include ideas from chapters 11 and 19. Double-check these chapters for the opening hours of specific attractions. You might also want to review the recommendations in chapter 1 to judge what experiences or sights have special appeal to you, and adjust your itinerary appropriately.

The itineraries below will highlight major attractions, such as Edinburgh's Royal Mile, but also direct you to less

celebrated spots, such as Alexander "Greek" Thomson's Holmwood House on Glasgow's Southside. The pace may look a bit breathless for some visitors. If so, skip a sight or two: These plans are suggestions, not requirements. You may also mix bits of one with highlights of another.

By combining the first and second itineraries, you'll have an instant plan for visiting both Glasgow and Edinburgh in 1 week (with a day to spare!). *Note:* The Edinburgh and Glasgow itineraries can be done on foot and by using public transportation in most cases; the side trips are best taken using a car, but can be adjusted to use trains and buses in some cases.

1 Edinburgh in 3 Days

Although it's impossible to see all of Edinburgh in 3 days, you can get a fairly good feel for the city during visits of less than a half-week.

Day ❶: The Royal Mile & Old Town ★★

After checking into a hotel or guest house, head straight to the **Royal Mile** (p. 84) in Edinburgh's Old Town. It stretches from **Edinburgh Castle** to the **Palace of Holyroodhouse.** Along the way you can stop at the historic **Gladstone's Land** or **St. Giles Cathedral,** as well as the modern **Scottish Parliament** building. Take your time and be sure to wander down some of the narrow alleys

and passageways that extend down the hill on either side of the Royal Mile, like ribs from a spine. Also, if you have time left over, check out the **Grassmarket** and take a detour to the **Museum of Scotland** (p. 89).

Day ❷: New Town & Scotland's National Galleries ★★

Having a grip on Edinburgh's Old Town, it's time to move to the city's **New Town,** which dates to the late 1700s. Begin with

Edinburgh in 3 Days

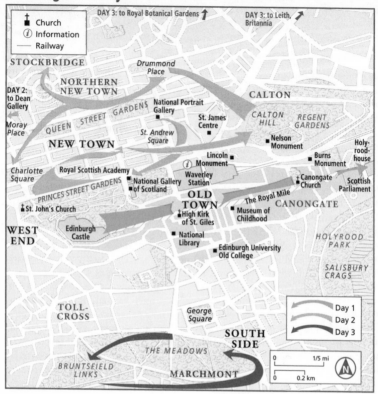

the **Princes Street Gardens** and then move on to **George Street,** with its panoply of shops and stylish bars. Climb up to **Calton Hill** (p. 94) at the eastern end of New Town for the views and from the western side of the district, take in **Charlotte Square** or wander down to **Stockbridge** on the Water of Leith. Depending upon your legs, you can follow a path along the Water of Leith to the **Dean Gallery,** part of the capital **National Galleries of Scotland** (p. 89). Catch the shuttle bus to any of the others, including the **National Portrait Gallery** or the main **National Gallery of Scotland** back in Princes Street Gardens.

Day ❸: To Leith & the Southside ☙
It is your last day, so let's move out of the city center and head to the sea. First stop,

however, is the marvelous **Royal Botanic Garden** (p. 95), where you might well spend a few hours wandering about the verdant paths. In **Leith,** you'll find the original port of Edinburgh, once an independent town in its own right. Diehard fans of golf should see **Leith Links,** one of the sport's historic landmarks or, if you are Royal fancier, go to see the *Britannia,* the yacht that Queen Elizabeth and family used until 1997. Come back towards central Edinburgh, but detour south to the **Meadows** and see some of the fine residential neighborhoods of Marchmont or Bruntsfield and get an idea of how Edinburghers live.

2 Glasgow in 3 Days

Even with only 3 days, you can still see a good portion of Scotland's largest city.

Day ❶: Central Glasgow ★★

Drop your bags at the hotel or guest house and get moving into the heart of Glasgow. The bustling **City Centre** offers a host of monumental Victorian buildings and a couple of landmarks designed by the great **Charles Rennie Mackintosh,** such as his **Glasgow School of Art** (p. 194). The city also boasts another great 19th-century design genius, **Alexander "Greek" Thomson.** Have a gander at his **St. Vincent Street Church,** with its exotic mix of Central Asian, Middle Eastern and Mediterranean influences. Just southeast of the city's commercial center is the **Merchant City,** Glasgow's version of New York's SoHo, with loft apartments and trendy bars. This is the historic core of the city, but alas most of its historic buildings are long gone. The strongest surviving remnant of Glasgow's rich Medieval history is **Glasgow Cathedral** (p. 193).

Day ❷: The West End ★★

Glasgow's West End is the most prosperous and attractive district in the city. Opening after a 3-year multimillion pound refurbishment, the **Kelvingrove Art Gallery and Museum** (p. 195) offers an expansive collection of paintings and artifacts—one of the best held by any city in Europe. Take a stroll through adjacent **Kelvingrove Park** and then stop at the **University of Glasgow,** where you can see at the **Hunterian Art Gallery** (p. 195) the complete interiors of the home where Mackintosh lived. The West End's "Main Street" is **Byres Road,** with bars, restaurants, shops and more. Detour onto cobbled **Ashton Lane,** or, on fine days, take in the city's **Botanic Garden** at the top of Byres Road.

Day ❸: The Southside ★

Glasgow is bisected by the River Clyde, and the city's Southside is considered, by some, to be the real Glasgow. Perhaps, but while mostly residential, there are some highlights to visit. First and foremost is the **Burrell** (p. 196), a custom-made museum holding the vast collection of art and artifacts collected by a local industrialist who bequeathed the entire wonderful lot to the city. If you find that "Greek" Thomson intrigues you, then definitely go to **Holmwood House** (p. 196); it's the best example of his sumptuous and timeless villas. Families will enjoy the **Science Centre** (p. 199) on the southern banks of the Clyde.

3 Edinburgh & Side Trips in 1 Week

Okay, you have more time and really should see some of the picturesque countryside that surrounds the capital of Scotland.

Days ❶ to ❸

Follow "Edinburgh in 3 Days" itinerary, above.

Day ❹: Fife & Linlithgow ★

If you're up early, you might scale **Arthur's Seat,** the ancient volcano that rises up above Edinburgh. From there you can see the Firth of Clyde, and crossing it takes you into the so-called Kingdom of **Fife** (p. 143). For a full-day's excursion, first go north to the seaside town of **St. Andrews** (p. 144), world famous for its golf but also an important historic site of Christian pilgrimage and

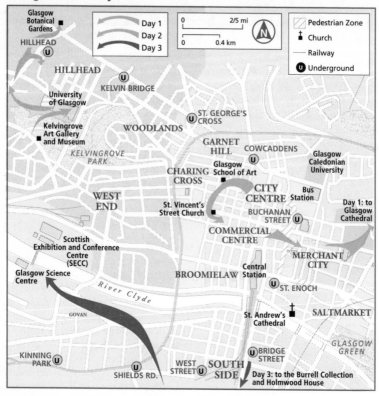

home of the first university in Scotland. Come back south along the coast, stopping briefly to see the excellent Scottish art collection in the **Kirkcaldy Museum** (p. 146). After this, you'll have just enough time to head back across the Forth and get to **Linlithgow** (p. 134) and its ancient palace, the birthplace of one of Scotland's most iconic figures: Mary Queen of Scots.

Day ⑤: East Lothian ✸

In the morning, head east out of the city for the town of North Berwick and its popular **Scottish Seabird Centre** (p. 138), where, thanks to a host of video cameras dotting the nearby islands and coastal cliffs, you can see a range of avian and sea-life colonies. Other highlights of the

region include two castle ruins, the romantic **Dirleton** (p. 137), in the cute village of the same name, as well as the magnificent **Tantallon** (p. 138) on bluffs above the sea. Golf buffs may want to see **Muirfield,** although others will settle happily for a stroll around nearby **Gullane** village and its sandy beaches (p. 138).

Day ⑥: South into the Borders ✸✸

Make another early start and head south towards Melrose. This village has **Melrose Abbey** (p. 141), which has inspired many—including writer Sir Walter Scott. His home, **Abbotsford** (p. 141), is next on the agenda. This mansion has a host of historical artifacts collected by Scott, and it is where he wrote many of his most enduring tales. Next up is the oldest continuously

Edinburgh & Side Trips in 1 Week

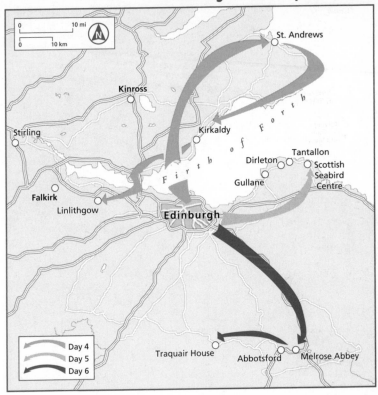

Map legend:
- Day 4
- Day 5
- Day 6

Locations shown: St. Andrews, Kinross, Kirkaldy, Stirling, Dirleton, Tantallon, Gullane, Scottish Seabird Centre, Falkirk, Linlithgow, Edinburgh, Firth of Forth, Traquair House, Abbotsford, Melrose Abbey

inhabited home in Scotland, the alluring **Traquair House** (p. 142).

Day ❼: Edinburgh's Other Attractions

Take it easy—you've had a busy week. It's time to see some of the other attractions that Edinburgh has to offer. Take in any museums or galleries not yet hit, such as the **Writer's Museum** or **Fruitmarket Gallery.** How about the **Edinburgh Zoo** (p. 91) or if you really enjoyed Dan Brown's *Da Vinci Code,* then you had better make the pilgrimage to **Rosslyn Chapel** (p. 136) on the southern fringes of the city. Otherwise, just hang out in Old Town or New Town.

4 Glasgow & Side Trips in 1 Week

Glasgow is a fairly big city with lots to offer, but one of its additional attractions is the ease of escaping the metropolis, finding fresh air and memorable scenery.

Days ❶ to ❸

Follow "Glasgow in 3 Days" itinerary, above.

Day ❹: Burns Country & Culzean ✪✪

Set out for Ayrshire and start with the town of **Ayr,** on the coast southwest of

Glasgow & Side Trips in 1 Week

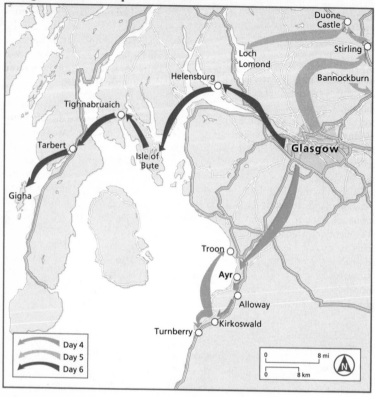

Duone Castle
Stirling
Loch Lomond
Bannockburn
Helensburg
Tighnabruaich
Glasgow
Tarbert
Isle of Bute
Gigha
Troon
Ayr
Alloway
Turnberry
Kirkoswald

Day 4
Day 5
Day 6

0 ___ 8 mi
0 ___ 8 km

N

Glasgow. This is the beginning of your tour of **Burns Country**—the historic stomping grounds of Scotland's most famous plowman poet. In nearby Alloway is the **Burn's National Heritage Park,** highlighted by the bard's birthplace, the **Burns Cottage and Museum** (p. 243). Depending on your time and interest, you can also visit other landmarks, such as **Souter Johnnie's Cottage** in Kirkoswald. But leave time for **Culzean Castle** and its magnificent **Country Park** (p. 246), with acres and acres to explore from sandy beachhead to a walled garden with exotic plants. If you fancy golf, however, you might prefer seeing world-famous **Troon** and **Turnberry** (p. 248).

Day ❺: Stirling, the Trossachs & Loch Lomond ✦

Roughly equidistant to Edinburgh and Glasgow is **Stirling,** site of much Scottish history and one-time home to royalty. Start with Stirling's Old Town, which has the impressive **Stirling Castle** (p. 254). Children will enjoy nearby **Stirling Jail** (p. 254), but history buffs should try to visit **Bannockburn,** where the Scots defeated English invaders in the 14th century. Stirling also has the towering monument to **William Wallace,** whose life inspired Mel Gibson's film *Braveheart.* Head west and see the well-preserved ruins of **Doune Castle** (p. 254) before hitting the rolling hills and small mountains of the Trossach's and then lovely **Loch Lomond** (p. 252) in the shadows of the southern Highlands.

Day 6: The West Coast ★★

This tour can take 2 days, depending upon your ambitions. Here are some highlights. West of Glasgow, on the north shores of the Clyde as it widens to the sea is Helensburgh and the superlative **Hill House,** designed by Charles Rennie Mackintosh. Across the Clyde, are the roads that lead to head-clearing ferry rides, such as to the **Isle of Bute**—one of the easiest islands to reach. On it is the mansion of **Mount Stuart** (p. 250) as well as plenty of country lanes and quiet beaches to explore. From Bute you can head further west to the Argyll peninsulas of **Cowal** and **Kintyre** (p. 251), each increasingly remote and sparsely settled. **Tighnabruaich** and **Tarbert** are two picturesque harbor villages worth stopping in. Finally, you might wish to really leave it all behind and go to the small island of **Gigha** (p. 251). Owned by a community trust, it is the southern-most of Scotland's inner Hebrides.

Day 7: Glasgow's Other Attractions

Unless you're still absorbing the refreshing air of the West Coast and haven't made it back to Glasgow, pick up where you left off in the city. Re-visit the **West End** for lunch and bit of shopping, or stay in the city center and see any museums missed earlier, such as the **Gallery of Modern Art** (p. 192) or the more contemporary offerings at the **CCA** (p. 197). If the weather's fine and dry, hike up to the **Central Necropolis,** (p. 194) near Glasgow Cathedral, or stroll through **Glasgow Green** (p. 201), along the River Clyde.

4

Getting to Know Edinburgh

Edinburgh has been called one of Europe's fairest cities and the Athens of the North. And what most experienced travelers to the U.K. say is true: if you can visit only two cities in all Great Britain, it's London first and Edinburgh second. Built on extinct volcanoes atop an inlet from the North Sea (the Firth of Forth) and enveloped by rolling hills, lakes, and forests, the Scottish capital began as a small, fortified settlement on a craggy hill. Indeed, because of its defensive attributes, Edinburgh (remember "burgh" is always pronounced "*burr*-a" in Scotland) became an important, protected place for the country's rulers. Somewhat ironically, the city today represents the virtual crossroads of Scotland for many visitors: the spot that they are likely to stop in or pass through while in Scotland.

Edinburgh is filled with historic, intellectual, and literary associations. Names such as Mary Queen of Scots and her nemesis Protestant reformer John Knox; pioneer economist Adam Smith and philosopher David Hume; authors Sir Walter Scott, Robert Louis Stevenson, and Sir Arthur Conan Doyle; as well as inventor Alexander Graham Bell: They are all part of Edinburgh's past.

Today the city is famous for its world-class cultural festival. The **Edinburgh Festival** is actually several festivals at once: films, books, comedy, drama, classical music, dance, and more. But this ancient seat of Scottish royalty has a year-round attraction: when the festival-goers have returned home, the city's pace is more relaxed, its prices are lower, and the inhabitants—though not celebrated for their bonhomie—are under less pressure and offer a hospitable welcome.

Edinburgh is a city that lends itself to walking. Its **Old Town** and **New Town** sport moody cobbled alleys, elegant streetscapes, handsome squares, and placid parks. From several hilltops, panoramic views can be enjoyed. The city's sunsets can be romantic—in the Scots language, the fading evening light is the "gloaming."

Edinburgh was long the cultural capital of the north, but that particular crown—in terms of contemporary culture—has been perhaps lost to Glasgow since the last few decades of the 20th century. However, the lively capital is staging a comeback. It will always be home to the several **National Galleries** of Scotland. And as a point for excursions, it's well placed.

Impressions

No situation could be more commanding for the head city of a Kingdom; none better chosen for noble prospects.

—Robert Louis Stevenson

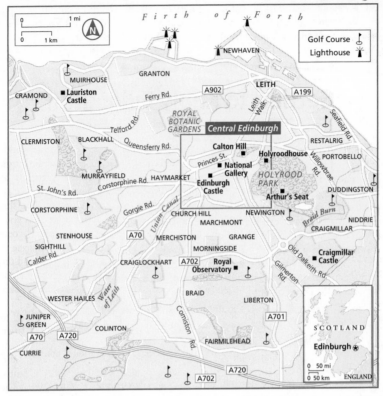

Notable nearby attractions include Linlithgow, where Mary Queen of Scots was born; the Borders, with rolling hillsides to the south; the Kingdom of Fife on the opposite shore of the Firth of Forth; and even St Andrews is not far.

1 Essentials

ARRIVING

BY PLANE   Edinburgh is only about an hour's flying time from London, which is 633km (393 miles) south. **Edinburgh International Airport** (ⓒ **0131/333-1000**) is about 10km (6 miles) west of the city's center and has become a growing hub of flights both within the British Isles as well as to and from continental Europe. Remember, however, that Glasgow International Airport is only about 90km (55 miles) away and should not be discounted as it traditionally greets more long-haul flights, especially from North America. From Edinburgh airport, the Airlink bus makes the trip to the city center about every 10 minutes during peak times, terminating at Waverley Bridge near the central railway station. The fare is £3 ($5.50) one-way or £5 ($9.25) round-trip. The trip from the airport into the heart of the city takes about 25 minutes (sometimes longer during rush hours). Overnight service is provided by Night Bus N22. Visit www.flybybus.com for details of service. A taxi into the city will cost about £12

($22) or more, depending on traffic, and the ride will take about the same time as the bus. Before heading into town, you might want to stop at the airport's **VisitScotland information and accommodations desk** (© **0131/473-3800**); it's generally open Monday to Saturday 6:15am to 7:45pm and Sunday 9am to 4:30pm.

BY TRAIN   The trains which link London to Edinburgh (via Newcastle) on the so-called East Coast Main Line are reasonably fast, efficient, and generally relaxing with restaurant and bar service as well as air-conditioning. Trains depart from London's Kings Cross Station (call **National Railway Enquiries** at © **0845/748-4950** for rail information) every hour or so and arrive in Edinburgh at **Waverley Station** in the heart of the city. The trip generally takes 4½ hours. "Off-peak" fares bought in advance can range widely, from around £25 to £93 ($46–$172) and the government is examining whether they should be less variable. "Off-peak" first class purchased in advance also ranges widely from about £30 to £100 ($55–$185), although the cheapest fares seem to be rarely available. A fully flexible "buy anytime, travel anytime" standard open single fare is upwards of £120 ($220). The Caledonian Sleeper service for overnight travel can cost about £100 ($185), but online bargains booked well in advance can mean the trip may cost as little as £19 ($35). Taxi and bus connections are easily made at Waverley Station, which also serves Glasgow with a shuttle service every 15 minutes during the day and every 30 minutes in the evening until about 11:30pm. The one-way fare during off-peak times (travel after 9:15am and not between 4:15am and 6:30pm) is £8.80 ($16).

BY BUS   **National Express** (© **0870/580-8080;** www.nationalexpress.com) runs buses daily (typically 9:30am, noon, and 11pm for direct service) from London's Victoria Coach Station to Edinburgh Bus Station near St. Andrew Square. Standard round-trip fare is about £45 ($83). Without stopovers, the trip should take less than 10 hours.

BY CAR   Edinburgh is 74km (46 miles) east of Glasgow and 169km (105 miles) north of Newcastle-upon-Tyne in England. No express motorway links London directly to Edinburgh. The M1 from London takes you most of the way north, but you'll have to come into Edinburgh via secondary roads: either the coastal A1 or inland A68. Alternatively, one can travel the well-used motorways in the west of the U.K. from London. Take the M1 to the M6 (near Coventry), which links to the M74 at Carlisle. Then travel to the M8 southeast of Glasgow, which takes you to Edinburgh's ring road or beltway. Allow 8 hours or more for the drive north from London.

VISITOR INFORMATION

Edinburgh Information Centre, atop the Princes Mall near Waverley Station (**Visit Scotland;** © **0131/473-3800** or 0845/225-5121; fax 0131/473-3881; www.edinburgh. org; bus: 22, 25, 3, 31, or 8), can give you sightseeing information and also arrange lodgings. The center sells bus tours, theater tickets, and souvenirs of Edinburgh. It also has racks and racks of free brochures. It's open year-round; typically the hours are Monday through Saturday from 9am to 7pm and Sunday from 10am to 7pm, though it is open later during the Festival and closes earlier in the winter months.

CITY LAYOUT

Central Edinburgh is divided into the **Old Town,** where the city began, and the larger **New Town,** where it expanded in the 1700s. Many visitors find lodgings in New Town and tend to visit Old Town for sightseeing, dining, and drinking (note that the local parlance generally drops the definite article "the" for both Old Town and New Town). There are accommodations, however, in historic core of the city on **High Street** and in the **Grassmarket.**

Most everyone planning to travel to Edinburgh has heard of the **Royal Mile,** the main thoroughfare of Old Town, running from Edinburgh Castle in the west to the Palace of Holyroodhouse in the east. Because of its once smoky skies, Old Town earned the city the nickname "Auld Reekie." Today, the air is fine and the district is chock-a-block with tourist attractions, shops, and sidewalks full of out-of-town visitors for most months of the year. Both British **Royalty** and Scotland's **Parliament** (revived in 1999) are based in Old Town, as are city government offices and the country's legal elite. Another more infamous street at the southern base of the castle is the Grassmarket, where convicted criminals were once hanged on the gallows. But now it is home to restaurants, pubs, and hotels.

New Town is actually fairly old. North of Old Town, across what is today Princes Street Gardens, was first settled in the 18th century—about a decade before the American declaration of independence was signed. By the end of that century, classic squares, streets, and town houses had been completed and the first New Town was soon expanded with more Georgian designs. The first New Town represents a "Golden Age of Edinburgh," with world-famous **Princes Street.** Today it is the city's main shopping precinct, with broad sidewalks and a park running its entire length—all with panoramic views of Old Town and Castle.

North of and running parallel to Princes Street is New Town's second great boulevard, **George Street.** It begins at St. Andrew Square and runs west to Charlotte Square, full of bars, restaurants, and posh shops. Directly north of George Street is another impressive thoroughfare, **Queen Street,** opening onto Queen Street Gardens on its north side with views of the Firth of Forth. You may also hear a lot about **Rose Street,** a lane between Princes Street and George Street—with many more pubs, shops, and restaurants.

Edinburgh's **Southside** and **West End** are primarily residential. The former is home to the city's well-regarded university (making parts of the area quite lively) and the sprawling park known as the Meadows. The West End includes the last of the New Town developments begun at the beginning of the 19th century. It has theaters, several small B&Bs, and swank boutique hotels as well as the city's most exclusive central neighborhoods.

Leith is Edinburgh's historic port where the Water of Leith meets the Firth of Forth. Leith briefly served as the Scottish capital and such was its strategic location that Oliver Cromwell's invading forces built a citadel here. It remained an independent burgh until the 20th century. Fans of Irvine Welsh (author of *Trainspotting*) will know that it has a rough and tumble reputation. But today most of its shipping and the sailors have gone, and lots of luxury apartments are being built. Still, it remains an evocative area and offers a good selection of seafood restaurants and nautical-themed pubs. It is also now the home of the Royal Yacht *Britannia.*

Edinburgh Neighborhoods

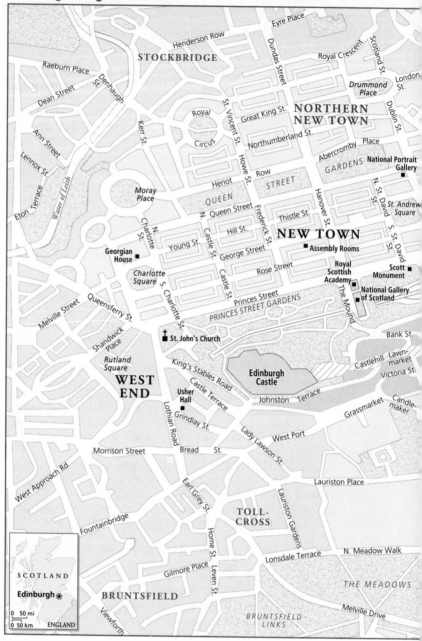

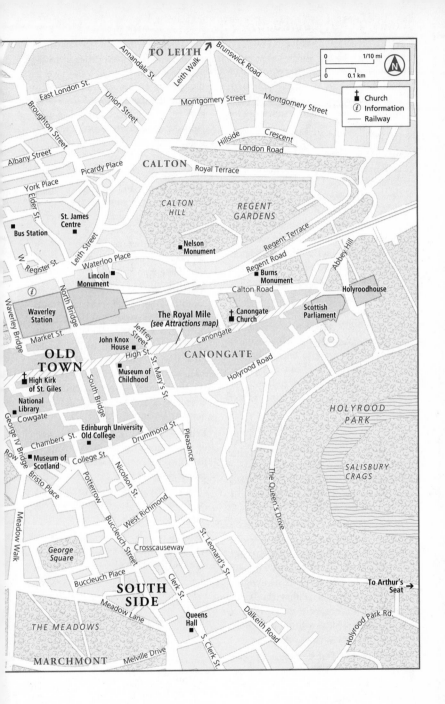

TO LEITH

Brunswick Road

Annandale St.

Leith Walk

East London St.

Union Street

Montgomery Street

Montgomery Street

Broughton Street

Hillside

Crescent

London Road

Albany Street

Picardy Place

CALTON

Royal Terrace

York Place

Elder St.

CALTON
HILL

REGENT
GARDENS

St. James
Centre

Bus Station

Leith Street

W. Register St.

Waterloo Place

Nelson
Monument

Regent Terrace

Regent Road

Abbey Hill

Lincoln
Monument

North Bridge

Burns
Monument

Calton Road

Holyroodhouse

ℹ

Waverley
Station

The Royal Mile
(see Attractions map)

✝ Canongate
  Church

Scottish
Parliament

Market St.

Jeffrey
Street

Canongate

OLD
TOWN

John Knox
House

High St.

St. Mary's St.

CANONGATE

Holyrood Road

✝ High Kirk
of St. Giles

South Bridge

Museum of
Childhood

HOLYROOD
PARK

National
Library

Cowgate

Chambers St.

Edinburgh University
Old College

Drummond St.

Pleasance

George IV Bridge

Museum of
Scotland

College St.

Nicolson St.

SALISBURY
CRAGS

Bristo Place

Potterrow

West Richmond

The Queen's Drive

Meadow Walk

George
Square

Buccleuch Street

Crosscauseway

Buccleuch Place

SOUTH
SIDE

Clerk St.

St. Leonard's St.

To Arthur's →
Seat

Meadow Lane

Holyrood Park Rd.

THE MEADOWS

Queens
Hall

S. Clerk St.

Dalkeith Road

MARCHMONT

Melville Drive

0   1/10 mi
0   0.1 km

✝ Church
ℹ Information
— Railway

EDINBURGH NEIGHBORHOODS IN BRIEF

Edinburgh has a host of districts—some of which appear to include only a few streets, and many that can be folded into the broader areas of the Old and New Towns.

Old Town This is where Edinburgh began. Its spine is the **Royal Mile,** a medieval thoroughfare stretching for about 1.6km (1 mile) from Edinburgh Castle downhill to the Palace of Holyroodhouse. The Royal Mile is one boulevard with four segments bearing different names: Castlehill, Lawnmarket, High Street, and Canongate. "This is perhaps the largest, longest, and finest street for buildings and number of inhabitants in the world," wrote English author Daniel Defoe. Old Town also includes the Grassmarket and Cowgate.

New Town Situated north of Old Town, the first New Town bloomed between 1766 and 1840 and is one of the largest Georgian developments in the world. It grew to encompass the northern half of the heart of the city. Home to at least 25,000 residents, it's also the largest historic conservation area in Britain. The New Town is made up of a network of squares, streets, terraces, and circuses, reaching from Haymarket in the west almost to Leith Walk in the east. The New Town also extends from Canonmills in the north to Princes Street, its most famous artery, on the south.

Stockbridge Part of the New Town today, northwest of the castle, Stockbridge is a one-time village that still rather feels like a small town near the heart of the city, with its own tight-knit community. Straddling the Water of Leigh, it is a good place for visitors to the city to relax, with some friendly cafes, pubs, restaurants, and shops.

Haymarket & Dalry West of the city center by about 1.5km (1 mile), these two districts may be off the beaten path for most visitors. Haymarket centers on the railway station (an alternative to Waverley for travelers to and from Glasgow or places much further north). Near the station is the Scottish national rugby stadium: Murrayfield. Dalry is slowly being gentrified.

Tollcross & West End Edinburgh's theater district and conference center are in the area west of the Castle. While the West End neighborhoods near Shandwick Place are rather exclusive, the district of Tollcross might appear a bit rough, although it is rapidly changing.

Marchmont About 1.5km (1 mile) south of High Street, this suburb was constructed between 1869 and 1914, offering new housing for people who could no longer afford to live in the New Town. Its northern border is the Meadows. Sometimes visitors go south to this neighborhood seeking an affordable B&B in one of the little homes that receive guests.

Bruntsfield This suburb to the west of the Meadows is named for Bruntsfield Links. Now a residential district, this is where James IV gathered the Scottish army he marched to its defeat at Flodden in 1513. Many lower cost B&Bs are found in this area.

Church Hill & Morningside South of Bruntsfield, Church Hill has the area nicknamed "holy corner" because of the concentration of churches at the junction of Bruntsfield, Colinton, and Chamberlain roads. Morningside is probably the poshest old suburb in the city, with leafy streets. If you venture this far, be sure and visit the historic pub Canny Man.

Calton Encompassing Calton Hill, with its Regent and Royal terraces, it

In Edinburgh, both street names and addresses might seem to have been created purposely to confuse visitors. Roads can change names for no apparent reason. To complicate matters, the city—with the exception of the Old Town—is checkered with squares, terraces, and circuses that interrupt whatever street you're trying to follow. Also the same name can be used for a lane, street, terrace, crescent, avenue, road, square, or garden: so make sure that you've not confused Argyll Place with Argyll Street.

House numbers can run sequentially on straight streets or clockwise or counterclockwise on circuses or squares—if they exist at all. Some places don't bother with numbers. Our advice: Get a map. If you're looking for a specific location, get the name of the nearest cross street. The good news is that the locals are generally glad to assist a bewildered foreigner.

skirts the so-called Pink Triangle. Edinburgh has a lively and engaged gay population, which focuses socially on an area from the top of Leith Walk to Broughton Street. It is not, however, a dedicated gay district such as San Francisco's Castro or Christopher Street in Manhattan's Greenwich Village. It is just part and parcel of this lively area with its bars, nightclubs, and restaurants.

Leith Walk Not precisely a neighborhood, but the main artery that connects Edinburgh's city center to Leith. Off it are Easter Road (home of Hibernian football club) and the districts of Pilrig and South Leith. An honest cross section of Edinburgh can be seen during a foray down Leith Walk.

Leith The Port of Leith lies only a few kilometers north of Princes Street and is the city's major harbor, opening onto the Firth of Forth. The area is currently being gentrified, and visitors come here for the restaurants and pubs, many of which specialize in seafood. The port isn't what it used to be in terms of maritime might; its glory days were back when stevedores unloaded cargoes by hand.

Newhaven Newhaven is a fishing village adjacent to Leith. Founded in the 1400s, this former little harbor with its bustling fish market was greatly altered in the 1960s. Many of its "bow-tows" (a nickname for closely knit, clannish residents) were uprooted, like the Leithers, in a major gentrification program.

2 Getting Around

Because of its narrow lanes, wynds, and closes, you can only honestly explore the Old Town in any depth on foot. Edinburgh is fairly convenient for the visitor who likes to walk (see chapter 8 for some tours), as most of the attractions are along the Royal Mile, Princes Street, or one of the major streets of the New Town.

BY BUS

As there is no underground or subway in Edinburgh and only limited commuter train service, the city's rather numerous buses provide the chief method of public transportation. There are lots of them, and most seem to go down Princes Street at some point on their route.

(Tips Look Both Ways!

Remember, you're in Great Britain, and cars drive on the left. So if you're cross-ing, traffic closest to you approaches from the right. Always look both ways before stepping off a curb. Lots of new arrivals practically commit suicide cross-ing the street because they forget which way to look for traffic.

Fares depend on the distance traveled, with the adult one-way (single) **minimum fare** £1 ($1.85) covering the central Edinburgh districts. If you plan multiple trips in 1 day, purchase a **Dayticket** that allows unlimited travel on city buses for 1 day at a cost of £2.30 ($4.25) adults. Children 5 to 15 are charged a flat rate of 60p ($1.10), but kids 13 to 15 are expected to carry a **teen card** (available in bus Travelshops—see below) as proof of age. Child Daytickets cost £2 ($3.70). Children 4 and under ride free. Be advised that bus drivers will not make change, so carry the correct amount in coins or expect to pay more. At Travelshops, 1-week **RideaCard** passes, which allow unlimited travel on buses, can be purchased for £13 ($24) adults, £11 ($20) students, and £9 ($17) juniors.

Also the tourist buses that terminate at Waverley Bridge offer hop-on, hop-off at any of their stops on the set circuit of primarily Old and New towns. Tickets—£9 ($17) for adults; £3($5.50) for children—can be used for 24 hours (although the buses' last journeys are made in the early evening).

Visitors can find advance tickets and further information in the city center at the **Waverley Bridge Travelshop,** Waverley Bridge, open Monday to Saturday 8:30am to 6pm and Sunday 9:30am to 5pm, or at **27 Hanover Street Travelshop,** open Monday to Saturday 8:30am to 6pm. For details on fares and timetables, call ✆ **0131/555-6363** or log on to **www.lothianbuses.co.uk**.

BY TAXI

You can hail a taxi or pick one up at a taxi stand. Meters begin at £1.45 ($2.70) in the day, and a typical trek across town might cost about £6 ($11). Taxi ranks are at High Street near North Bridge, Waverley and Haymarket stations, Hanover Street, North Sreet, Andrew Street, and Lauriston Place. Fares are displayed in the front of the taxi and charges are posted, including extra fees for night drivers or destinations outside the city limits. You can also call a taxi. Try **City Cabs** at ✆ **0131/228-1211** or **Central Radio Taxis** at ✆ **0131/229-2468**.

BY CAR

Unless absolutely necessary, don't drive in Edinburgh—it can prove to be a tricky and frustrating business, even for natives. Traffic-calming, one-way systems, and dedicated bus lanes are all good reasons to forego the automobile. Parking is expensive and also can be difficult to find. Metered parking is available, but you'll need the right change and have to watch out for traffic wardens who issue tickets. Some zones are marked PERMIT HOLDERS ONLY, meaning your vehicle will be towed if you have no permit. A double yellow line along the curb indicates no parking at any time. A single yellow line along the curb indicates restrictions, too, so be sure and read the signs on what the limitations are. Major parking lots (car parks) are at Castle Terrace (near Edin-burgh Castle), Waverley Station, and at St. James Centre (close to the east end of Princes St.).

You may want a rental car for touring the countryside or for heading onward. Many agencies grant discounts to those who reserve in advance (see chapter 2 for more information). Most will accept your foreign driver's license, provided you've held it for more than a year and are over 21. Most of the major car-rental companies maintain offices at the Edinburgh airport should you want to rent a car on the spot. In the city, try **Avis** on West Park Place near Haymarket Station (✆ **0870/153-9103**), **Hertz** on Picardy Place (✆ **0870/864-0013**), or **Thrifty** at 42 Haymarket Terrace (✆ **0131/337-1319**).

BY BICYCLE

Bicycles are more common in Edinburgh than in Glasgow. Nevertheless, biking is probably a good idea only for visitors in good shape, as the city is set on a series of ridges and the streets are often cobbled. Try **Rent-a-Bike Edinburgh,** 29 Blackfriars St., near High Street (✆ **0131/556-5560;** www.cyclescotland.co.uk; bus: 35). Depending on the type of bike, charges range from £10 to £15 ($19–$28) per day or up to £70 ($130) for the week. Part-day hires are possible. A credit card imprint will be taken as security. The same company runs **Scottish Cycle Safaris,** which organizes tours in the city and across Scotland. They can equip you for excursions, and because they have branches in places such as Oban, Inverness, and Skye, you can drop off your bike and equipment there if that is more convenient.

FAST FACTS: Edinburgh

American Express The office is at 69 George St. at Frederick Street (✆ **0131/718-2505**; bus: 13, 19, or 41). It's open Monday through Friday from 9am to 5:30pm and Saturday from 9am to 5pm; on Wednesday, the office opens at 9:30am.

Business Hours In Edinburgh, **banks** are usually open Monday through Friday from 9 or 9:30am to 4 or 5pm, with some branches sometimes shutting early on 1 day a week and open late on another. **Shops** are generally open Monday through Saturday from 9 or 10am to 6pm; on Thursday, retail stores are open late to 8pm. Food supermarkets generally keep later hours. Many shops are now open on Sunday, as well. In general, **business hours** are Monday through Friday from 9am to 5pm, though some offices will close early on Friday.

Currency Exchange Many banks in the Old and New towns will exchange currency. Post offices run *bureaux de change* as does the Edinburgh Information Office (see earlier in this chapter for hours). Major hotels will also exchange currency but charge a premium for the service. ATMs in the city center are linked to major banking systems such as Cirrus, and you may be able to draw money directly from your bank account at home.

Dentists If you have a dental emergency, go to the **Edinburgh Dental Institute,** 39 Lauriston Place (✆ **0131/536-4900**; bus: 35), open Monday through Friday from 9am to 3pm. Alternatively, call the **National Health Service Helpline** (✆ **0800/224-488**).

Doctors You can seek help from the **Edinburgh Royal Infirmary,** 1 Lauriston Place (✆ **0131/536-1000**; bus: 35). The emergency department is open 24 hours.

Embassies & Consulates All embassies are in London. There's a **U.S. Consulate** in Edinburgh at 3 Regent Terrace (© **0131/556-8315**), open Monday through Friday from 1 to 4pm. All other nationals have to use London to conduct their business: The **Canadian High Commission** is at MacDonald House, 1 Grosvenor Sq., London W1K 4AB (© **0207/258-6600**), open Monday through Friday from 8am to 4pm. The **Australian High Commission** is at the Strand, London WC2B 4LI (© **0207/379-4334**), open Monday through Friday from 9:30am to 3:30pm. The **New Zealand High Commission** is at New Zealand House, 80 Haymarket at Pall Mall, London SW1Y 4TQ (© **0207/930-8422**), open Monday through Friday from 9am to 5pm. The **Irish Embassy** is at 17 Grosvenor Place, London SW1X 7HR (© **0207/235-2171**), open Monday through Friday from 9:30am to 1pm and 2:15 to 5pm.

Emergencies Call © **999** in an emergency to summon the police, an ambulance, or firefighters.

Hospitals See "Doctors," above.

Hot Lines **Edinburgh and Lothian Woman's Aid** is at © **0131/229-1419**. **Lothian Gay & Lesbian Switchboard** (© **0131/556-4049**) offers advice from 7:30pm to 10pm daily; the **Lesbian Line** is © **0131/557-0751**. The **Rape Crisis Centre** is at © **0141/331-1990**.

Internet Access **EasyInternet Cafe** at 58 Rose St., between Frederick and Hanover streets (www.easyeverything.com; bus: 42) is open daily from 7:30am to 10:30pm. It has some 448 terminals.

Laundry & Dry Cleaning For your dry-cleaning needs, the most central service is probably at **Johnson's Cleaners, 23 Frederick St.** (© **0131/225-8095;** bus: 13, 19, or 42), which is open Monday through Friday from 8am to 5:30pm and Saturday from 8.30am to 4pm.

Luggage Storage & Lockers Given the tenor of the times, left luggage can prove problematic if an alert is on. Generally speaking, you can store luggage in lockers at **Waverley Station.**

Newspapers Published since 1817, *The Scotsman* is a quality daily newspaper with a national and international perspective, while its sister publication, the *Evening News,* concentrates more on local affairs. For comprehensive arts and entertainment listings and reviews of local shows, buy the *List* magazine, which is published every other Thursday—and weekly during the Festival. *Metro,* a free daily (Mon–Fri) available on buses and in train stations, also gives listings of daily events.

Pharmacies There are no 24-hour drugstores (called chemists or pharmacies) in Edinburgh. The one with probably the longest hours is the branch of **Boots** at 48 Shandwick Place, west of Princes Street (© **0131/225-6757;** bus: 12 or 25). It is open Monday through Friday from 8am to 8pm, Saturday from 8am to 6pm, and Sunday from 10:30am to 4:30pm.

Police See "Emergencies," above.

Post Office The Edinburgh Branch Post Office, St. James Centre, is open Monday through Saturday from 9am to 5:30pm. For general postal information and customer service, call © **0845/722-3344.**

Restrooms These are found at rail stations, terminals, restaurants, hotels, pubs, and department stores. Public toilets, often marked WC, are located at strategic corners and squares throughout the city. They're safe and clean but likely to be closed late in the evening.

Safety Edinburgh is generally thought to be safer than Glasgow—in fact, it's one of Europe's safest capitals for a visitor to stroll. But that doesn't mean crimes, especially muggings, don't occur. They do, largely because of Edinburgh's problems with drug abuse.

Weather For weather forecasts of the day and 24 hours in advance and for severe road-condition warnings, call the Met Office ⒸC **0870/900-0100.** An advisor will offer forecasts for the entire region and beyond.

5

Where to Stay in Edinburgh

Edinburgh offers many options for accommodations, from the super posh and fabulously pricey five-star hotels to down-and-dirty bunkhouses and youth hostels. It is a city that anticipates bundles of tourists and travelers, whether seasonal backpackers, school groups, and families—or professional types in the Scottish capital on commercial and governmental matters. Be warned, however. During the monthlong period of the Edinburgh Festival every August, the hotels, guesthouses, and B&Bs fill up. If you're planning a visit at that time, be sure to reserve your accommodation as far in advance as possible. Otherwise you may end up in a town or village as many as 40km (55 miles) from the city center. And don't be surprised if the standard rates for accommodation in Edinburgh are higher—in isolated cases twice as high—during August, particularly at smaller hotels.

The tourist board's **Edinburgh Information Centre** is near Waverley Station, atop the Princes Mall shopping center, 3 Princes St. (© **0845/225-5121** or 0131/473-3800, or 44-150/683-2121 from overseas; www.edinburgh.org or www.visitscotland.com; bus 3, 8, 22, 25, or 31). The local information center, in conjunction with the Scottish tourist board, compiles a lengthy list of small hotels, guesthouses, and private homes providing a bed-and-breakfast for as little as £20 ($37) per person. A £3 ($5.50) booking fee is charged for reservations made using the Booking Hotline and a 10% deposit is expected. It's open year-round; typically the hours are Monday through Saturday from 9am to 7pm and Sunday from 10am to 7pm, though it is open later during the Festival and closes earlier in the winter months.

The Scottish tourist board is also a source of star ratings, which are based largely on amenities. So the stars can be limited for smaller operations that may not offer all the mod conveniences but are still perfectly good places to stay. References to stars in the information below are those bestowed by VisitScotland.

The Internet can be a trove of discounted rates if you have the time and inclination to surf the Web. In some cases, the bargains are only available if using web-based booking services. Some of these special prices and promotions are noted below. Also check the Edinburgh Principal Hotel Association website, www.edinburgh-hotels.org. Finally, booking for multiple nights in one hotel is another way to reduce your accommodation bills.

If you have an early flight out and need a hotel convenient to the airport, consider the 244-unit **Edinburgh Marriott,** 111 Glasgow Rd. (© **0131/334-9191**), off A8 on Edinburgh's western outskirts. It offers doubles from about £150 ($277), including breakfast. Facilities include an indoor pool, gym, sauna, and restaurant.

1 New Town

VERY EXPENSIVE

Balmoral Hotel   When it first opened in 1902 as the North British Hotel, it was then—and remains today—one of the grandest hotels in Britain. Known as the Balmoral since the early '90s, the rooms received a £7-million ($13-million) refurbishment not long ago. Almost directly above the Waverley Rail Station, the building features a soaring clock tower that is one of the city's landmarks, famously set 5 minutes fast for the benefit of those on the way to the train. Kilted doormen supply the Scottish atmosphere from the start. Sumptuously furnished, the best of the units—such as room 520, the Dee Suite—can be distinguished and large, with an ample sitting room and a huge, well-appointed bathroom—not to mention fabulous views towards the castle. Dining options at the Balmoral include the elegant and Michelin-star-earning **Number One** (p. 69) and the more casual Hadrian's Brasserie. Afternoon tea is served in the high-ceilinged Palm Court. In addition to the standard rates, the hotel's website offers "Simply Balmoral" seasonal discounts among other package deals.

1 Princes St., Edinburgh EH2 2EQ. ✆ **800/223-6800** in the U.S., or 0131/556-2414. Fax 0131/557-3747. www.thebalmoralhotel.com. 188 units. £225–£290 ($416–$536) double; £245–£310 ($453–$573) superior double; from £465 ($860) suite. AE, DC, MC, V. Valet parking £15 ($27). Bus: 3, 8, 22, 25, or 30. **Amenities:** 2 restaurants; 2 bars; indoor pool; health club; spa; sauna; concierge; business center; room service; laundry service; dry cleaning. *In room:* A/C, TV, fax, dataport, minibar, hair dryer, safe.

Caledonian Hilton Edinburgh ✦   Completely renovated in 1991, the hotel remains one of the city's landmarks and offers commanding views towards the nearby Edinburgh Castle and over Princes Street Gardens. The public rooms are reminiscent of Edwardian splendor, and the guest rooms (many of which are exceptionally spacious) are conservatively styled with reproduction furniture. The fifth-floor rooms are the smallest. Bathrooms come with combination tub/showers. Although the accommodations are equal to those of other first-class, multistar hotels in Edinburgh, the competition has moved ahead with its leisure facilities. Fine dining meals are served in the Pompadour Restaurant. A traditional tea is featured in the high-ceilinged lounge. On the Internet, advance booking reaps savings.

Princes St., Edinburgh EH1 2AB. ✆ **0131/222-8888.** Fax 0131/222-8889. www.caledonian.hilton.com. 251 units. £180–£380 ($333–$703) double; from £340 ($630) suite. Children 15 and under stay free in parent's room. AE, DC, MC, V. Parking £10 ($19) per day. Bus: 33. **Amenities:** 2 restaurants; 2 bars; indoor pool; exercise room; room service; laundry service; dry cleaning. *In room:* TV, dataport, minibar, hair dryer, iron/ironing board, trouser press.

The Howard ✦✦   Dubbed one of the most discrete five-star hotels in the city, this lovely hotel links a set of Georgian terraced houses in the Northern New Town, just down the hill from the Queen Street Gardens. Some of the aura of a private home remains. Accommodations are midsize to spacious, each unit individually and rather elegantly decorated, with some of the best bathrooms in town, featuring power and double showers and, in some, a Jacuzzi. The decor is traditional and modern, using both antiques and reproductions. Service is a hallmark of the Howard, with a dedicated butler that can tend to your individual needs, even unpacking your luggage, should you so desire. To sum up: an oasis of Georgian charm and class. And if you're on a budget, weekend breaks can bring rates to £99 ($183) per person.

34 Great King St., Edinburgh EH3 6QH. ✆ **0131/557-3500.** Fax 0131/557-6515. www.thehoward.com. 18 units. £180–£275 ($333–$508) double; £243–£475 ($450–$878) suite. Rates include breakfast. AE, DC, MC, V. Free parking. Bus: 23 or 27. **Amenities:** Restaurant; room service; laundry service; dry cleaning. *In room:* TV, dataport, hair dryer.

Edinburgh Accommodations

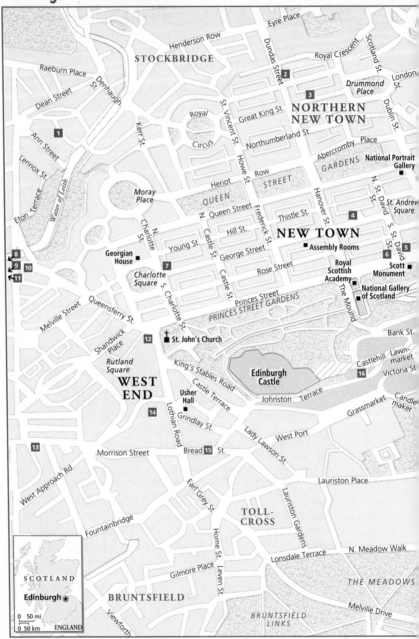

STOCKBRIDGE

Eyre Place

Dundas Street

Royal Crescent

Scotland St.

London St.

Henderson Row

Raeburn Place

Denhaugh St.

Dean Street

Kerr St.

Royal

Circus

St. Vincent St.

Great King St.

NORTHERN
NEW TOWN

Drummond
Place

Dublin St.

2

3

Ann Street

Lennox St.

Eton Terrace

Water of Leith

Moray
Place

Northumberland St.

Howe St.

Row

Heriot

STREET

Abercromby   Place

GARDENS

National Portrait
Gallery

QUEEN

N Queen Street

Frederick St.

Thistle St.

Hanover St.

NEW TOWN

N. St. David St.

St. Andrew
Square

S. St. David St.

Georgian
House

N. Charlotte St.

Young St.

Castle St.

Hill St.

George Street

Assembly Rooms

4

5

6

Charlotte
Square

Charlotte Square

S. Charlotte St.

Castle St.

Rose Street

Princes Street

PRINCES STREET GARDENS

Royal
Scottish
Academy

Scott
Monument

National Gallery
of Scotland

The Mound

7

Melville Street

Queensferry St.

St. John's Church

Bank St.

Shandwick
Place

Rutland
Square

WEST
END

King's Stables Road

Castle Terrace

Edinburgh
Castle

Johnston   Terrace

Castlehill

Lawn-
market

Victoria St.

Grassmarket

Candle
maker

12

8
9 10
11

Usher
Hall

Lothian Road

Grindlay St.

Lady Lawson St.

West Port

14

Morrison Street

Bread   St.

15

West Approach Rd.

Earl Grey St.

Home St.

Leven St.

Lauriston Gardens

Lauriston Place

TOLL-
CROSS

N. Meadow Walk

13

16

Fountainbridge

Gilmore Place

Lonsdale Terrace

THE MEADOWS

SCOTLAND

Edinburgh ⊛

0   50 mi
0   50 km   ENGLAND

BRUNTSFIELD

Viewforth

BRUNTSFIELD
LINKS

Melville Drive

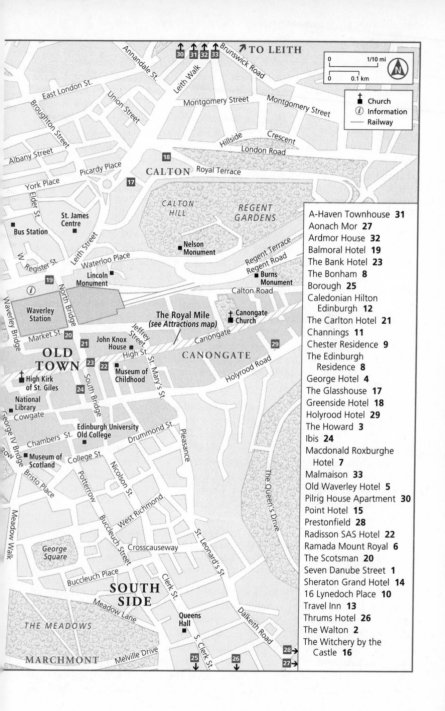

A-Haven Townhouse **31**
Aonach Mor **27**
Ardmor House **32**
Balmoral Hotel **19**
The Bank Hotel **23**
The Bonham **8**
Borough **25**
Caledonian Hilton Edinburgh **12**
The Carlton Hotel **21**
Channings **11**
Chester Residence **9**
The Edinburgh Residence **8**
George Hotel **4**
The Glasshouse **17**
Greenside Hotel **18**
Holyrood Hotel **29**
The Howard **3**
Ibis **24**
Macdonald Roxburghe Hotel **7**
Malmaison **33**
Old Waverley Hotel **5**
Pilrig House Apartment **30**
Point Hotel **15**
Prestonfield **28**
Radisson SAS Hotel **22**
Ramada Mount Royal **6**
The Scotsman **20**
Seven Danube Street **1**
Sheraton Grand Hotel **14**
16 Lynedoch Place **10**
Travel Inn **13**
Thrums Hotel **26**
The Walton **2**
The Witchery by the Castle **16**

EXPENSIVE

Channings ★★ Five Edwardian terrace houses combine to create this hotel, technically just outside New Town and near Stockbridge in a tranquil residential area. Channings maintains the atmosphere of a Scottish country house, with oak paneling, ornate fireplaces, molded ceilings, and antiques. The guest rooms are in a modern style; the front units get the views, but the rear ones offer more seclusion. The most desirable rooms are the "Executives," most of which have bay windows and wingback chairs. Even if you're not a guest, consider a meal here, as Channings offers some fine food while Ochre Vita is more casual and Mediterranean in orientation.

12–16 South Learmonth Gardens 15, Edinburgh EH4 1EZ. © 0131/623-9302. Fax 0131/332-9631. www.channings. co.uk. 46 units. £120–£185 ($222–$342) double. Rates include breakfast. AE, DC, MC, V. Parking on street. Bus: 37. **Amenities:** 2 restaurants; bar; room service; laundry service; dry cleaning. *In room:* TV, dataport, coffeemaker, hair dryer, iron/ironing board, trouser press.

The George Hotel ★ The buildings that house this inn were first erected in the 1780s, transformed with alterations of Corinthian and neo-Renaissance style during the next 150 years or so before becoming the posh George Hotel in 1950. In the summer of 2006, a whopping £12-million ($22-million) renovation was scheduled to be completed. While the public rooms will no doubt retain their elegance and old-fashioned comfort, the guest rooms were to be completely updated and made modern in the course of the refurbishment. A stylish new restaurant and bar, Tempus, replaces the previous catering options.

19–21 George St., Edinburgh EH2 2PB. © 0131/225-1251. Fax 0131/226-5644. www.principal-hotels.com 195 units. £100–£300 ($351–$508) double; from £460 ($851) suite. AE, DC, MC, V. Limited free parking. Bus: 24, 28, or 45. **Amenities:** Restaurant; bar; concierge; laundry service; dry cleaning. *In room:* TV, coffeemaker, hair dryer, iron/ironing board.

The Glasshouse ★★ *Finds* A recently developed property at the top of Leith Walk on the fringes of Calton Hill, this hotel is not only one of the most modern but is also among the top so-called "boutique" hotels of Edinburgh. It combines old and new, with an impressive stone church facade, which is the actual entrance to the hotel, coexisting in harmony with a modern glass structure. Many of the well-furnished bedrooms offer panoramic views of the city. A special feature of the Glasshouse is the rooftop bar and garden for hotel guests. The bedrooms are as modern as tomorrow, with sleek, well-styled furnishings and the beds closed off from the sitting area by wood panels.

2 Greenside Place, Edinburgh EH1 3AA. © 0131/525-8200. Fax 0131/525-8205. www.theetoncollection.com/ hotels/glasshouse. 65 units. £175–£195 ($323–$360) double; £225–£295 ($416–$545) suite. AE, DC, MC, V. Parking £13 ($24). Bus: 5, 14, or 22. **Amenities:** Bar; health club; concierge; room service; babysitting; laundry service; dry cleaning. *In room:* A/C, TV, dataport, minibar, coffeemaker, hair dryer, safe, trouser press.

Macdonald Roxburghe Hotel ★★ Housed in buildings that are part of the original New Town designed by Robert Adam, at the corner of Charlotte Square and fashionable George Street, the Roxburghe provides classy atmosphere reflected in the elegant drawing room with its ornate ceiling and woodwork, antique furnishings, and tall arched windows. Reopened in 2000 after a multimillion-dollar redevelopment, the hotel was enlarged into two neighboring buildings, tripling the original number of guest rooms, which vary in size. The largest are in the original building and maintain features such as their imposing fireplaces. The new rooms have more recent furnishings and more up-to-date plumbing. The hotel's Melrose restaurant features classic British cuisine and Scottish specialties.

38 Charlotte St. (at George St.), Edinburgh EH2 4HG. © 0870/194-2108 or 888/892-0038 (U.S. only). Fax 0131/240-5555. www.macdonaldhotels.co.uk/roxburghe. 197 units. £140–£180 ($259–$333) double; from £230 ($425) suite. AE, DC, MC, V. Parking £12 ($23). Bus: 13, 19, or 41. **Amenities:** Restaurant; bar; indoor pool; health club; spa, sauna; concierge; laundry service; dry cleaning; 24-hr. front desk. *In room:* TV, coffeemaker, hair dryer, iron/ironing board, trouser press.

Old Waverley Hotel   Opposite the Scott Monument, the Old Waverley dates from 1848, overlooking Princes Street Gardens and Old Town beyond. The refurbished guest rooms are well maintained and comfortable; some look directly onto the Scott Monument and the castle, and the corner rooms are the most impressive. Each unit comes with a combination tub/shower. Online bookings appear to offer significant savings over the standard rates.

43 Princes St., Edinburgh EH2 2BY. © 0131/556-4648. Fax 0131/557-6316. www.old-waverley-hotel.co.uk. 66 units. £130–£170 ($240–$314) double. Rates include breakfast. AE, DC, MC, V. Parking £10 ($19). Bus: 4, 12, 31, or 44. **Amenities:** Restaurant; bar; room service; dry cleaning; 24-hour reception. *In room:* TV, Internet access, coffeemaker, hair dryer.

Ramada Mount Royal   The seven-story, 158-room Mount Royal, a not very handsome remake of an 1860s hotel, is at the heart of Princes Street. The second floor reception area offers floor-to-ceiling windows that frame classic views of the Old Town and Edinburgh Castle. There aren't necessarily a lot of frills with the Ramada, but the comfort is genuine in the streamlined guest rooms. Just be aware that this hotel is a favorite of tour groups. The lounge, with views of the Scott Memorial and Princes Street, provides a wide range of savory and sweet snacks and beverages throughout the day, while the Arts Restaurant does breakfasts, lunches and dinners. Upgrades to provide a castle view are £20 ($37) per room per night.

53 Princes St., Edinburgh EH2 2DG. © 0131/225-7161. Fax 0131/220-4671. www.ramadajarvis.co.uk. 158 units. £125–£180 ($231–$333) double; £180–£250 ($333–$462) suite. AE, DC, MC, V. Parking available nearby. Bus: 4, 12, 31, or 44. Pets accepted. **Amenities:** Restaurant; bar; room service; laundry service; dry cleaning. *In room:* TV, coffeemaker, hair dryer, trouser press.

MODERATE

Seven Danube Street ⊛   This small three-unit B&B (one double, one twin, and one single) is in Stockbridge, the handsome and refined district just northwest of the bustling commercial center but miles away in ambience. The building is attributed to architect James Milne, who was responsible for the design of this section of the New Town developments in the 1820s. The spacious guest rooms boast artfully draped chintzes. A lavish breakfast in the dining room may include venison sausages, omelets prepared with free-range hen's eggs, homemade scones, and jams and marmalades. The owners, Fiona and Colin Mitchell-Rose also have a self-catering apartment on nearby Dean Terrace. No smoking is permitted.

7 Danube St., Edinburgh EH4 1NN. © 0131/332-2755. Fax 0131/343-3648. www.sevendanubestreet.com. 3 units. £100–£130 ($185–$240) double. Rates include breakfast. MC, V. Free parking nearby. Bus: 24, 29, or 42. **Amenities:** Laundry. *In room:* TV, coffeemaker, hair dryer.

The Walton ⊛ (Finds)   A real discovery, this guesthouse sits right at the heart of Edinburgh's northern New Town in a well-restored 200-year-old town house. A complete refurbishment and renovation has maintained the essential Georgian character and elegant features, but have revitalized and modernized the entire hotel. Bedrooms are

Kids Family-Friendly Hotels

A-Haven Townhouse With some guest rooms large enough to accommodate families, any brood should feel right at home in this small hotel in Leith. See p. 66.

The Carlton Hotel Kids will love the indoor pool. Parents will love the availability of extra-large units and the fact that cots are readily provided. It's right in the heart of town to boot. See below.

Thrums Hotel This Southside hotel takes its name from J. M. Barrie's name for his hometown of Kirriemuir. Barrie is best known to children as the author of *Peter Pan*. Kids are made especially welcome at Thrums and have room to play outside. See p. 65.

midsize, cozy, comfortable, and tranquil. In the morning you're served a superior breakfast. The location is only a short walk up the hill to the heart of New Town. A sister hotel, the **Glenora,** offers alternative accommodation on Rosebery Crescent near the Haymarket railway station.

79 Dundas St., Edinburgh EH3 6SD. © **0131/556-1137.** Fax 0131/557-8367. www.waltonhotel.com. 10 units. £80–£165 ($148–$305) double. Rates include breakfast. MC, V. Limited free parking. Bus: 23 or 27. *In room:* TV, coffeemaker, hair dryer, Wi-Fi.

INEXPENSIVE

Greenside Hotel Behind a chiseled sandstone facade on the slopes of Calton Hill, this four-story Georgian (designed by William Playfair), retains such features as high ceilings, cove moldings, and elaborate trim. Guests access their rooms via a winding staircase, illuminated by a skylight. The rooms have shower-only bathrooms. The Firth of Forth and the dramatic Forth bridges are just about seen from the uppermost front rooms; a sloping tiered garden, with a patio at the bottom, is visible from the rear units. Breakfast is served in a formal dining room.

9 Royal Terrace, Edinburgh EH7 5AB. ©/fax **0131/557-0022.** 15 units. £45–£110 ($83–$203) double. Rates include breakfast. AE, MC, V. Parking on street. Bus: 1, 4, 5, or 15. **Amenities:** Bar. *In room:* TV, coffeemaker, hair dryer.

2 Old Town

VERY EXPENSIVE

The Carlton Hotel *Kids* With Victorian turrets, Flemish gables, and severe gray stonework, this baronial pile (a former department store) rises from the east side of North Bridge, between the Royal Mile and the cavernous gap that separates Old Town from New Town. The Paramount group owners invested substantially to upgrade this hotel. Some bedrooms were removed to make units larger and more comfortable with private bathrooms with a tub and shower. Furnishings are tasteful with a subdued modern simplicity. In spite of its overhaul, some complaints of inadequate soundproofing for rooms facing the busy street have been made. Light sleepers should request rooms at the rear.

19 North Bridge, Edinburgh EH1 1SD. © **0131/472-3000.** Fax 0131/556-2691. www.paramount-hotels.co.uk. 189 units. £180–£250 ($333–$462) executive double. Children 14 and under stay free in parent's room. AE, DC, MC, V.

Parking £6 ($11). Bus: 3, 8, 14, or 29. **Amenities:** Restaurant; bar; indoor pool; health club; Jacuzzi; sauna; limited room service; babysitting; squash courts. *In room:* TV, coffeemaker, hair dryer, iron/ironing board, safe.

The Scotsman ⭐ Located on North Bridge just across from the Carlton, only minutes from the Royal Mile or Princes Street, this is one of the brightest and most stylish hotels to open in Edinburgh recently. Its name honors the newspaper that was
published here for nearly a century before relocating to modern facilities near Holyroodhouse. Traditional styling and cutting-edge design are harmoniously wed in the
1904 baronial limestone pile, a city landmark since it was first constructed. The 68
units, from the Study Room to the Baron Suite, vary in size (from 28 sq. m/300 sq.
ft. to a whopping 103 sq. m/1,110 sq. ft.) and aspect, such as views of the castle or
towards Calton Hill and Firth of Forth. They include state-of-the-art bathrooms and
such extras as two-way service closets, which means your laundry can be picked up virtually unnoticed. The two-floor Penthouse suite is in a category of its own, with a private elevator and balcony with barbecue. The in-house dining options include the
smart North Bridge Brasserie & Bar as well as the more exclusive fine-dining option
in the basement, Vermilion. In addition to standard rates, the hotel runs weekend
break promotions.

20 North Bridge, Edinburgh EH1 1DF. ℂ **0131/556-5565.** Fax 0131/652-3652. www.scotsmanhotels.com. 68 units.
£200–£350 ($370–$645) double; from £380 ($705) suite; £1,200 ($2,220) penthouse. AE, DC, MC, V. Valet parking.
Bus: 3, 8, 14, or 29. **Amenities:** 2 restaurants; bar; indoor pool; health club; spa; sauna; salon; room service; massage; babysitting; laundry service; dry cleaning. *In room:* TV, Internet, minibar, coffeemaker, hair dryer, iron/ironing
board, safe.

The Witchery by the Castle ⭐⭐ Part of the famous Edinburgh restaurant (p. 75),
the overnight accommodation in the Witchery offers romantic, sumptuous and
theatrically decorated rooms with Gothic antiques and elaborate tapestries. Most of
the hype about the suites is true: "the perfect lust-den," "Scotland's most romantic
hotel," "a jewel-box setting," and "one of the 50 best places in the world for honey-
mooners." *Cosmopolitan* and others have hailed this place as one of the world's "most
wonderful" places to stay. Each lavishly decorated suite (named the Library, Vestry,
Armoury, and the like) features splendid furnishings—"fit for a lord and his lady"—
and such extras as books, chocolates, a Bose sound system, and a complimentary bottle of champagne. Each suite has its own individual character. One called Sempill,
features an oak four-poster bed in a red-velvet-lined bedroom. The buildings near the
castle date to the 17th century, filled with open fires, opulent beds, and luxurious sitting areas. The list of celebrity guests includes Michael Douglas and Catherine Zeta
Jones, Simpson's creator Matt Groening, as well as Jack Nicholson.

Castlehill, The Royal Mile, Edinburgh, EH1 2NF. ℂ **0131/225-5613.** Fax 0131/220-4392. www.thewitchery.com. 7
suites. From £295 ($462). Rates include continental breakfast and champagne. AE, DC, MC, V. Parking nearby. Bus:
28. **Amenities:** Restaurant. *In room:* A/C, TV, fridge, coffeemaker, hair dryer, iron/ironing board, safe.

EXPENSIVE

Holyrood Hotel ⭐ This deluxe charmer provides contrast to the grand palace
hotels of Edinburgh. The Holyrood launched itself into the millennium by being pro-
claimed "Hotel of the Year for Scotland" by the Automobile Association. This impressive and stylish hotel stands near the new Scottish Parliament and the Palace of
Holyroodhouse and is only minutes from the heart of Old Town. Bedrooms are luxurious, with deluxe furnishings and elegant toiletries. The Club Floor is one of the

best retreats in Edinburgh for luxury-minded guests: It has its own private elevator, lounge, and library along with a champagne and canapé reception every night.

81 Holyrood Rd., Edinburgh EH8 8AU. © **0870/194-2106.** Fax 0131/550-4545. www.macdonaldhotels.co.uk. 156 units. £150–£250 ($277–$462) double; from £264 ($488) suite. Rates include buffet breakfast. AE, DC, MC, V. Limited parking £15 ($28). Bus: 35. **Amenities:** Restaurant; bar; indoor pool; health club; sauna; room service; laundry service; dry cleaning; club-level rooms. *In room:* A/C, TV, fax, dataport, minibar, coffeemaker, hair dryer, iron/ironing board, safe, trouser press.

Radisson SAS Hotel ⭐   Formerly the "Crowne Plaza," this is the preferred major hotel in Old Town for many visitors. The baronial style building lies midway along the Royal Mile, halfway between Edinburgh Castle and Holyroodhouse. In spite of the antique geography, the hotel is thoroughly modernized and offers first-class facilities (if lacking the old-world charm of some of Edinburgh's grand dame hotels). It's also one of the best-equipped hotels in the area, with such luxuries as a leisure club with a jet-stream pool and undercover parking. Most of the bedrooms are spacious and well-decorated; bathrooms contain tub/shower combinations and heated floors for those chilly Scottish mornings. Carrubbers restaurant specializes in steak, while the less formal Itchycoo Bar and Kitchen offers tapas style eating. Check the Radisson website for "special offers" and "best online price guarantee."

80 High St., Edinburgh EH1 1TH. © **0131/473-6590.** Fax 0131/557-9789. www.radisson.com. 238 units. £110–£230 ($203–$425) double. AE, DC, MC, V. Parking £7.50 ($14). Bus: 35. Pets accepted. **Amenities:** Restaurant; bar; indoor pool; health club; sauna; concierge; business center; room service; massage; laundry service; dry cleaning. *In room:* TV, Wi-Fi, minibar, coffeemaker, hair dryer, iron/ironing board, safe, trouser press.

MODERATE

The Bank Hotel *Value*   This hotel offers better value than many of its competitors in this congested area on the Royal Mile where the High Street intersects South Bridge, across from the Tron Kirk. From the 1920s to the 1990s, it was a branch of the Bank of Scotland, hence the name. You enter the hotel via the popular Logie Baird Bar. Once inside you'll discover high ceilings, well-chosen furnishings, and king-size beds; all but one guest room have a shower and a tub in the bathrooms. The units are dedicated to the works of a famous Scots, including rooms dedicated to Robert Burns, Robert Louis Stevenson, and Alexander Graham Bell.

1 South Bridge St., Edinburgh EH1 1LL. © **0131/622-6800.** Fax 0131/622-6822. www.festival-inns.co.uk. 9 units. £110 ($203) double; £140 ($260) executive room. Rates include breakfast. AE, MC, V. Parking nearby £8 ($16). Bus: 35. **Amenities:** Bar; laundry service. *In room:* TV, coffeemaker, hair dryer, trouser press.

Tips **Basic Chain Hotels**

If you're the type of traveler who thinks of hotels as just places to lay one's head at night, some of the better deals in town are found at the no-frills chains. In the heart of Old Town, try the **Ibis** (6 Hunter Sq., Edinburgh EH1 1QW; © **0131/240-7000;** www.accor-hotels.com) where rooms cost between £55 ($102) and £77 ($142). In the West End, the **Premier Travel Inn** (1 Morrison Link, Edinburgh EH3 8DN; © **0870/238-3319;** www.premiertravelinn.co.uk) is modern and functional with rooms at £77 ($142), although its Leith branch is cheaper still at £56 ($104).

---

3 West End

VERY EXPENSIVE

The Bonham 🎯🎯   One of Edinburgh's most stylish hotels, the Bonham is actually three connected West End town houses that functioned in the 19th century as a nursing home and then more recently as dorms for the university. In 1998, all that changed when a team of entrepreneurs poured millions of pounds into its refurbishment, pumped up the design, and outfitted each high-ceilinged guest room in a hip blend of old and new. Perhaps the jewel in the crown of the Townhouse Group of hotels in Edinburgh (which also includes The Edinburgh Residence, Howard, and Channings), the Bonham's rooms have an individual theme and plush upholsteries. Bathrooms are state of the art, with expensive toiletries. The Restaurant at the Bonham provides elegant, yet modern, dining rooms. In addition to the standard rates, mid- and off-season special rates that include breakfast are available for two people staying at least 2 nights.

35 Drumsheugh Gardens, Edinburgh EH3 7RN. 🕿 **0131/226-6050.** Fax 0131/226-6080. www.thebonham.com. 48 units. £195–£240 ($360–$444) standard double; £340 ($629) suite. Rates include continental breakfast. AE, DC, MC, V. Free parking. Bus: 19 or 37. **Amenities:** Restaurant; room service. *In room:* TV w/Internet, dataport, minibar, coffeemaker, hair dryer, iron/ironing board, trouser press.

The Chester Residence   Another option between self-catering and hotel accommodation is "serviced apartments," and those at the Chester Residence rate five stars according to the tourist board. Each luxury flat (save the studio-size "patio apartment") has a kitchen, separate sitting room, and full bathroom. The "garden apartment" includes a private walled garden for its guests.

9 Chester St., Edinburgh EH3 7RF. 🕿0131/226-2075. Fax 0131/226-2191. www.chester-residence.com. 5 units. £140–£230 ($260–$425) per apartment. Rates include continental breakfast. MC, V. Parking on street. Bus: 13. **Amenities:** *In room:* TV, dataport, Internet, CD/DVD player.

The Edinburgh Residence 🎯   Part of the Townhouse Group, this is one of the finest luxury hotels in Scotland, a series of elegant suites installed in a trio of architecturally beautiful and sensitively restored Georgian buildings in the West End. As you enter, grand staircases and classic wood paneling greet you, but the units have all the modern conveniences that befit five-star accommodation. This hotel is on the same level of its siblings—the Bonham, the Howard, and Channings. The rooms are the ultimate in comfort, with a trio of suites that have their own private entrances. All units are spacious. If you are traveling off season, it is worth inquiring about "short break" promotions that offer savings.

7 Rothesay Terrace, Edinburgh EH3 7RY. 🕿 **0131/226-3380.** Fax 0131/226-3381. www.theedinburghresidence.com. 29 units. £150–£265 ($277–$490) suite; £260–£395 ($481–$730) apt. Rates include continental breakfast. AE, MC, V. Free parking. Bus: 13. **Amenities:** Bar; room service. *In room:* TV, minibar, hair dryer, iron/ironing board.

Sheraton Grand Hotel 🎯   On the grounds of a former railway siding near Edinburgh's Usher Hall, Traverse, and Royal Lyceum theaters, this six-story postmodern structure houses a glamorous hotel and office complex. The Sheraton is elegant, with soaring public rooms and rich carpeting. Boasting a good location in the proverbial shadow of Edinburgh Castle—as well as state-of-the-art spa and leisure facilities (including a rooftop indoor/outdoor pool)—the hotel pretty much has it all. The spacious, well-furnished units have double-glazed windows; glamorous suites are available as are rooms for travelers with disabilities. The castle-view rooms on the top floors are best (and most expensive). The main restaurant, with views of the Festival Square, presents well-prepared meals and a lavish Sunday buffet, while an annex houses the Italian **Santini** restaurant (p. 72) below the spa.

1 Festival Sq., Edinburgh EH3 9SR. © 800/325-3535 in the U.S. and Canada, or 0131/229-9131. Fax 0131/228-4510. www.sheraton.com. 260 units. £150–£360 ($277–$666) double. AE, DC, MC, V. Parking nearby. Bus: 10, 22, or 30. **Amenities:** 3 restaurants; 2 bars; indoor and outdoor pools; exercise room; spa; sauna; concierge; room service; massage; babysitting; laundry service; dry cleaning. In room: A/C, TV, dataport, minibar, coffeemaker, hair dryer, iron/ironing board, trouser press.

EXPENSIVE

Point Hotel   With one of the most dramatic contemporary interiors of any hotel in Edinburgh, this is a stylish place not far from the Grassmarket. The decor has appeared in a book detailing the 50 premier hotel designs in the world, with a great emphasis on color and innovation, including a black stone floor at the front. The overnight accommodations are equally attractively furnished. Standard rooms may feel a bit small, but the premium rooms are more comfortable and spacious. Many units have views of the castle, but those in the rear do not, so be duly warned. If you like stainless steel and brushed chrome instead of Scottish tartan and antiques, this might be the place for you.

34 Bread St., Edinburgh EH3 9AF. © 0131/221-5555. Fax 0131/221-9929. www.point-hotel.co.uk. 140 units. £125–£160 ($231–$296) double; from £350 ($650) suite. AE, DC, MC, V. Parking on street. Bus: 2 or 28. **Amenities:** Restaurant; bar; limited room service; laundry service; dry cleaning. In room: TV, dataport (executive rooms only), hair dryer, iron/ironing board.

MODERATE

16 Lynedoch Place   The 1820 Georgian row house that houses this West End B&B near Dean Bridge has a flower-filled garden in the front, which is quite unusual for central Edinburgh, where buildings often go right up to the sidewalks. Inside are high ceilings with deep cove moldings, a cantilevered staircase illuminated by a glassed-in cupola, and family antiques. The midsize guest rooms are cozy and decorated with charm. The elaborate breakfasts are served in a formal dining room. Your hosts—Susie and Andrew Hamilton—are experts in planning itineraries through the Highlands.

16 Lynedoch Place, Edinburgh EH3 7PY. © 0131/225-5507. Fax 0131/226-4185. www.16lynedochplace.co.uk. 3 units. £75–£120 ($139–$222) double. Rates include breakfast. MC, V. Parking on street. Bus: 19. In room: TV, no phone.

4 Southside

EXPENSIVE

Prestonfield ✦✦   Prestonfield, rising in Jacobean splendor amid 5.3 hectares (13 acres) of gardens, pastures, and woodlands below Arthur's Seat, received a £3-million ($5.5-million) refurbishment in 2003 in the hands of James Thomson, who owns the Witchery (see review earlier in this chapter). The pile was built in the 17th century, serving first as the home of the city's Lord Provost (mayor), and has entertained such luminaries over the years as David Hume and Benjamin Franklin. More recently, it's been pop stars and actors such as Sean Connery and Minnie Driver. Guests should appreciate the traditional atmosphere and 1680s architecture as well as the peacocks and Highland cattle that strut and stroll across the grounds. The spacious bedrooms (now five-star-rated) hide all modern conveniences behind velvet-lined walls: Bose sound systems, DVD players, and flatscreen plasma TVs. The restaurant, Rhubarb, is as theatrical as they come. Sometimes, reduced midweek rates are available.

Priestfield Rd., Edinburgh EH16 5UT. (C) **0131/225-7800.** Fax 0131/668-3976. www.prestonfield.com. 28 units. £195–£225 ($360–$416) double; from £295 ($545) suite. Rates include breakfast. AE, MC, V. Free parking. Bus: 2, 14, 30. **Amenities:** Restaurant; bar; concierge; secretarial services; room service; babysitting; laundry service; dry cleaning. *In room:* TV, dataport, coffeemaker, hair dryer, iron/ironing board.

MODERATE

Aonach Mor   Near Prestonfield on the city's Southside, this guest house is located in a proud, if short, row of three-story Victorian terraced houses. Away from the hustle and bustle of the city center, some of the rooms offer views towards Arthur's Seat. Named after a Western Highland mountain, the Aonach Mor is family run, offering what they think is one of the best breakfasts in Edinburgh.

14 Kilmaurs Terrace, Newington, Edinburgh EH16 5DR. (C) **0131/667-8694.** www.aonachmor.com. 7 units. £60–£140 ($111–$260) double, depending on season. Rates include breakfast. MC, V. Parking on street. Bus: 3, 8, or 29. *In room:* TV, coffeemaker, hair dryer.

Borough   This stylish boutique hotel south of the Meadows near the antique shops of Causewayside is a warehouse conversion, designed by Britain's Ben Kelly who is best known for the famous Hacienda nightclub in Manchester. The rooms are admittedly on the small side, but they are individually designed and at least have high ceilings and casement windows as well as stylish looks. The bar and restaurant on the ground floor are equally fashionable.

72 Causewayside, Edinburgh EH9 1PY. (C) **0131/668-2255.** www.boroughhotel.com. 12 units. £80–£125 ($129–$230) double. Rates include breakfast. Limited parking. Bus: 3, 5, 7, or 31. **Amenities:** Restaurant; bar. *In room:* TV with DVD/CD, Wi-Fi.

INXPENSIVE

Thrums Hotel *Kids*   In the Newington district southwest of the Meadows, Thrums Guest House is a pair of connected Georgian buildings. The hotel contains high-ceilinged guest rooms with some antique furnishings. Children are particularly welcomed here. Some accommodations are set aside as family rooms, while the garden offers an outdoor play area. Six units come with a shower-only bathroom; the rest are equipped with combination tub and shower.

14–15 Minto St., Edinburgh EH9 1RQ. (C) **0131/667-5545.** Fax 0131/667-8707. www.thrumshotel.com. 15 units. £55–£110 ($101–$203) double. Rates include breakfast. MC, V. Free parking. Bus: 3, 8, 29. **Amenities:** Laundry service. *In room:* TV, coffeemaker, hair dryer.

5 Leith & North of New Town

EXPENSIVE

Malmaison *&&*   Leith's stylish boutique hotel, amid the old harbor district, Malmaison is only a few steps from the Water of Leith, the Edinburgh stream that empties into the sea here. It was converted from an 1883 seamen's mission/dorm and is capped by a stately, stone clock tower. A hip, unpretentious place has been created with a minimalist decor. Rooms are average in size but individually designed and well equipped. The leisure facilities are limited to an exercise room, but you'll find the brasserie and a cafe and wine bar favored by locals. Even during summertime, at least before the Festival begins, Malmaison's online reservation system offers good discounts.

1 Tower Place, Leith, Edinburgh EH6 7DB. (℗ **0131/468-5000.** Fax 0131/468-5002. www.malmaison.com. 100 units. £135–£195 ($250–$360) double. AE, DC, MC, V. Free parking. Bus: 16 or 35. **Amenities:** Restaurant; bar; exercise room; room service. *In room:* TV, dataport, minibar, coffeemaker, hair dryer.

MODERATE

Pilrig House Apartment   This self-catering two-bedroom apartment just south of Leith is in historic premises dating back to 1718. More recently, the author Robert Louis Stevenson played in its gardens as a child in the 1800s. Today, it will suit those travelers who want a bit of independence as well as some peace and quiet—though you're not far from the action, either. The accommodations sleep three, with two bedrooms, a sitting room, and its own, rather regal, entrance up steps passing through a Doric portico and double oak doors.

Pilrig House Close, Bonnington Rd. (north side of Pilrig Park), Edinburgh EH6 5RF (℗ **0131/554-4794.** www.pilrig houseapartment.co.uk. 1 unit. £80–£140 ($148–$260) triple. MC, V. Free parking. Bus: 11 or 36. *In room:* TV, DVD/CD player, hair dryer.

INEXPENSIVE

A-Haven Townhouse *(Kids)*   The A-Haven is a semidetached gray-stone Victorian in an up-and-coming neighborhood in Leith. The guest rooms vary in size (the biggest being on the second floor) and are outfitted with traditional furnishings and shower-only bathrooms. Some units overlook the Firth of Forth, while the opposite side of the building opens onto views of Arthur's Seat. Some rooms are large enough to accommodate families with cots. Recently a two-unit "lodge" was added to the rear of the property. David Kay extends a Scottish welcome in this family-type place.

180 Ferry Rd., Edinburgh EH6 4NS. (℗ **0131/554-6559.** Fax 0131/554-5252. www.a-haven.co.uk. 14 units. £60–£110 ($111–$203) double. Rates include breakfast. AE, MC, V. Free parking. Bus: 7, 14, 21. **Amenities:** Bar. *In room:* TV, dataport, coffeemaker, hair dryer, trouser press.

Ardmor House   This gay-owned, straight-friendly four-star guesthouse with nice gardens on a stretch of road with plenty of B&Bs was opened in 1999 by Robin Jack and Colin Lennox. Recently refurbished, it has moved into small boutique B&B terrain. Ardmor House has five overnight rooms, all with modern bathrooms, and large, firm beds. Bay windows and period settees befit this restored Victorian, just about halfway between the city center and Leith. Jack and Lennox also have two four-star self-catering apartments in New Town.

74 Pilrig St. (near Leith Walk), Edinburgh, EH6 5AS. (℗ **0131/554-4944.** www.ardmorhouse.com. 5 units. £65–£110 ($120–$203). Rates include breakfast. MC, V. Free parking. Bus: 11. **Amenities:** Garden. *In room:* TV, coffeemaker, hair dryer, no phone.

Where to Dine in Edinburgh

Cuisine in Scotland is perhaps the most misunderstood aspect of the country. Too many seem to think that food here begins and ends with haggis, which in itself is misunderstood. There is honestly a lot more to the country's larder than the famous traditional dish.

Edinburgh boasts some of the best restaurants in the country, and the choice in the capital is more diverse than ever. You'll find an array of contemporary Scottish restaurants; French, fish, and brasserie-style eateries; along with cuisine from around the world, particularly Indian and Thai food. Plus, the vegetarian options are not too bad.

Scotland's reputation for excellent fresh produce is growing. So look out for the following in season: shellfish such as langoustines (large prawns), oysters, mussels, or scallops; locally landed finned fish (such as halibut, bream, or sea bass); as well as lamb and Aberdeen Angus, or Highland, beef. Fresh vegetables include asparagus, peas, and, of course, potatoes—some claim that the spuds grown in Ayrshire's sandy soils are unparalleled for fluffy texture and rich taste.

Remember, a majority of the restaurants close in the afternoon, so don't plan to eat lunch too late in the day. The hours given in the information below reflect when food may be ordered; bars on the premises may keep longer hours. Many restaurants also close for business on either Sunday or Monday—sometimes both. But during the annual Edinburgh Festival from late July to the end of August, many also offer extended hours; given the crowds, always reserve a table in advance.

For ideas on dining options, buy *The List* magazine's comprehensive *Eating & Drinking Guide,* an annually updated publication that lists and reviews hundreds of restaurants, bars, and cafes in Edinburgh (and Glasgow).

PRICES In part because of the strength of the currency in the U.K., the cost of dining out may well seem expensive. Still, there is a range of choices for most budgets. The prices do include the 17.5% VAT, so there are no hidden surprises when the bill comes. If you're looking for bargains, inquire about pretheater special menus, which can be almost half the price of the regular dinner menu. Log onto www.5pm.co.uk for a selection of restaurants offering early dining deals.

TIPPING A gratuity of 10% is the average for service, although leave nothing if you were badly treated. On the other hand, if you were truly impressed, leaving up to 15% to 20% should be considered. In a few restaurants, service is included in the bill automatically. This can, however, be refunded if service was genuinely dreadful.

SMOKING All restaurants and bars are nonsmoking by law, following the pattern of Ireland, California, and New York City. Some have outdoor dining areas, however, where smoking is allowed.

1 Restaurants by Cuisine

AMERICAN
Bell's Diner ✦ (New Town, $, p. 74)
Calistoga (Southside, $$, p. 78)
Wannaburger (Old Town, $, p. 77)

CAFES
Plaisir du Chocolat ✦ (Old Town, $, p. 76)
Spoon ✦✦ (Old Town, $, p. 77)

SEAFOOD/FISH
Café Royal Oyster Bar ✦ (New Town, $$, p. 73)
Fishers Bistro (Leith and New Town, $$, p. 79)
The Shore Bar & Restaurant ✦ (Leith, $$, p. 79)
Sweet Melindas ✦ (Southside, $$, p. 78)

FRENCH
La Garrigue ✦ (Old Town, $$, p. 76).
Le Café St. Honoré (New Town, $$, p. 73)
Restaurant Martin Wishart ✦✦✦ (Leith, $$$$, p. 78)
The Vintners Rooms ✦✦ (Leith, $$$$, p. 79)

INDIAN
Kebab Mahal ✦ (Southside, $, p. 78)
Namaste ✦ (Old Town, $$, p. 76)

INTERNATIONAL
Atrium ✦✦ (West End, $$$, p. 69)
blue bar café (New Town, $$, p. 73)
Dome Grill Room and Bar (New Town, $$$, p. 69)
Marque Central ✦ (West End, $$, p. 73)

Oloroso ✦ (New Town, $$$, p. 72)
Zinc Bar & Grill (Leith, $$, p. 79)

ITALIAN
Santini (West End, $$$, p. 72).

SCOTTISH/MODERN BRITISH
Atrium ✦✦ (West End, $$$, p. 69).
blue bar café (New Town, $$, p. 72)
Forth Floor Restaurant ✦✦ (New Town, $$$, p. 69)
Haldanes Restaurant (New Town, $$$, p. 72)
The Grain Store ✦ (Old Town, $$$, p. 75)
Howies (Old Town, $$, p. 76)
The Marque Central (West End, $$, p. 73)
Number One ✦✦ (New Town, $$$$, p. 69)
Off the Wall (Old Town, $$$, p. 75)
Oloroso ✦ (New Town, $$$, p. 72)
Rhubarb (Southside, $$$, p. 77)
Sweet Melindas ✦ (Southside, $$, p. 78)
The Tower (Old Town, $$, p. 77)
The Witchery by the Castle (Old Town, $$$, p. 75)

SPANISH
Barioja (Old Town, $$, p. 75)

THAI
Dusit (New Town, $$, p. 73)
Time 4 Thai (New Town, $$, p. 74)

VEGETARIAN
Henderson's Salad Table (New Town, $, p. 74)
David Bann's Vegetarian Restaurant (Old Town, $$, p. 75)

Key to Abbreviations: $$$$ = Very Expensive $$$ = Expensive $$ = Moderate $ = Inexpensive

2 New Town & West End

VERY EXPENSIVE

Number One ✦✦ MODERN BRITISH/SCOTTISH   This is the premier restaurant in the city's premier central hotel, with a well-earned star for superior cuisine and service from the widely respected *Michelin Guide.* You can sample the likes of pan-seared Scottish monkfish with saffron mussel broth, or perhaps venison loin with juniper jus, red cabbage, and black truffle mash. Dessert brings some rather exotic choices, such as mulled wine parfait with a cinnamon sauce, and a variety of sorbets or mature cheeses. Wines are excellent, if pricey, but so is the meal. A special treat while you're in Edinburgh.

Balmoral Hotel, 1 Princes St. ✆ **0131/557-6727.** www.thebalmoralhotel.com. Reservations recommended. Fixed-price lunch £24 ($44); fixed-price dinner £55 ($102); fixed-price "chef's tasting menu" £65 ($120). AE, DC, MC, V. Mon–Fri noon–2pm and 7–10pm; Sat–Sun 7–10pm. Bus: 3, 8, 19, or 30.

EXPENSIVE

Atrium ✦✦ SCOTTISH/INTERNATIONAL   Since 1993, this has been one of the most acclaimed and stylish restaurants in Edinburgh. Meals are prepared using lots of local and some organic ingredients, displaying flair but not excessive amounts of fuss or fancy presentation. Favorites include dishes such as roasted sea bass with Dauphinois potatoes, baby spinach, charcoal-grilled eggplant, and baby fennel. Yum. Or how about seared scallops served with chiles and garlic on lemon linguini? The desserts are equally superb. The wine list is excellent but not cheap, with most bottles costing in excess of £20 ($37). Those on a tighter budget should try the **blue bar café** in the same premises (see review later in this chapter).

10 Cambridge St. (adjacent the Traverse Theatre, about a 5-min. walk from Princes St). ✆ **0131/228-8882.** www. atriumrestaurant.co.uk. Reservations recommended. Fixed-price lunch £14 ($26); dinner main courses £17–£22 ($31–$40). AE, MC, V. Mon–Fri noon–2pm and 6–10pm; Sat 6–10pm. Bus: 1, 10, 15, or 24.

Dome Grill Room and Bar INTERNATIONAL   Thanks to its restored Victorian-era Royal Bank of Scotland premises on posh George Street, with Corinthian columns, intricate mosaic-tile flooring, marble-topped bar, potted palms, and towering flower arrangements—all under an elaborate domed ceiling—it is only honest to say that most people come here for the look of the Dome Grill Room and Bar. It oozes class and elegance. Alas, the last time we visited, they rather ruined the ambience with a loud, modern pop/R&B soundtrack that belonged at the All Bar One branch across the street. The selection of food includes smoked salmon starters, bowls of mussels, or breast of duck. At the rear of the building is the garden cafe, which backs onto Rose Street.

14 George St. ✆ **0131/624-8624.** www.thedomeedinburgh.com. Reservations suggested. Lunch main courses £9–£16 ($17–$30); dinner £10–£22 ($19–$40). AE, DC, MC, V. Daily noon–10pm; bar Fri–Sat until 1am. Bus: 45.

Forth Floor Restaurant ✦✦ SCOTTISH/MODERN BRITISH   No that's not a misspelling of the name, this restaurant at the top of the Harvey Nichols boutique department store has excellent views of the Firth of Forth from the fourth floor of the building. It combines excellent contemporary Scottish cooking with those commanding vistas. While you do feel like you're dining in a department store annex (despite the slick, minimalist decor), the food can be phenomenal, whether a succulent and robust braised ox tail or a light salad with endive and seasonal truffles. The produce used by the kitchen is notably fresh. The brasserie menu, while less extensive than the restaurant's selections, offers good value with a fixed-price £14 ($26) lunch and serves

Edinburgh Dining

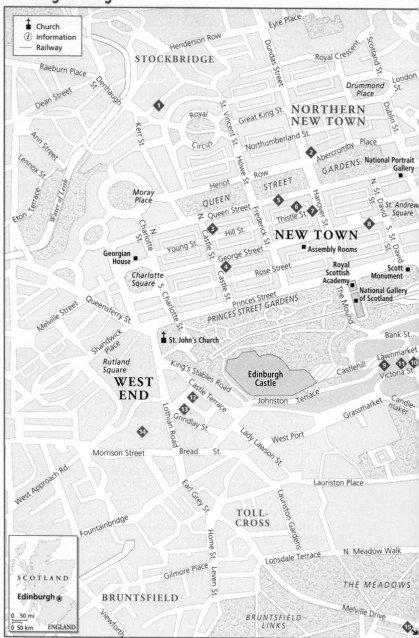

Legend:
- ✝ Church
- ⓘ Information
- — Railway

STOCKBRIDGE

Eyre Place

Henderson Row

Dundas Street

Royal Crescent

Scotland St.

Raeburn Place

Denhaugh St.

Drummond Place

London St.

Dean Street

Kerr St.

St. Vincent St.

Great King St.

NORTHERN NEW TOWN

Dublin St.

Ann Street

Royal Circus

Northumberland St.

Abercromby Place

Lennox St.

Eton Terrace

Water of Leith

Moray Place

Heriot Row

STREET

GARDENS

National Portrait Gallery

Howe St.

QUEEN

N. Charlotte St.

Queen Street

Hanover St.

Thistle St.

NEW TOWN

N. St. David St.

St. Andrew Square

Georgian House

Charlotte Square

Young St.

Castle St.

Hill St.

Frederick St.

S. St. David St.

Assembly Rooms

George Street

Scott Monument

S. Charlotte St.

Castle St.

Rose Street

Royal Scottish Academy

National Gallery of Scotland

Melville Street

Queensferry St.

Princes Street

PRINCES STREET GARDENS

The Mound

Bank St.

Shandwick Place

Rutland Square

WEST END

King's Stables Road

St. John's Church

Castle Terrace

Edinburgh Castle

Castlehill

Lawnmarket

Victoria St.

Candlemaker

Johnston Terrace

Grassmarket

Lothian Road

Grindlay St.

West Port

Lady Lawson St.

Morrison Street

Bread St.

Lauriston Place

West Approach Rd.

Earl Grey St.

Lauriston Gardens

TOLL-CROSS

Fountainbridge

Home St.

Leven St.

Lonsdale Terrace

N. Meadow Walk

THE MEADOWS

Gilmore Place

Viewforth

BRUNTSFIELD

BRUNTSFIELD LINKS

Melville Drive

Inset map:

SCOTLAND

Edinburgh ✶

0 — 50 mi
0 — 50 km

ENGLAND

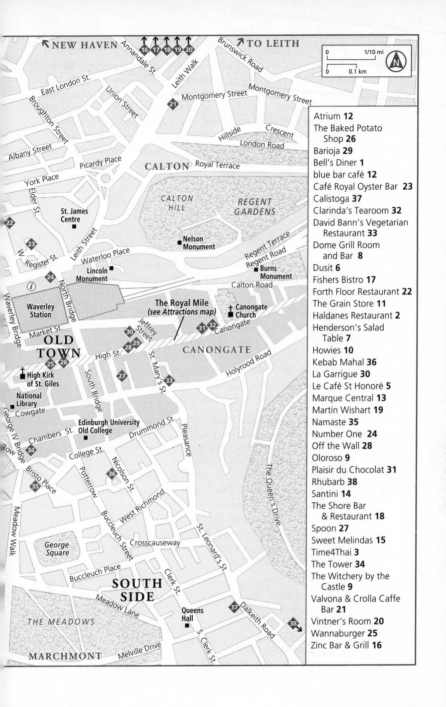

Map labels:

NEW HAVEN
TO LEITH
Annandale St.
Brunswick Road
East London St.
Leith Walk
Union Street
Montgomery Street
Montgomery Street
Broughton Street
Hillside Crescent
London Road
Albany Street
Picardy Place
CALTON
Royal Terrace
York Place
Elder St.
CALTON HILL
REGENT GARDENS
St. James Centre
Leith Street
Nelson Monument
W. Register St.
Waterloo Place
Regent Terrace
Regent Road
Lincoln Monument
Burns Monument
North Bridge
Calton Road
Waverley Station
The Royal Mile
(see Attractions map)
Canongate Church
Waverley Bridge
Market St.
Jeffrey Street
Canongate
OLD TOWN
High St.
St. Mary's St.
CANONGATE
Holyrood Road
High Kirk of St. Giles
South Bridge
National Library
Cowgate
George IV Bridge
Chambers St.
Edinburgh University Old College
Drummond St.
Pleasance
College St.
Potterrow
Nicolson St.
The Queen's Drive
Bristo Place
West Richmond
Buccleuch Street
Crosscauseway
St. Leonard's St.
Meadow Walk
George Square
Buccleuch Place
SOUTH SIDE
Clerk St.
Meadow Lane
Queens Hall
Dalkeith Road
THE MEADOWS
Melville Drive
S. Clerk St.
MARCHMONT

0   1/10 mi
0   0.1 km

Restaurant index:

Atrium **12**
The Baked Potato Shop **26**
Barioja **29**
Bell's Diner **1**
blue bar café **12**
Café Royal Oyster Bar **23**
Calistoga **37**
Clarinda's Tearoom **32**
David Bann's Vegetarian Restaurant **33**
Dome Grill Room and Bar **8**
Dusit **6**
Fishers Bistro **17**
Forth Floor Restaurant **22**
The Grain Store **11**
Haldanes Restaurant **2**
Henderson's Salad Table **7**
Howies **10**
Kebab Mahal **36**
La Garrigue **30**
Le Café St Honoré **5**
Marque Central **13**
Martin Wishart **19**
Namaste **35**
Number One **24**
Off the Wall **28**
Oloroso **9**
Plaisir du Chocolat **31**
Rhubarb **38**
Santini **14**
The Shore Bar & Restaurant **18**
Spoon **27**
Sweet Melindas **15**
Time4Thai **3**
The Tower **34**
The Witchery by the Castle **9**
Valvona & Crolla Caffe Bar **21**
Vintner's Room **20**
Wannaburger **25**
Zinc Bar & Grill **16**

71

King o' the Puddin' Race

Haggis, the much-misunderstood traditional dish of Scotland, may be an acquired taste, but it's honestly tasty. If you've come all this way—why not give it a try? **Macsween of Edinburgh** (www.macsween.co.uk) is a long-established family business specializing in Burn's "King o' the Puddin' Race." Macsween haggis includes lamb, beef, oatmeal, onions, and a special blend of seasonings and spices cooked together and stuffed into a natural casing. They also make a popular vegetarian version. Both are sold in vacuum-packed plastic bags and require only reheating in a microwave or simmering pan of water. You can find this company's product at a range of food stores and supermarkets throughout Edinburgh.

an "afternoon menu" between lunch and dinner. A recently added bar mixes some wonderful cocktails.

Harvey Nichols, 30–34 St. Andrew Sq. ℂ 0131/524-8350. www.harveynichols.com. Reservations suggested. Fixed-price lunch £25 ($45); dinner main courses £15–£20 ($28–$37). AE, DC, MC, V. Daily noon–10pm. Bus: 8, 10, 12, or 45.

Haldanes Restaurant SCOTTISH   Moving to new Northern New Town digs in 2006, the award-winning Haldanes still serves dinners that are conducted like meals in a private country house, with polite and deferential service. Owned by chef George Kelso and wife Michelle, Haldanes's cooking applies a light touch to mostly traditional ingredients, whether venison, wood pigeon, or salmon. The set-price lunch is a bargain, while the new layout is excellent for a romantic dinner for two.

13b Dundas St. ℂ 0131/556-8407. www.haldanesrestaurant.com. Reservations suggested. Fixed-price lunch £9.50 ($17); dinner main courses £16–£23 ($30–$42). MC, V. Tues–Sat noon–1:45pm and 5:30–9:30pm. Bus: 23 or 27.

Oloroso ✦ SCOTTISH/INTERNATIONAL   Oloroso's chef and owner, Tony Singh, is a Scottish-born Sikh with an imaginative approach to cooking Scottish produce. Here, in his rooftop restaurant with an ample veranda and excellent panoramic views, the feeling is contemporary and swanky. The space is sparsely decorated as the vistas provide enough interest. Frequently changing menus include dishes such as pan-seared marlin with stir-fried vegetables or chump of roast lamb with fondant potatoes and braised cabbage. There is also a grill menu with a variety of cuts of aged Highland beef. The bar, which mixes some mean cocktails, is usually open until 1am. To sample Singh's take on Indian cuisine, try his more recently launched **Roti** on the lane behind Oloroso.

33 Castle St. ℂ 0131/226-7614. www.oloroso.co.uk. Reservations suggested. Main courses £15–£22 ($27–$40). MC, V. Daily noon–2:30pm and 7–10pm. Bus: 24, 29, or 42.

Santini ITALIAN   This modern restaurant in a building adjacent the Sheraton Grand Hotel in the West End offers some of the capital's classiest Italian cooking. This small international chain, with the other branches in Milan and London, serves dishes such as fish antipasti with seared whitefish and chargrilled prawns or venison and pork belly. If you're in the mood for only pasta dishes or pizza, then opt for **Santini Bis**— the more casual option under the same roof.

8 Conference St. ℂ 0131/221-7788. Fixed-price 2-course lunch £21 ($38); dinner main courses £15–£22 ($28–$40). AE, MC, V. Mon–Fri noon–2:30pm and 6:30–10:30pm; Sat 6:30–10:30pm. Bus: 1, 2, 10, 24, or 34.

MODERATE

blue bar café INTERNATIONAL/MODERN BRITISH   In the building containing the Traverse Theatre in the West End, this attractive bistro is the less expensive sibling of **Atrium** (see review earlier in this chapter). You'll find a minimalist decor with touches of azure hues and a cheerful staff. The menu has dishes that can either serve as starters or a light main meal and a list of more substantial choices. Solid options include sausages with mash and onion gravy or goat-cheese tart with red-onion jam.

10 Cambridge St. ℂ **0131/221-1222.** www.bluebarcafe.com. Reservations recommended. Fixed-price lunch £9.95 ($18); main courses £10–£15 ($19–$28). AE, MC, V. Mon–Sat noon–3pm and 6–10:30pm. Bus: 1, 10, 15, or 24.

Café Royal Oyster Bar ℱ FISH/SEAFOOD   The Café Royal has been here for some 140 years and the many splendorous Victorian touches remain intact. The main menu offers more than just oysters: salmon, langoustines, and lobsters—as well as beef and rabbit—can be featured. The restaurant closes after lunch and reopens for dinner, but the ground-level **Circle Bar** is open throughout the day. The menu there is more limited but also less pricey. A highlight of the bar is the collection of tile pictures of notable inventors. Upstairs, a second drinking hole, the **Bistro Bar,** has an ornate ceiling although a less classy atmosphere.

17a W. Register St. ℂ **0131/556-4124.** Reservations recommended. Fixed-price 2-course lunch £15 ($27); dinner main courses £15–£20 ($27–$37). AE, MC, V. Daily noon–2pm and 7–10pm. Bus: 8 or 29.

Le Café St. Honoré FRENCH   A New Town favorite, this Parisian-style brasserie with the classic black-and-white-checkered floor is a deliberately rapid-paced place at lunchtime and more sedate at dinner. An upbeat and usually enthusiastic staff serves cuisine that might include baked oysters with smoked salmon, venison with juniper berries and wild mushrooms, local pheasant in wine and garlic sauce, or baked cod with asparagus. Pretheater prices from 5:30 to 6:45pm are a bargain.

34 NW Thistle St. ℂ **0131/226-2211.** Reservations recommended. Lunch main courses £8–£12 ($15–$22); dinner main courses £16–£20 ($30–$37). AE, MC, V. Daily noon–2:15pm and 6–10pm. Bus: 24, 29, or 42.

Dusit THAI *Finds*   Thistle Street, although little more than a slender lane with narrow sidewalks, has become a hot-bed for dining out, and this unassuming restaurant has quickly developed a reputation for being one of the best in the city for Thai cuisine. The menu is not typical and has a tendency towards modern dishes with occasionally prosaic translations, such as "A Pretty Duck" which is pretty delicious: chargrilled with nuts, mango, and shallots. Some of the main courses incorporate Scottish produce, such as venison, and the seafood options are plentiful.

49a Thistle St. ℂ **0131/220-6846.** www.dusit.co.uk. Reservations suggested. Main courses £10–£16 ($19–$30). AE, MC, V. Mon–Sat noon–3pm and 6–11pm; Sun 3–6pm. Bus: 24, 29, or 42.

The Marque Central ℱ SCOTTISH/INTERNATIONAL   The Marque Central is located in an annex of the Royal Lyceum Theater and is ideal for reasonably priced pre- and post-theater dinners at £15 ($27). Owned by former employees of Atrium, this is a popular place with locals. The cuisine can be ambitious and seductive. Main courses might include crispy cod fillet with prawn cocktail or medallion of beef with sausage cassoulet.

30b Grindlay St. ℂ **0131/229-9859.** www.marquecentral.co.uk. Reservations recommended. Fixed-price lunch £15 ($27); dinner main courses £13–£18 ($24–$33). AE, MC, V. Tues–Sat 11:45am–2pm and 5:30–10pm (till 11pm Fri–Sat). Bus: 1, 10, 15, or 24.

Time 4 Thai THAI There has been an extraordinary boom in Thai restaurants in Edinburgh over the past few years. Just when you think the market is saturated, another one seems to open. Why? Who knows, although it makes for a welcomed alternative to the Chinese eateries, with their proclivity to offer only bland Westernized meals (unless you can speak or read Chinese). This stylish New Town restaurant is relatively new, offering well-made and attractively presented curries and other Thai specialties. Everything is served with the accustomed grace and courtesy that Thai restaurants generally excel in.

45 N. Castle St. ✆ 0131/225-8822. Reservations recommended. Fixed-price lunch £9 ($17); dinner main courses £8–£16 ($15–$30). AE, MC, V. Mon–Thurs noon–2:30pm and 5–11pm; Fri–Sun 2:30–5pm. Bus: 24, 29, or 42.

INEXPENSIVE

Bell's Diner ✮ AMERICAN If you're desperate for a chargrilled patty of real ground beef, please resist any urge to visit the ubiquitous international fast-food chains. You can patronize them enough at home. Instead seek out wee Bell's Diner in Stockbridge. Open for some 30-odd years, the diner's burgers are cooked to order with a variety of toppings (cheese to garlic butter) and are served with fries, salad, and a full array of condiments. Its only drawback, aside from its limited space, is the limited hours of operation: only open in the evenings, save Saturdays when Bell's is open for lunch and dinner.

17 St. Stephen St. ✆ 0131/225-8116. Reservations recommended. Main courses £6.50–£9 ($12–$16). Sun–Fri 6–10:30pm; Sat noon–6pm. Bus: 24, 29, or 42.

Henderson's Salad Table Value VEGETARIAN Right in the heart of the New Town, Henderson's Salad Table (and Henderson's Bistro around the corner) are long-time stalwarts of healthy, inexpensive meat-free cuisine in Edinburgh. During the day, the Salad Table half of the operation offers counter service only. In the evening, however, the menu is expanded a bit and staff members wait on your table. Dishes, such as vegetable stroganoff or Greek moussaka complement what you might expect from the name: a wide array of salads. Wines include organic options.

94 Hanover St. ✆ 0131/225-2131. www.hendersonsofedinburgh.co.uk. Fixed-price 2-course lunch £8 ($14); dinner main courses £6–£8 ($11–$14). MC, V. Mon–Sat 8am–10:30pm. Bus: 13, 23, or 27.

⸢Kids⸣ Family-Friendly Fare

The Baked Potato Shop Children generally delight in being taken to this favorite lunch spot located at 56 Cockburn St., just off the High Street in Old Town (✆ 0131/225-7572). Here they can order fluffy baked potatoes with a choice of a half-dozen hot fillings along with all sorts of other dishes, including chili and a variety of salads. It's cheap, too. Open Monday to Sunday 9am to 9pm.

Valvona and Crolla Caffe Bar ✮ Located at 19 Elm Row, at the top of Leith Walk (✆ 0131/556-6066), this place is best known as one of the U.K.'s finest Italian delis. But if you can get past the tempting salamis, cheeses, and other delicacies, V&C offers a welcoming cafe handling children in that way that Italians seem to do best.

3 Old Town

EXPENSIVE

The Grain Store ✿ SCOTTISH/MODERN BRITISH   With its dining room up some unassuming stairs, and wooden tables set amid raw stone walls, the Grain Store capably captures some Old Town essence and atmosphere. The cooking of owner Carlo Coxon is ambitious and innovative: for example, the menu might include dishes such as a saddle of Scottish venison with a beetroot fondant or a medley of sea bass and scallops, served with fennel, olives, and tomato. Although the evening a la carte menu is not cheap, the fixed-price options are moderately priced.

30 Victoria St. © 0131/225-7635. www.grainstore-restaurant.co.uk. Reservations recommended. Fixed-price lunch £10 ($19); fixed-price dinner £18 ($33); dinner main courses £17–£25 ($31–$46). AE, MC, V. Daily noon–2pm and 6–10pm. Bus: 2, 41, or 42.

Off the Wall SCOTTISH/MODERN BRITISH   Another second-floor restaurant, this time looking right down on to the Royal Mile near the John Knox house, Off the Wall moved to this prestigious location a few years ago. Fresh fish and game dishes are often highlighted on a frequently changing menu. Sea bass might be served with buttered leeks and mussels. A saddle of rabbit can be accompanied by rich foie gras or venison with braised cabbage. The dining room is elegant without being stuffy—the same goes for service.

105 High St. © 0131/558-1497. www.off-the-wall.co.uk. Reservations recommended. Fixed-price lunch £17 ($30); dinner main courses £16–£22 ($30–$40). AE, MC, V. Mon–Sat noon–2pm and 6–10pm. Bus: 35.

The Witchery by the Castle SCOTTISH/MODERN BRITISH   The restaurant, so named because of historical connections to medieval executions nearby and lingering ghosts, serves classy Scottish food in classy surroundings, with dishes that feature ingredients such as Angus beef, Scottish lobster, or Loch Fyne oysters. Well-prepared old-time British favorites, such as an omelet Arnold Bennett (made with cream and smoked fish), contrast with specials such as pan-roasted monkfish with a thyme and lemon risotto. Atmospheric and good for special occasions, it is also ideal for a sumptuous late meal. In addition to the dining room nearest the street, there is also the "Secret Garden" farther down the narrow close. The premises also house a boutique hotel (see chapter 5).

Boswell Court, Castlehill, Royal Mile. © 0131/225-5613. www.thewitchery.com. Reservations required. Fixed-price 2-course lunch, pre- and post-theater dinner £10 ($19); dinner main courses £18–£25 ($33–$46). AE, DC, MC, V. Daily noon–4pm and 5:30–11:30pm. Bus: 28.

MODERATE

Barioja (Finds) SPANISH   Just off the Royal Mile (near the World's End Close) with views north to Calton Hill and the Royal High School, this tapas bar is the partner to the fine-food Spanish restaurant Iggs next door. Casual and staffed by natives of Spanish-speaking nations, Barioja is fun, friendly, and often lively. The kitchen's tapas come in reasonably substantial portions: whether tender fried squid, garlicky king prawns, or spicy chorizo sausages. Desserts are posted on the blackboard.

19 Jeffrey St. © 0131/557-3622. Fixed-price lunch £6.75 ($13); main courses £4–£10 ($7.50–$19). AE, MC, V. Mon–Sat 11am–11pm. Bus: 36.

David Bann's Vegetarian Restaurant ✿ VEGETARIAN   Chef David Bann has been at the forefront of meat-free cooking in Edinburgh for more than a decade. He

---

Moments **Tea for Two?**

If you're looking for a bit of a break while sightseeing in Old Town, try **Plaisir du Chocolat** *⚶*, 251–253 Canongate (© **0131/556-9524**). This is a modern representative of the Auld Alliance between Scotland and France—when England was the nemesis of both countries. There are more than 100 types of tea, but if you need a boost of energy, go for one of the cafe's specialties: hot chocolate—as effective as coffee, believe us. It's open daily 10am to 6pm. A more traditional choice is **Clarinda's Tearoom,** 69 Canongate (© **0131/557-1888**), for the classically British experience of afternoon tea: lace tablecloths, china, and Wedgwood plates on the walls. If you want a formal venue, try the Palm Court at the **Balmoral Hotel,** 1 Princes St. (© **0131/556-2414**).

---

comes from the school of thought that vegetarian meals can be *both* tasty and healthy: no need to sacrifice the former for the latter. The menu at his eponymous restaurant (located just a short stroll south of Royal Mile) is eclectic: Dishes have international influences, from Mexico to Thailand. The dining room is as stylish as the cooking, and to top it off, the prices are reasonable.

56–58 St. Mary's St. © 0131/556-5888. www.davidbann.com. Reservations recommended. Lunch main courses £7.50 ($16); dinner main courses £7.50–£10 ($16–$19). AE, MC, V. Daily 11am–10pm. Bus: 36.

La Garrigue *⚶* FRENCH   The chef and proprietor of La Garrigue, Jean Michel Gauffre, hails from the southern French region of Languedoc and he attempts to recreate the fresh and rustic cooking of his home here in Edinburgh. The feeling of the dining room is casual but smart, with some stylish handmade furniture and almost naïve paintings on the wall. The menu might feature a hearty roast or cassoulet (stew) with beans and meat as well as a more delicate pan-fried filet of bream. The wines are from southern France, too. Often, chef Gauffre will come in the dining room to see how it is going and have a friendly chat. He knows the small touches go a long way.

31 Jeffrey St. © 0131/557-3032. www.lagarrigue.co.uk. Reservations recommended. Fixed-price lunch £13 ($23); fixed-price dinner £20 ($36). AE, MC, V. Mon–Sat noon–2:30pm and 6:30–10:30pm. Bus: 36.

Howies SCOTTISH/MODERN BRITISH   David Howie Scott started his eponymous restaurant with modest ambitions (for example, guests brought their own wine) and then created a minor empire in Edinburgh, with a couple of branches elsewhere in Scotland as well. In the capital city, there are four. The one on Victoria Street, in Old Town, is probably the most convenient. The minichain's motto is "fine food without the faff"—and we might add "sold at reasonable prices," as well. Typical dishes include pan-seared supreme of chicken, honey cured Scottish salmon, or gnocchi with fresh basil pesto. You can still bring your own bottle, but the wine list at Howies is as reasonably priced as its menu.

10–14 Victoria St. © 0131/225-1721. www.howies.uk.com. Reservations suggested. Fixed-price 2-course lunch £8.95 ($16); fixed-price dinner £17 ($31). AE, MC, V. Daily noon–2:30pm and 6–10pm. Bus: 2, 41, or 42.

Namaste *⚶ Finds* INDIAN   In 2004, this unassuming restaurant, which features cuisine from the region of India's North Frontier, moved to this more central location near the Museum of Scotland. But that's about all that has changed. The feeling is still relaxed, and the cooking excellent. Unlike so many Indian restaurants, Namaste doesn't have a menu with 200-plus dishes. Instead it concentrates on a select number, whether the succulent tandoori fish starter or a spicy lamb jalfrezi. The vegetarian options are good, as well, with the black lentil stew (Dhal Mahkni) particularly recommended. Casual and cozy, Namaste is also open for lunches in the summer Monday to Friday.

15 Bristo Place. ⓒ 0131/225-2000. Reservations recommended. Main courses £6.25–£10 ($12–$19). MC, V. Daily 5:30–11pm. Bus: 2, 41, or 42.

The Tower SCOTTISH/MODERN BRITISH   Because the Tower is set at the top of the Museum of Scotland, it's worth requesting a window seat when making a reservation here. A sister operation to the Witchery (see above) and in some opinions superior, the kitchen here employs local ingredients to create some tasty fare: Hearty portions of steak, roast venison, and excellent seafood are featured on the menu. Dishes can include a pepper-encrusted monkfish served with baby leeks and a red wine sauce or quail stuffed with Spanish black pudding.

In the Museum of Scotland, Chambers St. ⓒ 0131/225-3003. www.tower-restaurant.com. Reservations required. Fixed-price lunch £10 ($19); dinner main courses £14–£22 ($26–$40). AE, DC, MC, V. Daily noon–11pm. Bus: 2, 41, or 42.

INEXPENSIVE

Spoon ✸✸ CAFE   This particular spoon is far from greasy. Instead, the contemporary cafe just off the High Street combines a relaxed ambience, first-rate espresso-based coffees, and the assured hand of a classically trained chef. The soups are superb, whether meat-free options—such as lentil and red onion or a roast pepper and eggplant—or Italian ham and pea soup. Sandwiches are prepared freshly, using quality ingredients, such as free-range chicken breast with tarragon on a toasted Italian roll. Alternatively, you can simply drop in for a piece of homemade cake: moist carrot or rich chocolate. Yum. (The same people now run the new cafe within the renovated Scottish Storytelling Centre, just round the corner on the Royal Mile.)

15 Blackfriars St. ⓒ 0131/556-6922. Soups from £2.80 ($5); sandwiches and salads from £4.50 ($8). MC, V. Mon–Sat 9am–6pm. Bus: 35.

Wannaburger AMERICAN   Previously called Relish, Wannaburger is a modern diner in the heart of Old Town serving what it says on the label: burgers. They come with a variety of toppings, presented on thick sesame-seed buns that can make eating them a challenge. Best of all, the chefs here don't seem to be afraid to cook them medium rare on the charcoal grill (whereas the norm at too many places is to serve beef burgers well-done). The meat is advertised as 100% Scottish, and chicken and veggie options are served as well as decent shakes.

217 High St. ⓒ 0131/225-8770. www.wannaburger.com. Burgers from £5.50 ($10). MC, V. Daily noon–9pm (till 10pm Fri–Sat). Bus: 35.

4 Southside

EXPENSIVE

Rhubarb SCOTTISH/MODERN BRITISH   Standing proud amid 5.3 hectares (13 acres) of private parkland and gardens, about 5km (3 miles) south of Edinburgh's city center, 17th-century Prestonfield House is the elegant home for this posh, almost theatrical, restaurant which first opened in 2003. Another venture from the owner of the Witchery by the Castle, Rhubarb shares its sense of drama and flair. And some might indeed find its plush, tassel-laden furniture just a bit over the top. The menu is a bit fancy as well.

Priestfield Rd. © 0131/225-1333. www.prestonfield.com. Reservations recommended. Fixed-price 2-course lunch £17 ($31); main courses £18–£25 ($33–$46). AE, DC, MC, V. Daily noon–3pm and 6–11pm. Bus: 2, 14, or 30.

MODERATE

Calistoga AMERICAN   Unique in Scotland, this restaurant attempts to recreate California cuisine here on the capital's less touristy side of town. In truth, they focus on Pacific Rim–style recipes, which can mean dishes as diverse as curried gazpacho, ginger-and-scallion-roasted monkfish, or a seven-peppered rib-eye steak. The wine list, however, is devoted to California vintages (plus two from Oregon) priced only £5 ($9) over retail—including Napa Valley chardonnays and Russian River pinot noirs. Casual and relaxed, with a West Coast radio station playing in the background, it's almost like being in L.A.

93 St. Leonard St. © 0131/668-4207. www.calistoga.co.uk. Reservations recommended. Main courses £13–£15 ($24–$28). AE. MC, V. Fri–Mon 12:30–2:30pm and 6–10pm (till 11pm Fri–Sat); Tues–Thurs 6–10pm. Bus: 14, 30, or 33.

Sweet Melindas ✦ SCOTTISH/FISH   The capital's Marchmont neighborhood, although just south of the Meadows, is far enough from the well-trod traveler's trail to seem miles away from touristy Edinburgh. This locally owned and operated restaurant is a neighborhood favorite and merits a visit from those outsiders who admire simple and amiable surroundings. The cooking tends to emphasize fish, which the chefs purchase from the shop next door, in dishes such as crispy squid salad or roast cod with a sesame and ginger sauce. But the menu is not limited to the fruits of the sea. Often there is seasonal game, whether wood pigeon or venison, and a reasonable selection of vegetarian options, as well.

11 Roseneath St. © 0131/229-7953. Reservations recommended. Lunch main courses £7 ($13); dinner main courses £10–£15 ($19–$28). AE, MC, V. Mon 6–10pm; Tues–Sat noon–2pm and 6–10pm. Bus: 24 or 41.

INEXPENSIVE

Kebab Mahal ✦ _Value_ INDIAN   The kebab is usually a late-night meal scarffed down by students standing in the streets after they have danced their heads off in the club. While the late weekend hours of this simple diner means they attract that clientele, too, Kebab Mahal is much more. Drawing a cross-section of the city, whether dusty construction workers on a break or tweed-clad professors grading papers, this basic Indian restaurant—where you may have to share your table with others—has become a landmark. Although the counter is full of hot food, most of the main courses are prepared separately in a kitchen to the rear. True to its Islamic owner's faith, Kebab Mahal doesn't have a license to serve alcohol, doesn't allow diners to bring their own, either, and also closes every Friday from 1 to 2pm for prayers.

7 Nicolson Sq. © 0131/667-5214. Main courses £4–£6 ($7.50–$11). No credit cards. Sun–Thurs noon–midnight; Fri–Sat noon–2am (except for Fri prayers). Bus: 3, 5, 29, 31, or 35.

5 Leith

VERY EXPENSIVE

Restaurant Martin Wishart ✦✦✦ MODERN FRENCH   Despite a vaunted Michelin star and local awards, chef and owner Martin Wishart is the antithesis of the high-profile prima donna or loud-mouthed TV chef. One of Scotland's leading chefs, he takes his accolades in stride and strives to improve the quality of his high-price establishment in this now fashionable part of the Leith docklands. The decor is minimalist, featuring modern art. The menu, which changes frequently, is kept short and sweet, taking advantage of the best of the season; think John Dory with leeks, salsify, and mussel and almond gratin. If you're not on a budget, push the boat out—as the Scots say—and go for the tasting menu. Ask the sommelier to open a different wine to match each course. It costs a month's wages but is heavenly.

54 The Shore. ✆ 0131/553-3557. www.martin-wishart.co.uk. Reservations required. Fixed-price lunch £21 ($38); dinner main courses £20–£25 ($37–$46); tasting menu (6 courses) £60 ($89–$102). AE, MC, V. Tues–Fri noon–2pm and 6:45–10pm; Sat 6:45–10pm. Bus: 22 or 36.

The Vintners Rooms ⏣⏣ FRENCH   This impressive stone building was constructed in the 17th century as a warehouse for the barrels and barrels of Bordeaux (claret) and port wine that came to Scotland from France. And that Auld Alliance carries on with this restaurant, one of the most romantic in Edinburgh. After a change in management a few years ago, its reputation has never been higher. The French-born chef uses Scottish produce in a host of confidently Gallic dishes. The menu might feature roast stuffed fig with goat's cheese and Parma ham, steamed halibut with a classic artichoke Barigoule, or roast cote de boeuf (for two) with béarnaise sauce. Wines are specially selected by Raeburn Fine Wines.

The Vaults, 87 Giles St. ✆ 0131/554-6767. www.thevintnersrooms.com. Reservations recommended. Fixed-price lunch £16 ($29); dinner main courses £18–£23 ($33–$43). AE, MC, V. Tues–Sat noon–2pm and 7–10:30pm; Sun noon–2:30pm. Bus: 22 or 36.

MODERATE

Fishers Bistro FISH   Seeing how you've come down to the shore, you might as well have some fish. This place is a favorite for its seafood and view of the harbor at Leith. Naturally, a nautical theme prevails with fish nets, pictures of the sea, and various marine memorabilia. The Miller family founded the restaurant in the early 1990s, and their chefs offer such enticing dishes as fresh Loch Fyne oysters, acclaimed as among Britain's finest, mussels in white-wine sauce, or breaded and crispy fish cakes. Of course the fresh fish depends on what's been landed: it might be shark, trout, or turbot. There is also a branch, **Fishers in the City,** in the New Town on Thistle Street (✆ **0131/225-5109**).

1 The Shore. ✆ 0131/554-5666. www.fishersbistros.co.uk. Reservations suggested. Main courses £12–£16 ($22–$30). AE, MC, V. Daily noon–10:30pm. Bus: 16, 22, 35, or 36.

The Shore Bar & Restaurant ⏣ FISH   Whether diners eat in the unassuming pub or in the only slightly more formal dining room to one side, they should appreciate the simplicity and ease of this operation, which is dedicated to fresh fish and seafood. The menu changes daily, offering unfussy dishes whether mussels with white wine, garlic, and onions or salmon filet with herby oil and balsamic vinegar reduction. And when food is not being served, the bar is still one of the best in Leith. It often has live music in the evenings, good ale on tap, and a sincere seaport ambience all the time.

3/4 The Shore. ✆ 0131/553-5080. Reservations recommended. Fixed-price lunch £17 ($31); dinner main courses £12–£18 ($22–$33). AE, MC, V. Daily noon–2:30pm and 6:30–10pm. Bus: 16, 22, 35, or 36.

Zinc Bar & Grill INTERNATIONAL   Here in the Ocean Terminal shopping mall, this bar and grill has vast picture windows with views of the Firth of Forth. On warm days or when the prevailing wind drops, an outdoor terrace comes in handy. Zinc offers the best choice for lunch or dinner in the shopping center—which is also the home of the Royal Yacht Britannia. Food includes an array of burgers, roast lamb, grilled chicken, fried sole, or salmon, along with steaks made from Angus beef.

Ocean Terminal, Victoria Dock. ℭ 0131/553-8070. Reservations recommended. Main courses £9–£14 ($17–$26). AE, DC, MC, V. Daily noon–10pm (till 11pm Fri–Sat). Bus: 11, 22, or 34.

6 Picnic Fare

The Edinburgh weather doesn't always lend itself to outdoor dining on an expanse of lawn, but there are certainly days when the sun shines warmly enough to enjoy a picnic at Princes Street Gardens, the Meadows, and Holyrood Park—or along the Water of Leith and in the Botanic Gardens.

If you're in the central area of town, the best place for deli goods is undoubtedly **Valvonna & Crolla,** 19 Elm Row (at the top of Leith Walk; ℭ 0131/556-6066). This Italian shop has an excellent reputation across the U.K. with a wonderful range of cheeses and cured meats, fresh fruit and vegetables, plus baked goods from rolls to sourdough loaves, all the condiments you might need, and wine as well. Another option in New Town is the food hall at the top of **Harvey Nichols** department store, 30–34 St. Andrews Sq. ℭ 0131/524-8388. Freshly prepared salads, lots of dried goods, plus fresh fruit and vegetables are stocked here.

In Stockbridge, **IJ Mellis Cheesemongers** on Bakers Place (ℭ 0131/225-6566) sells award-winning British and Irish cheeses. The Mellis staff members really know their stuff, and there are other shops in Old Town on Victoria Street and south of the city center on Morningside Road.

If you're on the south side of the city near the Meadows, **Peckham's** on Bruntsfield Place (ℭ 0131/229-7054) is a solid choice for filling a picnic basket. But if you like Mexican food—Monterrey Jack cheese, real tortillas, and the like—find **Lupe Pintos** in Tollcross at 24 Leven St. (near the King's Theatre; ℭ 0131/228-6241). The shop also stocks American goods, such as beef jerky, dill pickles, and peanut butter.

Heading towards the Botanic Gardens on the other side of town in Canonmills, at the roundabout, there is a Spanish deli called **Dionika** (ℭ 0131/652-3993).

7

Exploring Edinburgh

Edinburgh's reputation is enormous and the city essentially lives up to it. The second most popular destination after London for visitors to Great Britain, the Scottish capital is one of the most picturesque cities in Europe. Built on a set of hills, Edinburgh is unarguably dramatic. Its **Old Town** lies at the heart, with Edinburgh Castle at one end of **the Royal Mile,** which follows the spine of a hill down to the Palace of Holyroodhouse. For many visitors, this *is* Edinburgh, with its mews, closes, and alleyways. But across the valley to the north, now filled by the verdant Princes Street Gardens, is the city's **New Town,** which dates to the 1770s. Here are tidy streets and broad avenues, another popular focal point in Edinburgh, with restaurants, bars, shops, squares, and attractions, such as the **National Portrait Gallery.** New Town

reaches out to the village-like setting of Stockbridge—from which one can walk along the city's narrow meandering river, the Water of Leith—to Dean Village (another district that feels almost rural in nature) and the **National Gallery of Modern Art** and its sister arts venue, the Dean Gallery. South of Old Town is the sprawling Meadows, with its acres of grass, and the precincts of Edinburgh University and suburbs such as Marchmont. North is the port of **Leith** along the Firth of Forth, which empties into the North Sea.

Edinburgh's world famous annual cultural celebration—the **Edinburgh Festival**—brings in tourists and lovers of art of all forms from around the world. But if you prefer a bit more space and smaller crowds, avoid the month of August in Edinburgh.

SUGGESTED INTINERARIES

If You Have 1 Day

Stick to the city's famous Royal Mile and Edinburgh's Old Town. It is every bit a day's worth of activity, with plenty of history and attractions from Edinburgh Castle to the Palace of Holyroodhouse, shops, restaurants, and pubs. Wander down some of the alleys off the Royal Mile, too.

If You Have 2 Days

Take the hop-on hop-off bus tour that emphasizes the New Town. Your ticket is good for 24 hours (although the buses stop running in the late afternoon or

early evening). Get off at Calton Hill for the views, which Robert Louis Stevenson said were the best in the city. Amble down Princes Street for a bit of shopping, and afterwards, rest in Princes Street Gardens. Admire some art at one of the branches of the National Gallery.

If You Have 3 Days

Take in **Leith,** Edinburgh's once rough-and-tumble port. Now increasingly gentrified, it is still evocative of a historic seaside village. The Botanic Garden on your way back into the city

Edinburgh Attractions

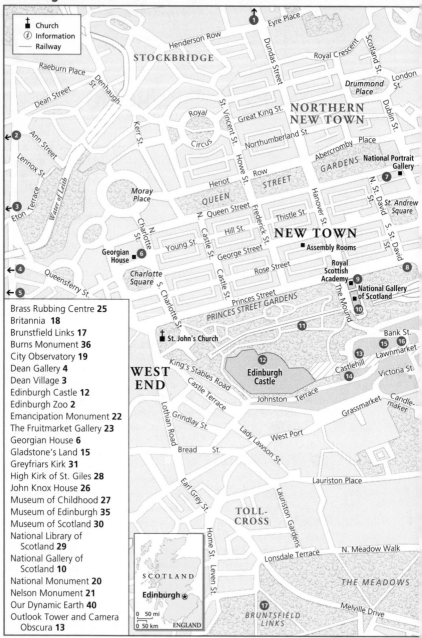

Brass Rubbing Centre 25
Britannia 18
Brunstfield Links 17
Burns Monument 36
City Observatory 19
Dean Gallery 4
Dean Village 3
Edinburgh Castle 12
Edinburgh Zoo 2
Emancipation Monument 22
The Fruitmarket Gallery 23
Georgian House 6
Gladstone's Land 15
Greyfriars Kirk 31
High Kirk of St. Giles 28
John Knox House 26
Museum of Childhood 27
Museum of Edinburgh 35
Museum of Scotland 30
National Library of
   Scotland 29
National Gallery of
   Scotland 10
National Monument 20
Nelson Monument 21
Our Dynamic Earth 40
Outlook Tower and Camera
   Obscura 13

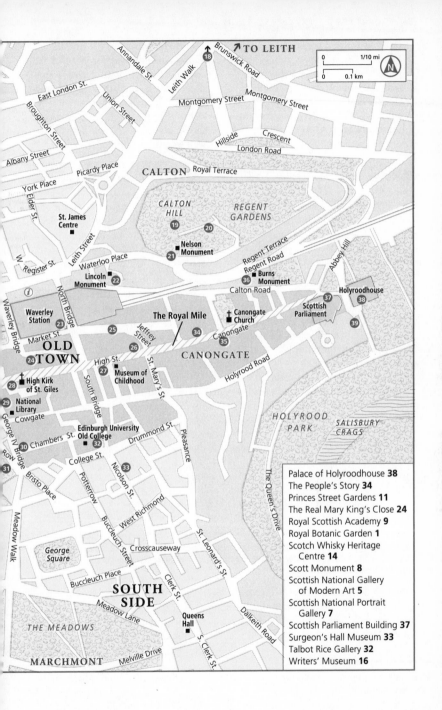

TO LEITH

| 0 | 1/10 mi |
| 0 | 0.1 km |

Annandale St.
Brunswick Road
East London St.
Union Street
Leith Walk
Montgomery Street
Montgomery Street
Broughton Street
Hillside
Crescent
London Road
Albany Street
Picardy Place
York Place
CALTON
Royal Terrace
Elder St.
St. James Centre
Leith Street
CALTON HILL
REGENT GARDENS
W. Register St.
Waterloo Place
Nelson Monument
Regent Terrace
Regent Road
Burns Monument
Abbey Hill
Lincoln Monument
Calton Road
Holyroodhouse
Waverley Station
North Bridge
Scottish Parliament
Waverley Bridge
The Royal Mile
Canongate Church
Market St.
Jeffrey Street
Canongate
OLD TOWN
CANONGATE
High St.
Holyrood Road
High Kirk of St. Giles
Museum of Childhood
St. Mary's St.
National Library
South Bridge
Cowgate
HOLYROOD PARK
SALISBURY CRAGS
George IV Bridge
Chambers St.
Edinburgh University Old College
Drummond St.
Pleasance
Bristo Place
College St.
Nicolson St.
The Queen's Drive
Potterrow
Buccleuch Street
West Richmond
St. Leonard's St.
Meadow Walk
George Square
Crosscauseway
Buccleuch Place
SOUTH SIDE
Clerk St.
Dalkeith Road
THE MEADOWS
Meadow Lane
Queens Hall
MARCHMONT
Melville Drive
S. Clerk St.

Palace of Holyroodhouse **38**
The People's Story **34**
Princes Street Gardens **11**
The Real Mary King's Close **24**
Royal Scottish Academy **9**
Royal Botanic Garden **1**
Scotch Whisky Heritage Centre **14**
Scott Monument **8**
Scottish National Gallery of Modern Art **5**
Scottish National Portrait Gallery **7**
Scottish Parliament Building **37**
Surgeon's Hall Museum **33**
Talbot Rice Gallery **32**
Writers' Museum **16**

center is worth a visit. It is one of the best in Britain—and that's saying something. If you have any time to spare, take one of the strolls outlined in chapter 8 and visit Stockbridge or the Meadows, which feel off the main tourist tracks.

If You Have 4 Days or More

Climb **Arthur's Seat** for views of the city and the sea, or if you have children, take the family to the **Edinburgh Zoo.** Explore the regions around the city, with excursions up to St Andrews, to the coast and North Berwick, or west to nearby, historic Linlithgow.

1 Some Top Attractions

ALONG THE ROYAL MILE

Old Town's **Royal Mile** 🐾🐾🐾 in an attraction in itself, stretching down the spine of a hill from Edinburgh Castle to the Palace of Holyroodhouse. It bears four names along its length: Castlehill, Lawnmarket, High Street, and Canongate. Walking along, you'll see some of the most interesting old structures in the city, with turrets, gables, and towering chimneys. Some of the highlights are listed here, in order from west to east.

Edinburgh Castle   Few places in Scotland can equal the lore associated with Edinburgh Castle. The very early history is somewhat vague, but in the 11th century, Malcolm III and his Saxon queen, later venerated as St. Margaret, founded a castle on this spot. The only fragment left of their original pile—in fact, the oldest structure in Edinburgh—is St. Margaret's Chapel; built in the Norman style, the oblong structure dates principally from the 12th century. After centuries of destruction, demolitions, and upheavals, the buildings that stand today are basically those that resulted from the castle's role as a military garrison in the past 300 years or so. It still barracks soldiers. And much of the displays are devoted to military history, which might limit the place's appeal for some. The castle vaults served as prisons for foreign soldiers in the 18th century, and these great storerooms housed hundreds of Napoleonic soldiers in the early 19th century. Some prisoners made wall carvings still seen today. Among the batteries of armaments that protected the castle is the medieval siege cannon, known as Mons Meg, which weighs more than 5 tons.

However, it is not all about war. Visitors can see where Mary Queen of Scots gave birth to James VI of Scotland (later James I of England). Scottish Parliaments used to convene in the Great Hall. Another highlight is the Scottish Crown Jewels, used at the coronations, along with the scepter and sword of state of Scotland and the infamous Stone of Scone. Note that last entry is 45 minutes before closing

Castlehill. ⓒ **0131/225-9846.** www.historic-scotland.gov.uk. Admission £10 ($19) adults, £8.50 ($16) seniors and students, and £4.50 ($8.50) children age 15 and under. Apr–Sept daily 9:30am–6pm; Oct–Mar daily 9:30am–5pm. Bus: 23 or 41.

Outlook Tower and Camera Obscura 𝑲𝒊𝒅𝒔   The 150-year-old periscope-like lens at the top of the Outlook Tower throws an image of nearby streets and buildings onto a circular table, which can be almost magically magnified with just a bit of cardboard. Guides reveal this trick and help to identify landmarks and discuss highlights of Edinburgh's history. In addition, the observation deck offers free telescopes, and there are several exhibits in the "World of Illusions" with an optical theme that will keep some children occupied. What is disappointing, however, is the dearth of information on the man responsible for the Camera Obscura, Sir Patrick Geddes, a polymath who worked tirelessly to improve the fortunes of the Old Town in the 19th and 20th centuries and

Frommer's Favorite Edinburgh Experiences

Contemplating the City and Environs from on High. At 250m (823 ft.) Arthur's Seat is presumably the best—unless you want your panorama to include Arthur's Seat; in which case you might prefer Castle Hill. But then you will miss the castle. Calton Hill affords views of all. And if you are not up for climbing, take the elevator in the Museum of Scotland, which has an observation deck atop its magnificent modern building.

Downing a Pint in an Edinburgh Pub. Whether sampling a pint of real ale— look for Dark Island from Orkney and the local Deuchar's IPA—or a dram of whisky (peaty island Laphroaig or smooth Highland Dalwhinnie), Edinburgh has numerous traditional pubs. Our favorites include the Bow Bar, Café Royal Circle Bar and, for something a bit more hip, Black Bo's.

Visiting the Royal Botanic Garden and National Galleries. The garden is not just for plant lovers (although that helps). There are paths and paths to stroll amid a variety of foliage and settings: from redwoods in a miniforest to rock gardens with a waterfall. The collections of the National Gallery are split between different museums and while the size of them is not exceptional, some of the works hanging in them are.

Strolling in Old Town or New Town. Take your pick of these two central and historically preserved districts, and don't be afraid to get off the beaten track of their main roads and boulevards. Explore the many cobbled side streets and alleyways for a feel of the real Edinburgh. Get a little lost. The city center is not so large that you'll go very far astray.

kept it from being torn down. The last camera presentation begins one hour before closing.

Castlehill. ⓒ **0131/226-3709.** www.camera-obscura.co.uk. Admission £6.45 ($12) adults, £5.15 ($9.50) seniors and students, and £4.15 ($7.75) children. Apr–June and Sept–Oct daily 9:30am–6pm; July–Aug daily 9:30am–7:30pm; Nov–Mar daily 10am–5pm. Bus: 23 or 41.

Gladstone's Land ⓖ   Run by the National Trust for Scotland, which rescued the property from demolition in the 1930s, this 17th-century merchant's house is decorated in period-style furnishings. It's not big and perhaps worth a visit if only to get the impression of how confined living conditions were some 400 years ago, even for the reasonably well off. Note, as well, how low the doorways are—don't bump your head. Gladstone (then spelled Gledstane) expanded the original 16th-century structure he purchased in 1617 both upwards and towards the street. On the second floor, in the front room that he added, you can see the original facade with its classical friezes of columns and arches. Here, as well, is the sensitively restored timber ceiling, looking suitably weathered and aged, with colorful paintings of flowers and fruit.

477B Lawnmarket. ⓒ **0131/226-5856.** www.nts.org.uk. Admission £5 ($9.25) adults, £4 ($7.50) seniors, students, and children, and £14 ($25) family. Apr 1–June 30 and Sept 1–Oct 31 daily 10am–5pm; July 1–Aug 31 daily 10am–7pm. Bus: 23 or 41.

Writers' Museum *Value*   This remnant of a 17th-century house contains a trove of portraits, relics, and manuscripts relating to Scotland's greatest men of letters: Robert Burns (1759–96), Sir Walter Scott (1771–1832), and Robert Louis Stevenson (1850–94). The Writers' Museum is often a surprisingly uncrowded space. The basement is perhaps best, with a good deal of items from the life of Stevenson (including his fishing rod and riding boots), as well as a gallery of black-and-white photographs taken when he lived in the South Pacific. The main floor is devoted to Scott with his dining room table from 39 Castle St., his pipe, chess set, and original manuscripts. Another set of rooms gives details of Burns's life (note his page-one death notice in a copy of London's *Herald* on July 27, 1796) along with his writing desk, rare manuscripts, portraits, and other items. The premises, Lady Stair's House, with its narrow passages and low clearances, were originally built in 1622 for Edinburgh merchant Sir William Gray.

In Lady Stair's House, off Lawnmarket. (℃) 0131/529-4901. www.cac.org.uk. Free admission. Mon–Sat 10am–5pm (also Sun noon–5pm in Aug). Bus: 23 or 41.

High Kirk of St. Giles *✦*   A brief walk downhill from Edinburgh Castle, this church—and its steeple in particular—is one of the most important architectural landmarks along the Royal Mile. Here is where Scotland's Martin Luther, John Knox, preached his sermons on the Reformation. Often called St. Giles Cathedral, the building combines a dark and brooding stone exterior (the result of a Victorian-era restoration) with surprisingly graceful buttresses. Only the tower represents the medieval era of the church. One of its outstanding features is Thistle Chapel, housing beautiful stalls and notable heraldic stained-glass windows.

High St. (℃) 0131/225-9442. www.stgilescathedral.org.uk. Free admission, but £2 ($3.75) donation suggested. May–Sept Mon–Fri 9am–7pm, Sat 9am–5pm, Sun 1–5pm; Oct–Apr Mon–Sat 9am–5pm, Sun 1–5pm. Bus: 23 or 41.

The Real Mary King's Close   Beneath the City Chambers on the Royal Mile lies a warren of hidden streets where people lived and worked for centuries. When the Royal Exchange (now the City Chambers) was constructed in 1753, the top floors of the existing buildings were torn down and the lower sections were left standing to be used as the foundations. This left a number of dark, mysterious passages largely intact.

Fun Fact **For Fans of Mr. Hyde**

Not far from Gladstone's Land is **Brodie's Close,** a stone-floored alley off the Lawnmarket. It was named after the well-respected cabinet-making father of the notorious William Brodie, who was a respectable councilor and deacon of trades by day—but a notorious thief and ne'er-do-well by night. Brodie's apparent split personality (actually he was simply calculating and devious) was apparently part of the inspiration for Robert Louis Stevenson's *The Strange Case of Dr. Jekyll and Mr. Hyde.* Brodie was finally caught and hanged in 1788. In a final irony, the mechanism used in the hangman's scaffold was perfected by none other than Brodie himself—and he tried to defy its action by secretly wearing a steel collar under his shirt. It didn't work. Across the street from Brodie's Close is one of the more famous pubs along the Royal Mile: **Deacon Brodie's Tavern,** 435 Lawnmarket ((℃) 0131/225-6531).

These underground "closes," originally very narrow walkways with houses on either side, date back centuries. In 2003, groups led by guides dressed up as characters from the past began to visit these dwellings for the first time in perhaps 250 years. During the tours, visitors return to the turbulent and plague-ridden days of the 17th century. Dim lighting and an audio track are intended to add to the experience.

2 Warriston Close, High St. © 0870/243-0160. www.realmarykingsclose.com. Admission £8 ($15) adults, £6 ($11) children 5–15. Advance reservations suggested. Apr–Oct daily 10am–9pm; Nov–Mar Sun–Fri 10am–4pm and Sat 10am–9pm. Closed Christmas Day. Bus: 23 or 41.

Brass Rubbing Centre *Finds*   Down Chalmers Close from the High Street (or pass through the breezeway of the Jury's Hotel from Jeffrey St.) and located in the remnants of the old Holy Trinity church is this lesser-known and calm attraction. Here you can make a wax rubbing (impression) from all sorts of designs, whether prehistorical Pictish motifs or Celtic crosses. Costs start from about £1.50 ($2.75) for simple rubbings that might take an hour or less to execute, though the cost is much more for elaborate brass plates that may occupy an entire day.

Chalmers Close. © 0131/556-4364. www.cac.org.uk. Free admission. Apr–Sept Mon–Sat 10am–5pm (also Sun noon–5pm in Aug); closed Nov–Mar. Bus: 36.

Museum of Childhood *Kids*   Allegedly the world's first museum devoted solely to the history of childhood, this popular and free museum is just past the intersection of High and Blackfriars streets. Contents of its four floors range from antique toys to games to exhibits on health, education, and costumes, plus video presentations and an activity area. Not surprisingly, this is often the noisiest museum in town.

42 High St. © 0131/529-4142. www.cac.org.uk. Free admission. Mon–Sat 10am–5pm; Sun noon–5pm. Bus: 35.

John Knox House   John Knox is acknowledged as the father of the Presbyterian Church of Scotland, the Protestant tenets of which he established in 1560. While some regard him as a prototypical Puritan, he actually proposed progressive changes in the ruling of the church and in education; as well as being quite renowned for sharp wit and sarcasm. But Knox lived at a time of great religious and political upheaval; he spent 2 years as a galley slave for agitating against papal authority and later lived in exile in Geneva (ruled by Jean Calvin). Upon his return, he became minister of St. Giles and worked to ensure the reformation's success in Scotland.

Knox was also a writer/historian, perhaps best known for the inflammatory treatise, *The First Blast of the Trumpet Against the Monstrous Regiment of Women*, written in exile and inspired by his loathing of the reign of three Roman Catholic queens in Scotland, France, and England. Even if you're not interested in the firebrand reformer (who may have never lived here anyway), you may want to visit this late-15th-century house. It's characteristic of the "lands" that used to flank the Royal Mile, and the house is noteworthy for its painted ceiling as well as its Knox history. Following three years of renovations, the house reopened in 2006 and is now integrated into the completely modernized **Scottish Storytelling Centre.**

43–45 High St. © 0131/556-9579. www.scottishstorytellingcentre.co.uk. Admission £3 ($5.50) adults; £1 ($1.85) children. Mon–Sat 10am–6pm (also Sun noon–6pm July–Sept). Bus: 35 or 36

The People's Story *Overrated*   As visitors continue walking downhill along Canongate toward Holyroodhouse (see later in this chapter), they'll see one of the most handsome buildings along the Royal Mile. Built in 1591, the Canongate Tolbooth was once the courthouse, prison, and center of municipal affairs for the burgh of Canongate. It

---

Moments **Canongate Kirkyard & Dunbar's Close**

Take a few minutes to wander about the graveyard that surrounds the Canongate Church and the neighboring walled garden in Dunbar's Close. If you use your imagination, they can evoke the past in a way that museums, audio loops, videos, and tour guides can't do half as well.

---

now contains this rather disappointing museum, which celebrates the social history of the inhabitants of Edinburgh from the late 18th century to the present, with lots of display cases and slightly naff dressed-up mannequins. Still, it offers a chance to get inside the old tollbooth.

163 Canongate. ℃ 0131/529-4057. www.cac.org.uk. Free admission. Mon–Sat 10am–5pm (also Sun noon–5pm in Aug). Bus: 35.

Museum of Edinburgh   Across from the Canongate Kirk and housed in part of historic Huntly House is the Museum of Edinburgh, another free museum run by the city. It, too, concentrates on the capital's history with a set of rooms on different levels featuring reproductions and original items to represent the city and its traditional industries, such as glassmaking, pottery, wool processing, and cabinetry. It even has Greyfriar Bobby's collar and feeding bowl.

142 Canongate. ℃ 0131/529-4143. www.cac.org.uk. Free admission. Mon–Sat 10am–5pm (also Sun noon–5pm in Aug). Bus: 35.

Scottish Parliament Building ⟨★⟩   After much controversy over its cost—the better part of £500 million ($925 million)—and the time it took to construct, the new Scottish Parliament finally opened in autumn 2004. Designed by the late Barcelona-based architect Enric Miralles, it is a remarkable bit of modern design and perhaps worth the expense and delays. The abstract motif repeated on the facade facing the Canongate was apparently inspired by Raeburn's painting of Rev. Walker skating on a Duddingston Loch, which hangs in the National Gallery of Art. The public can make a free visit and get tickets to seats in the main debating chamber or take a guided tour.

Holyrood Rd. ℃ 0131/348-5000. www.scottish.parliament.uk. Tickets for guided tour £3.50 ($6.50) adult, £1.75 ($3.25) seniors, students, and children over 5. Tues–Thurs 9am–7pm (all year business days); Mon and Fri (and weekdays when Parliament not in session) 10am–6pm (10am–4pm Nov–Mar); 10am–4pm weekends and public holidays. Last admission 45 min. before closing. Closed on Dec 25, 26; Jan 1, 2. Bus: 35.

Palace of Holyroodhouse ⟨★⟩   King James IV established this palace at the beginning of the 16th century adjacent to an abbey that King David I had founded in 1128. What you see today was mostly built for Charles II in the 1670s. The nave of the abbey church, now in ruins, still stands, though the north tower is the earliest bit of the palace that remains intact. This wing was the scene of Holyroodhouse's most dramatic incident when Mary Queen of Scots's Italian secretary, David Rizzio, was stabbed repeatedly by her jealous husband, Lord Darnley, and his accomplices. A plaque marks the spot where he died on March 9, 1566. And one of the more curious exhibits is a piece of needlework done by Mary depicting a cat-and-mouse scene. (Her cousin, Elizabeth I, is the cat.)

The palace suffered long periods of neglect, but it basked in brief glory during a ball thrown by Bonnie Prince Charlie in the mid–18th century, during the peak of his feverish (and doomed) rebellion to restore the Stuart line to monarchy. Later Holyrood's fortunes were revived—as were other royal holdings in Scotland—by Queen Victoria. Today the royal family stays here whenever they visit Edinburgh. When they're not in residence, the palace is open to visitors.

Highlights include the oldest surviving section, King James Tower, where Mary Queen of Scots lived on the second floor, with Lord Darnley's rooms below. Some of the rich tapestries, paneling, massive fireplaces, and antiques from the 1700s are still in place. The Picture Gallery boasts many portraits of Scottish monarchs. More recently, the **Queen's Gallery** (separate admission) opened to display works from the royal collection, whether Mughal art or Dutch paintings.

Behind Holyroodhouse is **Holyrood Park,** Edinburgh's largest. With rocky crags, a loch, sweeping meadows, and the ruins of a chapel, it's a wee bit of the Scottish countryside in the city, and a great place for a picnic. If you climb up Holyrood Park, you'll come to 250m-high (823-ft.) **Arthur's Seat,** from which the panorama is breathtaking. The name doesn't refer to King Arthur, as many people assume, but perhaps is a reference to Prince Arthur of Strathclyde or a corruption of *Ard Thor,* Gaelic for "height of Thor."

Canongate, at the eastern end of the Royal Mile. ℂ 0131/556-5100. www.royal.gov.uk. Admission (includes audio tour) £8.80 ($17) adults, £7.80 ($15) seniors and students, £4.80 ($9) children age 17 and under, £23 ($42) families (up to 2 adults and 3 children). Apr–Oct daily 9:30am–6pm; Nov–Mar 9:30am–3:45pm. Closed when Royal Family in residence, often 2 weeks in mid-May and 2 weeks in late Jun and Christmas. Bus: 35, open-top tours.

TOP MUSEUMS & MONUMENTS

Dean Gallery ℱ Opening in 1999 across the way from the Scottish Gallery of Modern Art, the Dean Gallery provides a home for surrealist art and includes a replication of the studio of Leith-born pop art pioneer Eduardo Paolozzi. He gave an extensive body of his private collection to the National Galleries of Scotland, including prints, drawings, plaster maquettes, and molds. The artist's mammoth composition of the robotic Vulcan dominates the entrance hall. Elsewhere works by Salvador Dalí, Max Ernst, and Joan Miró are displayed, while the Dean also hosts traveling and special exhibitions of modern art.

73 Belford Rd. ℂ 0131/624-6200. www.nationalgalleries.org. Free admission, except for some temporary exhibits. Daily 10am–5pm. Closed Dec 25–26. Bus: 13 or National Galleries shuttle.

The Fruitmarket Gallery Near Waverley Station, this is the city's leading independent, contemporary art gallery housed in an cavernous old market dramatically updated and modernized by architect Richard Murphy in the early 1990s. It hosts exhibits from both local and internationally renowned modern and conceptual artists, whether Louise Bourgeois, Cindy Sherman, and Yoko Ono—or Chad McCail and Nathan Coley. The Fruitmarket's bookshop and cafe are equally appealing. Across the street is the less innovative but still worthy city-run Edinburgh **City Art Centre** (2 Market St.; ℂ 0131/529-3993).

45 Market St. ℂ 0131/225-2383. www.fruitmarket.co.uk. Free admission. Mon–Sat 11am–6pm; Sun noon–5pm. Closed Dec 25–27. Bus: 36.

Museum of Scotland ℱℱ Opened in 1998, this impressive museum housed in an effective, modern, sandstone building not far from the Royal Mile follows the story of Scotland with exhibits on archaeology, technology, science, the decorative arts, royalty, and geology. On different floors, hundreds of millions of years of Scottish history are distilled. The museum has a total of some 12,000 items, which range from 2.9-billion-year-old rocks found on the island of South Uist to a cute Hillman Imp, one of the last 500 automobiles manufactured in Scotland. One gallery is devoted to Scotland's centuries as an independent nation. Another gallery, devoted to industry and empire from 1707 to 1914, includes exhibits on shipbuilding, whisky distilling, and the railways. The roof garden has excellent views, the **Tower Restaurant** (© 0131/225-3003) offers superb lunches and fine dinners, and the adjacent **Royal Museum** includes a well-preserved and airy Victorian-era Main Hall and some 36 more galleries.

Chambers St. © 0131/247-4422. www.nms.ac.uk. Free admission. Daily 10am–5pm. Bus: 2, 7, 23, 31, 35, 41, or 42.

National Gallery of Scotland ☆☆   Although the collection held by Scotland may seem small by the standards of larger countries, it has been chosen with great care and expanded by bequests, gifts, loans, and purchases. These galleries have only enough space to display part of the entire body of work. One recent major acquisition was Botticelli's *The Virgin adoring the Sleeping Christ Child.* The duke of Sutherland has lent the museum two Raphaels; Titian's two Diana canvases and *Venus Rising from the Sea.* The gallery also has works by El Greco and Velázquez and Dutch art by Rembrandt and van Dyck.

Impressionism and post-Impressionism are represented by Cézanne, Degas, van Gogh, Monet, Renoir, Gauguin, and Seurat. In the basement wing (opened in 1978), Scottish art is highlighted. Henry Raeburn is at his best in the whimsical *Rev. Robert Walker Skating on Duddingston Loch,* while the late-19th-century Glasgow School is represented by artists such as Sir James Guthrie.

Next door on the Mound is the **Royal Scottish Academy** (© 0131/624-6200), now connected by the Weston Link, which opened in summer 2004. The RSA was renovated and now hosts blockbuster exhibitions, such as for paintings by Monet or Titian.

2 The Mound. © 0131/624-6200. www.nationalgalleries.org. Free admission, except for some temporary exhibits. Fri–Wed 10am–5pm; Thurs 10am–7pm. Closed Dec 25–26. Bus: 23, 27, 41, 42, 45, or National Galleries shuttle.

Scott Monument   Resembling a church spire taken from a continental European cathedral, the Gothic-inspired Scott Monument is one of Edinburgh's most recognizable landmarks. In the center of the over 60m-tall (200 ft.) spire is a large seated statue of Sir Walter Scott and his dog, Maida, with Scott's heroes carved as small figures in the monument. You can climb 287 steps to the top for a worthwhile view: Look east and you can clearly see the **Burns Monument,** dedicated to Robert Burns and designed by Thomas Hamilton in 1830, along Regent Road.

East Princes St. Gardens, near Waverley Station. © 0131/529-4068. www.cac.org.uk. Admission £3 ($5.50). Apr–Sept Mon–Sat 9am–6pm, Sun 10am–6pm; Oct–Mar Mon–Sat 9am–3pm, Sun 10am–3pm. Bus: 3,10, 12, 17, 25, 29, 33, 41, or 45.

Scottish National Gallery of Modern Art ☆   Scotland's national collection of 20th-century art occupies a gallery converted from an 1828 school set on 4.8 hectares

---

Tips **A Note on Museum Hours**

During the Edinburgh Festival, some museums that are normally closed on a Sunday will be open, and hours can be generally longer. Some museums that open only in summer are also open on public holidays throughout the year.

> **Tips National Gallery Bus**
>
> If you plan to visit the various branches of the Scottish National Gallery, from the Dean to the Portrait, a good way to get around is by using the free shuttle bus service that stops at them all.

(12 acres) of grounds, about a 20-minute walk from the Haymarket train station. The collection is international in scope and quality, despite its modest size, with works ranging from Matisse, Braque, Miró, and Picasso to Balthus, Lichtenstein, and Hockney. Recently, the grounds in front of the museum were dramatically landscaped with grassy terraces and a pond into a piece of art itself called "Landform" by Baltimore, Maryland-born Charles Jencks. A cafe sells light refreshments and salads.

75 Belford Rd. (C) 0131/624-6200. www.nationalgalleries.org. Free admission, except for some temporary exhibits. Daily 10am–5pm. Closed Dec 25–26. Bus: 13 or National Galleries shuttle.

Scottish National Portrait Gallery Housed in a red-stone Victorian neo-Gothic pile designed by Robert Rowand Anderson at the east end of Queen Street, the country's portrait gallery gives you a chance to see many famous Scots. The portraits by Rodin, Kokoschka, Ramsay, and Raeburn, among others, include everybody from Mary Queen of Scots and Flora Macdonald to early golfers, authors, and enlightenment thinkers. But it's not all historical characters, as modern portraits include Sean Connery and Billy Connolly. In addition to paintings, sculptures, miniatures, and the National Photographic Collection are on display (although the latter is destined to have a home of its own).

1 Queen St. (C) 0131/624-6200. www.nationalgalleries.org. Free admission, except for some temporary exhibits. Fri–Wed 10am–5pm; Thurs 10am–7pm. Closed Dec 25–26. Bus: 4, 10, 12, 16, 26, or National Galleries shuttle.

2 Additional Attractions

Edinburgh Zoo *Kids* Scotland's largest animal collection is 4½ km (3 miles) west of Edinburgh's city center on 32 hectares (80 acres) of hillside parkland offering unrivaled views from the Pentlands to the Firth of Forth. Run by the Royal Zoological Society of Scotland, the zoo emphasizes its role in the conservation of wildlife and contains more than 1,500 animals, including endangered species: snow leopards, white rhinos, pygmy hippos, and others. The zoo boasts the largest penguin colony in Europe housed in the world's largest penguin enclosure. From April to September, a penguin parade is held daily at 2:15pm.

134 Corstorphine Rd. (C) 0131/334-9171. www.edinburghzoo.org.uk. Admission £10 ($19) adults, £7 ($13) children, £32 ($60) families. Apr–Sept daily 9am–6pm; Oct and Mar daily 9am–5pm; Nov–Feb daily 9am–4:30pm. Bus: 12, 26, 31, or Airport Express.

Georgian House Charlotte Square, designed by the great Robert Adam, was the final piece of the city's first New Town development. The National Trust for Scotland has two bits of property here: No. 28 on the south side of the square (its headquarters with a small gallery) and, on the northern side, this town house, which has been refurbished and opened to the public. The furniture is mainly Hepplewhite, Chippendale, and Sheraton, all from the 18th century. A sturdy old four-poster bed with an original 18th-century canopy occupies a ground-floor bedroom. The nearby dining room has a table set with fine Wedgwood china as well as the piss pot that was passed around after the women folk had retired.

7 Charlotte Sq. ℭ **0131/226-3318.** www.nts.org.uk. Admission £5 ($9.25) adults; £4 ($7.50) children, students, and seniors; £14 ($26) family. July and Aug 10am–7pm; Apr–Jun and Sept–Oct daily 10am–5pm; Mar and Nov daily 11am–3pm; closed Dec–Feb. Bus: 36.

Greyfriars Kirk   Although the churches of Scotland are not generally on the same scale as the cathedrals of the Continent, they do have their own slightly austere allure. Dedicated in 1620, this kirk was the first "reformed" church in Edinburgh and became the center of a good bit of history. It was built amid a cemetery that Queen Mary proposed in 1562 because there was no more burial space at St. Giles Cathedral on the Royal Mile. In 1638, the National Covenant, favoring Scottish Presbyterianism to the English Episcopacy, was signed here and an original copy is displayed. By the middle of the 17th century the church had become a barracks for Cromwell's forces, and then, in the 18th century, the original tower exploded when gunpowder stored there caught fire. Among the many restorations, one in the 1930s brought in California redwood to create the current ceiling. The kirkyard has a bit of the Flodden

The Father of Dr. Jekyll & Mr. Hyde

Robert Louis Stevenson (1850–94) was a restless character. Born in Edinburgh, he found the place unsuitable for his frail constitution. This, combined with his wanderlust, meant that he spent much of his life traveling and living outside his native Scotland. The author has been alternately hailed as Scotland's greatest writer and dismissed as nothing more than the creator of tall tales for children, though surely the former is more accurate.

He was the son of Margaret and Thomas Stevenson, born into a family famed for its Scottish civil engineering projects, especially lighthouses. RLS was a sickly child and, as a young adult, something of disappointment to his father. After he allowed his son to bow out of engineering and the lucrative family business, Thomas made Robert attend law school, vowing that "the devious and barren paths of literature" were not suitable. RLS, undaunted, became a writer and a bit of rogue. One of his favorite bars still stands today: Rutherford's on Drummond Street near South Bridge.

Determined to roam ("I shall be a nomad") and write, he went to France where he met and later married an American, Fanny Osborne, with whom he traveled to California. Following the success of *The Sea-Cook* (1881), which became the ever-popular *Treasure Island,* Stevenson produced *The Strange Case of Dr. Jekyll and Mr. Hyde,* an instant best-seller and his most famous work—thanks in no small part to later Hollywood adaptations. That was quickly followed by the classic *Kidnapped* (1886), his most evocative book. It reflects the troubled political times in Scotland after the failed 1745 rebellion of Bonnie Prince Charlie and the book takes its 16-year-old hero on an adventure across the Western Highlands.

Eventually RLS and Fanny settled in Samoa, hoping to find a climate that would suit his scarred lungs. While here, Stevenson worked on the unfinished classic, *Weir of Hermiston* (published posthumously in 1896). On December 3, 1894, at only 43 years old, he collapsed and died.

Britannia: The Royal Yacht

The royal yacht *Britannia* was launched on April 16, 1953, and traveled more than a million miles before it was decommissioned in December 1997. Several cities then competed to permanently harbor the ship as a tourist attraction. The port of Leith won, and today the ship is moored (somewhat controversially) next to the Ocean Terminal shopping mall about 3km (2 miles) from Edinburgh's center. Once on board, you're guided around by an audio tour. You can see where Prince Charles and Princess Diana strolled the deck on their honeymoon, visit the drawing room and the Royal apartments, as well as explore the engine room, galleys, and captain's cabin.

All tickets should be booked as far in advance as possible by calling ℂ **0131/ 555-5566.** The yacht is open daily except Christmas and New Year's Day, with the first tour from April to October beginning at 9.30am, the last tour at 4:30pm. From November to March, the hours are 10am to 3:30pm. Lasting at least 90 minutes, the tour is self-guided with the use of an audio headset. Adults pay £9 ($17), seniors £7 ($13), and children ages 5 to 17 £5 ($9.25); those age 4 and under visit for free. A family ticket, good for two adults and up to three children, is £25 ($46). From Waverley Bridge, take either Lothian buses 22, 34, or 35 or the Majestic Tour Bus operated by Edinburgh Bus Tours (see below).

Wall and it was the site of prison for Covenanters. Its collection of 17th-century monuments and grave stones is impressive. The most celebrated grave, however, contains a 19th-century policeman whose faithful dog, Bobby, reputedly stood watch for years. The tenacious terrier's first portrait (painted in 1867) hangs here while a statue of wee dog—made famous by Hollywood—is nearby at the top of Candlemaker Row, just outside the pub named in his honor.

Greyfriars Place. ℂ **0131/225-1900.** www.greyfriarskirk.com. Free admission. Apr–Oct Mon–Fri 10:30am–4:30pm; Sat 10:30am–2:30pm; Nov–Mar Thurs 1:30–3:30pm. Bus: 2, 23, 27, 41, 42, or 45.

National Library of Scotland   The country's central library hosts a year full of readings, activities, and exhibitions, such as one on the story of news, retracing its history from hand-printed single sheet circulars to the advent of the Internet. Each and every book published in the U.K. and Ireland is on the shelves here.

George IV Bridge. ℂ **0131/623-3700.** www.nls.uk. Exhibitions June–Oct. Mon–Sat 10am–5pm; Sun 2–5pm (till 8pm during the Festival). Bus: 2, 23, 27, 41, 42, or 45.

Our Dynamic Earth *(Kids)*   Under a futuristic tent-like canopy near the new Scottish Parliament, Our Dynamic Earth celebrates the evolution and diversity of the planet, with emphasis on the seismological and biological processes that led from the Big Bang to the world we know today. The presentation has been called "physical evolution as interpreted by Disney"—audio and video clips, buttons you can push to simulate earthquakes, meteor showers, and views of outer space. There is the slimy green primordial soup where life began and a series of specialized aquariums, some with replicas of early life forms, others with actual living sharks, dolphins, and coral. A simulated tropical rainforest has skies darken at 15-minute intervals, offering torrents of rainfall and creepy-crawlies underfoot. On the premises are a restaurant, a cafe, a children's play area, and a gift shop. Last entry is 1 hour and 10 minutes before closing.

Holyrood Rd. ℂ 0131/550-7800. www.dynamicearth.co.uk. Admission £8.95 ($17) adults, £5.45 ($10) seniors and children 5–15, £1.50 ($2.75) children 2–4. July and Aug daily 10am–6pm; Apr–June and Sept–Oct daily 10am–5pm; Nov–Mar Wed–Sun 10am–5pm. Bus 35 or 36.

Scotch Whisky Heritage Centre   This center makes the case for the Scottish national drink, whisky, by illuminating the traditions associated with its making. A holographic master blender's ghost and a whisky barrel ride showing historic moments in the whisky industry are included in admission. Last tours are 1 hour prior to closing.

354 Castlehill, near Edinburgh Castle. ℂ 0131/220-0441. www.whisky-heritage.co.uk. Admission £8.95 ($17) adults, £6.75 ($13) seniors and students, £4.75 ($9) children 5–17. Tours daily May–Sept 9:30am–6:30pm; Oct–Apr 10am–6pm. Closed Dec 25. Bus 23 or 41.

Surgeons' Hall Museums   Edinburgh's rich medical history and associations make this attraction worth a visit. Scotland's largest medical museum, it includes human anatomical specimens from the late 18th century as well as a section devoted to "Sport, Surgery and Well Being" that gives visitors a chance to use a keyhole surgery-training unit.

9 Hill Sq. ℂ 0131/527-1649. www.rcsed.ac.uk. Tickets £5 ($9.25). Mon–Fri noon–4pm. Bus: 3, 8, 29, or 49.

Talbot Rice Gallery   Part of the University of Edinburgh, housed in a wing of the Old College, the Talbot Rice contains the university's art collection in the Torrie gallery, with works by modern Scottish artists such as Joan Eardley, as well as paintings by the Scottish Colourists. Another boxy, modern exhibition space over two floors (the White Gallery) is reserved for temporary shows by significant contemporary artists.

Old College, South Bridge. ℂ 0131/650-2211. www.trg.ed.ac.uk. Free admission. Tues–Sat 10am–5pm. Bus: 3, 8, 29, or 49.

THE MONUMENTS ON CALTON HILL

Calton Hill 🔊, rising 106m (350 ft.), is partially responsible for Edinburgh's being called the "Athens of the North." It's a bluff of monuments. People visit the promontory not only to see them up close but also to enjoy the panoramic views of the Firth of Forth and the city spread beneath it. The Parthenon-like structure at the summit, the **National Monument,** was meant to honor the Scottish soldiers killed during the Napoleonic wars. However, the money ran out in 1829 and the William H. Playfair–designed structure (sometimes referred to as "Edinburgh Disgrace") was never finished.

The **Nelson Monument,** containing relics of the hero of Trafalgar, dates from 1815 and rises more than 30m (100 ft.) above the hill. A time ball at the top falls at 1pm Monday through Saturday; historically it helped sailors in Leith set their time-pieces. The monument is open April to September, Monday from 1 to 6pm and Tuesday through Saturday from 10am to 6pm; and October to March, Monday through Saturday from 10am to 3pm. Admission is £3 ($5.50).

The old **City Observatory** along the western summit of Calton Hill was designed in 1818 by Playfair, whose uncle happened to be the president of the Astronomical Institute, for which is was built. Nearby, the circular **Dougal Stewart's Monument** of 1831 (by Playfair, as well) is not dissimilar to colonnades of the 1830 **Burns Monument** designed by Thomas Hamilton on the southern slopes of Calton Hill. It replicates the Choragic Monument of Lysicrates in Athens, which was also the inspiration for his earlier attempt to honor the poet in Alloway (see chapter 19).

Down the hill towards Princes Street, in the Old Calton Burial Grounds, is a curiosity of special interest to visitors from the United States. The **Emancipation** or **Lincoln Monument,** erected in 1893, was dedicated to soldiers of Scottish descent who lost their lives in America's Civil War. It has a statue of President Abraham Lincoln with a freed slave at his feet. Some famous Scots are buried in this cemetery, too, with elaborate tombs honoring their memory (notably the Robert Adam–designed tomb for philosopher David Hume).

DEAN VILLAGE 🍿

Dean Village is a former grain-milling center dating from the 12th century, which occupies a valley about 30m (100 ft.) deep. Originally called the Water of Leith Village, it's located at the end of Bells Brae off Queensferry Street, along the Water of Leith. You can enjoy a celebrated view by looking downstream under the high arches of Dean Bridge (1833), designed by Thomas Telford.

The village's old buildings have been restored and converted into apartments and houses. You don't come here for any one particular site but to stroll around and enjoy the ambience, which feels a hundred miles away from bustling Princes Street or the Royal Mile. You can also walk for kilometers along the Water of Leith, one of the most tranquil strolls in the greater Edinburgh area.

3 Gardens & Parks

The Meadows   South of Old Town, separating the city center from the suburbs and leafy neighborhoods that popped up in the 18th and 19th centuries is this expansive public park. Tree-lined paths crisscross the playing fields, whether it's soccer, rugby, or cricket, with plenty of additional space for having a picnic or flying a kite. The park dates to the 1700s, when a loch here was drained. At the far western end of the Meadows is Bruntsfield Links, a short-hole course which has a hallowed place in the history of golf and can still be played today during the summer.

Melville Dr. Bus: 24 or 41.

Princes Street Gardens 🍿   Another drained loch created the land to the north of Old Town that is now filled by the Princes Street Gardens, the most used outdoor public space in the city. With Edinburgh Castle above, this is one of the most picturesque parks in Europe.

Princes St. Bus: 3, 10, 12, 17, 25, or 44.

Royal Botanic Garden 🍿🍿   This is one of the grandest gardens in all of Great Britain, which is certainly saying something. Sprawling across 28 hectares (70 acres), it dates from the late 17th century, when it was originally used for medical studies. In spring, the various rhododendrons, from ground cover to gigantic shrubs, are almost reason alone to visit, but the planting in various areas assures year-round interest,

---

(Fun Fact **Hume in Nor' Loch**

When Princes Street Gardens were still a bog, the great philosopher David Hume fell into it, couldn't remove himself, and called for help from a passing woman. She recognized him, pronounced him an atheist, and wouldn't offer her umbrella to pull him out of the mire until he recited the Lord's Prayer. He presumably did so.

whether in the rock garden or along the deep "herbaceous" borders elsewhere. When it comes to research, only Kew Gardens does more. The grounds include numerous glass houses, the Palm House (Britain's tallest) being foremost among them. Inverleith House is a venue for art exhibitions and has the Terrace Cafe, too.

20A Inverleith Row. ℂ 0131/552-7171. www.rbge.org.uk. Admission is by voluntary donation. Jan–Feb daily 10am–4pm; Mar and Oct 10am–6pm; Apr–Sept 10am–7pm; Nov–Dec 10am–6pm. Bus: 8, 17, 23, or 27.

4 Organized Tours

Edinburgh Bus Tours   For an entertaining 1-hour-long overview and introduction to the principal attractions of Edinburgh, consider the buses that leave every 20 minutes or so from Waverley Bridge from April to late October. You can see most of the major sights along the Royal Mile, the Grassmarket, Princes Street, George Street, and more from the double-deck open-top motor coaches. Three tours—Edinburgh Tour (green buses), City Sightseeing (red buses), and Mac Tours (vintage buses)—all cover roughly the same ground in Old Town and New Town. The Majestic Tour buses, however, make short work of the city center as they go down to Leith, as well. Tickets can be used for 24 hours, and you can hop on and hop off the bus at designated stops. The first tour is at 9:30am, and the last is usually around 5:40pm (till slightly later July–Sept).

55 Annandale St. ℂ 0131/220-0770. www.edinburghtour.com. £9 ($17) adults, £8 ($15) seniors and students, £3 ($5.50) children 5–15, £20 ($36) family of 2 adults and up to 3 children.

Edinburgh Literary Pub Tour   Trace the footsteps of such literary greats as Robert Burns, Robert Louis Stevenson, and Sir Walter Scott on this tour which goes into the city's taverns, highlighting the tales of Dr. Jekyll and Mr. Hyde or the erotic love poetry of Burns. They leave nightly at 7:30pm from the Beehive Inn on the Grassmarket from June to September; Thursday to Sunday in April, May, and October; and just on Friday from November to March. Tickets can be purchased at the Beehive.

97b West Bow ℂ 0131/226-6665. www.edinburghliterarypubtour.co.uk. Reservations are recommended in the high season. Tickets £7 ($13).

The Witchery Tours   Edinburgh's history is filled with tales of ghosts, gore, and witchcraft, and this tour is enlivened by characters who leap out of seemingly nowhere when you least expect it. Two tours—the 1½ hour "Ghost & Gore" and the 1¼ hour "Murder & Mystery"—overlap in parts. Scenes of horrific torture, murder, and supernatural occurrence in the Old Town are visited, under the cloak of darkness. The ghost tour (May–Aug) departs nightly at 7pm and 7:30pm, with the murder tour (year-round) leaving at 9pm and 9:30pm, all from the outside of the Witchery Restaurant on Castlehill.

84 West Bow. ℂ 0131/225-6745. www.witcherytours.com. Reservations required. Tickets £7.50 ($14).

Mercat Tours   This well-established company conducts popular walking tours of the city, covering a range of interests from "Secrets of the Royal Mile" to "Ghosts & Ghouls," which only takes place in the evenings. The tours leave from the Mercat Cross, outside of St Giles Cathedral on the Royal Mile.

Mercat House, 28 Blair St. ℂ 0131/255-5443. www.mercattours.com. Reservations recommended. Tickets around £7 ($13).

5 Special Events & Festivals

Edinburgh Festival ✰✰✰   The cultural highlight of Edinburgh's year comes every August during the Edinburgh Festival, which centers on the **Festival Fringe** and the

International Festival. Since 1947, the International Festival has attracted internationally accomplished performers in classical music, opera, ballet, and drama. The Fringe, which essentially runs simultaneously, has overtaken the International Festival in scope and popularity. In 2005, it presented some 1,800 shows at nearly 250 venues. It provides an opportunity for almost anybody—professional or nonprofessional, an individual, a group of friends, or a whole company—to put on a show wherever they can find an empty stage or street corner. For most visitors, the Fringe's attractions are first-rate comic acts, late-night revues, contemporary drama and performance art at the well-established Fringe venues, such as the Pleasance. Over the years, it has become increasingly established (and sponsored) if no less experimental and unexpected.

As if all that wasn't enough, Edinburgh also hosts at about the same time a variety of other festivals. In Charlotte Square, the international **Book Festival** has become a large annual event, drawing authors such as J.K. Rowling and Toni Morrison. There is also the international **Film Festival,** a **Jazz Festival,** and a **Television Festival.**

The International Festival box office is at The Hub, Castle Hill (© **0131/473-2000**; www.eif.co.uk). The Fringe is based in 180 High St. (© **0131/226-0000**; www.edfringe.com). Information on all the festivals is found at www.edinburghfestivals.co.uk. Ticket prices vary for Festival, Fringe, and other shows or events (£1–£50/$1.85–$93).

Military Tattoo   Occurring at the same time as the Festival, this is one of the more popular traditional spectacles. It features precision marching of not only Scottish regiments but also soldiers and performers (including bands, drill teams, and gymnasts) from dozens of countries on the floodlit esplanade of Edinburgh Castle.

The Tattoo Office is 32 Market St. © **08707/555-118**. www.edinburgh-tattoo.co.uk. Ticket prices vary (£11–£36/$21–$67).

Hogmanay   New Year's Eve in Scotland is traditionally bigger than Christmas and Edinburgh now hosts one of the biggest December 31 parties on the planet. In Scotland, the festivities traditionally don't really even begin until the clock strikes midnight, and then they continue until daybreak or later. In 1993, the Edinburgh City Council began a 3-day festival that features rock bands, street theater, and a lively procession. By 1997, the event had become so big that participation is reserved for ticket holders. For information, visit www.edinburghshogmanay.com.

Burns Night   On January 25, Scots the world over gather to consume the traditional supper of haggis, neeps (turnips), and tatties (potatoes), accompanied by a dram of whisky, while listening to recitals of the works of Scotland's Bard, Robert "Rabbie" Burns, whose birthday is being celebrated. Burns suppers are held all over town.

6 Sports & Outdoor Activities

SPECTATOR SPORTS

FOOTBALL

You might get swept up by the zeal that some residents have for their local soccer clubs: **Hearts** and **Hibs.** Heart of Midlothian Football Club (just Hearts or occasionally Jambos) home field is Tynecastle stadium on Gorgie Road (© **0131/200-7201;** www.hearts fc.co.uk), near Haymarket railway station. Hibernian FC (simply Hibs or sometimes Hibbies) play at Easter Road stadium, towards Leith (© **0131/661-2159;** www.hibs. co.uk). These cross-town rivals, when not battling each other in the Edinburgh "derby," take on other teams in the top Scottish soccer league. The season usually runs from August through May, and traditional playing time is Saturday afternoon at 3pm, although mid-week evenings and Sunday matches (which begin a bit after noon) are now common. Tickets range from £10 to £50 ($19–$93).

HORSE RACING

Place your bets at the **Musselburgh Racecourse,** Musselburgh Park (© **0131/665-2083;** www.musselburgh-racecourse.co.uk), about 6.5km (4 miles) east of Edinburgh. Admission is £15 to £20 ($28–$37).

RUGBY

The home of Scotland's National Rugby Team is **Murrayfield Stadium** (© **0131/346-5000;** www.scottishrugby.org), about 3km (2 miles) west of Edinburgh's city center (walking distance from Haymarket station). The sport is usually played from autumn to spring, usually on Saturdays. Some of the most passionate matches are those among teams in the annual Six Nations competition comprising Scotland, Wales, England, Ireland, Italy, and France. Ticket prices range from around £25 to £40 ($46–$74).

OTHER ACTIVITIES

BICYCLING

Bicycles are used by a surprising number of people in Edinburgh, despite the many hills and cobbled streets. The city is linked to the national cycle path system, and you can use it to get to many places on off-road and on-road lanes. Rent bikes from **Rent-a-Bike Edinburgh,** 29 Blackfriars St., near High Street (© **0131/556-5560;** www.cyclescotland.co.uk; bus: 35). Depending on the type of bike, charges range between £10 to £15 ($19–$28) per day or up to £70 ($130) for the week. Part-day hires are possible. A credit card imprint will be taken as security. The same company runs **Scottish Cycle Safaris,** which organizes tours in the city and across Scotland.

GOLF

Aside from the **Brunstfield Links,** where all you need is a ball, one lofted club, and a putter, Edinburgh's environs offer a host of attractive golf clubs and courses. It always pays to call a day or two, preferably, in advance to reserve a tee time and confirm greens fees. Among those run by the city are **Silverknowes Golf Course,** Silverknowes Parkway (© **0131/336-3843**), a 6,202-yard course above the Firth of Forth; **Braid Hills** (© **0131/447-6666**), about 5km (3 miles) south of Edinburgh's city center, just beyond Morningside; and **Carrick Knowe,** Glen Devon Park (© **0131/337-1096**), just west of Murrayfield stadium. Weekday rates for 18 holes are typically about £15 ($30), with rental clubs for about £16 ($30).

SAILING

Not far from Edinburgh is the **Port Edgar Sailing Centre** in South Queensferry (© **0131/331-3330;** www.portedgar.co.uk). From spring to autumn, it offers a range sailing instruction and boat rental to qualified sailors.

SPORTS COMPLEXES, GYMS & POOLS

The **Meadowbank Sports Centre,** London Road (© **0131/661-5351;** www.edinburgh leisure.co.uk) was built when the city hosted the Commonwealth Games in 1970. Then state-of-the-art, it still offers a good gym, track, and soccer fields. It costs about £5 ($9.25) to use the weight room. For swimming, the Olympic-size indoor pool at the **Royal Commonwealth Pool,** 21 Dalkeith Rd. (© **0131/667-7211**), is best in the city.

8

Edinburgh Strolls

Because Edinburgh is a relatively compact city, walking is one of the best ways to see it. This is especially true in the Old Town, where narrow passages and alleys—or in the local vernacular *closes* (pronounced "*clo*-zes") and *vennels*—run off both sides of the main street, like ribs from a spine. You really owe it to yourself to wander down a few of them to appreciate the medieval core of the Scottish capital. But beyond the Old Town to the north is the classic Georgian-era New Town, and another part of the city that now has UNESCO World Heritage Site status. In a bit of contrast to Glasgow, the main tourist attractions of Edinburgh are also quite contiguous. The strolls below are not definitive. They are intended to offer, however, a good sample of the city's key districts. Aside from Walk 1, they are virtually circular, so that you end up near to where you began your walk. Walk 3 is the longest and includes a few hills and should be done in segments if too strenuous. Always remember that traffic comes from the right as you cross streets, and it never hurts to look both ways—twice.

WALKING TOUR 1   THE ROYAL MILE

Start: Edinburgh Castle Esplanade.
Finish: Holyrood Park.
Time: About 1½ to 2 hours.
Best Times: Daytime.
Worst Times: Late at night.

This walk takes place in the historic heart of Old Town, the medieval city established as a royal burgh by King David I in the 12th century. Situated on a mile-long hill, Old Town (whose protective walls were knocked down and refortified throughout history) is, for many visitors, the most evocative district in Edinburgh. In large part, the city's current reputation for beauty and romance rests upon the appearance of the Royal Mile and its surrounding streets.

Start the walk at the esplanade of:
❶ Edinburgh Castle
The esplanade (now a car park) of Edinburgh Castle (p. 84) has the most accessible views of the city in practically all directions. The castle itself dates to the 11th century, although fortifications of some kind on Castle Rock may go back as far as the 6th century. In 1542, the castle ceased being a royal residence, having already begun to be used to as an ordinance factory. Today, military barracks are still on the grounds, although it is mainly a tourist attraction.

At the northeast corner of the esplanade is:

❷ Ramsay Garden

Not a garden but an innovative and charming set of buildings that date to the end of the 19th century, this bright and cheerful place was the brainchild of Sir Patrick Geddes. A polymath and city planner, Geddes almost single-handedly revived the fortunes of the Old Town, working to rid it of squalid living conditions while saving it from total destruction and redevelopment. Ramsay Garden's architecture is a mix of Scottish baronial and English cottage, combining corbels (the cantilevered round extensions), conical roofs, crow steps, and half-timber gable construction beautifully.

Move from the esplanade to:

❸ Castle Hill

Although the road that runs from the castle to the palace is generally called the Royal Mile, it has various names along the way. The first short section is Castle Hill, followed by the Lawnmarket, High Street, and Canongate. On the right as you move away from the castle grounds is Canonball House and Castlehill School, the Scotch Whisky Heritage Centre and then Boswell's Court, which was originally built around 1600 and now is the site of a sumptuous restaurant called The Witchery. Across the street is Geddes' observatory, which has his camera obscura, for unique views of the city.

At the roundabout, which marks the end of Castlehill, is the Tolbooth Church (now called The Hub). Completed in 1844, it doubled as a meeting hall for the General Assembly of the Church of Scotland.

Continue down the Royal Mile to the Lawnmarket and:

❹ Gladstone's Land

Lands are buildings, and between the 14th and 15th centuries, the plots (or *tofts*) on the Royal Mile were subdivided into forelands and backlands. Just past the entrances to James Court, Gladstone's Land (p. 85) dates to at least the 16th century and was purchased by Thomas Gladstone (then spelled Gledstane) in 1617. He expanded the building upwards and forward towards the Lawnmarket. Inside, you can see the original frontage as well as the painted ceiling in the second-floor front room. Nearby, Lady Stair's Close has the early-17th-century Lady Stair's House, the remnants of which now contain the Writer's Museum with exhibits dedicated to Burns, Scott, and Stevenson.

Across from Gladstone's Land is:

❺ Brodie's Close

Edinburgh's history has its fair share of rather dubious characters. None more so than craftsman William Brodie: upstanding gentleman and deacon of trades by day but thief and ne'er-do-well by night. Once captured, Deacon Brodie escaped arrest and fled to Holland, where he betrayed himself by his letter writing. Brought back to Edinburgh, in 1788 he was hung, ironically, on gallows of his own design. Robert Lewis Stevenson is said to have had a childhood nightmare about the two-faced Brodie, which later became inspiration for his character Dr. Jekyll and Mr. Hyde. Lest you worry about the morality of Edinburgh, the close is actually named after Brodie's father, Francis, a gifted cabinetmaker.

Continue down the Royal Mile, crossing Bank Street on the left and George IV Bridge on the right, to:

❻ St. Giles Cathedral

You're now on the High Street. There is nearly as much history around St. Giles, or the High Church, as the city itself (p. 86). Its origins date to the 12th century. It was burned by the English when they overran the city in 1385. Here, in the 1500s, John Knox laid down his uncompromising reforms, and, later, zealous followers destroyed and removed alters and relics. It's been rebuilt and

Walking Tour: Old Town & The Royal Mile

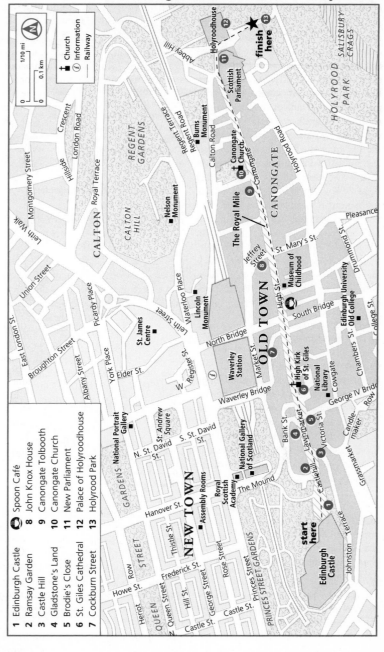

Legend:
1 Edinburgh Castle
2 Ramsay Garden
3 Castle Hill
4 Gladstone's Land
5 Brodie's Close
6 St. Giles Cathedral
7 Cockburn Street
8 John Knox House
9 Canongate Tolbooth
10 Canongate Church
11 New Parliament
12 Palace of Holyroodhouse
13 Holyrood Park

Spoon Café

renovated repeatedly. All that really remains of the 15th-century church is the spire, a familiar landmark of the city. Around St. Giles are the Law Courts of Parliament Square, featuring (since 1838) the designs of Robert Reid, though they were inspired by drawings by the great architect Robert Adam. In the sidewalk, note the heart-shaped arrangement of cobbles. This is meant to mark the site of the old tolbooth (where taxes were collected) and a city prison, the latter of which was made famous by Sir Walter Scott's *The Heart of Midlothian*. Spitting in the heart is meant to bring good luck. Further down and across the street is Edinburgh City Chambers, beneath which is Mary King's Close where tours reveal the Old Town underbelly: buildings as they looked before the mid-1700s. Nearby in the Anchor Close, the first edition of the Encyclopaedia Britannica was printed.

Continue down the Royal Mile to:

❼ Cockburn Street

Curving down the hill to the left, Cockburn Street is a relatively recent addition to the neighborhood, built in 1856 to improve access to Waverley railway station. Like Bank Street earlier, it interrupts the old closes and steps (such as those in the macabre-sounding Fleshmarket Close) that descend precipitously down the northern side of the hill. Cockburn Street has a variety of bars and restaurants, CD shops, tattoo parlors, and art galleries. Across the High Street is the Tron Kirk, a center for Old Town information. A tron was the beam used to weigh goods. The church was built atop a very old lane that today has been excavated.

Continue down the Royal Mile, crossing North Bridge on the left and South Bridge on the right to Blackfriars Street and:

TAKE A BREAK
Spoon Cafe (15 Blackfriars St.; ℰ **0131/556-6922**) is no greasy spoon, that's for sure. It's a modern and casual cafe with a talented chef in charge of the small and open kitchen. Sure, the selection is fairly modest: salads, soups, and sandwiches, plus cakes. But it's all freshly prepared—a rarity in our fast-food world—using some excellent and tasty ingredients. See p. 77 for a full review.

Return to High Street, turning right to:

❽ John Knox House

Jutting out into the wide sidewalk on the left side of the High Street is this apparently genuine 16th-century house, although any real link to the firebrand Protestant reformer (who surely resided in a church manse) has been discredited over the years. Still, the connection to Scotland's Martin Luther, however tenuous, is probably what's preserved this attractive building (p. 87). Next door (to the left) is Moubray House, which has some of the same details of Gladstone's Land. The rear portion might actually date to 1530, making it perhaps the oldest surviving dwelling in the city. Across the street, Tweeddale Court leads to Tweeddale House, a 16th-century survivor with the Doric porch added in the 18th century just before the printers Oliver & Boyd (whose name remains on the facade) occupied the building.

The patio is also the site of the infamous robbery and murder of one William Begbie in 1806. Apparently £3,000 ($5,500) of the £4,000 ($7,400) stolen was quickly recovered—but the assassin escaped justice. Next is the World's End Close, the final close on this stretch of the Royal Mile and indeed historically the last before the city's old wall, which protected the world within it.

Continue down the Royal Mile to:

❾ Canongate Tolbooth

Now, having crossed Jeffrey Street on the left and St. Mary's Street to the right, you are on the Canongate. The original settlement of the same name was only formally incorporated into the city of Edinburgh in 1856. Most of the buildings along the Canongate have been rebuilt over the years. The tower of the Tolbooth was built in the 1590s. The attractive clock that extends out over the street was added to the building in the 1880s. You can see a bit of the interior, which has been made into a not terribly impressive museum called the People's Story (p. 87).

Next door is:

❿ Canongate Church

The original parish church for the Canongate burgh was in Holyrood Abbey. But after James VII (James II of England) procured that space for different uses, a new kirk became necessary, and this one, with its bell-shaped roofline, was christened in 1691 (p. 88). It remains the church that today's royal family attends if staying at Holyrood Palace. The churchyard, with good views of the Royal High School on Calton Hill, has numerous monuments. Here is the grave of pioneering economic philosopher Adam Smith and possibly the murdered secretary to Mary Queen of Scots, David Riccio (whose body had to have been moved here more than 100 years after his death). Aficionados of the poet Robert Burns will know that he wrote the tribute on the headstone of fellow poet Robert Fergusson and that Mrs. Agnes McLehose (whom Burns addressed in umpteen letters as "Clarinda") was laid to rest in this cemetery, as well.

Continue on down the Royal Mile to the:

⓫ Parliament Building

Subject to seemingly endless debate—much delayed and way over budget—the Parliament Building for Scotland was designed by Enric Miralles, a Barcelona-based architect who died of cancer shortly after work on the building was started. The controversial complex (p. 88) was initially intended to open in 2001, but didn't host its first session until autumn 2004. In 2006, the bedeviled building suffered another setback when a beam in the main debating chamber came loose. The abstract motif, repeated on the facade along the Canongate, was apparently inspired by Raeburn's painting of Reverend Walker skating on Duddingston Loch, which hangs in the National Gallery of Art.

Continue to the foot of the Canongate and the:

⓬ Palace of Holyroodhouse

Rood means cross, and the abbey (now ruins) on the grounds of Holyroodhouse dates to King David I and 1128. The residence for royalty followed in the 15th century. Between 1426 and 1460, James II was born, crowned, married, and buried at the Palace (p. 88). Later, James IV expanded the buildings, as did his heir—all to be redone again in the 17th century by Charles II. A critical episode in the fraught reign of Mary Queen of Scots was played out here: the assassination of her loyal assistant David Rizzio. Young Pretender Bonnie Prince Charlie stayed at the palace briefly in 1745 during his nearly successful, but ultimately disastrous, rebellion. For many years, the palace remained empty most of the time and only since the first visit by Queen Victoria in 1842 have its lodgings been regularly used by members of the royal family. In 2002, the Queen's Gallery was opened for public displays of the royal collection of art.

Adjacent is:

⓭ Holyrood Park

If you have any energy left, these 160 plus hectares (400 acres) of open space allow plenty of ground to roam. From here you can scale Salisbury Crags and mount

Arthur's Seat, which rises some 251m (825 ft.) above Edinburgh. Nearby is the science-oriented and family-oriented tourist attraction, Our Dynamic Earth.

WALKING TOUR 2   SOUTH OF THE ROYAL MILE

Start: West Bow.
Finish: Grassmarket.
Time: About 1½ hours.
Best Times: Daytime.
Worst Times: Late at night.

The walls surrounding the medieval city of Edinburgh (first erected as much to deter smuggling as to protect inhabitants) were generally expanded each time the fortifications needed improving. So, eventually they were extended past the original Old Town boundaries to include districts such as the Grassmarket and ancient routes such as the Cowgate. This walk combines parts of Old Town with the historic settlements south of the original burgh, an area now dominated by the University of Edinburgh.

Start the walk at:

❶ West Bow

Initially this street zigzagged right up the steep slope from the Grassmarket to Castlehill. With the 19th-century addition of Victoria Street, however, it links more gently with the Royal Mile via George IV Bridge. The combination of Victoria Street and West Bow create a charming and winding road with unpretentious shops, bars, and restaurants. At the base of the street is the West Bow well, which was built in 1674. To the west is the Grassmarket.

But our walk goes southeast from Cowgate. Head up Candlemaker Row to:

❷ Greyfriars Church

Not the church you see ascending Candlemaker Row, but to the right at the top, Greyfriars Kirk (p. 92) was completed in 1620. It was built amid a cemetery that Queen Mary proposed in 1562 because burial space at St. Giles Cathedral was exhausted. Although Greyfriars was the first post-Reformation church constructed in Edinburgh, by the middle of the 17th century, it was being used as barracks. In 1718, the original tower exploded when gunpowder stored in it (a remnant of the 1715 rebellion) was ignited. After this point New Greyfriars was added to the western end of Old Greyfriars. The kirkyard has a bit of the Flodden Wall and is full of 17th-century monuments. Its most celebrated grave, however, contains a 19th-century policeman whose faithful dog, Bobby, reputedly stood watch at the plot for 14 years. Bobby's statue is at the top of Candlemaker Row, just outside the pub named in his honor.

Cross George IV Bridge to Chambers Street and the:

❸ Museum of Scotland

Directly in front of you as you leave Greyfriars is the impressive and modern Museum of Scotland (p. 89). It was designed by architects Benson and Forsyth and constructed mostly with sandstone from the northeast of Scotland. Opened in 1998, it was purpose-built for exhibitions that chart the history of Scotland: the land, wildlife, and its people. Next door is the Royal Museum. Chambers Street is named after a 19th-century lord provost (the equivalent of mayor), whose statue stands in front of the museum's Victorian Great Hall. Further down off Chambers Street on what is

Walking Tour: South of the Royal Mile

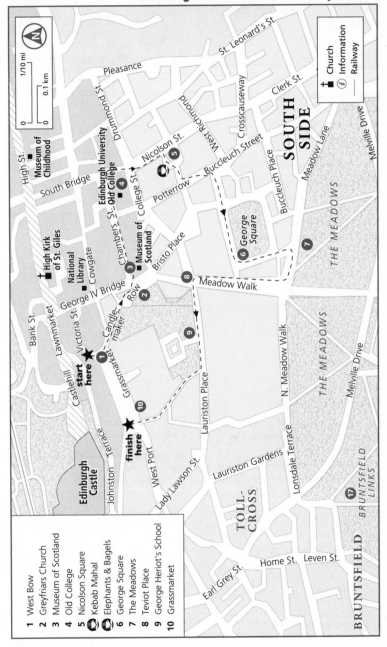

N

1/10 mi
0.1 km

Church
(i) Information
—— Railway

High St.

Pleasance

St. Leonard's St.

Clerk St.

Drummond St.

Museum of Childhood

South Bridge

Edinburgh University

Nicolson St. ⑤

Old College ④

West Richmond

Buccleuch Street

Crosscauseway

SOUTH SIDE

Chambers St.

College St.

Potterrow

Buccleuch Place

Meadow Lane

Melville Drive

High Kirk of St. Giles

National Library

Cowgate

Museum of Scotland ③

Bristo Place

George Square ⑥

THE MEADOWS

⑦

Bank St.

Lawnmarket

George IV Bridge

Candle-maker Row ②

Meadow Walk

⑧

N. Meadow Walk

THE MEADOWS

Victoria St.

Castlehill

start here ★①

Grassmarket

⑨

Lauriston Place

Melville Drive

Johnston Terrace

Edinburgh Castle

West Port

finish here ★

⑩

Lady Lawson St.

Lauriston Gardens

Lonsdale Terrace

TOLL-CROSS

BRUNTSFIELD LINKS

⑰

BRUNTSFIELD

Earl Grey St.

Home St.   Leven St.

1 West Bow
2 Greyfriars Church
3 Museum of Scotland
4 Old College
5 Nicolson Square
   Kebab Mahal
   Elephants & Bagels
6 George Square
7 The Meadows
8 Teviot Place
9 George Heriot's School
10 Grassmarket

today Guthrie Street, Sir Walter Scott was born.

Continue east on Chambers Street to South Bridge, turning right (south) and at this corner is the:

❹ Old College

The 1781 exteriors of the University of Edinburgh Old College have been called the greatest public work of architect Robert Adam. The university was first established in 1583 by James VI (James I of England), and this "Old College" actually replaced an earlier Old College. Construction of the quadrangle of buildings was suspended during the Napoleonic wars. William Playfair designed the Quad's interiors in 1819. In the southwest corner is the entrance to the Talbot Rice gallery. On nearby Drummond Street is one of Robert Louis Stevenson's favorite saloons—the Rutherford Bar—and a plaque commemorating his admiration for it is at the corner. Across Drummond Street there is more literary history—but of more recent vintage. A cafe here on the second floor is reputedly where J. K. Rowling began writing the *Harry Potter* series. More recently it became a Chinese restaurant.

At Drummond Street, South Bridge becomes Nicolson Street. Continue south on it to:

❺ Nicolson Square

The impressive neoclassical building you pass on the left (across from the modern Festival Theatre) before arriving at this square is the Surgeons' Hall, designed by William H. Playfair in the 1830s. Nicolson Square dates to 1756, and the buildings along its north fringe apparently were the first to be built here. In the square's park is the Brassfounders' Column, designed by James Gowans in 1886.

TAKE A BREAK
Along the northside of the square, **Kebab Mahal** (7 Nicolson Sq.; ☎ **0131/622-5214**) serves up inexpensive but tasty and generous portions of Indian food. Its simple and unpretentious surroundings draw a real cross-section of Edinburgh: professors, students, construction workers and visitors to the nearby central mosque. See p. 78 for a full review. Alternatively, you might try the cafe called **Elephants & Bagels** at the west side of the square.

Leave the square at the west on Marshall Street, turn left (south) on to Potterrow, turning right (west) at the parking lot entrance and Crichton Street to:

❻ George Square

Almost entirely redeveloped by the university in the 20th century, George Square originally had uniform, if less than startling, mid-18th-century town houses. It predates the city's New Town developments north of Old Town and some of the early buildings are still standing on the western side of the square. The park provides a quiet daytime retreat. The square was named after the brother of its designer, James Brown, and not a king. The writer Walter Scott played in the park as a child.

Exit the square at the southwest corner, turning right (west) into:

❼ The Meadows

This sweeping park separates the southern suburbs such as Marchmont, which were largely developed in the 19th century, from central Edinburgh. The area once had a loch, but today it is a green expanse crisscrossed by tree-lined paths (p. 95). At the Western end is Bruntsfield Links, which some speculate entertained golfers in the 17th century and still has a short course with many holes today.

Turn right after a short distance (at the black cycle network marker) on to a wide path for pedestrians and bicyclists—Meadow Walk—and

follow it north to:

❽ Teviot Place

The triangle of land formed by Teviot Place, Forrest Road, and Bristo Place is a hotbed of university life today, with its cafes and bars. To the right (east) is the Medical School. To the left (west) on Lauriston Place is the Royal Infirmary of Edinburgh. George Watson's Hospital on the grounds dates to the 1740s, but Scots baronial buildings superseded it in the 19th century, adopting the open-plan dictates of Florence Nightingale.

Walk west on Lauriston Place to:

❾ George Heriot's School

Heriot was nicknamed the Jinglin' Geordie and as jeweler to the James VI, he exemplified the courtiers and royal hangers-on who left Scotland and made their fortunes in London after the unification of the crowns. Heriot, at least, decided to pay some back by bequeathing several thousand pounds to build a facility for disadvantaged boys here. Of the 200-odd windows in the Renaissance pile, only two

are exactly alike. Today, it is a private school for young men and women.

Continue on Lauriston Place to the edge of the campus, turn right on Heriot Place and continue down the steps and path called the Vennel to the:

❿ Grassmarket

Just at the top of the steep steps of the Vennel is another piece of the Flodden Wall, the southwest bastion, indicating how the Grassmarket was enclosed in the fortified city by the 16th century. Now home to loads of bars and restaurants, the Grassmarket—in the shadow of the castle—held a weekly market for more than 400 years. The Grassmarket also was the site of public gallows until the 1780s: A place where zealous Protestants—known as the Covenators—were hung, as was Maggie Dickson who, according to legend, came back to life. She at least has a pub named after her today. At the nearby White Hart Inn, both Burns and Wordsworth are said to have lodged.

WALKING TOUR 3   NEW TOWN

Start: Royal Scottish Academy.
Finish: East Princes Street Gardens.
Time: About 2 to 3 hours.
Best Times: Daytime.
Worst Times: Late at night.

In 1767, the city fathers realized that the best way to relieve the increasingly cramped and unhygienic Old Town was to create a New Town. It is perhaps the definitive example of rational Georgian town planning. As hostilities with England (or between rebellious groups within Scotland) had ended, a fortified city was no longer needed. The loch to the north of Old Town was drained (becoming Princes Street Gardens), and the new roads on the other side were laid out in a strict grid. Subsequent additions to the original New Town created a new city center with fine housing, offices, and commercial space.

Begin the walk opposite the corner of Princes Street and Hanover Street at the:

❶ Royal Scottish Academy

Bisecting Princes Street Gardens, **The Mound** was created by earth moved during

the development of Edinburgh's New Town, and it effectively forms a ridge linking New and Old towns. Atop this hump are two galleries: the Royal Scottish

Academy and, to the south, the National Gallery of Art. Both buildings were designed with strong Greek Doric and Ionic styling by William H. Playfair around 1825 and 1850 respectively.

Cross Princes Street north to Hanover Street, walking up Hanover Street and turning left (west) onto:

❷ Rose Street

Not particularly significant historically, this lane was meant for "a better class of artisans" and at one point in the 1780s, a two-story limit was placed upon its buildings. The conversion of the street to an open-air pedestrian mall began in the late 1960s. Today Rose Street is best known for many popular pubs, such as the Abbotsford, Milne's, and the Kenilworth. The area has retail shops and restaurants, too.

Continue east on Rose Street to Frederick Street, turning right (north) to:

❸ George Street

All the street names in the first New Town were intended to celebrate the Hanoverian reign of George III (he who lost America). George Street is the central of three parallel avenues, and it runs along the ridge of the hill. Looking down it to the left (west) you can see the dome of West Register House in the distance and to the right (east) the column with Melville at the other end of George Street. Straight ahead are views of the Forth River. Today the wide boulevard (with parking down the center) is where most of the city's most expensive clothing shops are located. Here at the intersection with Frederick Street is the statue of Prime Minister William Pitt.

From the corner of Frederick Street, turn left and go west on George Street, turning left (south) on Castle Street and proceeding back to:

❹ Princes Street

Like Queen Street on the northern boundary of the first New Town, buildings were intentionally only constructed on one side of Princes Street. That has insured practically uninterrupted views of Old Town rising up the Castle: one of the most iconic panoramas in all of Europe. Despite the views, the original three-story homes on Princes Street were apparently not as nice or as desirable as the ones on George and Queen streets. Today, too much of Princes Street, the city's primary shopping street, is dominated by unattractive modern storefronts and some ghastly 20th-century monstrosities. But here at the western corner of Castle Street are three original buildings buried behind the much more recent facades.

Cross Princes Street to the statue of Guthrie and turn right (west) continuing to:

❺ St. John's & St. Cuthbert Churches

Episcopalians are Scottish (and American) Anglicans, and at the end of West Princes Street Gardens is St. John's, a Gothic house of Episcopal worship completed in 1818. Behind and below it is St. Cuthbert's Parish Church, which you enter from Lothian Road. Here, at the base of Castle Rock, a medieval church was apparently established in the 12th century. This one, dating to the 1890s, was at least the third to be constructed on the site. The churchyard offers plenty of handsome monuments and has the graves of the writer (and noted opium eater) Thomas DeQuincey as well as painter Alexander Nasmyth. In the church's vestibule is a memorial to John Napier of Merchiston, who invented logarithms. During the day, you can walk via a rear gate into West Princes Street Gardens.

But our stroll returns to Princes Street, crossing it, turning left (west), going a short distance and then turning right (north) on Hope Street to:

❻ Charlotte Square

This final bit of the first New Town, was designed by the preeminent Georgian era architect Robert Adam in 1791, just before his death. The central park was subsequently expanded from a circle to

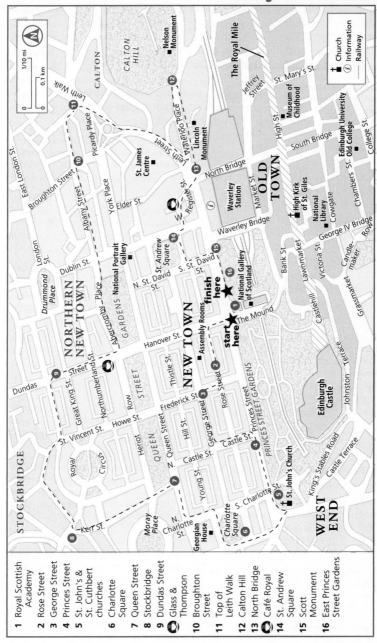

1 Royal Scottish Academy
2 Rose Street
3 George Street
4 Princes Street
5 St. John's & St. Cuthbert churches
6 Charlotte Square
7 Queen Street
8 Stockbridge
9 Glass & Thompson
10 Broughton Street
11 Top of Leith Walk
12 Calton Hill
13 North Bridge
14 Café Royal
15 St. Andrew Square
16 Scott Monument
16 East Princes Street Gardens

form an octagon in 1873, with the statue of Prince Albert added. On the west side, with the green copper dome, looking across the square and down George Street beyond, is West Register House, which was originally built as St. George's Church in 1814: a dubious revision of Adam's original plans by Robert Reid. It is worth detouring behind it to see the charming and unlikely half-timber, red-roofed house on Randolph Place by architect T. Duncan Rhind. On the south side of the square, at no. 42, the National Trust for Scotland has offices, a cafe, shop, and museum. Recent work on the building's foundations uncovered a can-nonball presumably shot in defense of the castle long before anything was built here. Across the square on the north side is Bute House, the official residence of the Scottish First Minister, and the Georgian House, decorated in that period and open to the public (p. 91).

From the northeast corner of the square go north 1 short block to North Charlotte Street, turning right at Albyn Place which then quickly becomes:

❼ Queen Street

This northern-most street of the original New Town development has the greatest amount of original buildings. Like Princes Street, town houses were only built on one side of what is today a very busy boulevard, with the private Queen Street Gardens running the length of the opposite side. At the far (eastern) end from here is the Scottish National Por-trait Gallery, in a smart red sandstone palace designed by R. Rowand Anderson in the 1880s. Nearby, north of the park on Heriott Row, Robert Lewis Stevenson lived as a young man.

Turn left (north) on Wemyss Place and continue on down the hill using Gloucester Lane and Gloucester Street to Bakers Place and:

❽ Stockbridge

Stockbridge, a charming village within the city along a bend in the Water of Leith, was something of a hippie enclave in the 1960s and 1970s. But today's property prices ensure that it is primarily home to the well-heeled. Its name comes from the Stock Bridge, which crosses the Water of Leith. Across it, Deanhaugh Street serves as the local main street. St. Stephen Street has a variety of places to shop and eat.

Leave Stockbridge via St. Stephen Street to St. Vincent Street, turning left (east) on Cumber-land Street and proceeding to:

❾ Dundas Street

Having passed Playfair's St. Stephen's church, you are now in the heart of the Northern New Town. Separated from the capital's first New Town by Queen Street Gardens, it was planned in the first years of the 19th century by Robert Reid and William Sibbald. The architecture remains uniform. At the bottom of Dundas Street, which has several art and antique shops, is Canonmills—originally the site of a milling settlement for the Abbey of Holyroodhouse. Beyond it are the Royal Botanic Gardens.

But we go up the hill of Dundas Street and:

> **TAKE A BREAK**
> **Glass & Thompson** (2 Dundas St.; ✆ 0131/557-0909) is a classic, upmarket cafe that feels part and parcel of Edinburgh's rather posh New Town. Local ingredients and Continen-tal goods are combined on platters with cheese, seafood, cold meats and salad. Open from 8am to late afternoon.

You can call it a day if tired and return to Princes Street by following Dundas Street through Queen Street Gardens (after which the road becomes Hanover St.).

Or, if you're still willing, carry on by turning left (east) on Abercromby Place, which (after cross-ing Dublin St.) becomes Albany Street, continu-ing to:

⑩ Broughton Street

This is one of the key places for nightlife in Edinburgh today, with traditional pubs, stylish bars, and some restaurants. At the bottom of the street at the roundabout is the former Bellevue Reformed Baptist Church (and before that, Catholic Apostolic), which the local community has actively tried to preserve, mainly for the sake of some colorful neo-Florentine interior murals by Phoebe Traquair. At the top of the street is Picardy Place, named after a weaver's village.

Cross Broughton Street to Forth Street, turning right on Union Street to Baxter's Place and the:

⑪ Top of Leith Walk

Facing the Theatre Royal bar, if you went left down Leith Walk you would end up at the port of Leith (See "Walking Tour 4: Leith," below). At this spot is the Playhouse, designed by a Glasgow architect for films and theater productions in the late 1920s (p. 124). Next to it, Lady Glenorchy's Low Calton Church was recently converted into a swank hotel. They no longer screen films at the Playhouse, but the glass Omni Centre just up the road has a multiplex cinema.

Having crossed Leith Walk, continue up the hill past the Omni Centre and further to Waterloo Place, turning left to reach:

⑫ Calton Hill

The first comparison of Edinburgh to Athens apparently was made in the mid-1700s. Given the city's key role in the Scottish Enlightenment, the moniker "Athens of the North" was later applied, too. But the city only made vain attempts to match the splendor of the Acropolis, ending up with a folly of the Parthenon on Calton Hill. Nearby (and clearly visible from Waterloo Place) is the towering Nelson Monument, whose ball drops every afternoon. Depending on your energy levels, you can scale Calton Hill. On its southern flank, facing Old Town,

is the monumental Royal High School, a key Greek Revival building by Thomas Hamilton completed in 1829. Robert Louis Stevenson reckoned the views from Calton Hill were the best as you can see both the castle and Arthur's Seat. Back along Waterloo Place is the Old Calton Burying Ground and its Emancipation Monument to honor Scottish-American Civil War soldiers with a statue of President Lincoln and a freed slave.

Follow Waterloo Place west towards Princes Street and:

⑬ North Bridge

As you look down the length of Princes Street westward, on the right is Wellington's Monument but on the left, leading to the Old Town, is North Bridge and another vantage point for looking at the castle. Curiously, few of Edinburgh's many bridges ever cross water. They rather link hills. The first North Bridge took some 9 years to complete in the 1760s, a beginning step to create the New Town. This broad span was designed in 1894.

Cross Princes Street, taking the West Register Street (to the left of Wellington's statue), following the lane and:

TAKE A BREAK
An oyster bar and restaurant at the **Cafe Royal** (17 West Register St.; ℂ **0131/556-4124**) has traded continuously since 1863. It retains a good deal of Victorian splendor. The restaurant closes after lunch and reopens for dinner, but the Circle Bar is open throughout the day. Some highlights of the room are the tile pictures of notable inventors. Upstairs, the Bistro Bar has an ornate ceiling but less ambience. See p. 130 for a full review.

Continue west on West Register Street to:

⑭ St. Andrew Square

Named for the patron saint of Scotland, this square is the eastern bookend to

George Street. Unlike Charlotte Square at the street's western terminus, it doesn't carry the same Georgian character. Up the column in the middle of the gated garden, some 38m (125 ft.) or more above, is Lord Melville.

From the southwest corner of the square, walk south on St. David Street, crossing Princes Street to the:

🅖 Scott Monument

Victorian critic John Ruskin hated this monument to Scotland's greatest novelist, describing it as the top of a church spire plunked on the ground. Never mind, the Gothic shrine remains one of the most notable landmarks in the city. The design was by George Meikle Kemp, who, apparently, was third in the 1836 competition but somehow got the commission after the committee requested more

drawings. It was meant to stand in Charlotte Square. The statue of Scott (with his trusty deerhound Maida) was hewn from a 30-ton block of marble by John Steell. From here you have good views up to Calton Hill's monuments.

Adjacent is:

🅖 East Princes Street Gardens

It took many years to completely drain the old Nor' Loch, and the park that now fills the valley was begun in 1830. The designs had to be altered in the wake of the construction of the railway lines into Waverley Station. The panoramic view of Old Town rising to Ramsay Gardens and the Castle are quite fine from here. West on the other side of the Mound, where this stroll began, is West Princes Street Gardens, with a band shell, fountain, carousel ride, and paths that scale Castle Rock.

WALKING TOUR 4   LEITH

Start: Foot of Leith Walk.

Finish: Newkirk Shopping Mall.

Time: About 1 hour.

Best Times: Daytime.

Worst Times: Late at night.

At Leith, Edinburgh's long-standing port, a natural harbor formed where the Water of Leith feeds into the Firth of Forth. Briefly, Leith was Scotland's capital during the interim rule of Mary of Guise. Her daughter, Mary Queen of Scots, landed here in 1561, and Oliver Cromwell built a fort almost 100 years after that, seized many years later by Highlanders trying to reinstate the Stuart Line of Kings. Leith was always an independent burgh, only incorporated into Edinburgh in the 20th century.

From the statue of Queen Victoria, walk north on Constitution Street, turning right (east) at Links Lane which leads to:

❶ Leith Links

Older than Bruntsfield Links in Edinburgh's Southside, Leith Links is, by some accounts, the birthplace of golf. A version of the sport was first played here in the 1400s. Charles I apparently got in a round or two in the early 1640s. In 1744, the first rules of the game were laid down

at Leith Links by the Honorable Company of Edinburgh Golfers. It was then a 5-hole course. Running adjacent to John's Place here was the first hole's fairway.

Go north down the west side of the park, turning left (west) on Queen Charlotte Street, and return to:

❷ Constitution Street

On the corner at the right is Leith Town Hall. Originally constructed as the Leith

Walking Tour: Leith

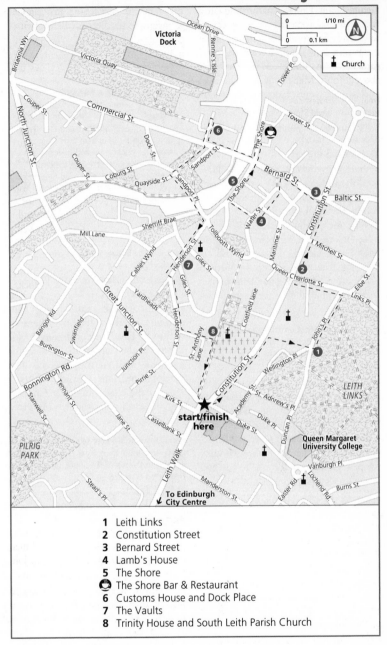

0   1/10 mi
0   0.1 km

✝ Church

1   Leith Links
2   Constitution Street
3   Bernard Street
4   Lamb's House
5   The Shore
☕ The Shore Bar & Restaurant
6   Customs House and Dock Place
7   The Vaults
8   Trinity House and South Leith Parish Church

Sheriff Court in 1828, adjoining property was incorporated later when the town became a parliamentary burgh. To the left, looking south down the street, is the fittingly named St. Mary Star of the Sea Catholic church as well as the modern Port of Leith Housing Association building.

Go right (north) on Constitution Street and continue to:

❸ Bernard Street

Bernard Street has been termed, architecturally speaking, Leith's "most formal space." At the corner to the right of the Burns statue, Leith Assembly Rooms include the original merchant's meeting place built in the 1780s. The Burn's Monument was erected in 1898, and the buildings from here west to the Water of Leith are Georgian and 19th-century commercial buildings, such as the former Leith Bank.

Go left from Constitution Street and walk west on Bernard Street, turning left on Carpet Lane (marked by tiles in the pavement) to:

❹ Lamb's House

The lane jogs a bit and becomes Water Street facing a handsome, harled red-roofed building with an odd window built into the corner of the facade. This 17th-century merchant's house is a masterpiece of the type and era, with crow-stepped gables and corbels. It has been restored repeatedly.

At Burgess Street, turn right to:

❺ The Shore

The port's first main street, running along the Water of Leith to the Firth of Forth, the Shore is now home to Michelin-star-winning Restaurant Martin Wishart and a clutch of pubs with outdoor seating. At Bernard Street, the King's Wark is a pub within a restored 18th-century building. The original King's Wark was believed to be a palace and arsenal

that James VI had rebuilt and given over to tavern-keeper Bernard Lindsay.

Cross Bernard Street and follow the Shore north and:

> **TAKE A BREAK**
> **The Shore Bar and Restaurant** (3/4 The Shore; ✆ 0131/553-5080) is one that feels as if it has been sitting here and receiving seafarers for years and years. In fact, it opened in the 1980s, but it remains the best unpretentious pub in Leith. Food—primarily fish—is served at the bar or in the adjoining dining room. See p. 79 for a full review.

Return to the bridge, turn right crossing it to Commercial Street and the:

❻ Customs House & Dock Place

Designed by Robert Reid in 1810, the Customs House has strong fluted columns. Nearby is the original entrance to the Old East Dock established by John Rennie at the start of the 19th century and the modern Commercial Quay development. This area also skirts the walls of the citadel built for Cromwell, with fragments apparently still part of Dock Street.

Cross Commercial Street to Sandport Street, going left on Sandport Place crossing the Water of Leith to the top of the Shore, turning right on Henderson Street to:

❼ The Vaults

Having passed the modern new apartments that are changing Leith's character, this handsome and broad stone warehouse dates to 1682, but the vaulted passage and cellar underneath may be 100 years older. Leith is where bottles and bottles of French wine were shipped. A link to that history is maintained by the Vintners Rooms restaurant and wine tastings that are held there. The Scotch Malt Whisky Society is located on the second floor.

Continue up Henderson Street, turning left at St. Anthony Place, passing the back of the Lidl supermarket to the Kirkgate and:

8 Trinity House & South Leith Parish Church

Trinity House is an early-19th-century survivor amid the urban renewal and tall apartment buildings of the 20th century. Owned by Historic Scotland, it is open to group tours by reservation. Across from it, a church has been standing since about 1480. This one was built in 1848. A plaque in the kirkyard details the intervening history. Almost back to the foot of Leith Walk (and the beginning of this perambulation) go through the Newkirkgate Shopping Mall, a mid-1960s development that now feels outdated.

Continue north through the mall and you're back where you started at the intersection of streets and the statue of Queen Victoria.

Several buses go up Leith Walk to the city center.

9

Edinburgh Shopping

Edinburgh may lack all of the shopping options available in Glasgow, but it has a combination of newfangled boutiques, souvenir shops, and traditional department stores, such as the classic John Lewis. With the addition a few years ago of the fashionista's favorite, Harvey Nichols, Edinburgh is certainly challenging the more style-conscious city to the west. New Town's **Princes Street** is a primary shopping artery in the Scottish capital, with leading department stores, whether the homegrown Jenners or the British staple, Marks & Spencer. But for the posher shops, such as Cruise or Laura Ashley, **George Street** tops the lot. For tourists, Old Town's **Royal Mile** can present the mother lode of Scottish souvenirs, whether it is tartan or trinkets.

1 The Shopping Scene

For visitors from abroad, prices in the U.K. may seem high. In recent years, the British currency has been strong relative to other major currencies, such as the U.S. dollar or the euro, which is, of course, now used by most countries in the European Union. Still, the prices for most retail goods in Scotland have not soared since the mid-1990s. Actually, in some cases—for example, clothes—costs to the consumer have come down in real terms. Nevertheless, many items carry the same numerical price in pounds as they would in American dollars. For example, a pair of hiking shoes that cost $100 in New York might well be priced £100 in Edinburgh, making it 50% to 100% more expensive.

BEST BUYS

Although you may find a bargain at the tourist-oriented shops along the Royal Mile, unique gifts are perhaps best found at the shops in the city's various national galleries or the one in the Museum of Scotland. Also, shops curiously tend to close earlier in the city center than the shopping malls in outlying districts. See chapter 7 for addresses and phone numbers of galleries and museums.

SHOPPING COMPLEXES

Ocean Terminal   Although it was designed by the Conran group, this is ultimately just another modern indoor mall. Debenhams, French Connection, Gap, and others have set out their stalls at this retail cathedral, which gets a lot of footfall from tourists because the royal yacht Britannia is moored here as well. Zinc Bar and Grill is the best dining option. Open till 8pm Monday to Friday. Ocean Dr., Leith. ✆ 0131-555-8888. www.oceanterminal.com.

Princes Mall   There's practically something for everyone—except a leading department store—at this tri-level mall next to Waverley Station and beneath the city's main tourist information center. In 2006, it was undergoing some refurbishments as part of changes being made to the railway station. There are about 80 shops selling fashions, accessories, gifts, books, jewelry, and beauty products; and a food court with typical fast-food outlets. Princes St. ✆ **0131/557-3759**. www.princesmall-edinburgh.co.uk.

St. James Centre   Slightly more upmarket than the Princes Mall, this shopping center has the anchor of the John Lewis department store, along with Dorothy Perkins, River Island, and Top Shop. Leith St. (at east end of Princes St.). ✆ **0131/557-0050**. www.stjamesshopping.com.

2 Shopping A to Z

Shopping hours in central Edinburgh are generally from 9 or 10am to 6pm Monday through Wednesday and on Friday and Saturday. On Sunday, shops open at 11am or noon and close around 5pm. On Thursdays, many shops remain open until 7 or 8pm.

ANTIQUES
The Bachelor Pad   A relative newcomer to St. Stephen Street, which is one of two roads in Edinburgh (the other is Causewayside on the Southside) that specialize in antiques and collectibles. This shop focuses on 20th-century design in furniture and accessories. 36 St. Stephen St., Stockbridge. ✆ **0131/226-6355**. www.thebachelorpad.org.

BOOKS
Blackwells   Once an outlet of the venerable, homegrown James Thin bookshop, Edinburgh's most respected seller, the outlet near the Royal Mile still has a knowledgeable staff and wide-ranging stock of fiction and nonfiction, despite being in a large U.K. chain operation now. 53 South Bridge. ✆ **0131/622-8222**. www.blackwells.com.

McNaughtan's Bookshop   Trading since 1957, this is one of the city's best antiquarian and second-hand book purveyors. A key stop for book lovers. 3a Haddington Place (at top of Leith Walk near Gayfield Sq.). ✆ **0131/556-5897**. www.mcnaughtansbookshop.com.

Waterstones   The giant Barnes & Noble–like operation with plenty of stock and lots of soft seats is the most prominent book retailer in the city center. It has a good Scottish section on the ground floor and branches in New Town at the western end of Princes Street and on George Street. 128 Princes St. (near Waverley Station). ✆ **0131/226-2666**.

CRYSTAL
Edinburgh Crystal   Some 16km (10 miles) south of Edinburgh, this place is devoted to handmade crystal glassware. The visitor center contains the factory shop where the world's largest collection of Edinburgh Crystal, and inexpensive factory seconds, are sold. Waterford may be a more prestigious name, but Edinburgh Crystal is a serious competitor. Eastfield, Penicuik (just off A701 to Peebles). ✆ **01968/672-244**. www.edinburgh-crystal.co.uk.

Tips Bring That Passport!

Take along your passport when you go shopping in case you make a purchase that entitles you to a **VAT (value-added tax)** refund.

Edinburgh Shopping

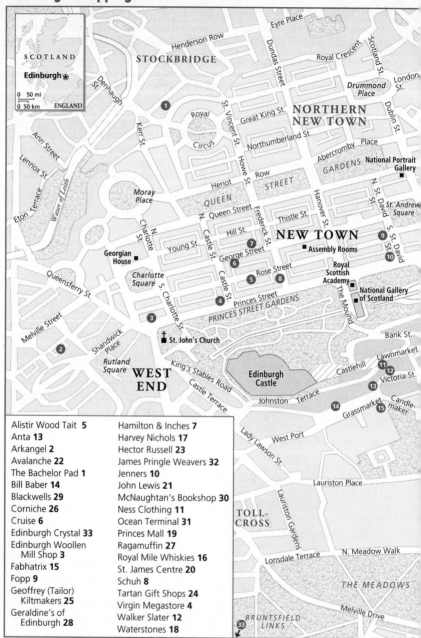

Alistir Wood Tait **5**
Anta **13**
Arkangel **2**
Avalanche **22**
The Bachelor Pad **1**
Bill Baber **14**
Blackwells **29**
Corniche **26**
Cruise **6**
Edinburgh Crystal **33**
Edinburgh Woollen
　Mill Shop **3**
Fabhatrix **15**
Fopp **9**
Geoffrey (Tailor)
　Kiltmakers **25**
Geraldine's of
　Edinburgh **28**

Hamilton & Inches **7**
Harvey Nichols **17**
Hector Russell **23**
James Pringle Weavers **32**
Jenners **10**
John Lewis **21**
McNaughtan's Bookshop **30**
Ness Clothing **11**
Ocean Terminal **31**
Princes Mall **19**
Ragamuffin **27**
Royal Mile Whiskies **16**
St. James Centre **20**
Schuh **8**
Tartan Gift Shops **24**
Virgin Megastore **4**
Walker Slater **12**
Waterstones **18**

THE TRAVELOCITY GUARANTEE

...THAT SAYS EVERYTHING YOU BOOK WILL BE RIGHT, OR WE'LL WORK WITH OUR TRAVEL PARTNERS TO MAKE IT RIGHT, RIGHT AWAY.

To drive home the point,
we're going to use the word "right" in every single sentence.

Let's get right to it. Right to the meat! Only Travelocity guarantees everything about your booking will be right, or we'll work with our travel partners to make it right, right away. Right on!

Here's a picture taken smack dab right in the middle of Antigua, where the Guarantee also covers you.

The Guarantee covers all but one of the items pictured to the right.

For example, what if the ocean view you booked actually looks out at a downright ugly parking lot? You'd be right to call – we're there for you. And no one in their right mind would be pleased to learn the rental car place has closed and left them stranded. Call Travelocity and we'll help get you back on the right track.

Now, you may be thinking, "Yeah, right, I'm so sure." That's OK; you have the right to remain skeptical. That is until we mention help is always right around the corner. Call us right off the bat, knowing our customer service reps are there for you 24/7. Righting wrongs. Left and right.

Now if you're guessing there are some things we can't control, like the weather, well you're right. But we can help you with most things – to get all the details in righting,* visit travelocity.com/guarantee.

*Sorry, spelling things right is one of the few things not covered under the Guarantee.

I'd give my right arm for a guarantee like this, although I'm glad I don't have to.

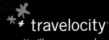

travelocity
You'll never roam alone.

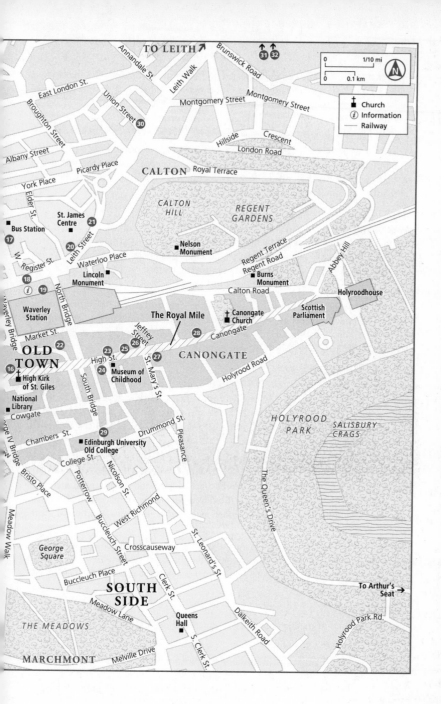

TO LEITH ↗

Brunswick Road

↑ ↑ **31** **32**

0 — 1/10 mi
0 — 0.1 km

✝ Church
ⓘ Information
— Railway

Annandale St.

Leith Walk

East London St.

Union Street

30

Montgomery Street   Montgomery Street

Broughton Street

Hillside

Crescent

London Road

Albany Street

Picardy Place

CALTON   Royal Terrace

York Place

**CALTON
HILL**

**REGENT
GARDENS**

Elder St.

St. James
Centre   **21**

■ **Bus Station**

17

■ **Nelson
Monument**

W. Register St.

Waterloo Place

20

Leith Street

18

Lincoln
Monument

Regent Terrace

Regent Road

Abbey Hill

Holyroodhouse

ⓘ **19**

North Bridge

■ **Burns
Monument**

Calton Road

Waverley
Station

Waverley Bridge

Market St.

The Royal Mile

Jeffrey Street

✝ Canongate
Church

**Scottish
Parliament**

**OLD
TOWN**

22

23 **25**

26

28

Canongate

CANONGATE

16

High St.

27

✝ **High Kirk
of St. Giles**

24   **Museum of
Childhood**

St. Mary's St.

Holyrood Road

**National
Library**

South Bridge

Cowgate

**HOLYROOD
PARK**

**SALISBURY
CRAGS**

George IV Bridge

Chambers St.

29

Drummond St.

Bristo Place

■ **Edinburgh University
Old College**

College St.

Pleasance

Potterrow

Nicolson St.

The Queen's Drive

Meadow Walk

Buccleuch Street

West Richmond

**George
Square**

Crosscauseway

St. Leonard's St.

Buccleuch Place

Clark St.

**SOUTH
SIDE**

Meadow Lane

**To Arthur's
Seat** →

THE MEADOWS

Queens
Hall
■

Dalkeith Road

Holyrood Park Rd.

Melville Drive

S. Clerk St.

MARCHMONT

CLOTHING
FASHION

Corniche   One of the more sophisticated boutiques in Edinburgh; if it's the latest in Scottish fashion, expect to find it here. Racks have included "Anglomania kilts" created by that once controversial lady of clothing design, Vivienne Westwood, as well as fashions by Gautier, Katherine Hamnett, and Yamamoto. Men's clothes are in the neighboring shop. 2 Jeffrey St. (near the Royal Mile). ✆ 0131/556-3707. www.corniche.org.uk.

Cruise   Commonly associated with Glasgow, this home-grown fashion outlet began in Edinburgh's Old Town—not generally considered fertile ground for the avant-garde. There is still a shop off the Royal Mile, but this New Town outlet is the focus for couture. 94 George St. ✆ 0131/226-3524.

MEN

Walker Slater   Well-made and contemporary (if understated) men's clothes, usually made of cotton and dyed in rich, earthy hues rule the roost here. It also carries Mackintosh overcoats and accessories for the smart gentleman about town. 20 Victoria St. (near George IV Bridge). ✆ 0131/220-2636. www.walkerslater.com.

WOMEN

Arkangel   William Street in the city's affluent West End offers a host of boutique shops. This one specializes in labels apparently exclusive not only to the Scottish capital but to all of Scotland. U.K. clothes designers include Clara Collins and Ginka. 4 William St., West End. ✆ 0131/226-4466. www.arkangelfashion.co.uk.

DEPARTMENT STORES

Harvey Nichols   Opening in 2002, the advent of Harvey Nics in Edinburgh was highly celebrated but a tad slow to catch on. Perhaps traditional shoppers were not quite prepared for floors of expensive labels and designers such as Jimmy Choo or Alexander McQueen. But they're learning. 30–34 St. Andrew's Sq. ✆ 0131/524-8388. www.harveynichols.com.

Jenners   Opening in 1838, this shop's neo-Gothic facade is almost as much of a landmark as the Scott Monument just across Princes Street. Although controversially sold in 2005 to House of Fraser, the store's array of local and international merchandise hasn't changed much. The food hall offers a wide array of gift-oriented Scottish products, including heather honey, Dundee marmalade, and a vast selection of shortbreads. 48 Princes St. ✆ 0870/607-2841.

John Lewis   The largest department store in Scotland, this branch of John Lewis is many people's first choice when it comes to shopping for clothes, appliances, furniture, toys, and more. St. James Centre (near Picardy Place at the top of Leith Walk). ✆ 0131/556-9121. www.johnlewis.com.

EDIBLES

See "Picnic Fare," in chapter 6, for a list of select food markets with Scottish specialties.

HATS

Fabhatrix   Keep your head warm and your whole body will stay warm. Well, so goes an old saying. But it is true and given the occasionally gusty weather in Edinburgh, a saying worth keeping in mind. This shop has hundreds of handmade felt hats and caps, many practical as well as attractive, and some downright frivolous but extremely fun. 13 Cowgatehead, Grassmarket. ✆ **0131/225-9222. www.fabhatrix.com.**

KILTS & TARTANS

Anta   Some of the most stylish tartans, especially cool minikilts and silk *earasaids* (oversize scarves) for women, are found at Anta. Woolen blankets and throws are woven from Shetland sheep wool. Crocket's Land, 91–93 West Bow. ✆ **0131/225-4616. www.anta.co.uk.**

Geoffrey (Tailor) Kiltmakers   Its customers have included Sean Connery, Charlton Heston, Dr. Ruth Westheimer, members of Scotland's rugby team, and Mel Gibson (who apparently favors the "Hunting Buchanan" tartan). It stocks 200 of Scotland's best-known clan patterns and is revolutionizing the kilt by creating so-called 21st-Century Kilts in different patterns such as pinstripe. 57–59 High St. ✆ **0131/557-0256. www.geoffreykilts.co.uk.**

Hector Russell   Bespoke—that is made to order—clothes made from tartan can be ordered from this well-known Highland-based kiltmaker, with shop on the Royal Mile and Princes Street. 137–141 High St. ✆ **0131/558-1254. www.hector-russell.com.**

James Pringle Weavers   The Leith mills produce a large variety of wool items, including cashmere sweaters, tartan and tweed ties, travel rugs, tweed hats, and tam o' shanters. In addition, it boasts a clan ancestry center with a database containing more than 50,000 family names. There's an outlet on the Royal Mile, as well. 70–74 Bangor Rd., Leith. ✆ **0131/553-5161.**

KNITS & WOOLENS

Bill Baber   This workshop turns out artfully modernized adaptations of traditional Scottish patterns for both men and women. Expect to find traditional knits spiced up with strands of Caribbean-inspired turquoise or aqua; rugged-looking blazers or sweaters suitable for treks or bike rides through the moors; and tailored jackets a woman might feel comfortable wearing to a glamorous cocktail party. 66 Grassmarket. ✆ **0131/225-3249. www.billbaber.com.**

Edinburgh Woollen Mill Shop   With several outlets in the capital and about 280 throughout the United Kingdom, the Edinburgh Woollen Mill Shop sells practical Scottish woolens, knitwear, skirts, gifts, and travel rugs. 139 Princes St. ✆ **0131/226-3840. www.ewm.co.uk.**

Ragamuffin   The staff here sells what is termed "wearable art," created by some 150 designers from all over the U.K. The apparel here is unique. Well, not exactly: Ragamuffin also has a shop way up north on the Isle of Skye. 276 Canongate, The Royal Mile. ✆ **0131/557-6007. www.ragamuffinonline.co.uk.**

GIFTS

Geraldine's of Edinburgh   Also known as the Doll Hospital, this is Edinburgh's doll and teddy bear factory, with more than 100 on display. Each of the heirloom-quality dolls requires days of labor to create and has a hand-painted porcelain head and sometimes an elaborate coiffure. 133–135 Canongate. ✆ **0131/556-4295. www.dollsand teddies.com.**

Ness Scotland   On the Royal Mile, Ness has two shops filled with knitwear, skirts, t-shirts, and whimsical accessories, scoured from areas around the country from the Orkney Islands to the Borders. You'll find hand-loomed cardigans and tasteful scarves,

Tracing Your Ancestral Roots

If you have a name beginning with Mac (which simply means "son of") or one of the other lowland Scottish names, from Burns to Armstrong, you are probably a descendant of Scotland and may have ties to a clan—a group of kinsmen of common ancestry. Clans and clan societies have their own museums throughout Scotland, and local tourist offices will have details about where to locate them. Bookstores throughout Scotland sell clan histories and maps.

Genealogical records are kept at the **General Register Office,** New Register House, 3 W. Register St. (✆ **0131/334-0380;** www.gro-scotland.gov.uk). It contains hundreds of thousands of microfiche and microfilm documents: details of every birth, marriage, and death in Scotland since 1855. The system is strictly self-service, and it gets crowded in summer. A fee of £10/£17 ($19/$31) for part/full day access is charged. Open Monday to Friday from 9am to 4:30pm. By the end of 2007, a new family history center is due to open (www.scotlandspeoplehub.gov.uk).

The official government source for genealogical data online is at **www. scotlandspeople.gov.uk**. Simply register to make searches of census records dating to 1841, births between 1855 and 1905, as well as wills and testaments filed as far back as 1513. A basic £6 ($11) fee is charged to look at details.

amid much more. In addition to the outlet near the castle, there is another on the High Street. 336 Lawnmarket. ✆ **0131/225-8155.** www.nessbypost.com.

Tartan Gift Shop   Tartan Gift Shop has a chart indicating the place of origin (in Scotland) of family names, accompanied by a bewildering array of hunt and dress tartans for men and women, sold by the yard. There's also a line of lambs wool and cashmere sweaters and all the accessories. 54 High St. ✆ **0131/558-3187.**

JEWELRY

Alistir Wood Tait   This jewelry store has a reputation for Scottish gems and precious metal such as agates, Scottish gold, garnets, and sapphires. Victorian collections include "Scottish Pebble" brooches while contemporary designs include Celtic bangles and Cairngorm handmade pin. 116A Rose St. ✆ **0131/225-4105.** www.alistirtaitgem.co.uk.

Hamilton & Inches   Since 1866, the prestigious Hamilton & Inches has sold gold and silver jewelry, porcelain and silver, and gift items. The company workshop is located above the shop, producing limited production pieces or custom-made jewelry. The watch selection is second only to Bond Street, London, shops. 87 George St. ✆ **0131/225-4898.** www.hamiltonandinches.com.

MUSIC

Avalanche   A bunch of harmless goth kids usually hang out in front of the branch of this excellent indie music CD shop where the steep steps of the Fleshmarket Close meet Cockburn Street. It's best for new releases of Scottish and U.K. bands and sec-ond-hand CDs. Another shop is on West Nicolson Street. 63 Cockburn St. (near the Royal Mile). © 0131/225-3939.

Fopp   DVDs; rock, pop, jazz, and dance CDs; books; and more are found in Fopp's Rose Street branch. Open until 9pm. Another outlet is located on Cockburn Street. 7–15 Rose St. © 0131/220-0310.

Virgin Megastore   Here you'll find one of the biggest selections of DVDs and CDs in Scotland. The shop has traditional and Scottish music, as well as the mainstream offerings. 125 Princes St. © 0131/220-2230. www.virginmegastores.co.uk.

SHOES
Schuh   Schuh (pronounced "shoe") has the latest in footwear, including some yel-low, red, and blue plaid boots made famous by a local rugby team. Expect fierce, funky finds as well as name brands. 6 Frederick St. © 0131/220-0290.

TARTANS
See "Kilts & Tartans," above.

WHISKY
Royal Mile Whiskies   The stock at this rather small shop on the Royal Mile is huge: some 1,000 different Scotch and other nation's whiskies are available. Prices range from around £20 ($37) to £900 ($1,665). Staff know their stuff, so tell them what you prefer (smoky, peaty, sweet, or whatever) and they'll find a bottle to please you. 379 High St. © 0131/622-6255. www.royalmilewhiskies.com.

10

Edinburgh After Dark

Every summer, the Scottish capital becomes the cultural capital of Europe—and the envy of every other tourist board in the U.K.—when it hosts the **Edinburgh Festival,** which encompasses the **Fringe, International Festival, Book Festival, Film Festival,** and **Jazz Festival.** All totaled, they bring in thousands upon thousands of visitors to see hundreds upon hundreds of acts—whether in comedy, dance, drama, music, and more. In August, the Scottish capital becomes a proverbial "city that never sleeps."

While the yearly Festival (www.edinburghfestivals.co.uk) is no doubt the peak of the year, Edinburgh offers a good selection of choices throughout the year when it comes to entertainment and activities after dark: from cinema to the clubs, theater or opera, the ballet, and other diversions, such as a night at the pub.

The most active areas for pubs and clubs are the **Cowgate** and **Grassmarket** in the Old Town and **Broughton Street** in New Town, although the university precincts on the south side of the city are lively, as are the pubs on the waterfront in the port of **Leith.**

The West End is the cradle of theater and music, with the legendary and innovative **Traverse Theatre,** as well as the **Royal Lyceum Theatre** and, for concerts, the classic **Usher Hall.** Nearby, the **Filmhouse** offers the best in independent and art-house cinema. Other venues for drama include the **Playhouse** and **Festival** theaters, while live music of a more contemporary vein takes place at venues such as the **Liquid Room** in Old Town. The folk scene centers on a couple of pubs (Sandy Bell's and the Royal Oak), and for jazz, your best bet is Henry's Jazz Cellar. Many of the city's pubs and bars are open until early hours of the morning during the Festival. Remember, all venues and bars are now nonsmoking.

For a complete rundown of what is happening in Edinburgh, pick up a copy of *The List,* a biweekly magazine available at all major newsstands and book shops. It previews, reviews, and gives the full details of arts events here—and in Glasgow.

1 The Performing Arts

The following venues are organized on the basis of the primary forms of performance—drama, opera, ballet, and such—that they host. But obviously, a stage that offers Shakespeare one week might be the home of Handel on another.

THEATER

Edinburgh Playhouse At the top of Leith Walk, this venue is best known for hosting popular plays or musicals and other mainstream acts when they come to town, whether Miss Saigon or Lord of the Dance. Formerly a cinema, it is, apparently, the largest theater in Great Britain with more than 3,000 seats. 18–22 Greenside Place. © 0131/ 524-3333. www.edinburgh-playhouse.co.uk. Tickets £8–£35 ($15–$65). Bus: 5 or 22.

Kings Theatre   This 1,300-seat late Victorian venue with a domed ceiling and rather Glasgow-style stained glass doors and red-stone frontage will be 100 years old in 2006. Located on the edge of Tollcross, southwest of the castle, it offers a wide repertoire, especially traveling West End productions, productions of the Scottish National Theatre, other classical entertainment, ballet, and opera. During December and January, it is the premier theater for popular pantomime productions in Edinburgh. 2 Leven St. © 0131/529-6000. www.eft.co.uk. Tickets £5–£25 ($9.25–$46) Bus: 11, 15, or 17.

Royal Lyceum Theatre ☆   No doubt, the Lyceum (built 1883) has a most enviable reputation with presentations that range from the most famous works of Shakespeare to new Scottish playwrights. It is home to the leading theater production company in the city, often hiring the best Scottish actors such as Brian Cox, Billy *(Lord of the Rings)* Boyd, and Siobhan Redmond—when they are not preoccupied with Hollywood scripts, that is. Grindlay St. © 0131/248-4848 for the box office, or 0131/238-4800 for general inquiries. www.lyceum.org. Tickets £7–£25 ($13–$46). Bus: 1, 10, 15, or 34.

Theatre Workshop   "Real theatre for real life" is the motto of this Stockbridge-based company highlighting performances by disabled professional actors—the first of its type in Europe. It often stages thought-provoking and political dramas at budget prices. 34 Hamilton Place. © 0131/225-7942. www.theatre-workshop.com. Tickets £3–£10 ($5.50–$19). Bus: 24, 29, or 42.

Traverse Theatre ☆☆   Around the corner from the Royal Lyceum, the Traverse is something of a local legend. Beginning in the 1960s as an experimental theater company that doubled as bohemian social club, it still produces contemporary drama at its height in Scotland—as well as premiering the best of the country's young playwrights. There are two theaters in this custom-made subterranean complex: seating 100 and 250 respectively on the benches. Upstairs the Traverse bar is where to find the hippest dramatists and actors (as well as their courtiers in tow). 10 Cambridge St. © 0131/228-1404. www.traverse.co.uk. Tickets £4–£15 ($7–$28). Bus: 11 or 15.

CLASSICAL MUSIC, BALLET & OPERA

Edinburgh Festival Theatre   This 1,900-seat theater, formerly the Art Deco Empire which dated to the 1920s, was reopened in 1994 after serious renovations in time for the Edinburgh Festival (hence the name). Located on the south side of the city, about a 10-minute walk from the Royal Mile and right near the University of Edinburgh Old Campus, it hosts the national opera and ballet, as well as touring companies and orchestras. 13–29 Nicolson St. © 0131/529-6000 for the box office, or 0131/662-1112 for administration. www.eft.co.uk. Tickets £5–£45 ($9.25–$83). Bus: 5, 7, 8, or 29.

CONCERT HALLS

Queen's Hall   About a mile or so south of the Royal Mile, the Queen's Hall dates to the 1820s and began life as the Hope Park Chapel but was altered in the 1970s (coinciding with Queen Elizabeth's silver jubilee) to accommodate concerts. Primarily a venue for classical works, it is busy during Edinburgh's Jazz and International festivals from late July through August. Occasionally it also hosts high-brow and brainy rock acts, such as Flaming Lips or John Cale. Clerk St. © 0131/668-2019. www.thequeens hall.net. Bus: 5, 7, 8, or 29.

Ross Theatre   The city council-managed band shell towards the western end of Princes Street Gardens, in the shadow of the castle, is open during the summer for

Edinburgh After Dark

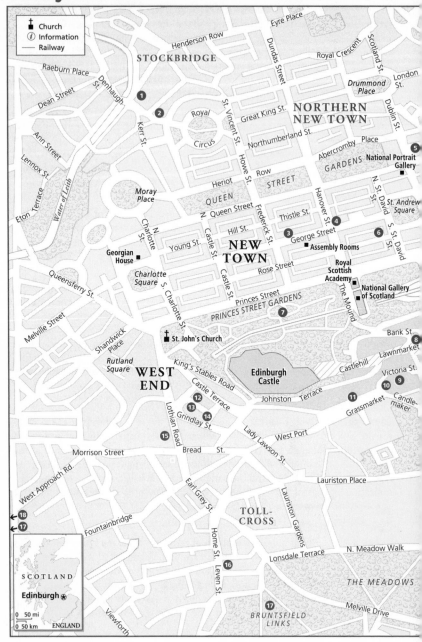

Church
(i) **Information**
— **Railway**

STOCKBRIDGE

Eyre Place

Henderson Row

Dundas Street

Royal Crescent

Scotland St.

Raeburn Place

Denhaugh St.

Dean Street

Royal/

Circus

Great King St.

Northumberland St.

Drummond
Place

London
St.

NORTHERN
NEW TOWN

Dublin St.

Ann Street

Kerr St.

GARDENS

Abercromby Place

National Portrait
Gallery

Lennox St.

Eton Terrace

Water of Leith

Moray
Place

Heriot

Howe St.

Row

STREET

N. St. David St.

St. Andrew
Square

QUEEN

N. Charlotte St.

N. Queen Street

Frederick St.

Thistle St.

Hanover St.

St. David St.

Georgian
House

Young St.

Castle St.

Hill St.

NEW
TOWN

George Street

Assembly Rooms

Royal
Scottish
Academy

National Gallery
of Scotland

Queensferry St.

Charlotte
Square

S. Charlotte St.

Castle St.

Rose Street

The Mound

Melville Street

Princes Street

PRINCES STREET GARDENS

Bank St.

Shandwick
Place

St. John's Church

King's Stables Road

Edinburgh
Castle

Castlehill

Lawnmarket

Victoria St.

Rutland
Square

WEST
END

Castle Terrace

Johnston   Terrace

Grassmarket

Candle-
maker

Lothian Road

Grindlay St.

West Port

Lady Lawson St.

Morrison Street

Bread   St.

West Approach Rd.

Earl Grey St.

Lauriston Place

Fountainbridge

TOLL-
CROSS

Lauriston Gardens

N. Meadow Walk

Home St.

Leven St.

Lonsdale Terrace

THE MEADOWS

BRUNTSFIELD
LINKS

Melville Drive

SCOTLAND

Edinburgh ✪

0   50 mi
0   50 km   ENGLAND

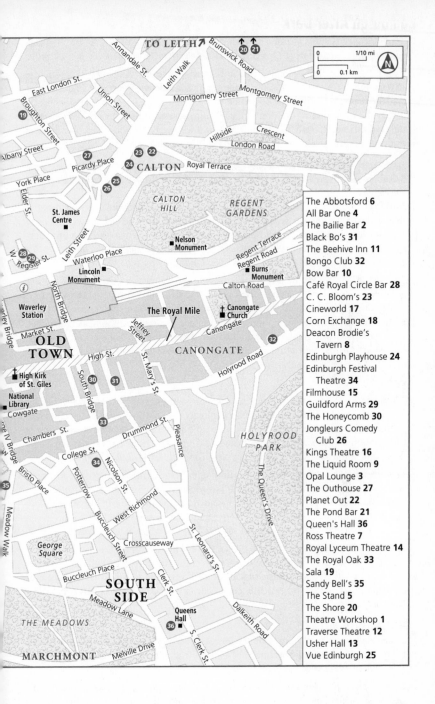

TO LEITH↗   Brunswick Road   ↑↑ 20 21

Annandale St.

East London St.
Union Street
Leith Walk

19 Broughton Street

Montgomery Street   Montgomery Street   Montgomery Street

Hillside   Crescent
London Road

Albany Street

27   Picardy Place

York Place

24 CALTON   Royal Terrace

26   25

Elder St.
St. James Centre ■

CALTON HILL

REGENT GARDENS

W 28 29 Register St.

Leith Street

Waterloo Place

Nelson Monument ■

North Bridge

Lincoln Monument ■

Burns Monument ■

Regent Terrace
Regent Road

Calton Road

ⓘ

Waverley Station

y Bridge   Market St.

OLD TOWN

The Royal Mile

Jeffrey Street

St. Mary's St.

† Canongate Church

Canongate

CANONGATE

32

High St.

■ High Kirk of St. Giles

South Bridge

30   31

Holyrood Road

National Library
Cowgate

33

Chambers St.

Drummond St.

Pleasance

HOLYROOD PARK

e IV Bridge

College St.

34

Nicolson St.

Bristo Place

35

Potterrow

West Richmond

The Queen's Drive

George Square

Buccleuch Street

Crosscauseway

SOUTH SIDE

Meadow Walk

Buccleuch Place

Clerk St.

Meadow Lane

Queens Hall

36 ■

St. Leonard's St.

Dalkeith Road

THE MEADOWS

MARCHMONT

Melville Drive

S. Clerk St.

0   1/10 mi
0   0.1 km   N

The Abbotsford **6**
All Bar One **4**
The Bailie Bar **2**
Black Bo's **31**
The Beehive Inn **11**
Bongo Club **32**
Bow Bar **10**
Café Royal Circle Bar **28**
C. C. Bloom's **23**
Cineworld **17**
Corn Exchange **18**
Deacon Brodie's
  Tavern **8**
Edinburgh Playhouse **24**
Edinburgh Festival
  Theatre **34**
Filmhouse **15**
Guildford Arms **29**
The Honeycomb **30**
Jongleurs Comedy
  Club **26**
Kings Theatre **16**
The Liquid Room **9**
Opal Lounge **3**
The Outhouse **27**
Planet Out **22**
The Pond Bar **21**
Queen's Hall **36**
Ross Theatre **7**
Royal Lyceum Theatre **14**
The Royal Oak **33**
Sala **19**
Sandy Bell's **35**
The Stand **5**
The Shore **20**
Theatre Workshop **1**
Traverse Theatre **12**
Usher Hall **13**
Vue Edinburgh **25**

outdoor concerts and sometime Scottish country-dancing dos, usually in the long, languid evenings. West Princes St. Gardens. ⓒ **0131/220-4351**. www.edinburgh.gov.uk. Bus: 3, 4, or 25.

Usher Hall ⊛   Built—thanks to the bequest of distiller Andrew Usher—in the 1890s, this Beaux Arts building is Edinburgh's equivalent of Carnegie Hall. During the International Festival, the horseshoe-shaped auditorium hosts such classic ensembles as the Cleveland or London Philharmonic orchestras. But it is not only a venue for classical music, with top touring jazz, world music, and pop acts playing here through the year. Lothian Rd. ⓒ **0131/228-1155**. www.usherhall.co.uk. Bus: 1, 10, 15, or 34.

2 The Club & Music Scene

COMEDY

Jongleurs Comedy Club   A corporate-owned entity from down south, with more than a dozen venues across the U.K., Jongleurs came to Scotland a few years back dragging along its own cadre of house funny men (and women) as well as some touring comedians from overseas. Omni Centre, Greenside Place (top of Leith Walk). ⓒ **0870/787-0707**. www.jongleurs.com. Tickets £4–£15 ($7.50–$28). Bus: 7 or 22.

The Stand ⊛   Given the importance today of the Edinburgh Festival Fringe, where good notices can launch a comedian's career, the stand-up is, umm, taken very seriously in the Scottish capital. The Stand, just down the hill from St. Andrew's Square, is the premier, purpose-built local venue. Big acts are reserved for weekend nights, while local talent tries its jokes and tales during the week. On Sunday you can combine yucks for free with brunch. 5 York Place. ⓒ **0131/558-7272**. www.thestand.co.uk. Tickets £1–£10 ($1.85–$19). Bus: 8 or 17.

FOLK

Although internationally touring folkies—performers such as Americans Gillian Welsh or Nanci Griffith are surprisingly big in Scotland—usually get booked into one of the music halls, the day-to-day folk scene in Edinburgh takes place in unassuming public houses. *Ceilidhs*—or Scottish country dance—are hosted at places such as the **Assembly Rooms** on George Street in New Town (ⓒ **0131/220-4349**).

The Royal Oak   Open most nights until 2am (4am during the festival), this pub, where Old Town meets the Southside, is just a few minutes walk from the Royal Mile. The Royal Oak, with ground floor and basement bars, is the home of live Scottish folk music. On Sunday from 8:30pm, various guests play at the "Wee Folk Club." 1 Infirmary St. ⓒ **0131/557-2976**. www.royal-oak-folk.com. Tickets £3 ($5.50). Bus: 3, 5, 8, or 29.

Sandy Bell's   Surprisingly, when there is not any live folk or traditional music being played here—as there is virtually every night from about 9pm and all day Saturday and Sunday—there is no music playing at all. This small pub near the Museum of Scotland is a landmark for Scottish and Gaelic culture. 25 Forrest Rd. ⓒ **0131/225-2751**. Bus: 2 or 42.

ROCK, POP & JAZZ

Usher Hall (see above) hosts some major rock and pop acts and, although not listed below, the **Murrayfield Stadium,** the national rugby stadium, hosts the biggest of acts—whether REM or the Rolling Stones.

Corn Exchange   A bit of a haul from the city center, this venue was meant to compete with the likes of Glasgow's infamous Barrowland ballroom, where touring groups

(Tips) Late-Night Eats

Okay, it's Friday or Saturday night. You've been out to a play, the pub, or dance club, and now you're utterly starving, but it's somewhere between 11pm and 2am. You're not exactly sure because your watch seems to be keeping Australian time at the moment. Food will help. If you're in the West End, Lothian Road is your best bet. Try **Lazio** (95 Lothian Rd.; ✆ **0131/229-7788**) for a bit of pizza or pasta. It is open until midnight during the week and until 2am on Friday and Saturday nights (that is Sat and Sun mornings).

In Old Town, another Italian eatery caters to night owls: **Gordon's Trattoria** on the High Street (✆ **0131/225-7992**) is open until 3am at the weekend. For something a bit more modern and trendy, **Favorit** is an NYC-style diner on Teviot Place (✆ **0131/220-6880**) that stays open until 3am.

---

absolutely love to appear. No comparison, really, but not a bad medium- to small-size hall (3,000 capacity) to see rock and pop performers (Radiohead or Justin Timberlake) and acts with more cultlike followings, such as the Raconteurs, Massive Attack, or the Streets. 11 New Market Rd. ✆ 0131/477-3500. www.ece.uk.com. Bus: 4 or 28. Suburban train: Slateford.

The Liquid Room With space for less than 1,000, this is Edinburgh's best venue for seeing the sweat off the brows of groups. Mostly booked by local bands, such as Mull Historical Society, and visiting indie acts, such as the Dandy Warhols. It is also a busy dance club when not hosting bands. 9c Victoria St. ✆ 0131/225-2564. www.liquid room.com. Bus: 35.

DANCE CLUBS

Clubbing is not quite as huge as it was in the 1980s and 1990s, but it probably draws more people than the folk, jazz, and classical music scene combined. Here is just a sampling of what is typically going on in the clubs around Edinburgh.

Bongo Club Offering a varied music policy throughout the week—funk, dub, and experimental—this venue has more reasonably priced drinks than many. Open daily 10pm to 3am. Moray House, 37 Holyrood Rd. ✆ 0131/558-7604. www.thebongoclub.co.uk. Cover up to £8 ($15). Bus: 35.

The Honeycomb Techno and electro, drum and bass, funk, and house. This is a stylish club off the Cowgate that also books some of the big-name DJs in the U.K., such as crossover celebrity Goldie. 15–17 Niddry St. ✆ 0131/530-5540. Cover up to £15 ($28). Bus: 35.

Po Na Na This is the Edinburgh branch of a successful chain of clubs in Britain. The theme is a Moroccan casbah with decor to match thanks to wall mosaics, brass lanterns, and artifacts shipped in from Marrakech. The dance mix is hip-hop and funk or disco and sounds of the '80s. Open daily to 3am. 43B Frederick St. ✆ 0131/226-2224. www.ponana.co.uk. Cover up to £5 ($9). Bus: 80.

3 Pubs & Bars

NEW TOWN

The Abbotsford Near the eastern end of Rose Street, just a short walk from Waverley Station, Abbotsford bartenders have been pouring pints since around 1900. The gaslight era is virtually still alive here, thanks to the preservation of dark paneling and ornate plaster ceiling. The ales on tap change about once a week, and there is a good selection of single malt whiskies, too. Drinks are served Monday through Saturday from 11am to 11pm. Platters of food are dispensed from the bar Monday through Saturday from noon to 3pm and 5:30 to 10pm. 3 Rose St. (C) **0131/225-5276.** Bus: 3, 28, or 45.

All Bar One   We resist the urge to promote characterless chain pubs, but the All Bar One operation is a well-run business, and the smart bar in New Town (a second outlet is off Lothian Rd.) offers a good selection of wines by the glass. Drinks are served Monday to Thursday from 11:30am to midnight; Friday and Saturday from 11:30am to 1am; and Sunday from 12:30 to 11pm. Food is available daily from opening until 9 or 10pm. 29 George St. (C) **0131/226-9971.** Bus: 24, 28, or 45.

The Bailie Bar   The Bailie is at the heart of the village of Stockbridge and feels as if it could substitute as a public meeting hall for the neighborhood. Newspapers are stacked on the counter at the front door of this sub-ground-level, traditional pub (and the day's news is posted in the men's restroom, as well). Often there is plenty of banter between the regulars and the staff, and no music ever drowns out the conversation here. A bit of live folk is often played on Sunday evenings, and a dining room is adjacent to the main lounge with its island bar. Drinks are served Monday to Thursday from 11am to midnight, Friday and Saturday from 11am to 1am, and Sunday from 12:30pm to 11pm. Food is available Monday to Thursday 11am to 10pm, Friday and Saturday from 11am to 5pm, and Sunday from 12:30 to 5pm. 2 St. Stephen St., Stockbridge. (C) **0131/225-4673.** Bus: 24, 29, or 42.

Cafe Royal Circle Bar   Another well-preserved, Victorian-era pub, the Cafe Royal was nearly demolished in the late 1960s. Thank goodness the wrecking ball wasn't used. Spacious booths combine with plenty of room around the island bar to create a comfortable and vaguely stylish place to drink. Hours for the bar are Monday through Wednesday from 11am to 11pm, Thursday from 11am to midnight, Friday and Saturday from 11am to 1am, and Sunday from 12:30 to 11pm. Above-average food from the same kitchen as the neighboring oyster bar/restaurant is served daily until about 1pm. 17 W. Register St. (C) **0131/556-1884.** Bus: 8 or 17.

Guildford Arms   This pub dates to the late 19th century, designed by architect Robert Macfarlane Cameron. Through the revolving door, you will find seven arched windows with etched glass and exquisite cornices. It's reasonably large and bustling, with a good deal of character. Separate dining facilities are upstairs on the mezzanine in the **Gallery** restaurant. The pub is open Monday through Thursday from 11am to 11pm, Friday and Saturday from 11am to midnight, and Sunday from 12:30 to 11pm. 1–5 W. Register St. (C) **0131/556-4312.** www.guildfordarms.com. Bus: 8 or 17.

Opal Lounge   If you want a sense of the so-called "style bar," then this is an excellent example of the genre. After opening in 2001, the Opal became the haunt of Prince William, when the handsome heir to the British throne attended St. Andrew's University. Several other stylish bars have popped up in its wake on trendy George Street, such as **Candy Bar, Le Monde,** and **Tigerlily.** The Opal draws a predominantly young, well-dressed, and affluent crowd, combining a long list of cocktails with a cavernous underground space that has several compartments around a central room, which eventually becomes the dance floor. Drinks are served from noon to 3am daily; food of an Asian-fusion nature is served from noon to 10pm daily. 51a George St. (C) **0131/226-2275.** www.opallounge.co.uk. Bus: 24, 29, or 42.

The Outhouse   Broughton Street has a mix of traditional places (such as Mathers) and modern bars (such as Baroque), keeping it one of the most lively streets to drink in Edinburgh, and a good road for a compact pub-crawl. The Outhouse, just down a lane off the street, is one of the more contemporary outfits, recently renovated with rich brown hues. During good spells of weather, a beer garden out back offers an excellent open-air retreat, and some outdoor heaters help take the chill off the night. Drinks are served daily from 11am to 1am. 12a Broughton St. Lane. ✆ **0131/557-6688.** Bus: 8 or 17.

OLD TOWN

The Beehive Inn   The Grassmarket is chock-a-block with bars, and this one's hardly exceptional, but there is plenty of space in three different rooms and, unlike so many others along the drag, the Beehive isn't trying to flog any dubious historic connections on a gullible public. (If that's what you're after, however, visit the White Hart Inn, where Burns stayed.) The literary pub tours of Edinburgh begin at the Beehive, which has a beer garden in the back as well as street-side seating. Drinks are served Monday to Sunday from 11am to 1am. Food is served until about 9pm. 18–20 Grass-market. ✆ **0131/225-7171.** Bus: 2.

Black Bo's   A stone's throw from the Royal Mile, this compact bar is slightly unconventional: It is neither traditional pub nor a particularly trendy, stylish place. Many will find its dark walls and mix-and-match furniture downright plain, but it does have a rather unforced hipness. And, due to its proximity to Blackfriars Street's hostels, Black Bo's often has chatty groups of college-age foreigners enjoying a pint or two. DJs play from Wednesday to Saturday; downstairs there is a pool room with jukebox, and next door is a mostly vegetarian restaurant—although no food is served in the bar itself. Drinks are served daily from 5pm to 1am. 57 Blackfriars St. ✆ **0131/557-6136.** Bus: 35.

Bow Bar   Below Edinburgh Castle near the Grassmarket, the compact Bow Bar is a rather classic Edinburgh pub, which appears little changed by time or tampered with by foolish trends. Surprise: it's only a few more than a dozen years old. Never mind. The pub looks the part and features some eight cask-conditioned ales, which change regularly. The gantry stocks some 140 single malt whiskies, as well. Food is limited to meat pies and toasties, served until they run out. Big groups will have trouble squeezing in and aren't generally encouraged. Open Monday through Saturday from noon to 11:30pm and Sunday from 12:30 to 11pm. 80 W. Bow. ✆ **0131/226-7667.** Bus: 2 or 35.

Deacon Brodie's Tavern   Deacon Brodie's Tavern is primarily populated by tourists wandering the Royal Mile and by members of the legal fraternity who come over from the nearby courts. Its name, of course, perpetuates the memory of William Brodie, good citizen by day and nasty robber by night: A real-life character of the 18th century, he may have inspired Robert Louis Stevenson's fictional Dr. Jekyll and Mr. Hyde. Certainly this traditionally styled pub would like you to think so. Open Sunday through Thursday from 10am to midnight and Friday and Saturday from 10am to 1am. Food is served in the bar from 10am to 10pm; in the restaurant upstairs, from noon to 10pm. 435 Lawnmarket. ✆ **0131/225-6531.** Bus: 35.

LEITH

The Pond Bar   A bit off the beaten track in Leith, between Salamander Street and the Edinburgh Dock, the Pond has been described as a transplanted Amsterdam brown bar. The name refers to the "water feature" in the ramshackle patio area in the rear. The decor of the pub inside is eclectic—as if furnished by the purchase of a lot in a blind auction. The highlights of the drinks selection are draft and bottled European lagers. No food is served. Drinks available Monday to Thursday 4pm to 1am, Friday and Saturday 2pm to 1am, and Sunday 12:30pm to 1am. 2–4 Bath Rd. (✆) **0131/467-3825.** Bus: 12.

The Shore 🕿🕿   Looking out on the oldest docks in Leith, this pub fits seamlessly into Leith's seaside port ambience, without resorting to a lot of the usual decorations of cork and netting. The place is small, but on nice days they put a few seats out front to soak in the afternoon sun. On 3 nights of the week, you'll find live folk and jazz music. Drinks are served Monday to Saturday from 11am to midnight and Sunday from 12:30pm to midnight. Food is served both in the bar and the adjoining dining room (p. 79). Monday to Friday from noon to 2:30pm and 6:30 to 10pm; Saturday and Sunday from 12:30 to 3pm and 6:30 to 10pm. 3–4 The Shore. (✆) **0131/553-5080.** www.theshore.biz. Bus: 16 or 36.

4 Gay & Lesbian Edinburgh

The heart of the gay community is the area northwest of **Calton Hill,** incorporating the top of **Leith Walk** around the Playhouse Theatre and **Broughton Street,** though it is hardly a district such as Manhattan's Christopher Street or San Francisco's Castro.

C. C. Bloom's   This club, apparently named after Bette Midler's character in *Beaches,* is one of Edinburgh's long-running and enduringly popular gay night spots. Given that there is no cover charge, the place is usually packed. The dancing is to a wide range of music. Open Monday to Sunday from 10:30pm to 3am. Next door, the glitzy **Habana,** 22 Greenside Place (✆) **0131/556-4349**), is a bar that draws a mixed gay crowd daily from noon to 1am. 23–24 Greenside Place. (✆) **0131/556-9331.** Bus: 7 or 22.

Planet Out   This bright bar draws a mixed crowd, attracting a slightly higher percentage of lesbians than most of its nearby competitors. It manages to combine a good, relaxed daytime trade—sort of a neighborhood pub—with a heady, hedonistic, late-night vibe after dark with popular local DJs like Trendy Wendy offering preclub warm-ups. Open Monday through Friday from 4pm to 1am and Saturday and Sunday from 2pm to 1am. 6 Baxters Place. (✆) **0131/524-0061.** Bus: 7 or 22.

Sala   Along with the nearby Blue Moon Cafe, this cafe bar (formerly known as Nexus) is the focus of gay cultural life on Broughton Street. It is also linked to the Lesbian, Gay, and Bisexual Centre, which is a useful resource for residents and visitors alike. Sala is open Tuesday to Thursday from 4pm to 11pm, Friday and Saturday from 4pm to midnight, and Sunday from 11am to midnight. 60 Broughton St. (✆) **0131/478-7069.** Bus: 8 or 17.

5 Cinema

Cineworld   Formerly UGC Cinemas, this chain of multiplex cinemas across the U.K. combines big releases and Hollywood blockbusters with art house and some foreign films, as well. Fountainpark, 130 Dundee St. (✆) **0871/200-2000.** www.ugccinemas.co.uk. Tickets £2.95–£5.50 ($5.50–$10). Bus: 34 or 38.

Filmhouse ⋒⋒   The capital's most important cinema, the Filmhouse is the focus of the Edinburgh Film Festival—one of the oldest annual film festivals in the world. The movies here are foreign and art house, classic and experimental, documentary and shorts. Plus, the Filmhouse hosts discussions and lectures with directors. The cafe bar remains open late and serves drinks and light meals. This is a must stop for any visiting film buff. 88 Lothian Rd. ⓒ 0131/228-2688. www.filmhousecinema.com. Tickets £1.20–£5.50 ($2–$10) Bus: 10, 22, or 30.

Vue Edinburgh   The big glass-fronted multiplex below Calton Hill at the roundabout near the top of Leith Walk is the most recent addition to the cinema scene, quickly changing its original moniker of Warner Village to Vue. It offers first-run, big commercial releases. Omni Centre, Greenside Place. ⓒ 0871/224-0240. www.myvue.com. Tickets £3.30–£5.60 ($6–$10). Bus: 7 or 22.

11

Side Trips from Edinburgh

Although Edinburgh has a full complement of attractions and plenty of activities visitors, there are also some worthwhile side trips you can take into the surrounding countryside. Whether in the Lothians and further south towards the Borders—or north across the Firth of Forth into the Kingdom of Fife—many attractions are no more than an hour's drive from the city. The closest regions are West and East Lothian, on either side of the city. The highlights include the impressive ruins of **Linlithgow Palace,** a favorite of the Stuart dynasty; 18th-century **Hopetoun House;** or the seaside town of **North Berwick,** with its views of Bass Rock. South in the Borders, the historic **Melrose Abbey** and **Abbotsford,** Sir Walter Scott's majestic home, beckon day-trippers.

One of the best excursions from the Scottish capital is north to Fife and places such as the golfing mecca of **St. Andrews,** with the oldest university in Scotland. There's also the ancient town and one-time capital of **Dunfermline.** It can be visited in a day, which will give you plenty of time to see its historic abbey as well as the Andrew Carnegie Birthplace Museum.

1 Linlithgow & West Lothian

In 1542, Mary Queen of Scots was born in Linlithgow in West Lothian, some 26km (16 miles) west of Edinburgh. Trains frequently depart from Edinburgh Waverley Station, and the 20-minute ride to the ancient royal burgh costs £6.30 ($12) for a standard round-trip ticket, although it's cheaper to travel off-peak. If you're driving from Edinburgh, follow the M8 toward Glasgow, taking exit 2 on to the M9, following the signs to Linlithgow.

Linlithgow Palace ⭐   Birthplace of Mary Queen of Scots, this was a favorite residence of Scottish royalty, and it is now one of the Scotland's most poignant ruins, set on the shores of Linlithgow Loch. Enough of the royal rooms are still intact so that visitors can get an idea of how grand the palace once was. It is a landmark bit of architecture in the country—the first building to be called a palace—and a romantic touchstone of Scottish history and lore. The English king Edward I occupied the tower in the 14th century, but Scots who had hidden in a load of hay retook it in 1313. Most of the structure was built by Scotland's King James I from 1425 to 1437. In 1513, Queen Margaret (a Tudor by birth) waited in vain here for husband James IV to return from the battle of Flodden. When their son, James V, also born here, wed Mary of Guise, the palace fountain ran with wine. In 1746, fire gutted the building when government troops who routed Bonnie Prince Charlie at Culloden were barracked in Linlithgow. Last admission 45 minutes before closing.

Linlithgow. ☎ **01506/842-896.** www.historic-scotland.gov.uk. Admission £4.50 ($8.40) adults, £3.50 ($6.50) seniors, £2 ($3.70) children. Apr–Sept daily 9:30am–6:30pm; Oct–Mar 9:30am–4:30pm.

Side Trips From Edinburgh

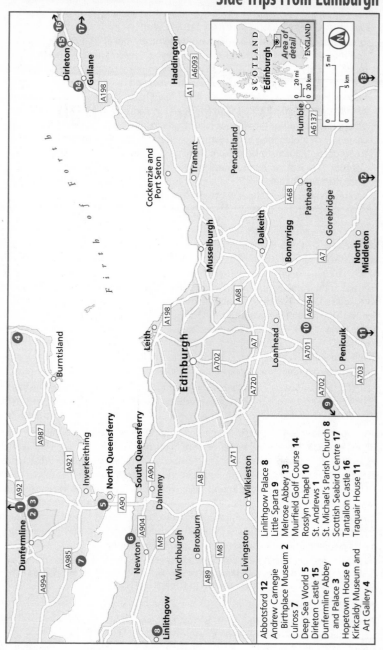

SCOTLAND

Edinburgh

Area of detail

ENGLAND

5 mi
20 km

5 km

Dirleton

Gullane

A198

Haddington

A6093

A1

Humbie

A6137

Pencaitland

Tranent

Cockenzie and
Port Seton

Dalkeith

Pathead

A68

Gorebridge

Bonnyrigg

A7

North
Middleton

F i r t h   o f   F o r t h

Musselburgh

A68

A198

Leith

A7

Loanhead

A6094

Penicuik

Edinburgh

A702

A720

A701

A703

A702

Burntisland

A987

Inverkeithing

North Queensferry

South Queensferry

Dalmeny

A90

A8

Wilkieston

A71

A921

A90

Newton

A904

M9

Broxburn

M8

Livingston

Winchburgh

A89

Dunfermline

A92

A985

A994

Linlithgow

Abbotsford **12**	Linlithgow Palace **8**
Andrew Carnegie	Little Sparta **9**
Birthplace Museum **2**	Melrose Abbey **13**
Culross **7**	Muirfield Golf Course **14**
Deep Sea World **5**	Rosslyn Chapel **10**
Dirleton Castle **15**	St. Andrews **1**
Dunfermline Abbey	St. Michael's Parish Church **8**
and Palace **3**	Scottish Seabird Centre **17**
Hopetown House **6**	Tantallon Castle **16**
Kirkcaldy Museum and	Traquair House **11**
Art Gallery **4**	

135

Rosslyn Chapel: The *Da Vinci Code* Effect

In no small thanks to the Dan Brown's blockbuster novel, *The Da Vinci Code*, and the Hollywood film, the elaborately carved Rosslyn Chapel south of Edinburgh is firmly on the trail of those who seek to retrace the historic and mythical path of the Knights Templar. Visitor numbers doubled in the run-up to the release of the movie, part of which was filmed here. The chapel was founded in 1446 by Sir William St. Clair and has been long noted for its architectural and design idiosyncrasies (though not all of those mentioned in Brown's tome). The chapel, undergoing long-term restoration works, is open to the public Monday to Saturday 9:30am to 6pm from April to September; 9:30am to 5pm from October to March; and on Sundays between noon and 4:45pm. Admission is £7 ($13). Rosslyn Chapel is in the village of Roslin, about 10km (6 miles) south of central Edinburgh, off the A701 to Peebles.

St. Michael's Parish Church   Next to Linlithgow Palace stands the medieval kirk of St. Michael, site of worship for many a Scottish monarch after its consecration in 1242. The biggest pre-Reformation parish church in Scotland, it was mostly constructed in the 15th century. In St. Catherine's Aisle, just before the battle of Flodden, King James IV apparently saw an apparition warning him against fighting the English. Perhaps he should have listened. Despite being ravaged by the disciples of John Knox (who chided followers for their "excesses") and transformed into a stable by Cromwell's forces, this remains one of Scotland's best examples of a parish church. While providing a dramatic focal point on the landscape, the aluminum spears projecting from the tower were added in the 1960s.

Adjacent to Linlithgow Palace. ℂ **01506/842-188.** www.stmichaelsparish.org.uk. Free admission. May–Sept daily 10:30am–4pm; Oct–Apr Mon–Fri 10:30am–1:30pm. On A706, on the south shore of Linlithgow Loch, 1km (½ mile) from Linlithgow railway station.

Hopetoun House ✦   On the margins of South Queensferry, amid beautifully landscaped grounds, Hopetoun House is one of Scotland's best examples of 18th-century palatial Georgian architecture, featuring design work by Sir William Bruce—and by no less than three members of the architecturally inclined Adam family. You can wander through splendid reception rooms filled with period furniture, Renaissance paintings, statuary, and other artworks. The views of the Firth of Forth are panoramic from the rooftop observation deck. After touring the house, visitors should try to take in the grounds, some 60 hectares (150 acres) of parkland with a walled garden, shorefront trail, and deer park. Last entry is 1 hour before closing.

South Queensferry. ℂ **01313/312-451.** www.hopetounhouse.com. Admission £8 ($15) adults, £7 ($13) seniors, £4.25 ($8) children, £22 ($40) family of 4. Mid-Apr to late Sept daily 11am–5:30pm. 3km (2 miles) from the Forth Rd. Bridge near South Queensferry, 16km (12 miles) from Edinburgh off A904.

WHERE TO DINE

The Boat House ✦ FISH/SEAFOOD   What a vista. This restaurant is down a few steps from the main street of South Queensferry, which means diners are closer to the sea and views of the marvelous Forth rail and suspension road bridges. Typical dishes are innovative but not overcomplicated. They might include grilled herring or monkfish, roasted with rosemary, garlic, and olive oil.

19b High St., South Queensferry. © 01313/315-429. Reservations recommended. Fixed-price lunch £12 ($22); dinner main courses £12–£18 ($22–$33). MC, V. Tues–Sat noon–2:30pm and 5:30–10pm; Sun 12:30–8pm.

Champany Inn SCOTTISH   You'll find some of the best steaks in Britain in this converted mill. The restaurant also serves oysters, salmon, and lobsters, but beef is the main reason why people dine here. Meat is properly hung before butchering, which adds greatly to its flavor and texture. Next to the main dining room is the Chop House, offering somewhat less expensive cuts. The wine list—some 2,000 bins—has won an award for excellence from the magazine, *Wine Spectator.* The inn also has some 16 handsomely furnished overnight rooms.

Champany Corner. © 01506/834-532. www.champany.com. Reservations required. Fixed-price lunch £17 ($31); main courses £18–£33 ($32–$60). AE, DC, MC, V. Mon–Fri 12:30–2pm; Mon–Sat 7–10pm. Main restaurant closed Sun. Take M9 until junction 3, then A904 until you reach the restaurant, 3km (2 miles) northeast of Linlithgow.

Livingston's MODERN SCOTTISH/FRENCH   This slightly hidden restaurant down an alley off the main street of Linlithgow includes a conservatory that overlooks a tidy little garden. On a seasonally changing menu, the saddle of venison is a favorite dish. Seared scallops with black pudding may appear on the menu, or perhaps wild duck breast and duck leg confit. An elegant dessert selection has, in the past, included a chilled soup of strawberries and champagne accompanied by a chocolate mousse. Diners can wash it all down with a selection from the ample wine and whisky lists.

52 High St., Linlithgow. © 01506/846-565. www.livingstons-restaurant.co.uk. Reservations recommended. Fixed-price lunch £20 ($37); fixed-price dinner £34 ($62). MC, V. Tues–Sat noon–2pm and 6–9pm. Closed first 2 weeks in Jan, 1 week in June, and 1 week in Oct.

2 North Berwick & East Lothian

The royal burgh of North Berwick (the "w" is silent) dates to the 14th century. But in more modern Victorian and Edwardian times, it was built to serve as an upmarket holiday resort, drawing visitors to its beaches, harbor, and golf courses where the Firth of Forth meets the North Sea. About 36km (21 miles) east of Edinburgh, the town is on a direct rail line from Edinburgh; the trip takes about 30 minutes. Standard one-way fare is £4.50 ($8.30). Bus service from Edinburgh takes a bit over an hour. An all-day ticket to North Berwick and the region around it costs £5.50 ($10). If you're driving, take the coastal road east from Leith, or use the A1 (marked THE SOUTH and DUNBAR) to the A198 (via Gullane) to North Berwick.

At the year-round **tourist office,** Quality Street (© 01620/892-197), you can get information on boat trips to offshore islands, including **Bass Rock,** a breeding ground inhabited by about 10,000 gannets, the second largest colony in Scotland, as well as puffins and other birds. It's possible to see the rock from the harbor, but the viewing is even better at **Berwick Law,** a volcanic lookout point that rises up behind the town.

Dirleton Castle 🐾   Run by Historic Scotland, the castle dates to the 13th century, with surrounding gardens—for some, the main attraction—that are apparently just as ancient. Reputed to have been completely sacked by Cromwell in 1650, another story holds that the building was only partially destroyed by his army but was further torn down by a local family. After building nearby Archerfield House, the owners desired a romantic ruin on their land, a grand garden feature. Highlights include the imposing gate house, vaulted arcades, and a 16th-century dovecot that resembles a beehive. The grounds include a herbaceous border that Guinness ranks as longest in the world.

Dirleton: Prettiest Village in Scotland?

Dirleton, midway between North Berwick and Gullane, has been cited as the prettiest village in Scotland. It's picture-postcard perfect, not like a real town at all, but one that appears to have been created for a movie set. Because the main road bypasses the village, there is little traffic. Even the railway station is closed: the last train ran through in the mid-1950s. Each cottage looks like it's waiting to be photographed, and home maintenance is, no doubt, high. The biggest news here occurred in the 1940s, when President Roosevelt and Sir Winston Churchill met to plan D-Day landings.

Dirleton ℂ **01620/850-330.** www.historic-scotland.gov.uk. Admission £4 ($7.50) adults, £3 ($5.50) seniors, £1.60 ($3) children. Apr–Sept daily 9:30am–6pm; Oct–Mar 9:30am–4:30pm. 5km (3 miles) west of North Berwick on the A198.

Scottish Seabird Centre *Kids*   From this popular attraction situated on a craggy outcropping in North Berwick, you can watch all the bird action out on Bass Rock, whether gannets and puffins, as well as guillemots on the island of Fidra or colonies of seals thanks to live video links—or in modern parlance: "Big Brother" cameras. The Seabird Centre also has a cafe/bistro and activities geared to the family.

The Harbour, North Berwick. ℂ **01620/890-202.** www.seabird.org. Admission £6.95 ($13) adult, £4.50 ($8.50) seniors, £19 ($35) family of 4. Apr–Oct daily 10am–6pm; Nov–Jan Mon–Fri 10am–4pm, Sat–Sun 10am–5:30pm; Feb–Mar Mon–Fri 10am–5pm, Sat–Sun 10am–5:30pm.

Tantallon Castle   After its construction in the 14th century on a bluff right above the sea, this became the stronghold of the powerful and somewhat trouble-making Douglas family—the Earls of Angus, who tended to side with England in their wars and disputes with Scotland in the 15th and 16th centuries. Both Stuart kings James IV and James V dispatched troops to Tantallon. Like most castles in the region, it endured a fair number of seizes, but the troops of Oliver Cromwell well and truly sacked it in the mid-1600s. Nevertheless, the ruins remain formidable, with a square five-story central tower.

Off the A198 (5km/3 miles east of North Berwick). ℂ **01620/892-727.** www.historic-scotland.gov.uk. Admission £4 ($7.50) adults, £3 ($5.50) seniors, £1.60 ($3) children. Apr–Sept daily 9:30am–6:30pm; Oct–Mar Sun–Wed and Sat 9:30am–4:30pm.

GULLANE & THE MUIRFIELD GOLF COURSE

Lying 8km (5 miles) west of North Berwick, about 28km (16 miles) east of Edinburgh in East Lothian, the pleasant and attractive village of Gullane (pronounced "*gill*-in" by many, "*gull*-an" by others) is another resort with a fine beach and a famous golf course. On the edge of the village, **Gullane Hill** provides a nature reserve and bird sanctuary, where over 100 species of birds have been spotted. Visitors cross a small wood footbridge from the car park to enter the reserve. There's no rail service into Gullane, but the Drem station is only about 4km (2½ miles) away; the train journey there from Edinburgh takes about 25 minutes. Buses for Gullane depart from the Edinburgh bus terminal near St. Andrew's Square (ℂ **0800/232-323** for information). They take about an hour.

Muirfield Golf Course ⛳   Ranked among the world's great golf courses, Muirfield has hosted the Open Championship in Great Britain 15 times. This is the home of the Honorable Company of Edinburgh Golfers—the world's oldest club—which began at the 5-hole Leith Links in Edinburgh and whose records date to 1744 when the first rules of golf were written. Developed on a boggy piece of low-lying land in 1891, Muirfield was originally a 16-hole course designed by the legendary Old Tom Morris. Visitors (with certified handicaps) to Muirfield are welcomed on Tuesday and Thursday only. Greens fees are steep: £145 ($270) for a single round and £180 ($333) for two in 1 day. Tee times go quickly, but there can be availability from mid-October to the end of March if you enquire in the summer.

Duncur Rd., Gullane. © 01620/842-123. Fax 01620/842-977. www.muirfield.org.uk. Visitor tee times 8:30–9:50am. From Edinburgh, take the A1 (marked THE SOUTH and DUNBAR) to the A198 and Gullane.

WHERE TO DINE & STAY

Creel Restaurant MODERN SCOTTISH/SEAFOOD   A two-story stone building near the harbor in Dunbar is home to the Creel restaurant. The casual bistro with modern decor emphasizes locally sourced produce whenever possible, including meat from a North Berwick butcher and cheese from nearby cheesemakers. Expect main courses in the evening such as lamb, chargrilled steak, and specials featuring fresh fish.

25 Lamer St., Dunbar. © 01368/863-279. www.creelrestaurant.co.uk. Reservations recommended. Fixed-price lunch (midweek) £10 ($19); dinner main courses £9–£12 ($17–$22). MC, V. Wed–Sun noon–2:30pm and 6–9:30pm.

Greywalls ⊛ MODERN SCOTTISH/FRENCH   This elegant Edwardian country house hotel was designed in 1901 by one of the most renowned architects of the day, Sir Edwin Lutyens. The grounds were laid out by one of England's most respected gardeners, Gertrude Jekyll. The guest rooms vary in size; some smaller ones are simply decorated, while the more spacious units are furnished with period pieces. The hotel's light, French-style dishes are served in the elegant dining room (which overlooks the Muirfield golf course), and they are almost as appealing to the eye as to the palate; specialties include fresh seafood, such as roast halibut or poached Gressingham duck.

Muirfield, Duncur Rd., Gullane, East Lothian EH31 2EG. © 01620/842-144. Fax 0162/084-2241. www.greywalls. co.uk. Reservations essential. Fixed-price dinner £45 ($83). 23 units. £285 ($527) superior double. Food served

Dunbar: Birthplace of John Muir

"Go to the wild places, and listen to what they have to say. Take time to look at the pattern of veins on a leaf, the perfect flight of a bird. Hear the music of the wind in the pines. Feel the life around you and in you."

—John Muir

The man who "discovered" Yosemite Valley in California, founded the Sierra Club, and was single-handedly responsible for establishing the national park system in the United States was born April 21, 1838, in the humble harbor town of Dunbar about 15km (9 miles) southeast of North Berwick. Ironically, Scotland is well behind when it comes to establishing national parks of its own amid the frequently spectacular countryside. There are two: the Cairngorms and Loch Lomond (with the Trossachs). Muir left the country as a child and only recently have Scots begun to recognize, celebrate—and also to capitalize on—Muir's international stature as an explorer, naturalist, and ground-breaking conservationist. In Dunbar, you can visit his birthplace (126 High St.; © 01368/865-899; www.jmbt.org.uk), which now houses a museum.

> *Tips*   **Guided Minitours from Edinburgh**
>
> Sightseeing tours from Edinburgh can give tourists a wee taste of the often stunning countryside as they whisk visitors on 1-, 2-, and 3-day excursions, whether to Stirling and Loch Lomond (see chapter 19) or further north to Glen Coe and the shores of Loch Ness. **Timberbush Tours** (555 Castlehill; ⓒ **01312/266-066**; www.timberbush-tours.co.uk) use minibuses to take small groups to the Highlands. Prices for a 2-day tour range from £58 ($107) in low season to £63 ($116) at the height of summer, and the prices only cover transportation and guide. **Heart of Scotland Tours** (37 Logie Green Rd.; ⓒ **01315/588-855**; www.heartofscotlandtours.co.uk) offers 1-day minibus tours of different regions, such as Loch Lomond, the Borders, or Fife. They depart from Waterloo Place near Calton Hill at 8am or 9am in the morning, returning to Edinburgh between 6pm and 8pm. Prices range from £27 to £32 ($50–$60). More intrepid adventurers might want to consider a "hop-on, hop-off" hostel bus service offered by **MacBackpackers** (105 High St.; ⓒ **01315/589-900**; www.macbackpackers.com). This bus does a circuit of Scotland stopping at Pitlochry, Inverness, Kyle of Lochalsh, Fort William, Oban, and Glasgow. The basic price is £75 ($139).

Mon–Thurs 7:30–9pm; Fri–Sun 12:30–2pm, 7:30–9pm. Rates include Scottish breakfast. AE, DC, MC, V. Parking available. Closed Oct 15–Apr 15. Follow the signs from A198 about 8km (5 miles) from North Berwick. **Amenities:** Restaurant; bar; putting green; tennis courts; limited room service; babysitting; laundry service garden. *In room:* TV, hair dryer.

La Potinière FRENCH   This rather legendary restaurant that once had a Michelin star closed briefly but found new owners, chefs Keith Marley and Mary Runciman, in 2003. The three-course lunches and four-course dinners offer dishes that are French-inspired, but the selection might also include a Thai-influenced soup, too. The menu is seasonal, and the produce is usually purchased locally, with everything freshly made on the premises.

Main St., Gullane. ⓒ **01620/843-214**. www.la-potiniere.co.uk. Reservations recommended. Fixed-price lunch £19 ($35); fixed-price dinner £37 ($68). MC, V. Wed–Sun 12:30–2pm and 7–9pm.

3 South of the City & the Borders

The romantic ruins and skeletons of Gothic abbeys in the **Borders** region stand as mute reminders of the battles that once raged between England and Scotland. For a long time, the "Border Country" was a no-man's land of plunder and destruction, lying south of the Moorfoot, Pentland, and Lammermuir hill ranges.

The Borders is also the land of Sir Walter Scott, master of romantic adventure, who topped the bestseller lists in the 19th century. And because of its abundant sheep-grazing land, the Borders is home of the cashmere sweater and the tweed suit. And in 2006, the Scottish Executive approved plans to reestablish a railway line between Edinburgh and the Borders.

MELROSE

Rich in history, the town of Melrose, about 60km (37 miles) southeast of Edinburgh, is one of the highlights of the region. It offers one of the most beautiful ruined abbeys in the country, as well as nearby Abbotsford, home of Sir Walter Scott, which is about 3km (2 miles) west. Melrose is on the Southern Upland Way, a trail that snakes across lower Scotland from Portpatrick in the southwest to the North Sea. You can take a hike along the section that runs near Melrose—a delightful and scenic trek. Among sports fans in the U.K., the town is most famous for its annual "Rugby Sevens" tournament, which began 1883.

Visitors may prefer to take the bus to Melrose from Edinburgh. Travel time is at least 90 minutes, departing twice an hour or so. Call © **0870/608-2608** for information. The nearest rail station is miles away in Berwick-upon-Tweed, from where you can catch a bus to Melrose. If you're driving from Edinburgh, you can reach the town by going southeast along the A68 or the more winding A7, which runs past the town.

The tourist office is at Abbey House, Abbey Street (© **01896/822-555**). It's open Monday through Saturday from April to October.

Abbotsford ⌖   Sir Walter Scott's home from 1817 until death, this is the mansion that he built and like his novels it quotes from history, too. Designed in the Scots baronial style, Abbotsford was constructed on land he acquired in 1811. After his literary works, it is considered the author's most enduring monument. Scott was a souvenir hunter, scouring the land for artifacts associated with the historical characters he rendered into fiction. Hence, Abbotsford contains many relics and mementos—whether Rob Roy's sporran or a purse made by Flora Macdonald. One of his other proud possessions is a sword given to the Duke of Montrose by Charles I for his cooperation (some say collaboration). The home itself has an entrance that mimics the porch at Linlithgow palace and a door from Edinburgh's tollbooth. Especially popular is Scott's small study, with writing desk and chair, where he penned some of his most famous works. There are also extensive gardens and grounds to visit, plus the private chapel, added after Scott's death.

B6360, near Galashiels. © **01896/752-043**. www.scottsabbotsford.co.uk. Admission £5 ($9.25) adult, £2.50 ($4.50) child. Late Mar–Oct daily 9:30am–5pm (closed Sun mornings Mar–May and Oct); Nov–Mar group bookings only Mon–Fri. 3km (2 miles) west of Melrose; just off the A6091 (between the A7 and A68) on the B6360.

Melrose Abbey ⌖⌖   These lichen-covered ruins, among the most evocative in Europe, are all that's left of an ecclesiastical community established by Cistercian monks in the 12th century. Though the soaring walls you see follow the lines of the original abbey, they were largely constructed in the 15th century. The Gothic design moved Sir Walter Scott to write in the *Lay of the Last Minstrel,* "If thou would'st view fair Melrose aright, go visit in the pale moonlight." The author was also instrumental in ensuring that the decayed remains were preserved in the 19th century. You can still view its sandstone shell, filled with elongated windows and carved capitals, and the finely decorated masonry. It is believed that, per his wishes, the heart of Robert the Bruce is interred in the abbey.

Abbey St., Melrose. © **01896/822-562**. www.historic-scotland.org.uk. £4.50 ($8.50) adult, £3.50 ($6.50) seniors, £2 ($3.50) children. Apr–Sept daily 9:30am–6:30pm; Oct–Mar daily 9:30am–4:30pm.

Little Sparta ✿ (Finds)   Not highlighted by many guide books, this garden was devised by one of Scotland's most intriguing artists in the 20th and 21st centuries, the late Ian Hamilton Finlay, who died on March 27, 2006. It is a surprisingly lush plot of land, given the harsh terrain of the Pentland Hills all around it. Dotted throughout the garden are stone sculptures (many with Finlay's pithy sayings and poems) created in collaboration with master stonemasons and other artists. Little Sparta has been called the "only original garden" created in Great Britain since World War II.

Stonypath, near Dunsyre, off the A702. ☎ **01899/810-252.** www.littlesparta.co.uk. Admission £10 ($19). Jun–Sept Fri and Sun 2:30–5pm. 32km (20 miles) southwest of Edinburgh

Traquair House ✿✿   Little changed since the beginning of the 18th century and dating in part to the 12th century, this is perhaps Scotland's most romantic house, rich in associations with ancient kings, Mary Queen of Scots and the Jacobite uprisings. The Stuarts of Traquair still live in the great mansion, making it, they say, the oldest continuously inhabited house in Scotland. One of the most poignant exhibits is in the King's Room: an ornately carved oak cradle, in which Mary rocked her infant son, who was to become James VI of Scotland and James I of England. Other treasures

Sir Walter Scott: Inventor of Historical Novels

Today it may be hard to imagine the fame that Walter Scott, novelist and poet, enjoyed as the best-selling author of his day. His works are no longer so widely read, but Scott (1771–1832) was thought to be a master storyteller and today he is considered the inventor of the historical novel. Before his Waverley series was published in 1814, no modern English author had spun such tales from actual events, examining the lives of individuals who played roles—large and small. He created lively characters and realistic pictures of Scottish life in works such as *The Heart of Midlothian.* Scott's name is also linked to the Trossachs, which he used as a setting for his poem "The Lady of the Lake" and his tale of Rob Roy MacGregor, the 18th-century outlaw.

Born into a Borders family who then settled in Edinburgh on August 14, 1771, Scott was permanently lame due to polio he contracted as a child. All his life he was troubled by ill health and later by ailing finances as well. He spent his latter years writing to clear enormous debts incurred when his publishing house and printers collapsed in bankruptcy.

Scott made his country and its scenery fashionable with the English, and he played a key role in bringing George IV to Edinburgh after many years when no British monarch set foot in Scotland. Although Scott became the most prominent literary figure in Edinburgh, his heart lay in the Borders. It was here he built his home and chose to live. Starting with a modest farmhouse, he created Abbotsford, a mansion that became a key tourist destination in the mid-1900s.

In 1831, heavily in debt and suffering from the effects of several strokes, Scott set out on a Mediterranean cruise to recuperate. He returned the following year to Abbotsford, where he died on September 21, 1832. Scott is buried at Dryburgh Abbey, sited in a loop of the Tweed River.

include embroideries, silver, manuscripts, and paintings. Of particular interest is the brewery, still in operation, producing very fine ales. On the grounds are craft workshops—such as wrought ironwork and woodturning—as well as a maze and woodland walks. There are three rather sumptuous overnight rooms, too, at £180 ($330) including full breakfast.

Innerleithen. ✆ **01896/830-323.** www.traquair.co.uk. Admission £6.20 ($12) adults, £5.60 ($10) seniors, £3.30 ($6) children, £18 ($32) family of 5. Apr–May and Sept daily noon–5pm; June–Aug daily 10:30am–5:30pm; Oct daily 11am–4pm. Nov Sat–Sun noon–4pm guided tours only. Closed Dec–Mar. 47km (29 miles) south of Edinburgh.

WHERE TO DINE & STAY

Burt's Hotel SCOTTISH   Within walking distance of Melrose Abbey, this family-run inn was built in 1722 to house a local dignitary. The traditional town house offers a taste of small-town Scotland, although much of the decor is modern, with an airy and restful feel. The restaurant menu offers main courses such baked halibut with crab and pea risotto or pan-seared pheasant with butter bean purée. In addition to the more formal dining room, Burt's serves meals in the bistro/bar with dishes such as king prawn Thai curry, grilled Toulouse sausages, or roast rib of Scotch beef. All guest rooms are well furnished and equipped with shower-only bathrooms. Alternative accommodations are offered across the street at the Townhouse hotel, with double rooms starting at £96 ($177).

Market Sq., Melrose. ✆ **01896/822-285.** Fax 01896/822-870. www.burtshotel.co.uk. Reservations recommended. Fixed-price dinner £32 ($58); bistro main courses £9–£14 ($16–$26). 20 units. £106 ($196) double. Rates include breakfast. AE, DC, MC, V. Free parking. **Amenities:** Restaurant; bar; room service; babysitting; laundry service. *In room:* TV, coffeemaker, hair dryer.

Chapters Bistro SCOTTISH/INTERNATIONAL   Cross the footbridge over the River Tweed to reach this unassuming bistro near Melrose, run by Kevin and Nicki Winsland. The menu ranges from the house stroganoff to scallops St. Jacques, red snapper to venison with juniper berries. Unfortunately, it's only open for dinner 5 nights a week.

Main St. (off the A6091), Gattonside by Melrose. ✆ **01896/823-217.** Main courses £10–£16 ($19–$30). MC, V. Tues–Sat 6:30–10pm.

Halcyon ✿ MODERN SCOTTISH   Stylish and contemporary, in decor and cuisine, Halcyon is a Borders restaurant that has people talking. Local suppliers are responsible for the raw ingredients, which end up in dishes such as rabbit rillottes with a caper, parsley and shallot salad, rump of lamb with aubergine pickle, or dark chocolate brownies. Many of the fruits and vegetables are organic.

39 Eastgate (off the A72), Peebles. ✆ **01721/725-100.** www.halcyonrestaurant.com. Reservations recommended. Main courses dinner £11–£20 ($20–$37). MC, V. Tues–Sat noon–2pm and 6–10pm.

4 North of Edinburgh to Fife

North of the Firth of Forth from Edinburgh, the region of Fife still likes to call itself a "kingdom," a distinction dating to Pictish prehistoric times when Abernethy was Fife's capital. Even today, the Kingdom of Fife evokes romantic episodes and the pageantry of Scottish kings. Indeed some 14 of Scotland's 66 royal burghs lay in this rather self-contained shire on a broad peninsula between the Forth and Tay rivers. The highlight for golfers is St. Andrews, which many consider the most sacred spot of the sport. But the town, named after the country's patron saint, is also of ecclesiastical and scholarly importance. St. Andrews is the site of Scotland's first university, founded in 1413. Closer to Edinburgh, Dunfermline was once the capital of Scotland, and its abbey witnessed the births of royalty and has the burial grounds for several, as well.

ST. ANDREWS: GOLF'S HALLOWED GROUND

The medieval royal burgh of **St. Andrews** in northeast Fife, about 80km (50 miles) from Edinburgh, was once filled with monasteries and ancient buildings, but only a few ruins of its early history survive. Once a revered place of Christian pilgrimage, the historic town by the sea is now best known for golf, which has been played here at least as early as the 1600s, though some believe much earlier. Today, the rules of the sport are reviewed, revised, and clarified in St. Andrews by the Royal and Ancient Golf Club, while its Old Course is perhaps the most famous 18 holes in the world. Golfers consider this town to be hallowed ground.

There is no train station in St. Andrews, but there is a stop some 13km (8 miles) away at the town of Leuchars. The trip from Edinburgh takes about an hour; the fare is £17 ($26) for a standard round-trip (return) ticket. Once at Leuchars, you can take a bus for the 10 minute ride to St. Andrews. Bus service from Edinburgh takes approximately 2 hours, and the same day roundtrip fare is £9 ($17). For information, call ℂ **0870/608-2608.** If you're driving from Edinburgh, head north across the Forth Road Bridge. Take A921 to the junction with A915 and continue northeast until you reach St. Andrews. Less scenic is the A92 north to A914 via Cupar. The tourist information center is at 70 Market St. (ℂ **01334/472-021**). It's open Monday to Saturday all year and on Sunday, too, during the high season.

St. Andrews Cathedral ⊛   Near the Celtic Church of Blessed Mary on the Rock, by the sea at the east end of town, is St. Andrews Cathedral. Once the largest church in Scotland, it was founded in 1161. The cathedral certified the town as the ecclesiastical capital of the country, but the ruins can only suggest its former beauty and importance. There's a collection of early Christian and medieval monuments, as well as artifacts discovered on the cathedral site. Admission allows entry to nearby **St. Andrews Castle,** where the medieval clergy lived.

A91, off Pends Rd. ℂ 01334/472-563. www.historic-scotland.gov.uk. Admission cathedral and castle £6 ($11) adults, £4.50 ($8.50) seniors, £2.70 ($5) children. Apr–Sept daily 9:30am–6:30pm; Oct–Mar daily 9:30am–4:30pm.

University of St. Andrews   This is the oldest university in Scotland and the third oldest in Britain after Oxford and Cambridge. Of its famous students, the most recent graduate was Prince William, heir to the throne after Charles. At term time, you can see packs of students in their characteristic red gowns. The university spreads throughout the town today, but the original site was centered in the districts just west of the Cathedral. The gate tower of St. Salvador College on North Street dates to the 15th century.

St. Andrews, Fife. www.st-andrews.ac.uk.

DUNFERMLINE & ITS ABBEY

The ancient town of Dunfermline, 23km (14 miles) northwest of Edinburgh, was a place of royal residence as early as the 11th century. The last monarch to be born in Scotland, Charles I, came into the world at Dunfermline. However, when Scottish and English crowns were joined three years later in 1603, the royal court departed for London and the burgh's fortunes declined—a process aided by a fire in 1624. Linen manufacturing in the 18th and 19th centuries provided a boost. In America, it's most famous product, however, is Andrew Carnegie, born in a weaver's cottage in 1835.

Hitting the Links

There are five 18-hole courses at St. Andrews (www.standrews.org.uk) and one course with only 9 holes for beginners and children, all owned by a trust and open to the public. They are:

1. **Old Course,** which is where the Open is frequently played and dates to the 15th century.
2. **New Course,** designed by Old Tom Morris in 1895.
3. **Jubilee Course,** opened in 1897 in honor of Queen Victoria.
4. **Eden Course,** opened in 1914.
5. **Strathtyrum Course,** the least testing 18 holes, designed for those with high or no handicaps.
6. **Balgove,** the 9-hole course designed for beginners and hackers. No reservations, just turn up and play (although not at busy times during weekends and holidays).

For the 18-hole courses, except the Old Course, you should try to reserve your tee time at least 1 month in advance—except for play at Jubilee, Eden, or Strathtyrum, which can be reserved 24 hours ahead (if you're lucky). The reservation office is at ℂ **0133/446-6666.** Online bookings for the New Course, Jubilee, Eden, and Strathtyrum can be made by logging on to www.linksnet.co.uk.

The Old Course, which hosted the Open in 2005, is a different kettle of fish: first you need a handicap of 24 for men and 36 for women. You apply in writing 1 year in advance and, even then, there are no guarantees. There is a daily ballot or lottery, which gives out about 50% of the tee times for the following day's play. Apply in person or by telephone before 2pm on the day before play. By post, send applications to Reservations Office, Pilmour House, St. Andrews KY16 9SF, Scotland. Single golfers wishing to play the Old Course should contact the reservations department at reservations@standrews.org.uk.

Greens fees vary from course to course and depending on the time of year. Generally speaking, for the 18-hole courses expect to pay between £16 (Strathtyrum in Mar) and £125 (Old Course in summer) ($40–$230). From November to March, it costs £61 ($112) to play the Old Course, using mats that protect the fairways, and between £12 and £32 ($22–$60) for the other 18-hole courses.

Facilities for golfers in St. Andrews are legion. Virtually every hotel in town provides assistance to golfers. The **Royal and Ancient Golf Club,** founded in 1754, remains more or less rigidly closed as a private-membership men's club, however. It does traditionally open the doors to the public on St. Andrews Day to view the trophy room. This usually falls on November 30.

Culross: Step Back in Time

Thanks largely to the National Trust for Scotland, this town near Dunfermline shows what a Scottish village from the 16th to 18th century was like. With its cobbled streets lined by stout cottages featuring crow-stepped gables, Culross may also have been the birthplace of St. Mungo, who went on to establish the cathedral in Glasgow. James IV made this port on the Firth of Forth a royal burgh in 1588. The National Trust runs a visitor center (© **0138/388-0359;** www. nts.org.uk) that is open daily noon to 5pm from Good Friday to the end of September, which provides access to the town's palace and other sites. Adult admission is £8 ($15).

Dunfermline is on the "Fife Circle" route from Edinburgh to the north, which means twice hourly connections to the Scottish capital on a 30-minute ride. By bus, the trip from Edinburgh takes about 40 minutes. If you're driving from Edinburgh, take A90 west, cross the Forth Road Bridge, and follow the signs north to the center of Dunfermline.

Dunfermline Abbey and Palace   This abbey was constructed on the site of a Celtic church and a priory church built under the auspices of Queen Margaret around 1070. Some 50 years later work began on a new priory, which can be visited as the Romanesque "Medieval Nave" today. Abbey status was bestowed in 1150, and thereafter a string of royalty, beginning with David I, was buried at the abbey, including Robert the Bruce. The newer sections of the abbey church were built in 1818, the pulpit was placed over the tomb and memorial to the Bruce. The remains of the royal palace are adjacent to the abbey. Only the southwest wall remains of this once-regal edifice.

St. Margaret's St., off the M90. © **01383/739-026.** www.historic-scotland.gov.uk. Admission £3 ($5) adults, £2.30 ($4.25) seniors, £1.30 ($2.50) children. Apr–Sept daily 9:30am–6:30pm; Oct–Mar daily 9:30am–4:30pm.

Andrew Carnegie Birthplace Museum   In 1835, American industrialist and philanthropist Andrew Carnegie was born just down the hill from Dunfermline Abbey. This museum is comprised of the 18th-century cottage where he lived as a child and a memorial hall funded by his widow, Louise. Displays tell the story of the weaver's son, who emigrated to the United States and became one of the richest men in the world. A union-busting industrialist, Carnegie nevertheless gave away hundreds of millions of dollars before his death in 1919. Dunfermline received the first of the 2,811 free libraries he provided throughout Britain and America and the town was also bequeathed Pittencrieff Park and Glen. A statue in the park honors Carnegie, who once worked as a bobbin boy in a cotton factory.

Moodie St., Dunfermline. © **01383/723-638.** www.carnegiebirthplace.com. Admission £2 ($3.70) adults, £1 ($1.85) seniors, free for children under 15. Apr–Oct Mon–Sat 11am–5pm, Sun 2–5pm.

KIRKALDY

Kirkcaldy Museum and Art Gallery ⊛ (Finds   The art collection in the second floor galleries here is among the single best gathering of works by Scottish artists. An entire room is devoted to the brightly hued still-life paintings and landscapes by "colourist" S.J. Peploe. There is more by Hornel, Hunter, and Fergusson. Another highlight of the collection is a range of paintings by William McTaggart. In addition, you can compare the abstract beauty of, say, Joan Eardley's "Breaking Wave" to a portrait by Scotland's currently best-selling, if critically panned, contemporary painter, Jack Vettriano. No comparison. This unassuming and humble attraction is arguably the best provincial art museum in Great Britain. What's more, all they request are donations from visitors.

War Memorial Gardens, next to the train station. © 01592/412-860. Free admission. Mon–Sat 10:30 am–5pm; Sun 2–5pm.

NORTH QUEENSFERRY

Deep Sea World *Kids*   In the early 1990s, a group of entrepreneurs sealed the edges of an abandoned rock quarry under the Forth Rail Bridge, filled it with sea water and positioned a 112m (370-ft.) acrylic tunnel on the bottom. Stocked with a menagerie of sea creatures, it is Scotland's most comprehensive aquarium. Now, compared to what you'll find in cities such as Baltimore or San Diego, this may seem amateurish. But from the submerged tunnel, you view kelp forests; sandy flats that shelter bottom-dwelling schools of stingray, turbot, and sole; and murky caves favored by conger eels and small sharks. Curiously, the curvature of the tunnel's thick clear plastic makes everything seem about 30% smaller than it really is. For £145 ($268), you can also arrange a "shark dive," however, and see them full size.

Battery Quarry, North Queensferry. © 01383/411-880. www.deepseaworld.com. Admission £8.55 ($16) adults, £6.30 ($12) children, £29 ($54) family of 4. Mon–Fri 10am–5pm; Sat–Sun 10am–6pm.

WHERE TO DINE & STAY

Keavil House Hotel   This tranquil country hotel in the Best Western chain is set on a dozen acres of forested land and gardens. The guest rooms are generous in size and well appointed, each with a bathroom (some with tubs). Master bedrooms contain four-poster beds. The hotel offers dining in its **Cardoon** Restaurant.

Main St., Crossford. © 01383/736-258. Fax 0138/362-1600. www.keavilhouse.co.uk. 47 units. £115 ($213) double. Rates include full breakfast. AE, DC, MC, V. Free parking. Take A994, 3km (2 miles) west of Dunfermline; the hotel is off the main street at the west end of village. **Amenities:** Restaurant; bar; finest health club in the area with pool, Jacuzzi, sauna, and steam room; room service; babysitting; laundry service. *In room:* TV, coffeemaker, hair dryer.

Ostlers Close *⚜* MODERN SCOTTISH   Fife has a host of good restaurants, and this charming one in a 17th-century building is one of the best. Located in the town of Cupar, west of St. Andrews, Ostlers Close emphasizes fresh and local produce. The daily changing menus can feature dishes such as seared Isle of Mull scallops, roast saddle of venison, or roast filet of Pittenweem cod. Only open for lunch on Saturday, however.

25 Bonnygate, Cupar. © 01334/655-574. Reservations recommended. Main courses £10–£18 ($19–$33). AE, MC, V. Tues–Fri 7–9:30pm; Sat 12:15–1:30pm and 7–9:30pm. Closed 2 weeks mid-May. From St. Andrews, go along A91 for 11km (7 miles) until you reach the village of Cupar.

Peat Inn *⚜* MODERN SCOTTISH/FRENCH   Also in Cupar, the Peat Inn came under new ownership in 2006. Luckily, it was taken over by chef Geoffrey Smeddle, who brought awards and accolades to his previous restaurant, étain, in Glasgow. The building dates to 1760, and refurbishment in 2007 was planned. Meals highlight local, seasonal ingredients in dishes such as seared scallops with fennel purée, roast filet of beef with chanterelle mushrooms, or tayberry and elderflower tart.

Cupar. © 01334/840-206. Fax 01334/840-530. www.thepeatinn.co.uk. Reservations suggested. Main course £16–£20 ($30–37). Tues–Sat 12:30–2pm and 7–9:30pm. 8 units. £165 ($305) suite for 2. Rates include continental breakfast. AE, MC, V. From St. Andrews, go along A91 for 11km (7 miles) until you reach the village of Cupar. **Amenities:** Restaurant; bar; bike rental; limited room service; dry cleaning. *In room:* TV, coffeemaker, iron/ironing board.

Old Course Hotel   The Old Course Hotel overlooks the 17th fairway—the infamous "Road Hole"—of its namesake (to which it has no formal connection). This hotel is world-class and has price tags to match. Spa facilities (for an extra £20/$37 per room) include a pool with waterfall. The eating options encompass the contemporary **Sands** seafood bar and restaurant and fine dining at the **Road Hole Grill,** where gentlemen are encouraged to wear jackets to dinner.

Old Station Rd., St. Andrews. ℭ **01334/474-371.** Fax 01334/477-668. www.oldcoursehotel.co.uk. 144 units. £220 ($407) double. Rates include full breakfast. Children under 12 stay free in parent's room. AE, DC, MC, V. **Amenities:** Restaurant; bar; pool; pro shop; spa; Jacuzzi; steam rooms; salon; room service; massage; babysitting; laundry service;. *In room:* TV, minibar, coffeemaker, hair dryer.

The Seafood Restaurant FISH/SEAFOOD   A second branch for owner Tim Butler and his business partner, chef Craig Millar, who began further down the coast in St. Monans. Here, the location on the seafront is spectacular, and given the restaurant is essentially housed in a glass box, there is no missing the views. Dishes range from crab risotto to pan-seared scallops, with plenty of fancy accompaniments on the side.

The Scores, St. Andrews. ℭ **01334/479-475.** www.theseafoodrestaurant.com. Fixed-price lunch £16 ($30); fixed-price dinner £30 ($55). AE, MC, V. Daily noon–2:30pm and 6–10pm.

12

Getting to Know Glasgow

Glasgow is only about 74km (46 miles) west of Edinburgh, but the contrast between the two cities is noticeable. Glasgow (pronounced "*glaaz*-go" by natives) doesn't offer a fairy-tale setting such as Edinburgh, but compensates with a lively culture, big-city feel, and gregarious locals.

Glasgow's origins are ancient, making Edinburgh seem comparatively young. Archaeologists have uncovered evidence of Roman settlements. In the 6th century, St. Kentigern (or St. Mungo) is believed to have begun a monastery at the site of **Glasgow Cathedral,** a hillside along a *burn* (creek) that feeds into the River Clyde. The site was logical for a settlement, as it was near a convenient point to ford the mighty Clyde before it widens on its way to the sea some 20 miles away. According to some translations, Glasgow, or *glascau*, means "dear green place."

Aside from the Cathedral itself, practically none of the medieval ecclesiastical center (including a university) remains. And much of its historical records (kept at the Cathedral) were swept away and lost during the Reformation.

The city became an economic powerhouse in the 18th century and quickly grew to be Scotland's largest city (as well

as the fourth most populous in the entire U.K.). The boom began in earnest with the tobacco trade to the New World, where Glasgow outpaced rivals such as London or Bristol. The city then became famous worldwide for shipbuilding and docks that produced the *Queen Mary* and other fabled ocean liners. It was the Second City of the Empire. But postindustrial decline gave Glasgow a poor reputation—particularly in contrast to the enduring charms of Edinburgh—and, internationally, it is still struggling to convince those who may have seen the city in the 1970s that it is today a safe, vibrant, and cosmopolitan city.

In the 1980s, the city reversed its fortune, becoming Scotland's contemporary cultural capital and drawing talent from across the U.K., whether in art or rock 'n' roll. Decades of grime were sandblasted away from its monumental Victorian buildings, and one of Europe's best collections of art—the **Burrell**—found a permanent home. In 1990, the city was named European Capital of Culture, thus certifying the changes that occurred.

That said, Glasgow is not a metropolis without flaws. Serious pockets of poverty remain in the city's peripheral housing projects (estates or schemes). A major

Impressions
The town of Glascow [sic], though not so big, nor so rich, yet to all seems a much sweeter and more delightful place than Edinburgh.
—Daniel Defoe, 1650

motorway cuts a scar through the center of town. Although the city still appears to prefer knocking buildings down and erecting new structures at the slightest opportunity, the splendor of what architectural critics hailed as "the greatest surviving example of a Victorian city" is evident.

Glasgow is a good gateway for exploring **Burns Country** in Ayrshire to the southwest. From Glasgow, visitors can also tour Loch Lomond and see some of the Highlands or travel less than an hour away to Stirling and Trossach mountains. Also on Glasgow's doorstep is the scenic estuary of the **Firth of Clyde,** with remote peninsulas and atmospheric islands only ferry rides away.

1 Essentials

ARRIVING

BY PLANE **Glasgow International Airport** (℡ **0870/040-0008** or 0141/887-1111) is at Abbotsinch, near Paisley, only about 16km (10 miles) west of the city via M8. Regular Glasgow **CityLink bus service** runs to and from the city center, terminating at the Buchanan Street Bus Station. The ride usually takes only about 20 minutes (but can be much longer at rush hour) and costs £5 ($9.25). A metered taxi to the city center costs about £17 ($31).

Monday to Friday, British Airways runs almost hourly shuttle service from London's Heathrow Airport to Glasgow. The first flight departs London at 7:15am and the last at 9:15pm; service is reduced on weekends, depending on volume. For flight schedules and fares, call British Airways in London at ℡ **0870/551-1155** or log onto www.ba.com, which offers a slight discount on ticket prices.

The schedule of direct flights from North America is subject to change. In recent years, **American Airlines** (℡ **800/433-7300** or 0845/778-9789; www.aa.com or www.americanairlines.co.uk) offered a daily nonstop flight to Glasgow from Chicago between mid-May and October, **Continental** has offered similar direct service from Newark International, and **US Airways** ran flights to Philadelphia. **Air Canada** has flown nonstop between Glasgow and Toronto.

BMI, formerly British Midland (℡ **0870/607-0555;** www.flybmi.com), offers internal U.K. and international flights. **Aer Lingus** (℡ **800/223-6537** or 0845/084-4444 at Dublin Airport; www.aerlingus.ie) flies daily from Dublin to Glasgow.

South of Glasgow is **Prestwick International Airport** (℡ **0871/223-0700**), favored by some of the low-budget airlines, such as **RyanAir.** It is on the railway line to Ayr, about a 45-minute (£5.70/$11) ride from Glasgow's Central Station. Remember, as well, that **Edinburgh International Airport** is not far away and should not be discounted as it greets many European and internal U.K. flights.

BY TRAIN Trains from London arrive in Glasgow at **Central Station** in the heart of the city (National Rail Enquiries: ℡ **0845/748-4950** for rail and fare info). The trains that directly link London and Glasgow (via Preston and Carlisle) on the West Coast Main Line don't have the same reputation for timeliness and efficiency as those going to Edinburgh do. The semiprivatized company responsible for railway maintenance, Network Rail, is spending literally billions to upgrade the line and create a faster service.

But work has been slow and while it's ongoing, travel is subject to delays. The trains (operated by Virgin; ℡ **0845/722-2333;** www.virgin.com/trains) on the West Coast Main Line depart from London Euston Station every hour or so, and the trip generally takes 5½ hours these days. If you plan a trip on the West Coast Main Line, however,

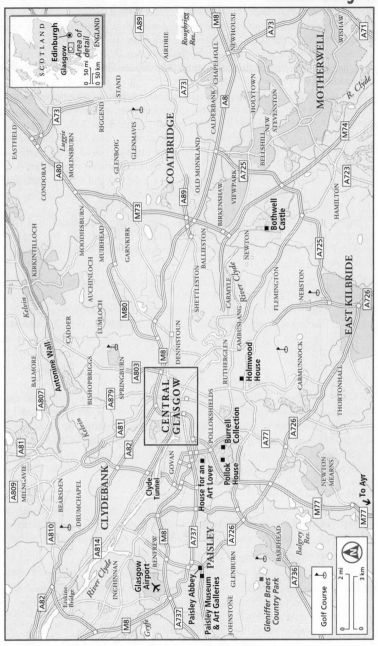

call and find out if any major "track works" are scheduled during your trip. If so, you can expect delays and the possibility of riding on a bus for a portion of the trip. Virgin prices, similar to all the U.K.'s train operating companies, are diverse and complicated. In general, you might get a one-way ticket for as little as £35 ($65) although the standard advance purchased ticket is more likely to be between £90 and £100 ($166–$185).

You might prefer trains—run by operators GNER—from London Kings Cross up the East Coast Main Line via Newcastle, Edinburgh, and across (via Motherwell) to Glasgow. The time it takes is about the same. See chapter 4 for details on fares.

Central Station is also the terminus for trains from the southwest of Scotland and a hub for numerous trains to city suburbs in most directions. A 10-minute walk away (or via shuttle bus no. 398) is **Queen Street Station.** From here, a **shuttle service** to and from Edinburgh runs every 15 minutes during the day and every 30 minutes in the evenings until about 11:30pm. The one-way fare during off-peak times (travel after 9:15am and not between 4:15 and 6:30pm) is £8.80 ($16).

Trains to the north (Stirling, Aberdeen, and such Highland destinations as Oban, Inverness, and Fort William)—as well as to Glasgow's suburbs—also run frequently through Queen Street Station. Glasgow has the biggest commuter rail network in Britain after London.

BY BUS   The journey from London to Glasgow by bus takes at least 8 hours. **National Express** (© 0870/580-8080; www.nationalexpress.com) runs buses daily (typically 9am, noon, and 10:30pm for direct service) from London's Victoria Coach Station to **Buchanan Street Bus Station** (© 0870-608-2608), about 2 blocks north of the Queen Street Station on North Hanover Street. The round-trip fare is £37 ($68), although cheaper if you book more than 7 days in advance. Scottish **CityLink** (© 0870/550-5050; www.citylink.co.uk) also has frequent bus service to and from Edinburgh, with a one-way ticket costing £3 to £5 ($5.50–$9.25).

BY CAR   Glasgow is 74km (46 miles) west of Edinburgh, 356km (221 miles) north of Manchester, and some 625km (388 miles) north of London. Motorways link London to Glasgow. From England and the south, Glasgow is reached by the M1 or M5 to the M6 in the Midlands, which becomes the M74 at Carlisle. The M74 runs north to southeastern conurbation of greater Glasgow, where drivers can link with the M8, which runs right through the city center before heading west. The M8 also links Glasgow and Edinburgh.

Other routes into the city are M77 (A77) from Ayr and A8 from the west (this becomes M8 around the port of Glasgow). A82 comes in from the northwest (the Western Highlands) on the north bank of the Clyde, and A80 also goes into the city. (This route is the southwestern section of M80 and M9 from Stirling.)

VISITOR INFORMATION
The **Greater Glasgow and Clyde Valley Tourist Board,** 11 George Sq. (© 0141/204-4400; Underground: Buchanan St.), is possibly the country's most helpful office. In addition to piles of brochures, there is a small bookshop, *bureau de change,* and hotel reservation service that charges a £2 ($3.70) booking fee for local accommodation. During peak season it is open Monday to Saturday from 9am to 7pm and Sunday from 10am to 6pm. Hours are more limited during winter months. Information

---

⟨Value⟩ "FirstDay" Bargain on the Buses

For £2.45 ($4.50), you can buy a FirstDay bus ticket that allows you to hop on and off coaches all day long. The ticket is valid daily from 9:30am to midnight. It's sold by drivers. For more information, check www.firstgroup.com.

---

about travel can be a bit more frustrating. Traveline ⓒ **0870/608-2608** offers bus timetable information and advice on routes but cannot tell you costs.

CITY LAYOUT

The monumental heart of Glasgow lies north of the **River Clyde.** The **City Center** is divided between the larger and mostly Victorian **Commercial Center** and the more compact district now designated the **Merchant City** (in honor of the tobacco and cotton "lords" who lived and ran businesses there from the 1700s). Glasgow is a vibrant modern city with art galleries, theaters, multiplex cinemas, music halls—not to mention hundreds of bars and restaurants. The Merchant City roughly is to Glasgow as SoHo is to Manhattan: full of warehouses converted to condos, stylish bars, and trendy restaurants. The City Centre offers loads of shopping opportunities on the pedestrian stretches of Argyle, Buchanan, and Sauchiehall streets. If the river creates a southern boundary for "downtown" Glasgow, the M8 motorway creates both its western and northern limits. The eastern boundary is set by the **High Street,** which is historically the core of the city.

Virtually all evidence of Glasgow's medieval existence was demolished by the well-meaning, if history-destroying, urban renewal schemes of late Georgian and Victorian Glasgow. Practically nothing remains to give any idea of how the city, before the 18th-century boom, looked. And, by some accounts, it was one Europe's most attractive medieval burghs. Still standing on the hill at the top of the High Street is **Glasgow Cathedral,** an excellent example of pre-Reformation Gothic architecture that dates, in part, to the 12th century, and across the square is Provand's Lordship, the city's oldest house, built in the 1470s. Down the High Street, you'll find the Tolbooth Steeple (1626) at Glasgow Cross, and nearer the River Clyde is **Glasgow Green,** one of Britain's first large-scale public parks.

The city's salubrious and leafy **West End,** home to the University of Glasgow, is just a short journey from central Glasgow, on the other side of the M8. The terraces of Woodlands Hill, rising to Park Circus, afford excellent views. Across Kelvingrove Park is a red sandstone palace, the city's **Art Gallery and Museum** (reopened after renovation in 2006). Nearby, the tower of the University of Glasgow dominates Gilmorehill. **Byres Road** is the social and entertainment destination in the West End, a street full of restaurants, cafes, bars, and shops.

The city's **Southside** sprawls from the River Clyde and is largely residential. Aside from the city's shiny **Science Centre,** on the south bank, there may be little of immediate interest to the casual visitor. But just over 5km (3 miles) southwest of central Glasgow in wooded **Pollok Country Park** is the vaunted **Burrell Collection.** This museum of antiquity and art has become one of Scotland's top tourist attractions. The commercial heart of the Southside is **Shawlands,** which offers an increasing number of good restaurants, and nearby **Queens Park** is a hilly classic of Victorian planning.

Glasgow Neighborhoods

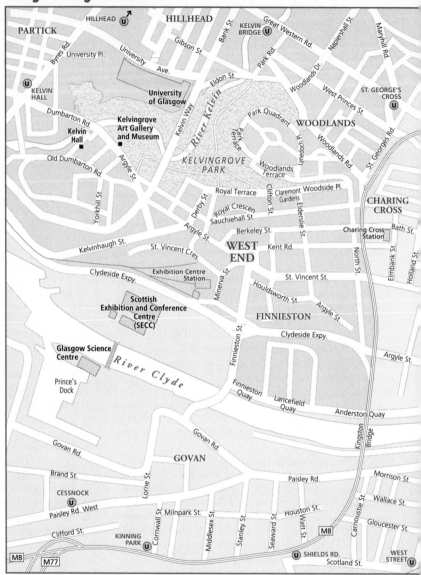

Glasgow's **East End** is only slowly redeveloping after its industrial heyday. Once the site of coal mining and steel production, it is the least affluent area of the city and, according to surveys, has the poorest and least healthy districts in all of Europe. But statistics don't tell the entire story. Visitors to the **Gallowgate** at the weekend should

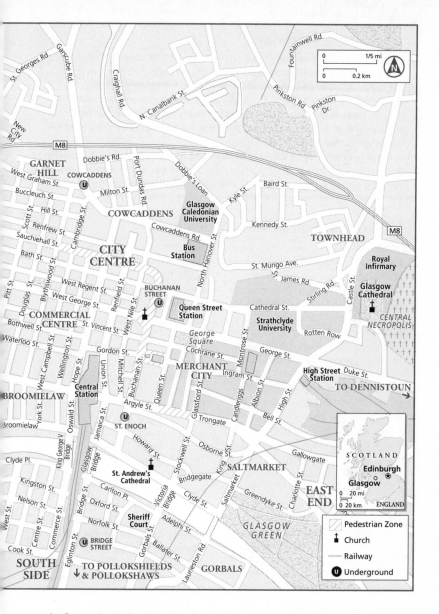

see the flea-market stalls of the **Barras.** Neighborhoods such as **Dennistoun** are gradually drawing young, creative types who can no longer afford apartments in the West End or on the Southside: a renaissance is simmering.

Tips Finding an Address

Glasgow was built in various sections over the years, and some historic districts, such as the infamous Gorbals, south of the city center, have been torn down in the name of slum clearance: streets have been completely reconfigured to accommodate modern traffic flows. Other central neighborhoods have fallen prey to freeway development. The central city is primarily laid out on a grid, which makes it easier to navigate, and in at least this part of the city, street names don't change every other block.

Get a detailed map of Glasgow before setting out. Always find the nearest cross street, and then look for your location from there. If it's a hotel or restaurant, the sign of an establishment is often more prominent than the number.

GLASGOW NEIGHBORHOODS IN BRIEF

City Centre

Cathedral (Townhead) This is where St. Mungo apparently arrived in A.D. 543 and built his little church in what's now the northeastern part of the city center. **Glasgow Cathedral** was once surrounded by a variety of prebendal manses, and the so-called Bishops Castle stood between the cathedral's west facade and the Provand's Lordship, which still exists largely in its original form. East of the Cathedral is one of Britain's largest Victorian cemeteries, Glasgow's Central Necropolis.

Merchant City The city's first New Town development—today southeast of the city's core—Merchant City, extends from Trongate and Argyle Street in the south to George Street in the north. As the medieval lanes and alleys off the High Street were regarded as festering sores, the affluent moved to develop areas to the west. Now, it has become one of few inner-city areas of Glasgow where people reside.

Gallowgate The beginning of the city's East End today was once one of the streets that prosperous city businessmen strolled. The Saracen's Head Inn stood here and took such distinguished guests as Dr. Samuel Johnson and James Boswell in 1774 after the

duo's famous tour of the Hebrides. Today the Gallowgate is best known for the Barras market and Barrowland, a one-time ballroom that now is a popular live-music venue.

Saltmarket While the first settlements in Glasgow were on the hill by the Cathedral, almost as early were dwellings in this area at the opposite end of the High Street along the banks of the Clyde. It served as the trading post where the river could be forded. The Bridgegate leads to the first crossing erected over the Clyde. Today it is Victoria Bridge. Constructed in the 1850s, it is the oldest Clyde crossing in Glasgow.

Commercial Center The biggest of the central districts of Glasgow, it includes areas of 19th-century development such as **Blythswood** and **Charing Cross** (although the latter was severed by the M8 freeway). This area offers Victorian architecture at its finest, and the city had a mind to tear it all to the ground until realizing in the middle to late 1960s that it had something of international interest.

Broomielaw It has been said: "The Clyde made Glasgow." From docks here, Glasgow imported tobacco, cotton, and rum and shipped its manufactured goods around the world. Today the Broomielaw, after becoming a rather lost and neglected part of the city center, is targeted for renewal, with luxury flats planned along the riverbank.

Garnethill Up the steep slopes north of Sauchiehall Street, this neighborhood is best known for the Charles Rennie Mackintosh–designed Glasgow School of Art. Developed in the late 1800s, Garnethill offers good views of the city and is also home to the first proper synagogue built in Scotland.

West End

Woodlands Centering on Park Circus at the crown of Woodlands Hill, this neighborhood is the first one just west of the M8 freeway. It is a mix of residential tenements and retail stretches, particularly on Woodlands and Great Western roads. South to the river lies the district of **Finnieston.** Its most visible landmark is the old shipbuilding crane, standing like some giant dinosaur. Along the Clyde is the Scottish Exhibition Centre. West of Woodlands is **Kelvingrove,** with the Art Gallery and Museum and the impressive park. Glasgow has more green spaces per resident than any other European city.

Hillhead With the Gilmorehill campus of the University of Glasgow, Hillhead is rather dominated by academia. Its main boulevard is Byres Road, which is the Main Street of the West End.

Partick The railway station at Partick is one of the few in the city to translate the stop's name into Gaelic: Partaig. Indeed there is a bit of Highland pride to the neighborhood, although no particular evidence that Highland people have settled here in great masses.

Partick is one of the less pretentious districts of the central West End. To the north are leafy and affluent **Hyndland** and **Dowanhill.**

Southside

Gorbals This neighborhood, just across the Clyde from the city center, developed a reputation for mean streets and unsanitary tenements; so, the city demolished it in the early 1960s, erecting sets of modern high-rise apartment towers, which, in turn, developed a reputation for unsavory and unpleasant conditions. Today they are coming down and the New Gorbals has been developed on a more human scale, although the fabric of the place still seems torn and frayed. It is home to the Citizens' Theatre, one of the most innovative and democratic in the U.K.

Govan Until 1912, this was an independent burgh and one of the key shipbuilding districts on the south banks of the Clyde. It was settled as early as the 10th century—another ecclesiastical focal point along with St. Kentigern's north of the river. The first shipyard, Mackie & Thomson, opened in 1840. But with the demise of shipbuilding, the fortunes of Govan fell too. Today, it is hoped that the Science Centre and other developments planned in the area, such as a new Transport Museum and new HQ for BBC Scotland, will revive Govan's fortunes.

Pollokshaws Along with **Pollokshields** and **Crosshill,** these neighborhoods form the heart of the city's more modern Southside suburbs. Pollok Park and the Burrell Collection are the primary tourist attractions, and Queens Park is perhaps better and more verdant than Kelvingrove Park, even if it lacks the monuments and statues of the West End's oasis.

2 Getting Around

One of the best ways to explore Glasgow is by foot. (See chapter 16 for walking tours.) The center of town is laid out on a grid, which makes map reading relatively easy. However, some of the city's significant attractions, such as the Burrell Collection, are in surrounding districts, and for those, you'll need to rely on public transportation or a car.

Remember: A one-way ticket is called "single" fare and a round-trip is a "return" journey.

BY BUS

Glasgow has an extensive (if somewhat confusing) bus service run by the privately owned **First Group.** Routes tend to run between east and west or north and south, with almost all buses coming though the city center on busy thoroughfares such as St. Vincent, Hope, Argyll, and Sauchiehall streets. Service is frequent during the day. After 11pm it is curtailed on most routes, but some (for example, no. 9, 12, 40, or 62) run all night long (at least on weekends), although there is a premium put on tickets. Typically, one-way (single) fares are about £1.15 ($2), and for £2.45 ($4.50) you can use the buses (after 9:30am) all day long with few restrictions. A weeklong ticket costs £12 ($22). The city bus station is the **Buchanan Street Bus Station.** The "Traveline" number (✆ **0870/608-2608**) gives timetable information (but not fares); you can also log on to www.firstgroup.com.

BY UNDERGROUND & SUBURBAN TRAIN

The Glasgow Underground, called affectionately the "Clockwork Orange," (due to the vivid hues of the trains, which travel in a virtual circle), offers a 15-stop system linking the city center, West End, and a bit of the Southside. During the day there is generally no more than a 5- to 8-minute wait for trains. Trains run on longer intervals on Sunday and at night. The one-way adult fare is £1 ($1.85). You can buy a 20-trip ticket for £15 ($28).The underground runs Monday to Saturday 6:30am to about 11:30pm and Sunday 11am to about 6pm.

The **Transcentre** (local ticket sales only) at the St. Enoch underground station, 2 blocks from the Central Station, is generally open Monday to Saturday from to 8:30am to 5:30pm, but it closes early on Wednesday. On Sunday, the hours are 10am to 5pm.

Glasgow and the region have the largest train network in Great Britain after London. Like the subway, it is operated by **Strathclyde Passenger Transport (SPT),** and service runs to both Central (upper and lower levels) and Queen Street (lower level only) stations. During the day, trains run as frequently as every 10 minutes or so to destinations in the West End and on the Southside. Service is less frequent after the evening rush hour, and it terminates at around midnight. While extensive, the trains are not cheap by European standards. A typical round-trip fare is £2 to £3 ($3.70–$6.30).

For families on an excursion, the **Daytripper** ticket is excellent. For £15 ($28) two adults and up to four children (5–15 years old) can travel anywhere in the system (including broad swaths of Ayrshire) by suburban train, the underground, most buses, and even a few ferries. For one adult and two children, the fare is £8.50 ($16).

The main SPT switchboard is ✆ **0141/332-6811.** Hours are Monday to Saturday 9am to 5pm, or log onto www.spt.co.uk.

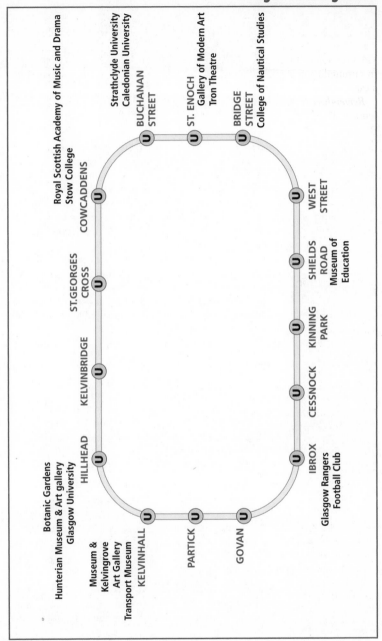

BY TAXI

Metered taxis are the same excellent ones found in Edinburgh or London: the Fast Black, which you can hail or pick up at taxi ranks in the city center. Alternatively you can also reserve one by calling **Glasgow Taxis Ltd** (© **0141/429-7070**). Fares are displayed on a meter next to the driver. When a taxi is available on the street, a sign on the roof is lit. Most taxi trips within the city cost between £5 and £15 ($9–$28). A surcharge is imposed for late-night/early-morning runs. There are also **Private Hire** cars, but they cannot be hailed. Call © **0141/774-3000.**

BY CAR

To get around the city, you're better off using public transportation (especially at rush hour), but Glasgow goes a long way towards encouraging car use with several multi-story parking lots. Metered parking is available, but expensive, and you'll need plenty of coins to feed the meter, which issues a ticket that you must affix to the windshield. Some zones in residential areas are marked PERMIT HOLDERS ONLY—your vehicle may be towed if you lack a permit. A double yellow line along the curb indicates no parking at any time. A single yellow line along the curb indicates restrictions, too, so be sure and read the signs on what the limitations are.

If you want to rent a car, it's best to arrange it in advance (see chapter 2). But if you want to rent a car locally, most companies will accept your foreign driver's license. All the major rental agencies are represented at the airport. In addition, **Avis Rent-a-Car** is at 70 Lancefield St. (© **0870/608-6339**); **Budget Rent-a-Car** is at 101 Waterloo St. (© **0800/212-636**); and **Arnold Clark** is at multiple locations (© **0845/607-4500**).

BY BICYCLE

Though bikes are not as widely used in Glasgow as in Edinburgh, most parts of the city are fine for biking. For what the Scots call "cycle hire," go to a well-recommended shop in the West End, just off Byres Road: **West End Cycles,** 16–18 Chancellor St. (© **0141/357-1344;** Underground: Hillhead or Kelvinhall; bus: 9 or 18). It is close to the National Cycle Trail that leads to Loch Lomond and rents bikes well-suited to the hilly terrain of Glasgow and surrounding areas. The cost is £15 ($28) per day, and a cash deposit of £100 ($185) or the imprint of a valid credit card is necessary as security. In the city center, **Alpine Bikes** in the TISO Outdoor Centre, 50 Couper St., near Buchanan Bus Station (© **0141/552-8575**) offers limited cycle rental. Prices start at £8 ($15).

FAST FACTS: Glasgow

American Express The office is at 115 Hope St. (© **0141/222-1401;** Underground: St. Enoch), and it's open Monday to Friday 8:30am to 5:30pm (Wed from 9:30am) and Saturday 9am to noon.

Business Hours Most **offices** are open Monday to Friday 9am to 5 or 5:30pm. Some companies close at 4:30pm on Friday. Most **banks** are usually open Monday through Friday from 9 or 9:30am to 4 or 5pm, with some branches sometimes closing early on 1 day a week and open late on another. Opening times can vary slightly from bank to bank. **Shops** are generally open Monday to Sunday 10am to 6pm. On Thursday, many remain open until 8pm.

Currency Exchange The tourist office at 11 George Sq. (℗ **0141/204-4400**) and the American Express office (see above) will exchange major foreign currencies. Thomas Cook operates a currency exchange at Central Station (generally open until 6pm). Many city center banks operate *bureaux de change*, too, and nearly all will cash traveler's checks if you have the proper ID. Most city center ATMs (cash points) will also draw money directly from your bank account at home.

Dentists In an emergency, go to the Accident and Emergency Department of **Glasgow Dental Hospital**, 378 Sauchiehall St. (℗ **0141/211-9600**). Its hours are Monday to Friday 9:15am to 3:15pm and Sunday and public holidays 10:30am to noon. For additional assistance call the **National Health Service** line (℗ **0800/ 224-488**).

Doctors The main hospital for emergency treatment (24-hr.) in the city is the **Royal Infirmary**, 82–86 Castle St. (℗ **0141/211-4000**).

Embassies & Consulates All embassies are in London. There's a **U.S. Consulate** in Edinburgh at 3 Regent Terrace (℗ **0131/556-8315**), open Monday through Friday from 1 to 4pm. All other nationals have to use London to conduct their business: The **Canadian High Commission** is at MacDonald House, 1 Grosvenor Sq., London W1K 4AB (℗ **0207/258-6600**), open Monday through Friday from 8am to 4pm. The **Australian High Commission** is at the Strand, London WC2B 4LI (℗ **0207/379-4334**), open Monday through Friday from 9:30am to 3:30pm. The **New Zealand High Commission** is at New Zealand House, 80 Haymarket at Pall Mall, London SW1Y 4TQ (℗ **0207/930-8422**), open Monday through Friday from 9am to 5pm. The **Irish Embassy** is at 17 Grosvenor Place, London SW1X 7HR (℗ **0207/235-2171**), open Monday through Friday from 9:30am to 1pm and 2:15 to 5pm.

Emergencies Call ℗ **999** in an emergency to summon the police, an ambulance, or firefighters.

Hospitals See "Doctors," above.

Hot Lines The **Centre for Women's Health** is at Sandyford Place, Sauchiehall Street (℗ **0141/211-6700**). Gays and lesbians can call the **Strathclyde Gay and Lesbian Switchboard** at ℗ **0141/847-0447**. The **Rape Crisis Centre** is at ℗ **0141/ 331-1990**.

Internet Access You can send or receive e-mail and surf the Net at **EasyInternet Cafe**, 57–61 St. Vincent St. (www.easyeverything.com; Underground: Buchanan St.). This outlet offers more than 350 computers and good rates. Open Monday to Friday from 7am to 10pm; Saturday and Sunday 8am to 9pm.

Laundry & Dry Cleaning The most central service is **Garnethill Cleaners**, 39 Dalhousie St. (℗ **0141/332-2387**; Underground: Cowcaddens), open Monday to Saturday from about 7:30am to 6:30pm and Sunday from 8am to 5pm.

Library The **Mitchell Library** is on North Street at Kent Road (℗ **0141/287-2999**; suburban train: Charing Cross; bus: 9 or 16). One of the largest reference libraries in Europe, it's a massive 19th-century pile. Newspapers and books, as well as miles of microfilm, are available. It's open Monday to Thursday 9am to 8pm; Friday and Saturday 9am to 5pm.

Newspapers & Magazines Published since 1783, the *Herald* is the major newspaper with national, international, and financial news, sports, and cultural listings; the *Evening Times* offers local news. The *Daily Record* is for tabloid enthusiasts only. For complete events listings, the *List* magazine is published every other week. On the buses and trains, pick up a free *Metro,* which also has listings. For international newspapers, go to Borders Books, 98 Buchanan St. ((*C* **0141/222-7700;** Underground: Buchanan St.).

Pharmacies The best bet is **Boots,** 200 Sauchiehall St. ((*C* **0141/332-1925**), open Monday to Saturday 8am to 6pm (till 7pm Thurs), and Sunday 11am to 5pm.

Police In a real emergency, call (*C* **999.** For other inquiries, contact Strathclyde police headquarters on Pitt St. at (*C* **0141/532-2000.**

Post Office The main branch is at 47 St. Vincent's St. ((*C* **0141/204-3689;** Underground: Buchanan St.). It's open Monday to Friday 8:30am to 5:45pm and Saturday 9am to 5:30pm. For general postal information, call (*C* **0845/722-3344.**

Restrooms Public toilets can be found at rail stations, bus stations, air terminals, restaurants, hotels, pubs, and department stores. Glasgow also has a system of public toilets, often marked wc. Don't hesitate to use them, but they're likely to be closed late in the evening.

Safety Although Glasgow may be the most dangerous city in Scotland, it's relatively safe when compared to cities of its size in the United States. Muggings do occur, and they're often related to Glasgow's drug problem. The famed razor gangs of Calton, Bridgeton, and the Gorbals are no longer around to earn the city a reputation for violence, but you still should stay alert.

Weather For weather forecasts of the day and 24 hours in advance, and for severe road-condition warnings, call the **Met Office** at (*C* **0870/900-0100.** An advisor will offer forecasts for the entire region and beyond.

13

Where to Stay in Glasgow

The tourist trade in Glasgow is less distinctly seasonal than in Edinburgh, with fewer visitors overall coming to Scotland's largest city. However, the increase in budget-airline flights from the European continent has increased the overall number of tourists, while the city continues to be a popular spot for business conferences. If, therefore, an international association of dentists is in town, finding accommodation can be more difficult. Until recently, many tourism industry observers said Glasgow suffered from a shortage of hotel rooms, but new places such as the Radisson SAS have changed the equation.

Whenever you're coming, it's recommended that you reserve a room in advance. Some rates are predictably high (especially so if the pound remains strong), but many business-oriented hotels offer bargains on weekends and the number of budget options is increasing.

Plus, the Internet can be a real treasure trove of reduced room rates and multiple-night stays also can bring price cuts. The Glasgow and Clyde Valley tourism office, in conjunction with the Scottish tourist board (www.seeglasgow.com or www.visitscotland.com), offers an **Information & Booking Hot Line** (✆ **0845/225-5121** from within the U.K., or 44-1506/832-121 from outside the U.K.; fax 0150/683-2222). Lines are open (local time) Monday to Friday from 8am to 8pm, Saturday from 9am to 5:50pm, and Sunday from 10am to 4pm. The fee for this booking service is £3 ($5.50).

The Scottish tourist board is also a source of ratings, which are based largely on amenities. The stars can be limited for smaller operations that may not offer all the mod cons, but these establishments are still perfectly good places to stay. References to stars in the information below are those bestowed by Visitscotland.

1 Merchant City & East End

MODERATE

Babbity Bowster ✧ Housed in a reconstructed late-18th-century "five-bay house," the Babbity Bowster is a small inn with fairly large character. Some of this is due to the classic design by brothers James and Robert Adam, and some comes courtesy of the acerbic wit of owner Fraser Laurie (he with the eye patch). The units are modest if reasonably well-appointed: a couple of guest bathrooms have only showers. But the Babbity Bowster is designed to appeal to travelers who do not spend too much time in their rooms. The location is convenient to the many local pubs and restaurants in the nightlife hotbed of the Merchant City—and it is only a 5- to 10-minute walk to the heart of central Glasgow. The ground-level pub of the same name (p. 237) is convivial and notably civilized, with a sheltered beer garden, excellent bar meals, and live acoustic Scottish folk sessions on Saturdays. The second-floor restaurant—**Schottische** (p. 179)—offers French-influenced cooking in the evenings only.

Glasgow Accommodations

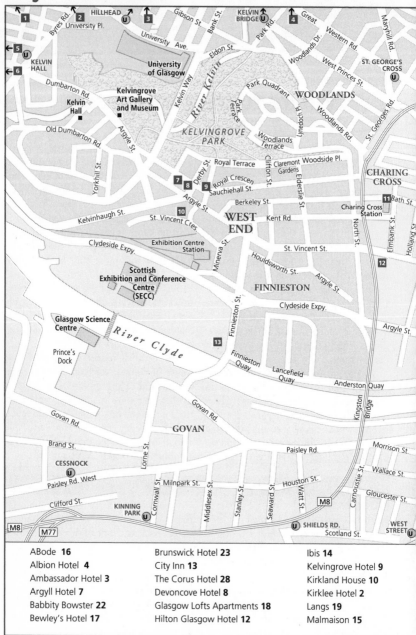

ABode **16**	Brunswick Hotel **23**	Ibis **14**
Albion Hotel **4**	City Inn **13**	Kelvingrove Hotel **9**
Ambassador Hotel **3**	The Corus Hotel **28**	Kirkland House **10**
Argyll Hotel **7**	Devoncove Hotel **8**	Kirklee Hotel **2**
Babbity Bowster **22**	Glasgow Lofts Apartments **18**	Langs **19**
Bewley's Hotel **17**	Hilton Glasgow Hotel **12**	Malmaison **15**

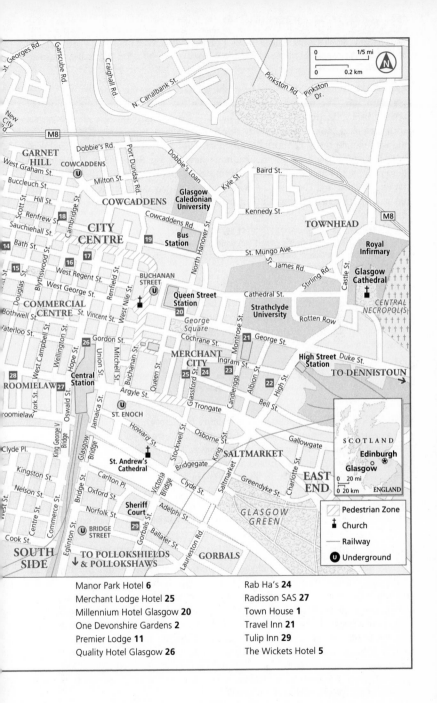

Manor Park Hotel **6**	Rab Ha's **24**
Merchant Lodge Hotel **25**	Radisson SAS **27**
Millennium Hotel Glasgow **20**	Town House **1**
One Devonshire Gardens **2**	Travel Inn **21**
Premier Lodge **11**	Tulip Inn **29**
Quality Hotel Glasgow **26**	The Wickets Hotel **5**

16–18 Blackfriars St. (off High St.), Glasgow G1 1PE. ☎ **0141/552-5055.** Fax 0141/552-7774. 5 units. £80 ($148) double. AE, MC, V. Free parking. Underground: Buchanan St. Suburban train: High St. Bus: 40. **Amenities:** Restaurant; bar. *In room:* No phone.

Brunswick Hotel ☞   In the heart of the Merchant City, this is one of the hippest places to stay. The modern, minimalist design has aged well since the Brunswick opened in 1990s: from the popular cafe/bar—Brutti Ma Buoni—to the bedrooms with their sleek look. The units may be on the small side but are soothing and inviting with neutral tones, comfortable mattresses, and adequate bathrooms (several with both tub and shower). For all its trendiness, however, the Brunswick is far from pretentiously run. The owners are fun-loving cosmopolitans. Indeed the cafe's name means, literally, "ugly but good"—which may accurately describe the misshapen pizzas that the kitchen churns out but actually says more about the place's sense of humor.

106–108 Brunswick St., Glasgow G1 1TF. ☎ **0141/552-0001.** Fax 0141/552-1551. www.brunswickhotel.co.uk. 18 units. £55–£100 ($100–$185) double; £400 ($740) penthouse suite. Rates include buffet breakfast. AE, DC, MC, V. Parking on street. Underground: Buchanan St. **Amenities:** Restaurant; bar; 24-hr. reception; laundry service; dry cleaning. *In room:* TV, dataport, coffeemaker.

Merchant Lodge Hotel   Located in a historic building, tucked down a narrow street in the heart of the Merchant City, this three-star hotel has five floors (and no elevator) of fairly basic rooms. While ideally situated for city center accommodations and attractively priced, a complaint from guests (and, indeed, the hotel itself) is the noise of late-night revelry on seemingly sedate Wilson Street as local nightclubs dispense their guests in the wee, small hours of the morning.

52 Virginia St., Glasgow G1 1TY. ☎ **0141/552-24224.** Fax 0141/552-4747. www.merchantlodgehotel.com. 40 units. £62 ($115) double. Rates include breakfast. AE, MC, V. Underground: Buchanan St. Bus: 40 or 62. *In room:* TV, coffeemaker, hair dryer.

Rab Ha's *Finds*   Similar in size to the Babbity (see above), this small boutique hotel has a quartet of overnight rooms above a popular and urbane pub on the ground level, as well as a modern restaurant in the basement. The recently redesigned units have dark slate flooring in the bathrooms, specially commissioned glass, photographic prints, and flatscreen televisions. The location in Merchant City, southeast of George Square is good.

83 Hutcheson St., Glasgow G1. ☎ **0141/572-0400.** Fax 0141/572-0402. www.rabhas.com. 4 units £65–£75 ($120–$138) double. Rates include continental breakfast. AE, DC, MC, V. Parking on street. **Amenities:** 2 restaurants; bar. *In room:* TV, coffeemaker, hair dryer.

INEXPENSIVE

Travel Inn   Backing onto churchyard behind the Ramshorn Theatre, this former tax office (Montrose House) is a branch of an inexpensively priced chain of hotels. As such, it is functional if not particularly full of character. There's a fair amount of new construction going on in the area, so the neighborhood can be noisy during the day. Rooms that overlook the old kirkyard and cemetery are preferable to those facing busy George Street and the Strathclyde University parking lot across the road. It's convenient to George Square and Glasgow Cathedral, as well.

187 George St., Glasgow G1 1YU. ☎ **0870/238-3320.** Fax 0141/553-2719. www.travelinn.co.uk. 254 units. £56–£59 ($103–$109) double. AE, DC, MC, V. Parking on street. Suburban train: High St. Bus: 40 or 41. **Amenities:** Restaurant; bar. *In room:* TV, coffeemaker, safe, trouser press.

2 Commercial Center

VERY EXPENSIVE

Hilton Glasgow Hotel ✦ Glasgow's first-class Hilton is centrally located but oddly situated over the stretch of M8 freeway that slashes through the city of Glasgow. Perhaps the caliber of guests ensures that they all take taxis or have private cars because actually trying to get to and from the place on foot can be a bit of a nightmare. Still, it is a dignified and modern hotel; one that has a good deal of class and shine. The numerous units—plush and conservative—in the 20-story building offer fine city views. Those staying on the executive floors enjoy the enhanced facilities of a semiprivate club. Dining options include a casual New York deli–style buffet, **Minsky's** as well as the posh **Camerons** with first-rate and expensive modern Scottish cuisine.

1 William St., Glasgow G3 8HT. ℂ **800/445-8667** in the U.S. and Canada, or 0141/204-5555. Fax 0141/204-5004. www.hilton.co.uk/glasgow. 331 units. £100–£180 ($185–$333) double; from £140 ($260) suite. Weekend discounts often available. AE, DC, MC, V. Parking £5 ($9.25). **Amenities:** 2 restaurants; bar; indoor heated pool; exercise room; sauna; concierge; business center; salon; room service; massage; babysitting; laundry service; dry cleaning. *In room:* A/C, TV, minibar, coffeemaker, hair dryer, iron/ironing board, safe, trouser press.

EXPENSIVE

ABode Formerly the Arthouse hotel, this handsome Edwardian building, only a few blocks from both Central and Queen Street train stations, was originally built to house school board offices. Today, it is a striking boutique hotel in the city center. Dramatic colors and textures blend in perfectly with the older structure while commissioned art and period pieces evoke some of the original splendor. The eponymously named fine-dining restaurant, **Michael Caines @ ABode,** is under the direction of a Michelin-starred chef in England (p. 181), while more a more casual cafe bistro is located in the basement, alongside the "Vibe Bar."

129 Bath St., Glasgow G2 2SZ. ℂ **0141/221-6789.** Fax 0141/221-6777. www.abodehotels.co.uk/glagsow. 65 units. From £125 ($231) double. AE, DC, MC, V. Parking on street. Underground: Buchanan St. **Amenities:** Restaurant; bar; salon; room service; laundry service; dry cleaning. *In room:* TV, dataport, coffeemaker, hair dryer, safe.

Glasgow Loft Apartments *Finds* These serviced apartments near the heart of Glasgow offer the comforts of home: range and oven, fridge, dishwasher, washing machine. All the modern one-bedroom and two-bedroom flats have floor to ceiling windows that face back to the city center, appointed in black leather upholstered sofas, power shower/Jacuzzi bathrooms and dining tables that seat six.

134 Renfrew St. Glasgow G2. ℂ **0141/332-1976.** www.glasgowloftapartment.co.uk. 10 units. £90–£120 1-bedroom; £125–£145 ($231–$268) 2-bedroom. MC, V. Parking £18 ($34). Underground: Cowcaddens.

Langs ✦ This contemporary and reasonably new hotel close to Glasgow Royal Concert Hall calls itself an "urban oasis." Indeed the main public space is called **Oshi,** a Zen-influenced bar and restaurant with a 12m (40-ft.) pool of water that runs between a waterfall and cauldron of fire. Very impressive, if just a little over the top. A medley of bedrooms in various shapes, sizes, and configurations are available, and each attempts to offer a certain flair. The smallest units are the studios, but guests can opt for a duplex, theme room, or a large suite. The beautifully-kept bathrooms have power showers with body jets. And if that doesn't relax visitors, there is the option of more individual pampering at the hotel's own spa. In addition to Oshi, with its Asian fusion cuisine, Aurora offers excellent Scottish produce such as Aberdeen Angus or fresh fish in the evenings, Tuesday to Saturday. Good discounts are offered through an online reservations service.

2 Port Dundas Place, Glasgow G2 3LD. ℂ **0141/333-1500.** Fax 0141/333-5700. www.langshotels.co.uk. 100 units. £148 ($273) double; £173 ($320) suite. AE, DC, MC, V. Parking nearby. Underground: Buchanan St. **Amenities:** 2 restaurants; bar; exercise room; spa; sauna; room service; massage; laundry service; dry cleaning. *In room:* TV, minibar, coffeemaker, hair dryer, iron/ironing board.

Malmaison ☆☆   Today there are hip and sophisticated Malmaisons across the U.K., but it began in Scotland. This converted church with its fine Greek-styled exterior (though not Greek Orthodox as Malmaison says but Episcopal) offers only a few of the original details on the inside—the decor is sleek and modern. In 1997, an annex designed to complement the architectural character of the facade was added to provide additional guest rooms. Units vary in size from quite cozy to average, but all are chic and well appointed with special extras such as CD players, some specially commissioned art, and top-of-the-line toiletries. In the vaulted spaces below reception is the popular brasserie of the same name (p. 182) and champagne bar. Internet reservations can secure a double for £99 ($180).

278 W. George St., Glasgow G2 4LL. ℂ **0141/572-1000.** Fax 0141/572-1002. www.malmaison-glasgow.com. 72 units. From £140 ($260) double; £165 ($305) suite. AE, DC, MC, V. Parking nearby £7 ($14). Suburban train: Charing Cross. **Amenities:** Restaurant; 2 bars; exercise room; room service; babysitting; laundry service; dry cleaning. *In room:* A/C, TV, dataport, minibar, coffeemaker, hair dryer, iron/ironing board, safe.

Millennium Hotel Glasgow   Following a $5 million upgrade, this landmark hotel, once called the Copthorne and erected at the beginning of the 19th century, has been modernized with all the amenities and services you'd expect of highly rated hotels. Technically just off the boundary of the Merchant City and adjacent to Queen Street Station (where trains for Edinburgh and the north of Scotland terminate), the hotel has a conservatory space for dining and drinks. It faces onto the city's central plaza, George Square, and offers views of the opulent Glasgow city chambers. The best units are at the front of the building, as well; those in the rear offer no views worth writing home about.

The ground-floor restaurant, Brasserie on George Square, offers an elegant, neo-colonial—but not stuffy—dining ambience, while the hotel's more recently recast Georgics bar has an excellent selection of wines, many served by the glass.

George Sq., Glasgow G2 1DS. ℂ **0141/332-6711.** Fax 0141/332-4264. www.millenniumhotels.com. 117 units. From £185 ($342) double; from £230 ($425) suite. AE, DC, MC, V. Parking £5 ($9.50). Underground: Buchanan St. **Amenities:** Restaurant; 2 bars; concierge; car-rental desk; business center; room service; babysitting; same-day laundry service; same-day dry cleaning. *In room:* A/C, TV, dataport, coffeemaker, hair dryer, iron/ironing board, safe, trouser press.

MODERATE

Bewleys Hotel   Located in the center of the financial district, just around the corner from the Mackintosh-designed Willow Tea Rooms, Bewley's hotel rises impressively from the street, with oddly angled windows that appear to look down on the ground below. Run by an Ireland-based group, Bewley's basic room rate applies to larger units that can accommodate families. At 38 Bath St., Bewleys also lets one and two-bedroom apartment suites suitable for families from £99 to £129 ($183–$239).

110 Bath St., Glasgow G2 2EN. ℂ **0141/353-0800.** Fax 0141/353-0900. www.bewleyshotels.com. 103 units. £69 ($127) double. AE, DC, MC, V. Parking nearby. Underground: Buchanan St. **Amenities:** Restaurant; bar; room service. *In room:* TV, dataport, coffeemaker, hair dryer, trouser press.

No Frills in the City Center

For basic, inexpensive accommodation from the better-known chains, Glasgow has a few options. Near Sauchiehall Street in the Charing Cross district is the **Ibis** (220 West Regent St., G2 4DQ; ✆ **0141/225-6000**) with rooms from £48 ($88) plus a restaurant and bar. Across the Clyde in the gentrified New Gorbals, the **Tulip Inn** (80 Ballter St., G5 0TW; ✆ **0141/429-4233**) offers double rooms from £59 ($109) and has lots of free car parking. Above the Charing Cross railway stop is a 278-unit **Premier Lodge** (10 Elmbank Gardens, G2 4PP; ✆ **0870/700-1394**) with rooms at £ 51 ($94).

Corus Hotel   Two blocks west of Central station, this contemporary seven-story hotel was once surrounded by dreary commercial buildings, but the neighborhood is slowly changing. It is a viable option near the center of Glasgow. You check into a rather cramped area, but once upstairs, the rooms are more inviting—although they, too, are small.

377 Argyle St. (opposite Cadogan Sq.), Glasgow G2 8LL. ✆ **0870/609-6166.** Fax 0141/221-1014. www.corushotels. co.uk. 121 units. From £74 ($137) double. AE, DC, MC, V. Parking nearby. Underground: St. Enoch. **Amenities:** Restaurant; bar; room service; laundry service; dry cleaning. *In room:* TV, hair dryer.

Quality Hotel Glasgow   When this hotel in Glasgow's Central Station first opened in the 1880s, it was perhaps the grandest the city had ever seen and subsequent guests included Churchill and JFK. In 2006, another refurbishment costing £3 million ($5.5 million) revamped the hotel's leisure center, restaurants, bars, reception and overnight rooms. Traditionalists are likely to take a shine to its historic attributes: whether the baronial, highly polished wooden staircase or the elaborate Victorian cornices and pilasters. The guest rooms, with high ceilings and large windows, now have interactive TVs and modernized facilities.

99 Gordon St., Central Station, Glasgow G1 3SF. ✆ **0141/221-9680.** Fax 0141/226-3948. www.quality-hotels-glasgow. com. 222 units. £70–£125 ($129–$231) double. AE, DC, MC, V. Reduced-rate parking nearby. Underground: St. Enoch. **Amenities:** Restaurant; bar; indoor pool; exercise room; Jacuzzi; sauna; room service; laundry service; dry cleaning. *In room:* TV, dataport, coffeemaker, hair dryer.

Radisson SAS 🐾   Still shiny since its November 2002 opening, the Radisson has set down architectural markers for any other hotels to open in Glasgow. Its dramatic and curving facade is just a stone's throw from Central Station, on the fringe of a portion of the city center that is still being redeveloped. Contemporary units with blonde wood details and Scandinavian cool have all the modern conveniences. The 1394-sq.-m (15,000 sq. ft.) club and fitness facility includes a 15m (49-ft.) pool and state-of-the-art gym. Collage and TaPaell'ya offer two distinct dining options.

301 Argyle St., Glasgow G2. ✆ **0141/204-3333.** Fax 0141/204-3344. www.radissonsas.com. 250 units. From £105 ($194) double. AE, DC, MC, V. Reduced-rate parking nearby. Underground: St. Enoch. **Amenities:** 2 restaurants; 2 bars; fitness facility; pool. *In room:* TV, dataport, minibar, coffeemaker, iron/ironing board, safe.

3 The West End

EXPENSIVE

One Devonshire Gardens 🐾🐾 *Kids*   This hotel has become the most glamorous the city has to offer: the place where the great and good traditionally stay, whether gorgeous George Clooney or Michael Jackson. The town houses along this lane are parallel to the always busy Great Western Road. Built in 1880, they are possibly more elegant today than in their heyday. Of the units, no. 29, the so-called "luxury town house," is the most impressive. The suite—£495 ($915) per night—includes a sitting room (with its own toilet); a separate dressing chamber; a master bedroom with a four-poster bed; and a full bathroom with spa, separate shower with computerized controls, and twin basins. In summer 2006, new owners, Hotel du Vin, took over.

1 Devonshire Gardens, Glasgow G12 0UX. © **0141/339-2001.** Fax 0141/337-1663. www.onedevonshiregardens. com. 38 units. From £155 ($286) double. AE, DC, MC, V. Free parking. Underground: Hillhead. **Amenities:** 2 restaurants; bar; room service; laundry service; dry cleaning. *In room:* TV, minibar, hair dryer, iron/ironing board, safe.

MODERATE

Albion Hotel   This unpretentious small hotel was renovated in April 2004. Originally two nearly identical beige-sandstone row houses, it sits in a convenient and leafy district of the West End. High-ceilinged guest rooms have modern furniture and a shower-only bathroom. If your hotel needs are straightforward, you'll likely be happy here, where they particularly pride themselves on friendliness.

405–407 N. Woodside Rd., Glasgow G20 6NN. © **0141/339-8620.** Fax 0141/334-8159. www.glasgowhotelsand apartments.co.uk. 20 units. £66 ($122) double without breakfast; £74 ($137) double with breakfast. AE, DC, MC, V. Free parking. Underground: Kelvin Bridge. **Amenities:** Bar; laundry service. *In room:* TV (VCR and DVD on request), dataport, coffeemaker, hair dryer, iron/ironing board, safe, trouser press.

Ambassador Hotel ⭐ *(Value)*   Across from the Botanic Gardens, and overlooking the Kelvin River, this small hotel in a circa-1900 Edwardian town house is owned by the same people as the Albion. After a refurbishment in 2002, the hotel is looking quite stylish. Each of the individually decorated and attractively furnished bedrooms has a well-maintained bathroom with tub and/or shower. The hotel is well-situated for exploring the West End, with many good restaurants or brasseries nearby on Byres Road. Suites are spacious enough to accommodate five to seven guests.

7 Kelvin Dr., Glasgow G20 8QJ. © **0141/946-1018.** Fax 0141/945-5377. www.glasgowhotelsandapartments.co.uk. 16 units. £66 ($122) double without breakfast; £74 ($137) double with breakfast. AE, DC, MC, V. Free parking. Underground: Hillhead. **Amenities:** Bar; laundry. *In room:* TV (VCR and DVD on request), coffeemaker, fridge, hair dryer, iron/ironing board, safe, trouser press.

Argyll Hotel *(Kids)*   It's hard to miss the hanging baskets and creeping ivy of this hotel on one of the main avenues from the city center to the West End. Only a short walk to the University or Kelvingrove Park and the Kelvingrove Art Gallery and Museum, the Argyll lives up to its Scottish name—full of tartan and the like. You almost expect this traditional feel to be part of a Highland lodge rather than urban inn. There is a clutch of spacious family rooms, and one double has a firm four-poster bed and corner-filling bathtub. Sutherlands is the basement restaurant with a seasonally changing menu. The Argyll also hosts "Mackintosh in Style Weekends" where guests tour many of the buildings designed by the great architect.

969–973 Sauchiehall St., Glasgow G3 7TQ. © **0141/337-3313.** Fax 0141/337-3283. www.argyllhotelglasgow.co.uk. 38 units. £78 ($144) double; £160 ($296) family room. Rates include breakfast. AE, MC, V. Limited free parking. Underground: Kelvin Hall. Bus: 18, 62, or city sightseeing bus. **Amenities:** Restaurant (nonsmoking); bar; room service (till 10pm); laundry service; same-day dry cleaning; nonsmoking rooms; porter (24-hr). *In room:* TV, coffeemaker, hair dryer.

City Inn   Right on the River Clyde and near the conference and exhibition center in Finnieston southwest of the commercial center, this smart hotel with its waterside terrace is not exactly in the heart of the action. But neither is it very far away. Part of a

---

Kids **Family-Friendly Hotels**

Argyll Hotel (p. 170)   The family rooms are basic but spacious enough, and the real advantage is the hotel's location: its proximity to Kelvingrove Park and the popular tourist attractions in the West End.

Kirklee Hotel (p. 172)   This small hotel lies in the leafy residential area near the Botanic Gardens, where guests often go for a stroll or a picnic. Some of its comfortably and attractively furnished bedrooms are big enough to house small families.

One Devonshire Gardens (p. 169)   Although this expensive hotel is full of antiques and attracts celebrities, it also caters to families with toys, cots, and highchairs. An interconnecting bedroom is perfect for families to book. Children are offered appropriate videos, and there are special facilities for heating food and sterilizing bottles.

---

small chain with other hotels in London, Birmingham, Bristol, and Manchester, City Inns are modern and contemporary with good facilities. Rooms have power showers.

Finnieston Quay, Glasgow. ✆ **0141/240-1002.** www.cityinn.com. 164 units. £99 ($91) double. AE, DC, MC, V. Limited free parking. Suburban train: Exhibition Centre. **Amenities:** Restaurant; bar; health club; room service. *In room:* A/C, TV, dataport, coffeemaker, hair dryer, trouser press.

Devoncove Hotel   With the closure of the Kelvin Park Lorne Hotel in 2004, the Devoncove is left to provide the more modern if basic hotel accommodation on this stretch of Sauchiehall Street, west of the M8 freeway. Units are comfortable if not huge, although by some local standards the singles here are downright roomy; no need to stand on the bed in order to open the closet door. The more spacious rooms face the street, which is typically quite busy although double-pane windows muffle most of the noise. Extension in 2006 planned to add another 30 rooms and a new restaurant.

931 Sauchiehall St., Glasgow G3 3TQ. ✆ **0141/334-4000.** Fax 0141/339-9000. www.devoncovehotel.com. 45 units. £60 ($111) double; £75 ($139) family. Some discounts available for groups. Rates include Scottish breakfast. AE, MC, V. Free parking. Bus: 18, 62, or city sightseeing bus. **Amenities:** Restaurant; bar; laundry service; dry cleaning; non-smoking rooms. *In room:* TV, fridge, coffeemaker, hair dryer, safe.

Kelvingrove Hotel ✦ *Finds*   Three generations of women in the Somerville family have made a difference to this guest house since buying it in October 2002. They are welcoming hoteliers with 30 years experience running small lodges in Edinburgh, Inverness, and the isle of Arran. Usually Muriel, Valerie, or Mandy are on duty during the day, orienting new arrivals, answering questions, booking cabs, or just generally conversing with visitors. The rooms are comfortable with mainly modern furnishings, set within the converted flats on the ground and garden levels. Room 24 is a particularly bright and reasonably spacious family room with kitchenette.

944 Sauchiehall St., Glasgow G3 7TH. ✆ **0141/339-5011.** Fax 0141/339-6566. www.kelvingrove-hotel.co.uk. 22 units. £60 ($111) double. Rates include Scottish breakfast. MC, V. Parking on street. Underground: Kelvin Hall. Bus: 18, 62, or city sightseeing bus. **Amenities:** Laundry service; dry cleaning; Internet access (evenings); night porter (24-hr.). *In room:* TV, coffeemaker.

Kirklee Hotel *Kids*   A red-sandstone Edwardian terraced house, with elegant bay windows, near the West End's diverse night life on Byres Road and the Botanic Gardens, the Kirklee is often recommended locally. Overlooking a private garden, the Edwardian guest lounge has period furniture. The high-ceilinged overnight rooms are average in size, but some are large enough to accommodate families. For guests who request it, the filling breakfast is served in their room.

11 Kensington Gate, Glasgow G12 9LG. 🕐 0141/334-5555. Fax 0141/339-3828. www.kirkleehotel.co.uk. 9 units. £72 ($133) double; £80–£95 ($148–$176) family room. Rates include Scottish breakfast. MC, V. Parking nearby. Underground: Hillhead. **Amenities:** Bar. *In room:* TV, coffeemaker, hair dryer.

Manor Park Hotel   This impressive West End town house was a private home when it was built in 1895. In 1947, the late Victorian was converted into a hotel, and it has been much improved and upgraded since that time. In the Broomhill district of the West End, the family-run Manor Park is slightly out of the way. Decor offers a blend of modern and traditional furnishings, including beechwood pieces set against a background of floral wallpaper. Each guest room comes with a neat little bathroom with either tub or shower; top floor units are the largest.

28 Balshagray Dr., Glasgow G11 7DD. 🕐 **0141/339-2143.** Fax 0141/339-5842. www.manorparkhotel.com. 9 units. From £65 ($120) double. Rates include full breakfast. AE, DC, MC, V. Free parking. *In room:* TV, coffeemaker, hair dryer, trouser press.

Town House *★★* *Value*   This remains one of the most charming of the city's B&Bs—a less expensive alternative to One Devonshire Gardens, which is just around the corner. The terraced stone Victorian house faces on to the rugby fields of Hillhead sports grounds; the finely corniced entry hall and landing are decorated with original art works. The sitting room features a coal fire, while the hotel provides a computer with high-speed Internet access. The only possible gripe about the individual units may be the box rooms in several that contain shower, sink, and toilet in order to make all units en suite. But otherwise, the hospitality, comfort, and ambience are excellent.

4 Hughenden Terrace (near Great Western and Hyndland rds.), Glasgow G12 9XR. 🕐 **0141/357-0862.** Fax 0141/ 339-9605. www.thetownhouseglasgow.com. 10 units. £72 ($133) double. Rate includes full breakfast. MC, V. Free parking. Underground: Hillhead. **Amenities:** Bar; limited room service; laundry service. *In room:* TV, dataport, coffeemaker, hair dryer, iron/ironing board.

The Wickets Hotel   Given that it overlooks the verdant pitch of the West of Scotland Cricket Club, there is perhaps good reason why the Wickets hotels feels more Gloucester than Glasgow. The pile, which dates to 1890, is something of an undiscovered West End gem. The units are reasonably spacious, with a cheerful decor. Behind the building is the Beer Garden, terraced over several levels. The plastic chairs and tables or wooden picnic tables are not luxurious, but the space is pleasant and peaceful, especially in the spring when the rhododendrons are in blossom and birds in song. The Conservatory restaurant serves fairly priced regional and Continental fare.

52–54 Fortrose St. (off Dumbarton Rd.), Glasgow G11 5LP. 🕐/fax **0141/334-9334.** www.wicketshotel.co.uk. 11 units. £70 ($130) double; £80 ($148) family room. Rates include full breakfast. AE, MC, V. Free parking. Underground: Partick. **Amenities:** Restaurant; 2 bars; room service; laundry service; dry cleaning. *In room:* TV, coffeemaker.

INEXPENSIVE

Kirkland House   On a quiet street in the Finnieston district, about a 10- to 15-minute walk from the Kelvingrove Art Gallery and Museum, the university, and the Scottish Exhibition Centre, this guest house is part of a well-maintained 1832 Victorian crescent of buildings. A mix of antiques and reproductions are used in the large units, where guests are served breakfast. Not many hotels boast their membership in the Harry James Appreciation Society and display a collection of 78rpm gramophone records. You're welcome to listen to sounds of James, Benny Goodman, and many others.

42 St. Vincent Crescent, Glasgow G3 8NG. ⓒ **0141/248-3458**. Fax 0141/221-5174. www.kirkland.net43.co.uk. 5 units. £50–£65 ($92–$120) double; £65–£90 ($120–$166). Rates include continental breakfast. No credit cards. Free parking. *In room:* TV, coffeemaker, no phone.

14

Where to Dine in Glasgow

Like Edinburgh, the dining scene in Glasgow has improved considerably since the days when many local residents thought spaghetti Bolognese was exotic. There has been tremendous growth in the number of restaurants since the mid-1990s, and the choice is excellent. Although the city may not be able to boast about the Michelin stars that a couple of Edinburgh restaurants have earned, Glasgow has some seriously stylish dining rooms, budget-minded bistros, and a mix of ethnic eateries.

Today some of the best fresh Scottish produce is served up here, whether it is shellfish and seafood from the nearby West Coast sea lochs, Ayrshire meat such as pork and lamb, or Aberdeen Angus steaks. There are an ever-increasing number of ethnic restaurants. The immigrant groups who have most influenced cuisine in the city are Italians and families from the Asian subcontinent, mainly the Punjab region. There is a surfeit of Italian and Indian restaurants, as well as a good choice of Chinese and Greek restaurants, too.

A lot of restaurants close on Sunday or on Monday (sometimes both), and many lock up after lunch, reopening again for dinner at around 6pm. The hours listed here are when food is served. Bars on the premises may stay open longer.

For more ideas on dining options, buy *The List* magazine's annual *Eating & Drinking Guide,* a comprehensive review of hundreds of eateries in Glasgow (and Edinburgh).

PRICES Especially given the strength of the currency in the U.K. since 2002, prices will seem high. Still, there is a range of choices for most budgets. The prices include the 17.5% VAT, so there are no hidden surprises when the bill comes. If you're looking for bargains, inquire about pretheater special menus, which can be half the cost of the regular dinner menu. Log onto **www.5pm.co.uk** for a selection of restaurants offering early dining deals.

TIPPING A gratuity of 10% is the rule, although diners can leave nothing if badly treated. On the other hand, if you were truly impressed, a 15% or 20% tip should be considered. In a few restaurants, service is included in the bill automatically. This can be, however, amended or deleted, if service was dreadful.

SMOKING Following a pattern set by nearby Ireland, as well as California and New York City, smoking is prohibited by law from all enclosed public spaces in Scotland, which includes restaurants and bars. Some, however, may provide outdoor seating where smoking is allowed.

1 Restaurants by Cuisine

ASIAN

Café Mao (Merchant City, $$, p. 178)

Wagamama (Commercial Center, $$, p. 183)

CAFE

Where the Monkey Sleeps (Commercial Center, $, p. 183)

CHINESE

Ho Wong (Commercial Center, $$$, p. 181)

Dragon-i ✿ (Commercial Center, $$, p. 182)

CONTINENTAL

Cafe Gandolfi ✿ (Merchant City, $, p. 179)

FISH/SEAFOOD

City Merchant (Merchant City, $$$, p. 178)

Harry Ramsden's (Southside, $$, p. 187)

Gamba ✿✿ (Commercial Center, $$$, p. 181)

Mussel Inn (Commercial Center, $$, p. 182)

Rogano (Commercial Center, $$$, p. 181)

Two Fat Ladies ✿ (West End, $$, p. 186)

FRENCH

Brian Maule at Chardon d'Or (Commercial Center, $$$, p. 180)

The Buttery (Commercial Center, $$$, p. 184)

étain ✿ (Commercial Center, $$, p. 180)

Malmaison (Commercial Center, $$, p. 182)

Michael Caines @ ABode ✿ (Commercial Center, $$$, p. 181)

Schottische (Merchant City, $$, p. 179)

GREEK

Konaki (West End, $$, p. 186)

INDIAN

Balbir's ✿ (West End, $$, p. 185)

The Dhabba ✿ (Merchant City, $$, p. 179)

Mother India ✿ (West End, $$, p. 185)

Wee Curry Shop ✿✿ (Commercial Center, $, p. 183)

INTERNATIONAL

Corinthian (Merchant City, $$, p. 179)

Stravaigin Café Bar ✿ (West End, $, p. 187)

Urban Grill (Southside, $$, p. 188)

ITALIAN

Bella Napoli (Southside, $$, p. 187)

Fratelli Sarti ✿ (Commercial Center, $, p. 183)

La Parmigiana ✿ (West End, $$, p. 186)

JAPANESE

Wagamama (Commercial Center, $$, p. 183)

RUSSIAN

Café Cossachok ✿ (Merchant City, $$, p. 178)

SCOTTISH

Art Lover's Café (Southside, $$, p. 187)

Brian Maule at Chardon d'Or (Commercial Center, $$$, p. 180)

The Buttery (West End, $$$, p. 184)

Cafe Gandolfi ✿ (Merchant City, $, p. 179)

City Merchant (Merchant City, $$$, p. 178)

étain ✿ (Commercial Center, $$, p. 180)

No. Sixteen ✿ (West End, $$, p. 185)

Key to Abbreviations: $$$$ = Very Expensive $$$ = Expensive $$ = Moderate $ = Inexpensive

Glasgow Dining

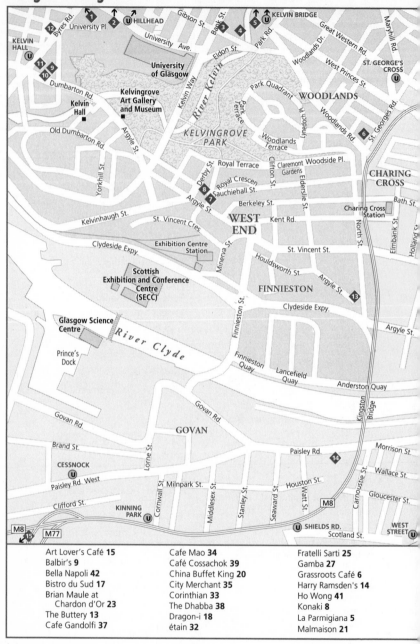

Art Lover's Café **15**
Balbir's **9**
Bella Napoli **42**
Bistro du Sud **17**
Brian Maule at
    Chardon d'Or **23**
The Buttery **13**
Cafe Gandolfi **37**

Cafe Mao **34**
Café Cossachok **39**
China Buffet King **20**
City Merchant **35**
Corinthian **33**
The Dhabba **38**
Dragon-i **18**
étain **32**

Fratelli Sarti **25**
Gamba **27**
Grassroots Café **6**
Harry Ramsden's **14**
Ho Wong **41**
Konaki **8**
La Parmigiana **5**
Malmaison **21**

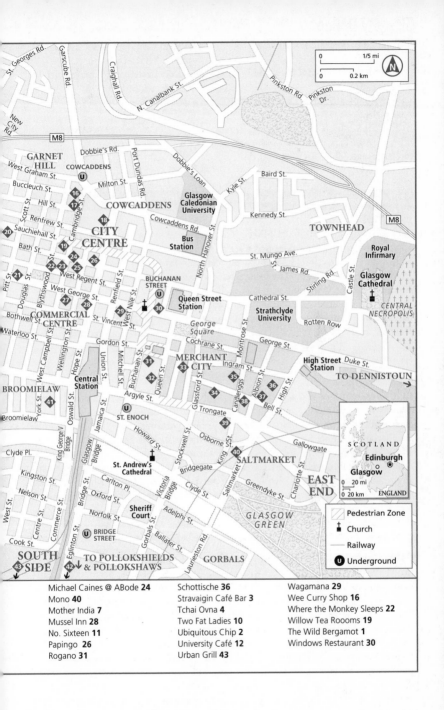

Michael Caines @ ABode **24**	Schottische **36**	Wagamana **29**
Mono **40**	Stravaigin Café Bar **3**	Wee Curry Shop **16**
Mother India **7**	Tchai Ovna **4**	Where the Monkey Sleeps **22**
Mussel Inn **28**	Two Fat Ladies **10**	Willow Tea Roooms **19**
No. Sixteen **11**	Ubiquitous Chip **2**	The Wild Bergamot **1**
Papingo **26**	University Café **12**	Windows Restaurant **30**
Rogano **31**	Urban Grill **43**	

Papingo (Commercial Center, $$, p. 182)

Schottische (Merchant City, $$, p. 179)

Stravaigin Café Bar ⊛ (West End, $, p. 187)

Two Fat Ladies ⊛ (West End, $$, p. 186)

Ubiquitous Chip ⊛ (West End, $$$, p. 184)

The Wild Bergamot ⊛⊛ (West End, $$$, p. 185)

Windows Restaurant (Commercial Center, $$, p. 183)

VEGETARIAN

Grassroots Café ⊛ (West End, $, p. 186)

Mono (Merchant City, $, p. 179)

2 Merchant City

EXPENSIVE

City Merchant FISH/SCOTTISH   This restaurant in the heart of the Merchant City combines friendly service and a set of menus that highlight fresh fish, seafood, and meat. Not exactly old-fashioned but certainly favored by businessmen and for family events, the restaurant's cuisine tends to be more reliable than mind-blowingly stunning. Try the whopping platter of shellfish served on ice or one of the "catch-of-the-day" main courses. Also tempting are seared scallops as well as the classic smoked haddock soup, known as Cullen skink. If you're not in the mood for some fruits of the sea, roast breast of duck, rack of lamb, or an escalope of venison can substitute.

97–99 Candleriggs. ✆ **0141/553-1577**. www.citymerchant.co.uk. Reservations recommended. Dinner main courses £16–£22 ($30–$41). AE, DC, MC, V. Mon–Sat noon–10:30pm. Underground: Buchanan St.

MODERATE

Café Cossachok ⊛ *(Finds)* RUSSIAN   A combination of small restaurant and gallery space, where live music frequently is played, the Atlas family's Café Cossachok has chefs that concentrate on hearty Slavic fare: primarily Russian, Georgian, and Ukrainian specialties. Come here to feast on famous dishes such as borscht beet root soup with sour cream or some savory blinis—the Russian equivalent of pancakes. In addition, for the full Russian experience, a variety of vodka bottles inhabit the freezer for a refreshing shot to throw down with your meal. Redevelopment of King Street may mean the operation has moved temporarily to Albion Street, while Café Gramofon across the way is run by the same people.

10 King St. ✆ **0141/553-0733**. www.cossachok.com. Reservations recommended. Main courses £7–£14 ($13–$26). MC, V. Tues–Thurs 11:30am–9:30pm; Fri–Sun 4pm–late. Underground: St. Enoch.

Café Mao ASIAN   This is a lively place for a meal situated north of the Trongate in the Merchant City district. What with the big Andy Warhol–style portraits of Chairman Mao prominently displayed in the window-filled corner location, you can't really miss the place. Part of a small chain of Asian eateries, curiously based in Ireland, the Mao formula mixes the casual setting of a spacious, modern, and stylish bistro with dishes from East Asia. The place can be quiet during lunch times, but it is almost always hopping at night, with a buzz you would expect at a popular bar. Dishes include starters, such as spring rolls stuffed with pumpkin, and main courses, such as Indonesian nasi goreng or Vietnamese beef and noodles, all prepared in the open kitchen where you can see flames licking at the chefs' bibs.

84 Brunswick St. ✆ **0141/564-5161**. www.cafemao.com. Reservations suggested. Fixed-price lunch £9.50 ($18); main courses £8.50–£12 ($16–$22). AE, MC, V. Daily noon–11pm. Underground: St. Enoch.

Corinthian INTERNATIONAL   This bar/restaurant/club in a one-time Bank of Scotland building is probably as popular for its stunning and fully restored Victorian looks, such as a 7.5m (25-ft.) glass dome or crystal chandeliers, as it is for anything else. If you feel like getting dressed up and going to a place where you can have a cocktail, dinner, and then dance—all under one roof—then come here. The restaurant menu ranges from glazed Oriental pork belly to twice-baked cheddar cheese soufflé.

191 Ingram St. ℰ **0141/552-1101.** www.corinthian.uk.com. Reservations recommended. Main courses £12–£22 ($22–$40). AE, MC, V. Sun–Fri 5–10pm; Sat noon–11pm. Bar and club open to 3am daily. Underground: Buchanan St.

The Dhabba ℱ INDIAN   Glaswegians love their Indian food, as visitors can tell from the number of Indian restaurants alone. This one, which opened in late 2002, however, is not your typical Glasgow curry house. It is a bit more refined, slightly more expensive, and considerably more stylish than the norm. It specializes in North Indian dishes and largely foregoes the bright food coloring that so many other restaurants use. In addition to spicy dishes featuring lamb, chicken, and prawns, there is also an excellent selection of vegetarian dishes, which are noticeably less costly than the meat options. Marinated fish cooked in tandoori spices is recommended, as are the many baked breads, whether naan, rotis, or parathas. Up Candleriggs and on the other side of the street is Dhabba's sister restaurant, Dakhin, which specializes in Southern Indian food.

44 Candleriggs. ℰ **0141/553-1249.** www.thedhabba.com. Reservations recommended. Main courses £8–£15 ($15–$28). AE, MC, V. Daily noon–2pm and 5–11pm; Sat–Sun 2–5pm. Underground: St. Enoch.

Schottische SCOTTISH/FRENCH   Housed above the popular **Babbity Bowster** (p. 237) pub in the small hotel of the same name, Schottische has a rustic feel with a coal fire at one end of the cozy room and hand-written menus. The ingredients are typically Scottish in origin, whether lamb, venison, or sea bass. But given that the chef was born in France, the cuisine usually displays hearty Gallic influences—in addition to excellent wines. For simpler but tasty meals from the same kitchen, stick to the pub on the ground floor.

16–18 Blackfriars St. (just off High St.) ℰ **0141/552-5055.** Reservations recommended. Dinner main courses £10–£14 ($19–$26). AE, MC, V. Tues–Sat 6:30–9:30pm. Suburban railway: High St.

INEXPENSIVE

Cafe Gandolfi ℱ SCOTTISH/CONTINENTAL   For many local foodies in the Merchant City, this is their favorite: it offers solid cooking at the right price and a friendly ambience. Owner Seumas MacInnes hails from a Highland/Hebridean family and so the black pudding comes down from Stornoway on the Isle of Lewis while the haggis hails from Dingwall. Particularly recommended is the black pudding, Gandolfi's creamy Cullen skink (smoked haddock chowder), or one of the light pasta dishes. Although if you're hungry, go for the steak sandwich. The ground floor room has original, organic, and comfortable wooden furniture created by the Tim Stead workshop in Scotland. A recent addition to the premises is **Bar Gandolfi** up the steel staircase in the attic space. With a ceiling skylight, however, it is anything but dark and dank.

64 Albion St. ℰ **0141/552-6813.** www.cafegandolfi.com. Reservations recommended. Main courses £6–£12 ($11–$22). MC, V. Mon–Sat 9am–11:30pm; Sun noon–11:30pm. Underground: Buchanan St.

Mono VEGAN/VEGETARIAN   Technically outside the Merchant City in the nearby Saltmarket district closer to the River Clyde, Mono does basic dairy- and meat-free meals in laid-back surroundings. Not only a cafe/restaurant with a bar, Mono also houses a store selling free-trade goods and a CD shop with the latest in indie rock and nonmainstream music. It is a welcoming and casual place with a mixed and varied clientele. Home-made soups or veggie burgers with fries are typical. The owners also stock a selection of organic wines. Live music, mostly but not exclusively of an acoustic nature, is featured regularly and the kitchen may close early on gig nights.

12 Kings Ct. © 0141/553-2400. Main courses £5–£7 ($9–$13). AE, MC, V. Daily noon–9pm. Underground: St. Enoch.

3 Glasgow Commercial Center

EXPENSIVE

Brian Maule at Chardon d'Or FRENCH/SCOTTISH   Chef Brian Maule was born in Ayrshire near Glasgow, but he trained as a young man with some of the best chefs in France. He became part of the team working with the highly respected Roux brothers in London. After rising in rank to head chef at their vaunted Michelin-star-winning Gavroche restaurant, he decided to go north and return to Scotland, opening his own restaurant in Glasgow in 2001. It is considered among the finest in the city, with excellent ingredients and an ambience that is classy but not at all stuffy. Fresh fish and lamb dishes come highly recommended.

176 West Regent St. © 0141/248-3801. www.brianmaule.com. Reservations recommended. Main courses £20–£24 ($37–$44). AE, MC, V. Mon–Fri noon–2:30pm and 6–10pm; Sat 6–10:30pm. Underground: Buchanan St.

étain ✿ FRENCH/SCOTTISH   Adjacent to a branch of Zinc Bar & Grill, étain (French for pewter) offers fine dining at the top of the Princes Square shopping center. You enter the restaurant either through the mall and via Zinc, or by using a dedicated glass elevator from a rear ally accessed by Queen Street. However you arrive, the

---

⌒Kids   Family-Friendly Fare

Bistro du Sud   Just off Sauchiehall Street, at 97 Cambridge St. (© 0141/ 332-2666), the small, locally owned cafe/bistro loves to have children in its midst. Don't be lulled by the familiar multinational chain operations and try something tasty at this modern Italian/French eatery instead. Open daily 8:30am to 10pm (from noon on Sun).

China Buffet King   Just like in Edinburgh, the buffet-only Chinese restaurant has taken Glasgow by storm. This one is centrally located, at 349 Sauchiehall St. (© 0141/333-1788), with a good variety of Chinese food and some European dishes, at all-you-can-eat discount prices that lower even more for children. Open daily noon to 11pm.

University Café   I scream, you scream, we all scream for ice cream. "Knickerbocker Glory" is the king of the ice-cream sundae in Scotland, and few places do it better than this Art Deco landmark at 87 Byres Rd., in the West of Glasgow (© 0141/339-5217), with all original features from booths to counters. Open Wednesday to Monday 9am to 10pm (or so).

food will feature contemporary French cooking using Scottish produce: whether lobster, lamb, scallops, crab, or venison. Memorable little touches include handmade truffles served after dinner. Service is generally excellent although perhaps a bit sniffy on occasion.

The Glass House, Princes Square, Springfield Ct. ℂ **0141/225-5630**. Reservations recommended. Fixed-price lunch £16 ($30); dinner main courses £14–£20 ($26–$37). AE, MC, V. Mon–Fri noon–2:30pm and 7–11pm; Sat 6–11pm; Sun noon–3pm. Underground: St. Enoch.

Gamba ★★ FISH/SEAFOOD   For many, Gamba is Glasgow's best on the strength of its fresh fish and seafood dishes prepared by chef and co-owner Derek Marshall—complemented by the professional and cordial staff. The basement venture is modern and stylish without feeling excessively fancy. Starters include Marshall's signature fish soup or sashimi, with succulent slices of salmon and scallops. Main courses may include whole lemon sole in browned butter or delicate pan-seared sea bream. And desserts are not an afterthought either, whether smooth panna cotta or ice cream infused with Scotch whisky. If you're on a tight budget, however, try the lunch or pretheater fixed-price menu.

225a West George St. ℂ **0141/572-0899**. www.gamba.co.uk. Reservations required. Fixed-price lunch £16 ($30); dinner main courses £19–£26 ($35–$48). AE, MC, V. Mon–Sat noon–2:30pm and 5–10:30pm. Underground: Buchanan St.

Ho Wong CHINESE   One of the city's fanciest Chinese restaurants, this classy establishment is on a rather inauspicious block between the river and Argyle Street, just southwest of Glasgow's Central Station. The ambience is refined and even a bit romantic. There are traditionally at least eight duck dishes on the menu, along with a few types of fresh lobster, plenty of fish options, and some sizzling platters as well. If you have trouble deciding, the banquet option (starting at £27/$43) makes life a bit easier.

82 York St. ℂ **0141/221-3550**. www.ho-wong.com. Reservations recommended. Fixed-price lunch £9.50 ($18); main courses £12–£20 ($22–$37); fixed-price banquet (5 courses) £27 ($43). AE, MC, V. Mon–Sat noon–2:30pm; daily 5:30–11:30pm. Underground: St. Enoch.

Michael Caines @ ABode ★ FRENCH   Opened in 2005, this restaurant has ambitions to be the best in the city. Chef/owner Michael Caines has already earned Michelin stars in England, and the staff he hired for this fine-dining operation at the ABode Hotel (formerly the Arthouse; p. 167) has similar aspirations. It is hard to find fault with cooking and presentation, such as seared red mullet with slivers of zucchini, daubs of tomato sauce, and some eggplant purée rounded off with a frothy fennel cream. The dining room is modern and stylish, as you would expect in a boutique hotel such as ABode. In addition to this fine-dining restaurant, there is a cafe/bar in the basement.

129 Bath St. ℂ **0141/572-6011**. www.abodehotels.co.uk. Reservations recommended. Fixed-price lunch £14 ($25); main courses £18–£25 ($33–$46); tasting menu £60 ($111). AE, MC, V. Mon–Sat noon–2:30pm and 7–10pm. Underground: Buchanan St.

Rogano FISH/SEAFOOD   Sold to new owners in 2006, Rogano boasts a well-preserved Art Deco interior patterned after the Queen Mary ocean liner that dates back to the opening of the oyster bar here in 1935. Since then, the space has expanded, and Rogano has hosted virtually every visiting celebrity to the city. You can enjoy dinner amid etched mirrors, ceiling fans, semicircular banquettes, and potted palms. Service is attentive and informed. The menu emphasizes seafood, such as halibut in champagne-and-oyster sauce or lobster Thermidor. While these are traditional if possibly old-fashioned recipes, they have their fans. A less-expensive menu is offered downstairs in the less-exclusive Cafe Rogano, where the price of main courses hover around the £12 ($22) mark.

11 Exchange Place. © **0141/248-4055.** www.rogano.co.uk. Reservations recommended. Fixed-price lunch £18 ($33); dinner main courses £17–£34 ($31–$63). AE, DC, MC, V. Daily noon–2:30pm and 6:30–10:30pm. Underground: Buchanan St.

MODERATE

Dragon-i ⚘ CHINESE   Although the location is convenient for the Theatre Royal, this contemporary Chinese/Far Eastern restaurant would be a bigger hit if it were on a different, more central street. But only a few minutes walk from Sauchiehall Street, it is hardly way out of the way. Expect the unexpected at the elegant Dragon-i, whose cuisine never falls into the bland or typical chow mein or sweet-and-sour standards. Instead, the menu has dishes such as tiger prawns with asparagus in a garlic chardonnay sauce or chicken with sautéed apples and pineapples. The wine list is also excellent.

313 Hope St. © **0141/332-7728.** www.dragon-i.co.uk. Reservations recommended. Fixed-price lunch £10 ($19); dinner main courses £11–£16 ($20–$30). AE, MC, V. Mon–Sat noon–2pm; daily 5–10pm. Underground: Cowcaddens.

Malmaison Brasserie FRENCH   In the vaulted basement of this hip boutique hotel (p. 168), the brasserie offers an atmospheric place to dine. Here, in the crypt, the cuisine sometimes has to compete with the surroundings. Food arrives in generous portions and may include rack of lamb with garlic crushed potatoes, grilled swordfish, or Malmaison's signature steak frites. The wine list features only French wines, specially selected by Malmaison. The adjacent atrium-like bar is a good place for a champagne cocktail.

278 W. George St. © **0141/572-1001.** www.malmaison.com. Reservations recommended. Fixed-price lunch £13 ($23); dinner main courses £11–£17 ($20–$31). AE, DC, MC, V. Daily noon–3pm and 5:30–10:30pm. Suburban train: Charing Cross. Bus: 62.

Mussel Inn FISH/SEAFOOD   Sister restaurant to the original on Rose Street in Edinburgh, the Mussel Inn has the distinction of being owned by shellfish farmers in the west of Scotland. The kilo pot of mussels you eat here on any given evening might have been harvested only earlier the same day. The feel at the Glasgow unit is casual, with an open kitchen, light wood tables, and high ceilings, re-creating the feel you might find if it were located right at the sea shore. In addition to the house specialty of steamed mussels served with a choice of broths (from spicy to white wine with garlic), the queen scallop salad is fine and refreshing, creamy chowders hearty and filling, and the menu always features a fresh "catch of the day."

157 Hope St. © **0141/572-1405.** www.mussel-inn.com. Main courses £8–£14 ($15–$26). AE, MC, V. Mon–Fri noon–2:30pm and 5:30–10pm; Sat noon–10pm; Sun 5–10pm. Underground: Buchanan St.

Papingo SCOTTISH   This has become a stalwart of solid, consistent dining in the city center of Glasgow. It is not flashy—or even necessarily fashionable—but it rarely strikes an out-of-tune note. It is what the British people might term a "safe pair of hands." The name is lowland Scots for "parrot," and motifs of the tropical bird abound in this basement space. The food is modern Scottish and brasserie-style fare, with starters, such as a creamy pâté served with tangy chutney, and main courses, such as grilled lamb chops with tomato and tarragon gravy. The pretheater prices are noteworthy.

104 Bath St. ✆ **0141/332-6678**. www.papingo.co.uk. Reservations recommended. Main courses £9–£15 ($17–$28). AE, MC, V. Mon–Sat noon–10pm; Sun 4–10pm. Underground: Buchanan St.

Wagamama (Value) ASIAN/JAPANESE Based in London, where there are several outlets, the Wagamama Japanese noodle bar formula has proved successful in its first venture into Scotland. Casual seating is at long tables and benches, where waitresses key your order into handheld devices that transmit it to the cooks. Dishes come as they are prepared, rather than as starters and main courses. It is one of the best places in the city center to get a quick bite before a show or the cinema.

97–103 W. George St. ✆ **0141/229-1468**. www.wagamama.com. No reservations. Dishes £5–£10 ($9.25–$19). Daily noon–11pm (till 10pm Sun). Underground: Buchanan St.

Windows Restaurant SCOTTISH Unlike Edinburgh, Glasgow doesn't have many restaurants with views from on high. In fact, not counting the cafe on top of the Lighthouse Center for Architecture, it has one. This one. Here, on the top floor of the Carlton George Hotel, this restaurant is aptly named, as it opens onto panoramic views of Glasgow's city center near George Square and the City Chambers. Diners get a "Taste of Scotland" with such dishes as seared scallops or the grilled filet of Scottish beef with mushrooms.

In the Carlton George Hotel, 44 W. George St. ✆ **0141/354-5070**. Reservations recommended. Fixed-price lunch £12 ($22); main courses £13–£16 ($24–$30). AE, MC, V. Daily noon–2:30pm and 5–9:30pm. Underground: Buchanan St.

INEXPENSIVE

Fratelli Sarti ✺ (Kids) ITALIAN Owned by the Sarti brothers, the dual restaurant and cafe feels like a family-run cafe/bistro crossed with a delicatessen. Indeed, you can still buy dry goods and wines here, although they discontinued the deli meats and cheeses a couple years ago. The pizza is excellent, with thin, crispy crust and modest amounts of sauce, cheese, and toppings, which prevent it from becoming a sloppy mess. Pasta dishes, such as "al forno" with penne, sausage, and spinach, are filling. Come here if you just want a real Italian espresso and pastry, too. If you desire a slightly more formal setting, try the Fratelli Sarti on Renfield Sreet (✆ **0141/572-7000**).

133 Wellington St. ✆ **0141/204-0440**. Reservations recommended. Main courses £6–£10 ($11–$19). AE, MC, V. Mon–Fri 8am–10:30pm; Sat 8am–11pm; Sun noon–10.30pm. Underground: Buchanan St.

Wee Curry Shop ✺✺ (Value) INDIAN This tiny place is hardly big enough to swing a cat in, but the aptly named Wee Curry Shop offers the best, low-cost Indian dishes in the city. Just about five tables are crammed between the front door and the open kitchen, where the chefs prepare everything to order. The menu is concise with a clutch of opening courses, such as fried pakora, and a half dozen or so main courses, such as spicy chile garlic chicken. Portions are large even if prices are cheap. While it may feel off the beaten track, the Wee Curry Shop is actually only a short walk from the shopping precincts of Sauchiehall Street. There is a second branch on Ashton Lane, in the West End.

7 Buccleuch St. (near Cambridge St.). ✆ **0141/353-0777**. Reservations recommended. Fixed-price lunch £4.75 ($9); main courses £5–£7 ($9.25–$13). Mon–Sat noon–2pm and 5:30–10pm; Sun 5–10pm. Underground: Cowcaddens.

Where the Monkey Sleeps CAFE Downstairs near Blythswood Square, this singular cafe-cum-gallery is one of the best daytime places for cappuccinos, soups, and sandwiches in the commercial center of Glasgow. You know you've found it when you

---

Moments **Tea for Two**

For tea and a snack, why not join the rest of the tourists in Glasgow and try to secure a table at the landmark **Willow Tea Rooms,** 217 Sauchiehall St. (*C* **0141/332-0521;** Underground: Cowcaddens). When the famed Mrs. Cranston opened the Willow Tea Rooms in 1904, it was something of a sensation due to its unique Charles Rennie Mackintosh design. The building's white facade still stands out from the crowd more than 100 years later. The dining room, one floor above street level, is open Monday to Saturday 9am to 5pm and Sunday noon to 5pm. A second branch on Buchanan Street is similarly appointed if less authentic.

For a more contemporary experience, in the West End overlooking the River Kelvin, **Tchai Ovna,** 42 Otago St. (*C* **0141/357-4524**), has a selection of some 80 teas, served in fairly eccentric and bohemian surroundings. In the evenings, there may be live music, poetry, or comedy. Tchai Ovna is open daily from 11am to 11pm.

---

see all the bikes of messengers who seem to live here when they are not on the streets delivering special letters and business packages. As the name might indicate, this is no ordinary cafe. It is owned and operated by artistic types (including two graduates from the nearby Art School) who learned their barista skills at Starbucks but wanted to be free of corporate constraints.

182 W. Regent St. *C* **0141/226-3406.** www.wtms.co.uk. Soups £2.50 ($4.75); sandwiches £1.80–£3.50 ($3.30–$6.50). Mon–Fri 8am–5pm; Sat 10am–6pm. Underground: Buchanan St.

4 The West End

EXPENSIVE

The Buttery SCOTTISH/FRENCH   West of the M8 freeway but not precisely in the West End, this is one of the best-known and long-established restaurants in Glasgow. This Victorian tenement has been standing here since 1870 or so, although most remnants of the neighborhood are now gone. The Buttery continues to exude old-world charm from its rich, sumptuous bar and lounge to the wood-paneled dining room with white linen. Although the setting is traditional, the cooking is progressive: rabbit served with roasted coriander seed sauce or halibut with a pea purée.

652 Argyle St. *C* **0141/221-8188.** www.eatbuttery.com. Reservations recommended. Fixed-price lunch £16 ($30); fixed-price dinner £34 ($63). AE, DC, MC, V. Tues–Fri noon–2pm and 6–9:30pm; Sat 6–9:30pm. Suburban train: Anderston.

Ubiquitous Chip *★* SCOTTISH   No other restaurant has been more responsible for the culinary renaissance in Scotland than the Ubiquitous Chip. Opening the "Chip" in 1971, chef/owner Ronnie Clydesdale was ahead of the curve, bringing the best Scottish ingredients into his kitchen—and then to the attention of diners. To this day, the menus state the provenance of the produce, a practice now commonplace in better restaurants. Inside the walls of a former stable, the recently renovated dining room focuses on an interior courtyard with a fountain and masses of climbing vines. The menu may feature free-range chicken, Aberdeen Angus beef, shellfish with crispy seaweed snaps, or wild rabbit. Upstairs, the friendly pub and small brasserie (Upstairs at the Chip) serves similar quality fare at a fraction of the price.

12 Ashton Lane, off Byres Rd. ℰ **0141/334-5007**. www.ubiquitouschip.co.uk. Reservations recommended. Fixed-price lunch £23 ($42); fixed-price dinner £34 ($63). AE, DC, MC, V. Daily noon–2:30pm and 5:30–11pm. Underground: Hillhead.

The Wild Bergamot ✸✸ *Finds* SCOTTISH   Chef and proprietor Alan Burns took over this tiny restaurant, formerly known as Gingerhill, in the northwestern suburbs of Glasgow and has put it on the culinary map. The cooking is assured and innovative, with emphasis placed on seasonal Scottish ingredients. A small lounge serves canapés and takes dinner orders before guests move to the cozy dining room. Dishes change regularly and can include almond-crusted halibut with braised oxtail or rump roast and lavender-braised shoulder of Scottish lamb. Intermediate courses add a special touch. It's worth finding your way to Milngavie to eat here.

1 Hillhead St., Milngavie ℰ **0141/956-6515**. www.thewildbergamot.co.uk. Reservations required. Fixed-price lunch £15 ($28); fixed-price dinner £30 ($56); tasting menu £45 ($83). MC, V. Wed–Sun 7–9:30pm; Fri and Sat noon–2pm. Near Milngavie railway station; off the A81, about 9km (6 miles) northwest of Glasgow city center.

MODERATE

Balbir's ✸ INDIAN   After taking a break from running restaurants in Glasgow, Balbir Singh Sumal returned in 2005 to open this sprawling place, serving first-class curries and other Indian specialties. Dishes are lighter than the norm, as his chefs eschew ghee in favor of low-cholesterol rapeseed oil. The tandoori oven is used to good effect with dishes, especially a starter of barbecued salmon, served with freshly made chutney. Fans of *Seinfeld* will appreciate the portrait of Kramer, proudly if rather incongruously hung on one wall of this otherwise stylish dining room.

7 Church St. ℰ **0141/339-7711**. Main courses £6–£12 ($11–$22). AE, MC, V. Daily 5–10pm. Underground: Kelvinhall.

Mother India ✸ INDIAN   After more than a decade in business, this restaurant seems to have established itself as the most respected Indian restaurant in Glasgow. The menu is not overloaded with hundreds of different dishes. Oven-baked fish, which comes wrapped in foil, is seasoned with aromatic spices, while chicken and zucchini squash is served with a sauce that favors pan-roasted cumin and cardamom. Whether seated on the ground floor or in the dining room above, diners will find the staff to be courteous and attentive. Down the road, towards the heart of the West End, a second branch—**Mother India's Café** (1355 Argyle St.; ℰ **0141/339-9145**)— offers less expensive, tapas-style dishes.

28 Westminster Terrace (Sauchiehall St. at Kelvingrove St.). ℰ **0141/221-1663**. www.motherindia.co.uk. Reservations required. Main courses £7.50–£12 ($14–$22). No credit cards. Mon–Fri 5–10:30pm; Sat–Sun 1–10:30pm. Underground: Kelvinhall.

No. Sixteen ✸ SCOTTISH   No. Sixteen has a neighborhood feel to it, small and slightly cramped with dining on the ground floor and a tiny mezzanine above. But its appeal extends far beyond those who happen to live nearby. The story's been told of a couple visiting Glasgow, who came here on their first night in town for dinner and returned every subsequent night because they were so pleased with the food. Near the base of Byres Road, this Scottish bistro offers inventive cooking of local ingredients: braised pig cheek with purple endive or pan-fried filet of mackerel with olive crushed potatoes, for example, on daily changing menus. The pretheater menu offers excellent value.

16 Byres Rd. ⓒ **0141/339-2544**. Reservations recommended. Fixed-price lunch £12 ($20); main courses £12–£20 ($22–$37). AE, MC, V. Daily noon–2:30pm and 5:30–9:30pm. Underground: Kelvinhall.

La Parmigiana ⚇ ITALIAN   This remains the favorite fine-dining Italian restaurant in Glasgow, providing a cosmopolitan and Continental atmosphere. A well-established, quarter-of-a-century-old business of the Giovanazzi family, Parmigiana is often recommended for its fish and meat dishes, whether grilled salmon with honey-roasted vegetables, pan-fried pork cutlet with caramelized apple, or roast breast of guinea fowl stuffed with porcini mushrooms. A highlight of the pasta options is lobster ravioli with basil cream sauce. The house wine is excellent, but the list affords the opportunity to sample some fine vintages at corresponding costs. Service by waiters in smart black vests is usually impeccable.

447 Great Western Rd. ⓒ **0141/334-0686**. www.laparmigiana.co.uk. Reservations required. Fixed-price lunch £12 ($21); dinner main courses £15–£20 ($28–$37). AE, DC, MC, V. Mon–Sat noon–2:30pm and 5:30–10:30pm. Underground: Kelvinbridge.

Two Fat Ladies ⚇ FISH/SCOTTISH   This ranks high on the list of many locals' favorite restaurants. The "Two Fat Ladies" is a reference to its street number—a nickname for the number 88 when called out in bingo games. The kitchen is placed right at the front door; the decor of the small dining space to the rear is fairly minimalist. Specialties include red-onion-and-goat-cheese tart, pan-seared bream, filet of sea bass served on mashed potatoes with spring onions, a balsamic roasted breast of chicken, and sticky toffee pudding. In addition to the West End flagship, a second outlet has opened in the commercial center at 118a Blythswood St. (ⓒ **0141/847-0088**).

88 Dumbarton Rd. ⓒ **0141/339-1944**. Reservations recommended. Fixed-price lunch £11 ($20); fixed-price pre-theater dinner £13 ($24); dinner main courses £14–£18 ($26–$33). MC, V. Mon–Sat noon–3pm; daily 5–10:30pm. Underground: Kelvinhall.

INEXPENSIVE

Grassroots Café ⚇ VEGETARIAN   Tied to the organic food shop located just around the corner on Woodlands Road, Grassroots is the city's leading vegetarian restaurant. The feel is casual and relaxed, with some sofas at the front of the dining space and booths separated by gauzy curtains along one wall. A good selection of non-alcoholic fruit drinks as well as organic wine and beer from Britain complement a menu that has international influences. Cakes of risotto-style rice with goat's cheese and pine nuts, tempura-battered and fried vegetables, and a Middle Eastern tagine with couscous offer examples of what you'll find here.

93–97 St. Georges Rd. (parallel the M8 Fwy.). ⓒ **0141/333-0534**. www.grassrootsorganic.com. Main courses £5–£8 ($9–$15). MC, V. Mon–Fri 10am–10pm; Sat–Sun 10am–3:45pm and 5–10pm. Underground: St. George's Cross.

Konaki *Finds* GREEK   This simple and unassuming Greek taverna midway between the city center and the heart of the West End, convenient to the moderately priced hotels and guesthouses nearby, has slowly developed a reputation for good, hearty food at relatively inexpensive prices. Unlike most of the city's Greek restaurants, which are primarily Cypriot, the owners of Konaki hail from the island of Crete instead. The menu includes phyllo pastry stuffed with goat's cheese, slow-cooked meats, and char-grilled kebabs. For a sample of Greek delicacies such as stuffed grape leaves and hummus dip, opt for the meze platter. Some Friday nights feature dancing and Greek plate-smashing for some lively entertainment.

920 Sauchiehall St. © 0141/342-4010. www.konakitaverna.com. Fixed-price lunch £7 ($13); dinner main courses £10 ($19). MC, V. Mon–Sat noon–2:30pm; daily 5–11pm. Underground: Kelvinhall.

Stravaigin Café Bar ★ *Value* SCOTTISH/INTERNATIONAL   The motto of Stravaigin, which roughly translates from the Scottish vernacular to "wanderin'" in English, is "think global, eat local." While the basement restaurant here is an award-wining enterprise, the ground level pub/cafe, with its recently expanded balcony, offers less expensive but still memorable food. Every afternoon and evening, people squeeze in for a drink and a meal. Scottish produce gets international twists: for example, cheese and herb fritters with sweet chile sauce or roast lamb served with coriander couscous. But there are also staples such as hearty fish and chips. The atmosphere is always cordial, and prices are lower still during the busy pretheater seating. If you like Stravaigin, you might consider its sister bistro near Byres Rd., called appropriately enough, **Stravaigin 2** (Ruthven Lane; © 0141/334-7156).

28 Gibson St. © 0141/334-2665. www.stravaigin.com. Main courses £6–£10 ($11–$19). AE, MC, V. Daily 11am–10:30pm. Underground: Kelvinbridge.

5 The Southside

MODERATE
Art Lover's Café SCOTTISH   The House for an Art Lover is a creation by contemporary builders and architects working with some very basic drawings left by Charles Rennie Mackintosh. It is a testament to the architect's latent popularity that this pile was built so many years after his demise. In addition to being a stop for hardcore Mackintosh fans, it also is home for a popular cafe. Next to the gift shop is a stylish, ivory-colored dining room with arching windows that look out on to the gardens. The cafe's modern Scottish cuisine—dishes such as salad of seared scallops, black pudding, and crisp pancetta—is occasionally inspired, and the place at lunchtime on the weekend is rarely less than full.

House for an Art Lover, Bellahouston Park, 10 Dumbreck Rd. © 0141/353-4779. Reservations recommended. www.houseforanartlover.co.uk. Fixed-price lunch £12 ($21). AE, MC, V. Daily noon–4pm. Bus: 9, 54, or 56.

Bella Napoli ITALIAN   Set in the heart of the Shawlands district, the main commercial area of Glasgow's Southside, Bella Napoli looks from the street to be a bright, shiny Italian cafe. But to the rear and down a few steps, a more refined but still casual dining room is hidden. The family-run business is friendly, and the staff is efficient as well. Starters include melon with prawns or minestrone soup, with the rest of the menu offering a range of pasta dishes as well as risotto and meaty main courses. Up front, the cafe is best for lunch food such as calzones filled with vegetables, cheese, and tomato sauce.

85 Kilmarnock Rd. © 0141/362-4222. Fixed-price lunch £8 ($15); dinner main courses £8–£12 ($15–$22). MC, V. Mon–Fri noon–3pm and 5–10:30pm; Sat–Sun noon–10:30pm. Bus: 38 or 45.

Harry Ramsden's *Kids* FISH   Near the multiplex cinema on the Clyde, Harry Ramsden's is something of a British institution. The restaurant chain began humbly in the north of England, with branches spreading in all directions today. While fish and chips in Scotland (more commonly called a "fish supper" if ordered to go and a "fish tea" when eating in) usually involves battered and deep-fried haddock, in England the common white fish used is cod. Here at Harry's you can get either—as well as plaice and other options. All meals are huge, with french fries and peas, and the obligatory plate of white bread with butter. For the children there is a special menu and outdoors play area.

251 Paisley Rd. (© 0141/429-3700. www.harryramsdens.co.uk. Main courses £7–£10 ($13–$19). AE, MC, V. Daily noon–10pm. Bus: 9 or 54.

Urban Grill INTERNATIONAL   Bringing a bit of cosmopolitan sophistication to the heart of the Southside, Urban Grill is owned by the same people behind Gamba (see above). Not devoted to seafood but rather offering a widely ranging menu—sticky pork ribs to roast cod with prawn and chick pea curry—this bar and restaurant also offers live piano playing in the evenings.

61 Kilmarnock Rd. (© 0141/649-2745. www.urbangrill.co.uk. Main courses £8–£15 ($15—28). MC, V. Daily noon–10pm.

6 Picnic Fare

The "dear green place" has no shortage of spots for a picnic, whether in sprawling Glasgow Green, along the Clyde near the city center, Kelvingrove Park or the Botanic Gardens in the West End, not to mention Pollok Country Park or Queens Park on the Southside.

If you're in the city center, gravitate towards **Pekhams** in the Merchant City near George Square, 61 Glassford St. (© **0141/553-0666**), which has a full delicatessen, fresh bread, and a wine shop. In the West End, the options include the exceptional **Heart Buchanan Fine Food and Wine,** near the Botanic Gardens at 380 Byres Rd. (© **0141/334-7626**), which also has a small cafe. **Delizique,** 66 Hyndland St. (© **0141/ 339-2000**), is another superior food shop, while there's another branch of **Pekhams** at 124 Byres Rd. (© **0141/357-1454**). Nearby is the cafe and deli, **Kember & Jones Fine Food Emporium,** 134 Byres Rd. (© **0141/337-3851**).

For some of the best cheese in the U.K., visit the **IJ Mellis Cheesemonger** branch in Glasgow on Great Western Road (© **0141/339-8998**), and just further towards the city center is the Glasgow branch of **Lupe Pintos,** 313 Great Western Rd. (© **0141/ 334-5444**), for Mexican and American foodstuffs. On the Southside in the Shawlands district near Queens Park, the **1901 Deli,** 11 Skirving St. (© **0141/632-1630**), has a good supply of goodies for any outdoor feast.

Exploring Glasgow

In the main, Glasgow is a compact and contiguous city—roughly the size of San Francisco. The part that U.S. visitors might describe as downtown, Glasgow's "city center," is laid out rather American-style on a grid, so the commercial heart of the city is user friendly. Most visits begin here, amid the rich Victorian architecture, whether it be 19th-century banks (many of which have been converted to other uses such as restaurants and bars), office buildings, warehouses, and churches. Culturally, the options in the heart of Glasgow include the **Gallery of Modern Art (GOMA)**, **The Lighthouse** (devoted to design and architecture), and the **Centre for Contemporary Art (CCA)**. There are also the **Royal Concert Hall** and **Theatre Royal** (see chapter 18). These attractions are all within a fairly short walking distance. Three main boulevards—Argyle, Buchanan, and Sauchiehall streets—form a Z shape and have been made into predominantly car-free pedestrian zones, which offer a wealth of shopping opportunities.

Adjacent to the commercial center is the Merchant City, where loft conversions over the past 20 years have created a hip, happening quarter with many lively bars and restaurants. This district skirts the historic heart of Glasgow, but little if anything remains of the medieval city—most has been knocked down over the years in various urban renewal schemes. But at either end of the historic High

Street—**Glasgow Cathedral,** which dates to the 13th century, and the Renaissance **Tolbooth** steeple—are two of the city's more ancient landmarks.

The affluent and urbane West End has the city's top university, its most desirable homes, and plenty of restaurants, bars, and shops. This area is trendy and lively, with some of city's best nightlife. Leafy and attractive, with the **Kelvingrove Art Gallery and Museum** fabulously refurbished and reopened in 2006, the West End is many visitors' favorite place to explore.

Of course, a river runs through Glasgow, and the city has yet to capitalize fully on the real potential of the **Clyde.** The shipbuilding industry that made the river famous is long gone. Yet, there isn't even an active, attractive marina for leisure boats today. Near the city center, development of the waterfront with concrete paths and plazas towards the end of the 20th century has not aged particularly well, though there is a certain derelict urban charm to the riverbank, which has a national cycle path.

On the other side of the Clyde, the Southside spreads out with well-established suburban neighborhoods. Some say this is the "real" Glasgow. While mostly residential, it is home to at least one major, arguably world-class, attraction—the **Burrell Collection**—that merits an excursion south of the River Clyde.

Glasgow Attractions

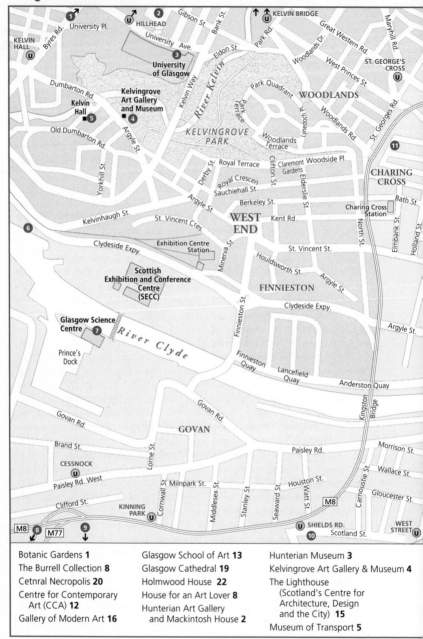

Botanic Gardens **1**

The Burrell Collection **8**

Cetnral Necropolis **20**

Centre for Contemporary
Art (CCA) **12**

Gallery of Modern Art **16**

Glasgow School of Art **13**

Glasgow Cathedral **19**

Holmwood House **22**

House for an Art Lover **8**

Hunterian Art Gallery
and Mackintosh House **2**

Hunterian Museum **3**

Kelvingrove Art Gallery & Museum **4**

The Lighthouse
(Scotland's Centre for
Architecture, Design
and the City) **15**

Museum of Transport **5**

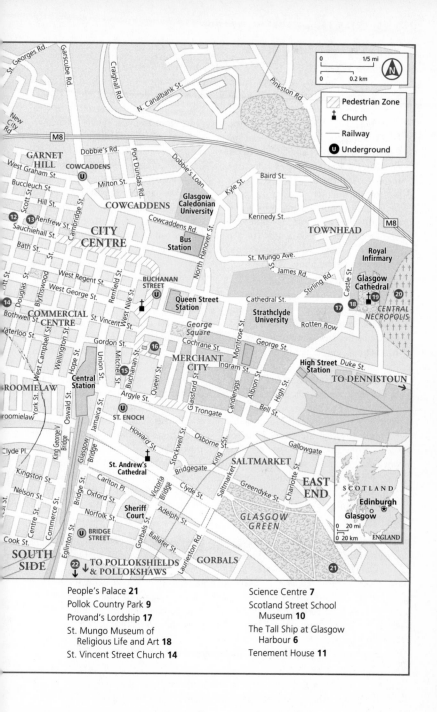

People's Palace **21**
Pollok Country Park **9**
Provand's Lordship **17**
St. Mungo Museum of
  Religious Life and Art **18**
St. Vincent Street Church **14**

Science Centre **7**
Scotland Street School
  Museum **10**
The Tall Ship at Glasgow
  Harbour **6**
Tenement House **11**

SUGGESTED ITINERARIES

If You Have 1 Day

From George Square, the city's main plaza in front of Glasgow City Chambers, catch one of the open-topped **tour buses.** The trip, from historic **Glasgow Cathedral** in the east to **Glasgow University** and trendy **Byres Road** in the west, can be as entertaining as it is informative. It's also the best way to get oriented. Tickets are valid for 24 hours, and you can get off and on as much as you desire. Visit at least one of the city-run museums (they're free) and a bona-fide Glasgow pub, such as the **Horse Shoe.**

If You Have 2 Days

Follow one of the strolls outlined in chapter 16. Try to take in a bit of real **Charles Rennie Mackintosh** architecture, whether an organized tour of the **Art School** on Garnethill or a visit to the interiors of his family house reconstructed at the **Hunterian Art Gallery.** Spend more time in the **West End** and check out the recently renovated **Kelvingrove Art Gallery and Museum.** Or go south and visit the vaunted **Burrell Collection.** Its art and artifacts from ancient to modern are the pride of the city, housed in an attractive, contemporary building amid verdant Pollok Country Park.

If You Have 3 Days

Architecture buffs should discover more about **Alexander "Greek" Thomson,** who preceded Mackintosh by two generations and was equally innovative and important. Try **Holmwood House** on the city's Southside. After London, Glasgow is the second city of shopping in the entire U.K. But don't be content with the familiar department stores: seek out the designer labels in the Merchant City or some funky shop off Byres Road in the West End. God after Mammon, so don't miss the Cathedral and if the weather's fine, hike around the nearby **Central Necropolis.** The city's main graveyard occupies a hill, so the views are grand.

If You Have 4 Days or More

Those more interested in social history might visit the **People's Palace** museum while those attuned to contemporary arts have not only the **CCA** but also the **Arches** and **Tramway** to consider. On the weekend, lovers of flea markets owe the **Barras** stalls a visit. An excursion away from the city is in order, either down the Clyde towards the sea and across to the Western peninsulas and islands, or up the road to **Loch Lomond** and the beginnings of the Highlands. In most directions, it takes less than 30 minutes to find wide-open countryside.

1 Some Top Attractions

CITY CENTER & MERCHANT CITY

The proverbial heart of Glasgow is **George Square,** onto which looks the seat of local government, the **City Chambers** that Queen Victoria opened in 1888. The building's interiors have been used for movie sets (sometimes to represent the Kremlin) and the lavishly decorated **Banqueting Hall** is sometimes open to the public. Of the several statues in George Square, the most imposing is the 25m (80-ft.) Doric column with Sir Walter Scott at the top. It was the first such monument built in the author's honor, about 5 years after his death.

Gallery of Modern Art   GOMA, as it is better known, is housed in the former Royal Exchange at Royal Exchange Square, where Ingram Street meets Queen Street. The building—originally surrounded by farmland—was built as a mansion for an

Frommer's Favorite Glasgow Experiences

Taking the Mackintosh "Trail" and Discovering Greek Thomson   Architecture in Glasgow has not always been appreciated, and city planners after World War II had a mind to accomplish what German bombers had not: that is, knock down the city's glorious Victorian structures. Luckily they were stopped. In the 19th century, the city spawned two singular stars of architecture with the now-famous Charles Rennie Mackintosh as well as lesser-known, but equally talented, Alexander "Greek" Thomson.

Visiting the Kelvingrove Art Gallery and Burrell Collection   The artistic pièces de résistance of Glasgow (and some say in all of Scotland), the Kelvingrove—restored in 2006—and Burrell are two of the city's major attractions. The former showcases the excellent municipal art collection. The latter shows what a virtually unlimited budget, acquired during the lifetime of shipping baron Sir William Burrell, can purchase.

Hanging Out in the West End   From dining in trendy bistros to shopping at vintage clothing or antiquary book shops—or just strolling the streets near the University and around the Botanic Gardens, Glasgow's West End is bound to have something to interest the erudite explorer.

Downing a Dram in a Glasgow Bar   Whether sipping a 12-year-old single malt whisky from the island of Islay or nursing a pint of lager, you should find that Glasgow's many bars are the best places to connect with the local population. In contrast to the essay by the 20th-century poet Hugh MacDiamid, the city's drinkers are generally not "dour" but rather friendly if occasionally direct.

18th-century tobacco magnate. Later it was expanded by one the city's busy 19th-century architects, David Hamilton, who added a dramatic portico to the front. Now the pile and its square are at the heart of the city, near George Square and Buchanan Street. The galleries on different floors are slightly pretentiously named after earth, fire, air, and water. The permanent collection has works by Stanley Spencer and John Bellany as well as art from the "new Glasgow boys" who emerged in the 1980s, such as Peter Howson, Ken Currie, and Steven Campbell. Before controversially becoming the museum in the mid-1990s, the pile was used as a public library and recently the basement was converted to that function again.

Royal Exchange Sq., Queen St. ✆ **0141/229-1996**. www.glasgowmuseums.com. Free admission. Mon–Wed and Sat 10am–5pm; Thurs 10am–8pm; Fri and Sun 11am–5pm. Underground: Buchanan St. Bus: 12, 18, 40, 62, or 66.

Glasgow Cathedral ✿   Also known as the cathedral of St. Kentigern or St. Mungo's, Glasgow Cathedral dates to the 13th century. The edifice is mainland Scotland's only complete medieval cathedral—the most important ecclesiastical building of that era in the entire country. Unlike other cathedrals across Scotland, this one survived the Reformation practically intact, although 16th-century protestant zeal did purge it of all Roman Catholic relics (as well as destroying plenty of historical documents). Later, misguided architectural "restoration" led to the demolition of its western towers, forever altering the cathedral's appearance.

The lower church is where Gothic design reigns, with an array of pointed arches and piers. The Laigh Kirk (lower church), whose vaulted crypt is said to be one of the finest in Europe, also holds St. Mungo's tomb, where a light always burns. Mungo's death in 612 was recorded, but the annals of his life date to the 12th century. Other highlights of the interior include the Blackadder aisle and the 15th-century nave with a stone screen (unique in Scotland) showing the seven deadly sins.

For one of the best views of the cathedral (and the city, too, for that matter), cross the ravine (through which the Molendinar Burn once ran before being diverted underground) into the **Central Necropolis** ✺. Built on a proud hill and dominated by a statue of John Knox, this graveyard (patterned in part on the famous Père Lachaise cemetery in Paris) was opened in the 1830s. Coincidentally emblematic of the mixing of ethnic groups in Glasgow, the first person to be buried here was Jewish, as Jews were first to receive permission to use part of the hill for burial grounds.

Glasgow Cathedral, Cathedral Sq., Castle St. ✆ 0141/552-6891. www.historic-scotland.gov.uk. Free admission. Apr–Sept Mon–Sat 9:30am–6pm, Sun 1–5pm; Oct–Mar Mon–Sat 9:30am–4pm, Sun 1–4pm. Sun morning service at 11am. Suburban train: High St. Bus: 11, 36, 37, 38, 42, or 89.

Glasgow School of Art ✺✺✺ Architect Charles Rennie Mackintosh's global reputation rests in large part on this magnificent building on Garnethill above Sauchiehall Street, a highlight of the Mackintosh trail that legions of his fans from across the world follow through the city. Completed in two stages (1899 and 1909), the building offers a mix of ideas promoted by the Arts and Crafts and Art Nouveau movements. Given its quality, what's more amazing is that Mackintosh was not yet 30 when he designed the place. It is still a working—and much respected—school whose graduates continue to make their mark in the international art world. Guided tours are the only way to see the entire building, a highlight of which has to be the library. If you just drop in, however, the first floor offers a gift shop. The airy landing one flight up serves as the school's exhibition space: the Mackintosh Gallery.

167 Renfrew St. ✆ 0141/353-4526. www.gsa.ac.uk. Tours £6.50 ($12). Advance reservations suggested. Apr–Sept daily 10:30am, 11am, 11:30am, 1:30pm, 2pm, 2:30pm; Oct–Mar Mon–Sat 11am, 2:30pm. The Mackintosh Shop Mon–Fri 10am–5pm; Sat 10am–noon. Underground: Cowcaddens. Suburban train: Charing Cross. Bus: 16, 18, 44, or 57.

St. Vincent Street Church ✺ This should be a three-star, must-see attraction, but access to the public is limited by the evangelic reformed Free Kirk of Scotland congregation that worships here. Nevertheless, the church remains the most visible landmark attributed to the city's other great architect, Alexander "Greek" Thomson. Built originally for Presbyterians in 1859, the stone edifice offers two classic Greek porticos facing north and south, aside which a clock tower rises, decorated in all manner of exotic yet curiously sympathetic Egyptian, Assyrian, and even Indian-looking motifs and designs. The interior is surprisingly colorful.

265 St. Vincent St. Sunday services at 11am and 6:30pm. www.greekthomsonchurch.com.

Tenement House ✺ (Finds Tenements (or apartment buildings) are what many Glaswegians lived in from the middle of 19th century. And many still do so today. Run by the National Trust for Scotland, this "museum" is a typical flat, preserved with all the fixtures and fittings from the early part of the 20th century: coal fires, box bed in the kitchen, and gas lamps. Indeed, the resident, Miss Agnes Toward, apparently never threw out anything from 1911 to 1965, so there are displays of all sorts of memorabilia, from tickets stubs and letters to ration coupons and photographs from trips down the Clyde.

145 Buccleuch St. ℂ **0141/333-0183**. www.nts.org.uk. Admission £5 ($9.25), £4 ($7.50) children, £14 ($26) family. Mar 1–Oct 31 daily 1–5pm. Closed Nov–Feb. Underground: Cowcaddens. Bus: 20 or 66.

WEST END

Hunterian Art Gallery ☆   The University of Glasgow inherited the artistic estate of James McNeill Whistler, with some 60 of his paintings bestowed by his sister-in-law and many hanging in this gallery. The main space exhibits 17th- and 18th-century paintings (Rembrandt to Rubens) and 19th- and 20th-century Scottish works, including works by the so-called "Glasgow Boys" and the Scottish Colourists, such as Cadell, Hunter, and Fergusson. Temporary exhibits, selected from Scotland's largest collection of prints, are presented in the print gallery. The Hunterian also boasts a collection of Charles Rennie Mackintosh furnishings, and one wing of the building has a re-creation of the architect's Glasgow home from 1906 to 1914—startling then and little less so today. The **Mackintosh House** ☆☆ covers three levels, decorated in the original style of the famed architect and his artist wife Margaret Macdonald. All salvageable fittings and fixtures were recovered from the original home before it was demolished in the mid-1960s. The aspect of this re-creation mimics the original house; the sequence of the rooms is identical.

University of Glasgow, 22 Hillhead St. ℂ **0141/330-5431**. www.hunterian.gla.ac.uk. Free gallery admission. Mackintosh House admission £3 ($5.50); free Wed after 2pm. Mon–Sat 9:30am–5pm. Closed Sun and public holidays. Underground: Hillhead. Bus: 44 or 59.

Hunterian Museum   First opened in 1807, this is Glasgow's oldest museum. It's named after William Hunter, its early benefactor, who donated his private collections in 1783. The original home was a handsome Greek revival building near the High Street across town on the Old College campus, none of which survives today. Now housed in the main Glasgow University buildings, the collection is wide-ranging: from dinosaur fossils to coins to relics of the Roman occupation and plunder by the Vikings. The story of Captain Cook's voyages is pieced together in ethnographic material from the South Seas.

University of Glasgow, Main/Gilbert-Scott Building. ℂ **0141/330-4221**. www.hunterian.gla.ac.uk. Free admission. Mon–Sat 9:30am–5pm. Closed Sun and public holidays. Underground: Hillhead. Bus: 44 or 59.

Kelvingrove Art Gallery and Museum ☆☆   Although the Burrell Collection (see below) may be the star, the newly refurbished Kelvingrove Art Gallery and Museum presents the stirring soul of the city's collection, one of the best amassed by a municipality in Europe. Reopened in 2006 after a 3-year and several million pound refurbishment, the Kelvingrove can boast that it is the most visited gallery and museum in Scotland—the most popular in the U.K. outside of London. The space features French impressionists and 17th-century Dutch and Flemish paintings. One painting of particular note is *Christ of St. John the Cross* by Spanish surrealist Salvador Dalí. Purchased at great expense by the city, it has been returned to its original position in the hall after a stint at the city's St. Mungo Museum (see later in this chapter). Other highlights include paintings by the Scottish Colourists and the Glasgow Boys, a wing devoted to Mackintosh, as well as more recent art by Anne Redpath and Joan Eardley. But there is more than art, with exhibits on Scottish and Glasgow history, armory and war, as well as natural history and nature—often mixing all to good educational effect, such as showing how human armor copied the natural protection of some animals, such as the armadillo. There are plenty of interactive display and touches of humor, too, such as the creature that supposedly is responsible for the traditional dish, haggis. The building itself, built for the 1901 Glasgow International Exhibition, is magnificent, as well. In the semibasement is a new cafe/restaurant.

Argyle St. ✆ 0141/276-9599. www.glasgowmuseums.com. Free admission, except for some temporary exhibits. Mon–Thurs and Sat 10am–5pm; Fri and Sun 11am–5pm. Underground: Kelvinhall. Bus: 9, 16, 42, or 62.

Museum of Transport   This museum contains a collection of all forms of transportation and related technology. Displays include a simulated 1938 Glasgow street with period shop-fronts, era-appropriate vehicles, and a reconstruction of one of the Glasgow Underground stations. The varied ship models in the Clyde Room reflect the significance of Glasgow and the River Clyde as one of the world's foremost areas of shipbuilding and engineering. By 2008, the museum should be in a new flashy building on the city's Southside along the River Clyde.

1 Bunhouse Rd., Kelvin Hall. ✆ 0141/287-2720. www.glasgowmuseums.com. Free admission. Mon–Thurs and Sat 10am–5pm; Sun and Fri 11am–5pm. Underground: Kelvin Hall. Bus: 9, 16, 18, 42, or 62.

SOUTHSIDE

The Burrell Collection 🞵🞵   This custom-built museum houses many of the 9,000 treasures left to Glasgow by Sir William Burrell, a wealthy ship owner and industrialist who had a lifelong passion for art and artifacts. He started collecting at age 14 and only stopped when he died at the age of 96 in 1958. His tastes were eclectic: Chinese ceramics, French paintings from the 1800s, tapestries, stained-glass windows from churches, even stone doorways from the Middle Ages. Here you can see a vast aggregation of furniture, textiles, ceramics, stained glass, silver, art objects, and pictures. Ancient artifacts, Asian art, and European decorative arts and paintings are featured. It is said that the collector "liked just about everything," and landed one of the very few original bronze casts of Rodin's *The Thinker.* The dining room, hall, and drawing room of Sir William's home, Hutton Castle at Berwick-upon-Tweed, have also been reconstructed and furnished with more items from his collection. A cafe is on site, and you can roam through surrounding Pollok Country Park, some 5km (3 miles) south of the River Clyde.

Nearby **Pollok House** (✆ 0141/616-6521) dates to the 18th century. Now managed by the National Trust for Scotland on behalf of Glasgow, it features interiors as they were in the Victorian/Edwardian era. Open daily with an admission of £8 ($15) for adults.

Pollok Country Park, 2060 Pollokshaws Rd. ✆ 0141/287-2550. www.glasgowmuseums.com. Free admission. Mon–Thurs and Sat 10am–5pm; Fri and Sun 11am–5pm. Suburban train: Pollokshaws West. Bus: 45, 47, 48, or 57.

Holmwood House 🞵 *Finds*   This villa, designed by Alexander "Greek" Thomson and built in 1858, is probably the best example of his innovative style as applied to stately Victorian homes. Magnificently original, its restoration (which is ongoing) has revealed that the architect was apparently concerned with almost every element of the house's design, right down to the wallpaper and painted friezes. Now operated by the National Trust for Scotland, visitors have access to most parts of the building and surrounding gardens. Most impressive is the overall exterior design, as well as the home's parlor, with its circular bay window, the cupola over the staircase, and the detailed cornicing around the ceiling in the dining room. There are also 2 hectares (5 acres) of grounds and small kitchen garden.

61–63 Netherlee Rd., Cathcart (about 6km/4 miles south of the city center). ℂ 0141/637-2129. www.nts.org.uk. Admission £5 ($9.25) adults, £4 ($7.50) seniors, students, and children, and £14 ($25) family. Apr 1–Oct 31 Thurs–Mon noon–5pm. Closed Tues–Wed and Nov–Mar. Suburban train: Cathcart. Bus: 44 or 66.

2 Additional Attractions

Centre for Contemporary Art (CCA)   One of three premier venues in Glasgow for the exhibition of contemporary art—usually of a conceptual nature by both local artists and those of international reputation. The main central and atrium-like space is actually given over to the CCA's cafe, but there are other exhibition rooms, plus a small theater, where art-house and foreign films coordinated by the Glasgow Film Theatre are screened. Housed in a building designed by Alexander "Greek" Thomson, the CCA annually hosts art by the nominees for the Beck Futures Awards, which has become one of the leading judges of young talent in Britain.

350 Sauchiehall St. ℂ 0141/352-4900. www.cca.org. Free admission. Tues–Fri 11am–6pm; Sat 10am–6pm. Closed Sun–Mon and 2 weeks during Christmas and New Year's holidays. Underground: Cowcaddens. Suburban train: Charing Cross. Bus: 16, 18, 44, or 57.

House for an Art Lover *(Overrated*   This house, which opened in 1996, was based on—or rather inspired by—an unrealized and incomplete 1901 competition entry of Charles Rennie Mackintosh. The building, with its elegant interiors, is therefore really a modern architect's interpretation of what Mackintosh had in mind. The tour includes the main hall, the dining room, with its gesso panels, and the music room. Mackintosh devotees flock here, but it is not the same as the real thing. On the plus side, however, is the popular **Art Lover's Cafe** (p. 187) as well as gift shop, all surrounded by a parkland setting adjacent to Victorian walled gardens.

Bellahouston Park, 10 Dumbreck Rd. ℂ 0141/353-4770. www.houseforanartlover.co.uk. Admission £3.50 ($5.60) adults, £2.50 ($4) for children, students, and seniors. Apr 1–Sept 30 Mon–Wed 10am–4pm, Thurs–Sat 10am–1pm; Oct 1–Mar 31 Sat–Sun 10am–1pm, call for weekday times. Cafe and shop daily 10am–5pm. Underground: Ibrox. Bus: 9 or 54.

The Lighthouse   The Lighthouse (Scotland's Centre for Architecture, Design and the City) opened in 1999, a year when the city hosted an international celebration of its architecture. It is housed in Charles Rennie Mackintosh's first public commission, home of the *Glasgow Herald* newspaper, from 1895. Unoccupied for 15 years, the building is now a seven-story, state-of-the-art exhibition space devoted to architecture and design. The Mackintosh Interpretation Centre on the third level is The Lighthouse's only permanent exhibition, which provides an overview of Mackintosh's art, design, and architecture. Visitors can ride an elevator to a viewing platform that offers a unique panorama of the city. The facility includes a cafe: the Doocot.

11 Mitchell Lane. ℂ 0141/221-6362. www.thelighthouse.co.uk. Admission £3 ($5.50). Mon and Wed–Sat 10:30am–5pm; Tues 11am–5pm; Sun noon–5pm. Underground: St. Enoch. Bus: 40, 61, or 62.

People's Palace *(Rids*   This museum covers the social history of Glasgow, with exhibits on how "ordinary people" have lived in the city, especially since the industrial age. It also attempts to explain the Glasgow vernacular, speech patterns, and expressions that even Scottish folk from outside the city have trouble deciphering. Also noteworthy are the murals painted by new "Glasgow Boy" Ken Currie. In front of the museum is the recently restored Doulton Fountain, which was moved here from another spot on Glasgow Green. The spacious **Winter Gardens,** to the rear of the building in a restored Victorian glass house with cafe facility, offer a good retreat.

Ahead of His Time: Charles Rennie Mackintosh

Although he is legendary today, Charles Rennie Mackintosh (1868–1928) was largely forgotten in Scotland at the time of his death. His approach, poised between Art and Crafts and the Art Nouveau eras, had its fans, however, and certainly history has compensated for any slights he received during his lifetime. Mackintosh's work is recognized today as one of the city's great architectural treasures.

Born in 1868, Mackintosh began his career as a draftsman for the architectural firm of Honeyman & Keppie. Glasgow had become the "second city" of the British Empire, and the era marks a golden age in the city's built heritage. In 1896, Mackintosh's design for the **Glasgow School of Art** won a prestigious competition. Forms of nature, especially plants, inspired his interior design motifs, which offered a pared down simplicity and harmony that was far from the Victorian fashions of the day. Acclaim came from central Europe and the Vienna Secessionists, in particular, as well as the Arts and Crafts movement in England and America. The reaction in Glasgow was mixed and he left the city in 1914.

Other landmark buildings in the city include the exterior of the old Glasgow Herald building, now **The Lighthouse,** the **Willow Tea Rooms** on Sauchiehall Street, the **Scotland Street School,** and the **Mackintosh Church at Queens Cross** (which was being renovated in 2006). His own West End home (1906–14) with wife and collaborator Margaret Macdonald, was itself a work of art, eschewing the fussy clutter of the age for clean, elegant lines. Its interiors have been re-created by the University of Glasgow's Hunterian Gallery. Forty kilometers (25 miles) west of Glasgow, in Helensburgh, is perhaps his greatest singular achievement: **Hill House,** which was designed for publisher Walter Blackie in 1902.

Leaving Glasgow, he moved to Walberswick on the southern coast of England (where friendships with German-speaking artists caused undue concern during World War I) and later to Port Vendres in France. In both places, lacking architecture or design commissions, his artistic talents were put in a different direction. He painted watercolors of flowers and landscapes that are nearly as distinctive and individual as his architectural and interior design work. His hand as a master draftsman was confirmed.

For more information on the buildings to visit, visit the website of the Charles Rennie Mackintosh Society, www.crmsociety.com, or call ℂ **0141/ 946-6600.**

Glasgow Green. ℂ **0141/554-0223.** www.glasgowmuseums.com. Free admission. Mon–Thurs and Sat 10am–5pm; Fri and Sun 11am–5pm. Bus: 16, 18, 40, 61, 62, 64, or 263.

Provand's Lordship   Glasgow's oldest house, built in the 1470s, and the only survivor from what would have been clusters of medieval homes and buildings in this area of the city near Glasgow Cathedral. It is named after a church canon who once resided here. Thanks to the 17th-century furniture from the original collection of Sir

William Burrell, it shows what the interiors would have been like around the date 1700.

3 Castle St. ℂ **0141/552-8819.** www.glasgowmuseums.com. Free admission. Mon–Thurs and Sat 10am–5pm; Fri and Sun 11am–5pm. Suburban train: High St. Bus: 11, 36, 37, 38, 42, or 89.

St. Mungo Museum of Religious Life and Art   Opened in 1993, this eclectic museum of spirituality is next to Glasgow Cathedral on the site where the Bishop's Castle once stood. It embraces a collection that spans the centuries and highlights various religious groups. It has been hailed as rather unique in that Buddha, Ganesha, and Shiva, among other spiritual leaders, saints, and historic figures are treated equally. A more recent acquisition is Kenny Hunter's statue of Jesus. The grounds include a Zen garden of stone and gravel.

2 Castle St. ℂ **0141/553-2557.** Free admission. Mon–Thurs and Sat 10am–5pm; Fri and Sun 11am–5pm. Suburban train: High St. Bus: 11, 36, 38, 42, or 89.

Science Centre (Kids)   This was called Britain's most successful "millennium project"—although there were so many stinkers constructed across the U.K. to commemorate the year 2000 that this compliment can be read as faint praise. Indeed, the millennium jinx even hit here. The tall, slender tower, atop which an observatory room was designed to give breathtaking views, closed shortly after the Science Centre opened in 2000, and in 2006, it remained off-limits. Still, on the banks of the River Clyde and opposite the Scottish Exhibition and Conference Centre, this futuristic-looking edifice is a focal point of Glasgow's drive to redevelop the rundown former dock lands. The overall theme of the exhibitions is to document 21st-century challenges, as well as Glasgow's contribution to science and technology in the past, present, and future. Families should enjoy the hands-on and interactive activities: whether taking a three-dimensional head scan or starring in their own digital video.

The Science Centre also is home to a planetarium and the silver-skinned **IMAX Theatre,** which uses a film with a frame size some 10 times larger than the standard 35mm film. The planetarium and theater charge separate admission.

50 Pacific Quay. ℂ **0141/420-5010.** www.glasgowsciencecentre.org. Admission £6.95 ($13) adults, £4.95 ($9) students and seniors, £19 ($35) family pass. Daily 10am–6pm. Underground: Cessnock. Suburban train: Exhibition Centre and walk across the footbridge over the Clyde. Bus: 89 or 90.

Scotland Street School Museum   Another of Charles Rennie Mackintosh's designs, this building, commissioned by the local school board near the beginning of the 20th century, celebrated its centenary in 2005. Given that it is surrounded by light-industrial parks and faces the M8 motorway, it seems an odd location for a school. But that's only because all of the surrounding apartment buildings were torn down, which is why the school had only about 90 pupils when it closed in 1979. The museum that occupies this admittedly lesser work from the great architect is devoted to the history of education in Scotland, with reconstructed examples of classrooms from the Victorian, World War II, and 1960s eras. It also has displays of Mackintosh's design for the building.

225 Scotland St. ℂ **0141/287-0500.** www.glasgowmuseums.com. Free admission. Mon–Thurs and Sat 10am–5pm; Fri and Sun 11am–5pm. Underground: Shields Rd. Bus: 89 or 90.

MARITIME GLASGOW
The Tall Ship at Glasgow Harbour   Here you'll have a chance to board one of the last remaining Clyde-built sailing ships, the *SV Glenlee.* Built in 1896, it circumnavigated

Unappreciated Genius: Alexander "Greek" Thomson

Although architect and designer Charles Rennie Mackintosh (1868–1928) is well-known and his worldwide popularity has spurred a cottage industry of "mock-intosh" fakes from jewelry to stationary, a precursor to him was perhaps even more important and innovative. Alexander "Greek" Thomson (1817–75) brought a vision to Victorian Glasgow that was unrivaled by his contemporaries. While the influence of classical Greek structures—the Greek Revival—was nothing new, Thomson did not so much replicate Grecian design as hone it to essentials, and then mix in Egyptian, Assyrian, and other Eastern-influenced motifs. Like Mackintosh later, Thomson increasingly found himself out of step with fashion, which architecturally was moving towards Gothic Revival (such as the University of Glasgow on Gilmorehill, which Thomson apparently despised).

While a number of structures created by the reasonably prolific and successful Thomson have been tragically lost to the wrecker's ball, some key works remain: terraced houses, such as **Moray Place** (where he lived) on the city's Southside and **Eton Terrace** in the West End; churches, such as the embarrassingly derelict **Caledonian Road Church** and still-used **St. Vincent Street Church;** detached homes, such as the **Double Villa** or **Holmwood House;** and commercial structures, such as the **Grecian Buildings** (which today houses the CCA) or **Egyptian Halls** near Central Station. Just as a Mackintosh trail has been created so that fans can revisit his works, Thomson deserves no less and, in time, may receive his full due.

Ironically, for all of his interest in the exotic, Thomson himself never traveled abroad. He was planning to visit Italy when he died in his home on Moray Place on March 22, 1875, at the age of 57. Less than a decade later, the "Alexander Thomson Traveling Studentship" was created in his honor, to send young architects abroad. The second recipient was none other than 22-year-old Charles Rennie Mackintosh.

Cape Horn 15 times. Restored in 1999, the vessel is one of only five Clyde-built sailing ships that remain afloat. You can explore the ship and, while onboard, take in an exhibition detailing *Glenlee*'s cargo-trading history.

If maritime topics float your boat, consider **Clydebuilt Scottish Maritime Museum,** in the Braehead Shopping Centre (℅ **0141/886-1013;** tickets £4.25/$8 adults, £2.50/$4.50 children and seniors).

100 Stobcross Rd. ℅ **0141/222-2513.** www.thetallship.com. Admission £4.95 ($9) adults, £3.75 ($7) seniors, students, and children. Mar–Oct daily 10am–5pm; Nov–Feb daily 10am–4pm. Suburban train: Exhibition Centre. Bus: Tour buses.

3 Gardens & Parks

Botanic Gardens *(Moments* Glasgow's Botanic Gardens are not as extensive or exemplary as the Royal Botanic Gardens in Edinburgh, but they nevertheless cover some 11 hectares (28 acres). There is an extensive collection of tropical plants in Kibble Palace, the Victorian cast iron glasshouse, which was being restored in 2006. The plant collection includes some rather acclaimed orchids and begonias. This is a good place to unwind and wander, whether through the working vegetable plot or along the banks of the River Kelvin. The Botanic Gardens are open daily from dawn to dusk. The greenhouses are open 10am to 4:45pm (until 4:15pm in the winter).

Great Western Rd. © 0141/334-2422. Free admission. Daily 7am–dusk. Underground: Hillhead. Bus: 20, 66, or 90.

Glasgow Green *Kids*   This is the city's oldest park by some distance and dates in part probably to medieval times. Running along the River Clyde, southeast of the commercial center, this huge stretch of green had paths laid and shrubs planted in the middle of the18th century but formally became a public park some 100 years later. Its landmarks include the **People's Palace** (see above) social history museum and adjoining Winter Garden, Doulton Fountain, and Nelson's Monument. At the eastern end, the influence of the Doges' Palace in Venice can be seen in the colorful facade of the old Templeton Carpet Factory. Near here is a large children's play area. The southern side of Glasgow Green offers dulcet walks along the river.

Greendyke St. (east of Saltmarket). © 0141/287-5098. www.glasgow.gov.uk. Free admission. Daily dawn–dusk. Underground: St. Enoch. Bus: 16, 18, 40, 61, 62, or 64.

Pollok Country Park *Kids*   On the Southside of the city, this hilly and large expanse of open space is the home to both the Burrell Collection and Pollok House but merits a visit for its own attributes. Rhododendrons, Japanese maples, and azaleas are part of the formal planting—created at the end of the 19th century by Sir John Stirling Maxwell, whose family long-resided in Pollok House—but the park is best-known for its glens and pastures, which have Highland cattle grazing.

2060 Pollokshaws Rd. © 0141/632-9299. www.glasgow.gov.uk. Free admission. Daily dawn–dusk. Suburban train: Pollokshaws West. Bus: 45 or 57.

4 Organized Tours

City Sightseeing Glasgow   These brightly colored and open-topped buses depart from George, and in addition to live commentary, which can be quite entertaining and informative, visitors can hop on and off at some 22 designated stops such as Glasgow Green, the University, or the Royal Concert Hall. Passes are good for 2 consecutive days.

153 Queen St. at George Sq. © 0141/204-0444. www.scotguide.com. Tickets £9 ($17) adults, £3 ($5.50) kids, £20 ($37) family. Apr 1–Oct 31 9:30am–5pm (buses leave every 15–20 min.). Underground: Buchanan St.

Mercat Glasgow   If you prefer to keep your feet on the ground and your focus on the more ghoulish aspects of Glasgow, the Mercat walking tours are happy to oblige

---

Fun Fact **Buddy, You're Steamin'**

A common euphemism for having too much to drink is "steamin'," as in the line: "I can't remember what happened last night, I was steamin'." Apparently this quaint expression came from the experience of taking the steamships down the Clyde from Glasgow, which was dry on a Sunday. The ships were exempt from any restrictions on alcohol, a situation of which passengers took full advantage. One paddle steamer, the *Waverley* (© 0845/130-4647; www.waverleyexcursions.co.uk) still plies the Clyde on excursion trips.

202 CHAPTER 15 · EXPLORING GLASGOW

you. Guides re-create macabre Glasgow with a parade of goons such as hangmen, ghosts, murderers, and body snatchers. The tours take about 1½ hours, departing every evening from the Tourist Information Centre at George Square. The company also does Historic Glasgow tours for those not interested in a fright.

25 Forth Rd., Bearsden. ℭ 0141/586-5378. www.mercat-glasgow.co.uk. Tickets £7–£10 ($13–$19). Tours depart at 7 and 8pm. Underground: Buchanan St.

Waverley Excursions The *Waverley*, considered the world's last "seagoing" paddle steamship, was built on the Clyde in 1947. During the summer and depending on weather conditions, it continues to ply the river. One-day trips, beginning at Anderston Quay in Glasgow, take passengers "doon the watter" to historic and scenic places along the Firth of Clyde, sometimes going as far as the Isle of Arran. As you sail along, you can take in what were once vast shipyards, turning out more than half the earth's tonnage of oceangoing liners.

Waverley Terminal, Anderston Quay, Broomielaw. ℭ 0141/221-8152 or 0845/130-4647. www.waverleyexcursions. co.uk. Boat tours cost £8.95–£30 ($17–$55).

5 Some Special Events

Celtic Connections ✦ The best attended annual festival in Glasgow, and the largest of its kind in the world, Celtic Connections kicks off the year every January. The main venue for performances is the Royal Concert Hall, which produces the event. Guests include traditional acts, folk music, and dance, as well as contemporary artists.

ℭ 0141/353-8000. www.celticconnections.com.

Doors Open Days ✦ *Value* For a couple weekends every September, this event arranges for the doors at buildings normally closed to the public to be opened. Thus it affords visitors rare opportunities to see the interiors of architecturally significant and historic edifices across the city.

ℭ 0141/248-1188. www.doorsopendays.org.uk.

Glasgow International Jazz Festival This annual event, usually running from the last week of June through the first days of July, brings a few top jazz acts to Glasgow. In recent years, the festival featured saxophonist David Murray and singer/songwriter Van Morrison, as well as showcasing more locally based talent, such as singers Carol Kidd and Tommy Smith. Free events are always included in the "Fringe" schedule.

ℭ 0141/552-3552. www.jazzfest.co.uk.

Piping Live! A lone piper playing a Scottish lament in a Highland glen can bring a tear to the eye, for sure. But a band full of bagpipes blown in unison is one of the most stirring sounds on the planet. The best pipers from around the world converge on Glasgow in August of every year for the **World Pipe Band Championships** on Glasgow Green, the culmination of a weeklong festival with concerts across the city.

30–34 McPhater St. ℭ 0141/353-8000. www.pipingfestival.co.uk.

West End Festival The city's West End celebrates every summer with a host of music and cultural events for 2 weeks in June. The centerpiece is a Mardi Gras Carnival and parade that draws thousands if it turns out to be a hot day.

www.westendfestival.co.uk.

6 Sports & Outdoor Activities

FOOTBALL

Glasgow's Southside is the site of Scotland's national football (soccer) stadium, **Hampden Park** (✆ 0141/620-4000; bus: 75 or 89). It seats just over 52,000 fans and is used for Scotland internationals as well as annual cup matches. There is also a football museum here.

The city's two big clubs are **Celtic** and **Rangers.** Celtic play in the East End at their stadium in Parkhead (✆ 0141/556-2611; www.celticfc.net). Rangers are based south of the Clyde at Ibrox Stadium (✆ 0870/600-1972; www.rangers.co.uk). Two relatively smaller soccer clubs also play their home games in Glasgow: Partick Thistle at Firhill in the West End and Queen's Park at Hampden.

OTHER ACTIVITIES

BICYCLING

In principal you can cycle from Glasgow east to Edinburgh, west to the Clyde coast, and north to Loch Lomond and beyond to Inverness using the national cycle routes. They combine off-road paths and on-road lanes, the latter of which are sometimes poorly marked. The tourist office, however, provides maps with overviews and details.

Rentals are available off Byres Road at **West End Cycles,** 16–18 Chancellor St. (✆ 0141/357-1344; Underground: Hillhead or Kelvinhall; bus: 9 or 18). It is close to the National Cycle Trail that leads to Loch Lomond and rents bikes well-suited to the hilly terrain of Glasgow and surrounding areas. The cost is £15 ($28) per day, and a cash deposit of £100 ($185) or the imprint of a valid credit card is necessary as security. In the city center, **Alpine Bikes,** in the TISO Outdoor Centre, 50 Couper St., near Buchanan Bus Station (✆ 0141/552-8575), offers limited cycle rental. Prices start at £8 ($15).

GOLF

The city of Glasgow operates five municipal golf courses, of a reasonable standard. The best-kept 18-hole courses are probably the 5,005-yard **Linn Park,** on the Southside (✆ 0141/633-0337), and 6,364-yard **Littlehill,** north of the city center (✆ 0141/772-1916). Two 9-hole courses are **Alexandra Park,** Alexandra Parade (✆ 0141/556-1294), and **Knightswood,** Lincoln Avenue (✆ 0141/959-6358). None have dress codes, and greens fees are modest: £10 ($19) adult and £5 ($9) juvenile between 5 and 17 during the week for 18-hole courses and about half those rates for the 9-hole courses. For additional information, log onto **www.glasgow.gov.uk**.

Tips The "Old Firm"

Glasgow has Scotland's two largest professional soccer teams—Celtic and Rangers—and they are collectively called the "Old Firm." These clubs are among the biggest in Europe, and both have passionate, if not fanatical, followers. Alas, given the clubs' histories, fans are also drawn into sectarian (religious/political) disputes that have little to do with modern politics or religion but can become violent. The best bet for visitors is to politely avoid discussions regarding the Old Firm, unless extremely well versed. A safe bet if pressed is to say you prefer Partick, Glasgow's small West End club with no sectarian ties.

Of course, Glasgow has private clubs and around the city are a host of more courses. Southwest of Glasgow, Ayrshire offers the best concentration of links-style golf in the country (see chapter 19).

SPORTS COMPLEXES, GYMS & POOLS

Kelvin Hall International Sports Arena is on Argyle Street (© **0141/357-2525;** Underground: Kelvinhall), near the River Kelvin. This is the country's major venue for national and international indoor sports competitions; check with the tourist office for any events scheduled for the time of your visit. The facility is open daily with a weight room and fully equipped gym.

Scotstoun Leisure Centre, further west on Danes Drive (© **0141/959-4000;** bus: 9), offers a gym, indoor and outdoor tennis, and a five-lane pool. In the East End, **Tollcross Park Leisure Centre** (© **0141/763-2345;** bus: 61) has the city's 50m (164-ft.), Olympic-size swimming pool. For hours, admission, and further information, log onto **www.glasgow.gov.uk**.

16

Glasgow City Strolls

Glasgow is set on fairly gentle hills rising up from the basin created by the River Clyde, so the city is amenable to walking. Most "perambulations" don't involve the scaling of many steep streets—although in order to obtain good vistas, a climb is sometimes obligatory. Like in any bustling metropolis now rather overly dependent on the use of automobiles, pedestrians should always exercise caution at intersections and other crossing points. Remember, look both ways. Glasgow drivers (including those behind the wheels of city buses) can be a tad aggressive at times. Still, some streets have been made into pedestrian malls. Most of the

city's buildings in the central districts are neither especially tall nor exceptionally imposing. It is quite easy to get off the beaten track and away from crowds, should that be your desire. Plus, the "dear green place" has plenty of parks and open spaces. And given the multitude of bus routes, the circular subway, and various suburban trains, getting back to where you began is typically easy, even if your route is not a convenient loop. If you have all day to spare, walks 1 to 3 listed below can be combined to create one pleasant stroll right across Glasgow from the Merchant City to the West End.

WALKING TOUR 1   THE MERCHANT CITY & THE EAST END

Start:	Central Necropolis.
Finish:	Royal Exchange Square.
Time:	About 1 to 2 hours.
Best Times:	Daytime.
Worst Times:	Late at night.

This walk takes in Glasgow's historic heart, whose medieval districts were first lost to the designs of the city's initial "New Town" developments in the 1700s—the beginnings of the area now known as the Merchant City. But there are hints to the past, and the Merchant City is almost to Glasgow as SoHo is to Manhattan, with loft apartments and trendy bars.

Start the walk at:

❶ The Necropolis

As big graveyards go—with monuments, crypts, and views—Glasgow's Central Necropolis is difficult to beat. Fashioned on Paris's famous Père Lachaise, it was the third of its kind in Britain, opening in

1833 (after St. James's in Liverpool and London's Kensal Green) although a Jewish burial ground had been established here 3 years earlier. The most sought-after plots of the day were near the monument to John Knox, which had been standing on the hill since 1825.

Cross the bridge to Cathedral Square and:

❷ Glasgow Cathedral

The Cathedral (p. 193) is considered the best example of 13th-century religious architecture in Scotland, although visitors may be disappointed to find there's no evidence of the settlement that once surrounded it. To the north is the sprawling Royal Infirmary. Across Castle Street, Provand's Lordship (p. 198) was built in 1471 by Bishop Andrew Muirhead. It miraculously managed to avoid demolition during Glasgow's robust urban renewals of the 19th and 20th centuries. The tall and modern buildings beyond are part of Strathclyde University.

Walk south on High Street to:

❸ Glasgow Cross

Down gently curving High Street, the red sandstone tenements (or apartment buildings) you pass are exemplary of those constructed in the late-Victorian era by the Civic Improvement Trust. After crossing Duke Street comes the College Bar (nearly opposite the High St. railway station) whose name is a reminder that the original Glasgow University campus was nearby here. The historic landmark at Glasgow Cross is the eight-story Tolbooth Steeple completed in 1627, around which traffic up and down the High Street snakes today.

At the steeple go east (left) and walk along the:

❹ Gallowgate

"Gate" in Scots essentially means "road to"—but don't worry, the gallows are long gone. The Gallowgate today hints at the working class nature of the city's East End. If it's a weekend, visit the Barras (or Barrows) market, full of antiques, junk, and Glasgow character. The old dancing ballroom called Barrowland has become one of the most famous and popular places to see rock bands in Scotland. Also worth noting is the Saracen Head (or as the locals say Sarry Heid) pub. It has historic connections to an inn of the same name that hosted Johnson and Boswell as well as Wordsworth.

Walk south from Gallowgate, crossing London Road to:

❺ Glasgow Green

Running along the River Clyde, this huge stretch of green became a public park in the middle of the 19th century, although paths had been laid and shrubs planted out 100 years earlier. Its landmarks include the **People's Palace** social history museum (p. 197) and adjoining Winter Garden, Doulton Fountain, and Nelson's Monument. To the east, the influence of the Doges' Palace in Venice is obvious in William Leiper's colorful facade of the old Templeton Carpet Factory. The southern side of Glasgow Green offers walks along the river as it begins its upstream meandering and the northwestern flank now features cool modern apartments opened in the late 1990s as the so-called "City for the Future."

Walk west on Greendyke Street, turning right (north) on Turnbull Street to:

❻ St. Andrew's Square

Styled after St-Martins-in-the-Field, London, and indeed once surrounded by open space, the impressive sandstone St. Andrew's parish church was completed in 1756. Today, it houses a center for traditional Scottish music and dance. Around the corner, the only remaining bit of 18th-century residential property on Charlotte Street (no. 52) is now available to rent as vacation accommodation from the National Trust for Scotland.

Make your way back to Glasgow Cross and proceed west on the Trongate to:

❼ Tron Steeple

The steeple with arches through which pedestrians can walk on the south side of the street dates to 1592, although the original Tron or Laigh Kirk was founded 8 years before Columbus "discovered" the New World, just over a century earlier. The tron was a beam used for weighing goods. The Tron Theater, which occupies the site today, favors inventive new plays, as well as hosting musical events (p. 232). The theater's modern bar (facing Chisholm St.)

Walking Tour: The Merchant City & the East End

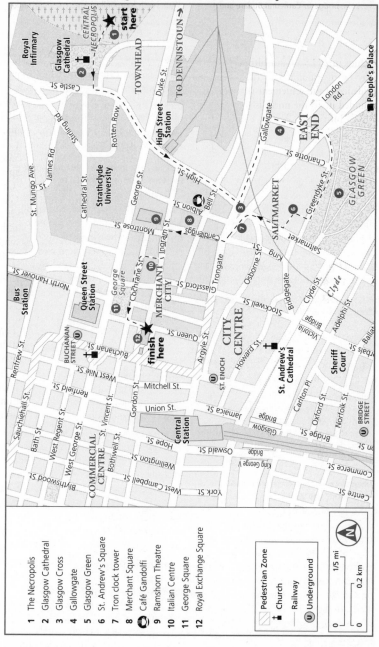

Legend / Tour Stops:

1 The Necropolis
2 Glasgow Cathedral
3 Glasgow Cross
4 Gallowgate
5 Glasgow Green
6 St. Andrew's Square
7 Tron clock tower
8 Merchant Square
9 Café Gandolfi
10 Ramshorn Theatre
11 Italian Centre
12 George Square
13 Royal Exchange Square

Map labels:

Pedestrian Zone
Church
Railway
Underground

N

1/5 mi
0.2 km

and Victorian-style pub and restaurant are well-known hangouts for creative people.

Cross the Trongate and go north (right) on Candleriggs to Bell Street and the:

⑧ Merchant Square & City Halls

The old covered markets of Glasgow have been converted into trendy spots. The Cheese Market is now a bar and nightclub, while more of the original character of the old Fruit Market has been retained by the Merchant Square development. A diverse array of bars and restaurants share the communal and cavernous interior space on the cobbles. Just north of it is the renovated **City Halls,** with acoustically celebrated performance spaces (p. 233). All around, since the 1980s, warehouses have been turned into loft apartments, while new condos have been constructed more recently.

From the east exit of the Merchant Square, cross Albion Street and:

TAKE A BREAK
In a bit of the old Cheese Market, **Café Gandolfi** (64 Albion St.; ✆ **0141/552-6813**) is one of the more popular places in the Merchant City. It is relaxed, friendly, and at times very busy. But with the recent addition of a bar on the top floor, you almost always find space. Food is Scottish and European. See p. 179 for full review.

Return to Candleriggs and continue north to Ingram Street and the:

⑨ Ramshorn Theatre

Yes, it's another former church (the handsome Gothic revival of Thomas Rickman's St. David, built in the 1820s) that has been turned into an arts venue, hosting mainly student productions. Round the side and to the rear, an atmospheric graveyard dates to 1719.

Go west on Ingram Street to John Street and the:

⑩ Italian Centre

Shopping anyone? The facade of this mid-19th-century warehouse has been

retained while an interior courtyard, upstairs condos, and retail space for flashy clothing shops were created in the late 1980s. The Italian Centre is home now to Emporio Armani, while car-free and cobbled John Street is where outdoor dining and drinking is possible. At the corner of Ingram and John streets is Hutcheson's Hall, designed by David Hamilton in 1802 to combine French neoclassical with English baroque.

Walk north on John Street, turn left (west) on Cochrane Street, and continue to:

⑪ George Square

The city's main civic plaza, dating to 1782, was altered somewhat controversially in recent years, when most of the lawn and permanent trees were removed. It was repaved in a red, spongy, asphalt-like material, though the color is oddly appropriate, as this is the historic focal point of labor and left-wing demonstrations. Glasgow City Chambers, designed by William Young in 1882 as the seat of municipal authority, rise majestically at the eastern side of George Square. Facing the western end of the plaza are attractive Victorian and Edwardian-era buildings, which were originally uniform in height. Inside Queen Street railway station, the arching iron roof over the high-level platforms is impressive, but the exterior that faces the square is an eyesore. The square's statues include Robert Burns (whose plinth includes reliefs depicting a few of his tales), the bulky Cenotaph (honoring war casualties), the seated figure of Scottish engineering pioneer James Watt, and the towering monument to Sir Walter Scott.

Leave George Square from the southwest corner and go south on Queen Street to:

⑫ Royal Exchange Square

Invariably, the statue of the Duke of Wellington in front of the city's Gallery of Modern Art (GOMA) will be wearing an orange traffic cone. The pile he guards was originally built in 1778 as a mansion on what was then farmland. In 1832, architect David Hamilton converted the building into the Royal Exchange. He added an imposing classical portico to the front and a matching "newsroom" to the back. The building sits squarely in the middle of the square, surrounded by cafes with outdoor seating and shops.

Start:	Royal Exchange Square.
Finish:	Charing Cross.
Time:	About 1½ to 2 hours.
Best Times:	Daytime.
Worst Times:	Late at night.

There is no definitive route to see the Glasgow City Centre. For some visitors, it may be better to simply wander. Given the grid system, anyone with a map would be hard-pressed to get completely lost. The pride of the city is its Victorian architecture. Many—indeed most—of the city's stone facades have been cleaned of decades of grime. This stroll includes buildings by the city's two greatest architects: Charles Rennie Mackintosh and Alexander "Greek" Thomson.

This walk begins at the west side of:
① Royal Exchange Square
At the west end of the square, behind the Gallery of Modern Art, are two archways, both leading to Buchanan Street. Just past the southern one is a restaurant landmark: the Rogano. Its Art Deco interiors were fashioned after the Queen Mary ocean liner in 1935. The building between the arches, which now houses an expansive Borders bookstore, is the former Royal Bank of Scotland (from Charles Wilson's 1850 designs), which faces Gordon Street, leading to Central Station.

Go through one of the arches, and north (right), walking up Buchanan Street to:
② St. Vincent Street
Buchanan Street was turned into a car-free pedestrian zone in the mid-1970s, although it has long been a primary shopping street. Just before St. Vincent Street is a bronze, table-high scale model of central Glasgow's streets and buildings. To the right (east) toward George Square is St. Vincent Place and its handsome late-19th- and early-20th-century structures. Mid-block, the former Anchor Line

office includes some maritime-themed interiors by the same designer who worked on rooms for the ill-fated SS *Lusitania*. To the left, running west is St. Vincent Street. Its commercial architecture, which replaced terraced houses in the mid-1800s, has been called "monumental."

Continue north up Buchanan Street to:
③ Nelson Mandela Place
Just before St. George's Tron Church, on the left (west) side of Buchanan Street, is the attractive sandstone and Gothic facade of the former Stock Exchange by John Burnet in 1875. Roundels mark Science, Art, and Engineering. The slender square (formerly St. George's Place) that engulfs the church dates to 1810 and was renamed in honor of the South African leader, who was awarded the Freedom of the City in August 1981.

Continue up Buchanan Street to:
④ Buchanan Galleries
Before the next intersection, after entrances to the underground, comes the southern wing of the rather unremarkable Buchanan Galleries shopping center. Indoors, it is

equally predictable, a mall that could be almost anywhere in the Western world. Ahead is the modern and similarly brutalist Royal Concert Hall, which now terminates Buchanan Street—effectively cutting off a direct path to the bus station and Glasgow Caledonian University beyond. The concert hall's outdoor steps, however, offer good views down Buchanan Street towards St. Enoch Square. Just in front of those broad stairs is a statue of Scotland's first First Minister, Donald Dewar, who opened the new Parliament in 1999 but died before his initial term in office was over.

Turn left (west) and proceed on:

❺ Bath Street

Bath Street got its name from the public baths that opened here in the early 19th century. Today, it is home to several popular bars and restaurants. At the next intersection, West Nile Street, looking south (left), one can see the first of three buildings by Alexander "Greek" Thomson (p. 200) on this walk. Today housing a barbershop, this modest warehouse displays some design signatures of Thomson, Glasgow's underappreciated yet visionary Victorian-era architect. At the intersection after the next, again just south of Bath Street, is another minor architectural landmark at 172 Hope Street: the Lion Chambers. Recently trussed in chick-wire after many years behind scaffolding, the eight-story gabled building resembles a Scottish castle keep. It is built on a plot measuring only 10 by 14m (33 by 46 ft.) with artist studios at the top.

At Hope Street, turn right (north) 1 block to:

❻ Sauchiehall Street

Sauchiehall Street is probably Glasgow's most famous street. Today, for several blocks west of Buchanan Street, it is pedestrianized and popular for shopping. Just over the rise of Hope Street to the north, one gets a glimpse of the Italian styling of the Piping Centre (formerly St.

Stephen's church). Nearby is the Theatre Royal (p. 233).

Go left (west) on Sauchiehall Street and continue to:

❼ Willow Tea Rooms

On the south side of Sauchiehall Street, between West Campbell and Blythswood streets, is one of the signature works by architect Charles Rennie Mackintosh (p. 198). The spare white exterior, clean lines, and asymmetrically arranged windows certainly stand out from anything else on the street. The ground floor is now a jeweler's shop but above are tea rooms in Mackintosh's ground-breaking 1904 design. Much of it has been reconstructed, but a few original details remain. Around the corner and north up Rose Street is the **Glasgow Film Theatre,** the city's only dedicated art and repertory cinema (p. 239). In the other direction, 2 blocks away, is Blythswood Square, a fenced park at the top of Blythswood Hill and part of a New Town development that dates to the 1820s.

TAKE A BREAK
We cannot honestly recommend the food at the Willow Tea Rooms, but near Blythswood Square down some steps is a cafe/gallery called **Where the Monkey Sleeps** (182 West Regent St.; © 0141/226-3406). As the name might indicate, this is no ordinary cafe. It is owned and operated by artistic types (including two graduates from the nearby Art School) who learned their barista skills at Starbucks but wanted to be free of corporate constraints. Excellent cappuccino can be complemented by freshly prepared sandwiches. See p. 183 for full review.

Our walk continues west on Sauchiehall Street to Dalhousie Street, turning right (north), and climbing steep Garnethill to the:

❽ Glasgow School of Art

Our second Mackintosh masterpiece is on the left as you ascend Garnethill. Even from this approach along the most

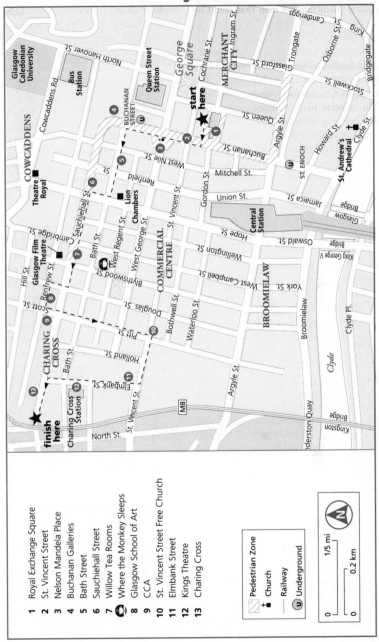

Glasgow Caledonian University

North Hanover St.

Cowcaddens Rd.

Bus Station

COWCADDENS

Theatre Royal

Queen Street Station

George Square

BUCHANAN STREET

start here

MERCHANT CITY

Cochrane St.

Ingram St.

Candleriggs

King

Trongate

Glassford St.

Osborne St.

Bridgegate

Stockwell St.

Clyde St.

St. Andrew's Cathedral

Howard St.

Queen St.

Argyle St.

Buchanan St.

West Nile St.

Renfield St.

Mitchell St.

Union St.

Gordon St.

St. ENOCH

Jamaica St.

Glasgow Bridge

Cowcaddens Rd.

Sauchiehall St.

Cambridge St.

Lion Chambers

Bath St.

West Regent St.

St. Vincent St.

Hope St.

Central Station

Oswald St.

King George V Bridge

Hill St.

Glasgow Film Theatre

Renfrew St.

Scott St.

Blythswood St.

West George St.

COMMERCIAL CENTRE

West Campbell St.

Wellington St.

York St.

BROOMIELAW

Clyde Pl.

Broomielaw

Clyde

CHARING CROSS

Pitt St.

Douglas St.

Bothwell St.

Waterloo St.

Bath St.

Holland St.

Argyle St.

Elmbank St.

Charing Cross Station

St. Vincent St.

M8

Kingston Bridge

finish here

North St.

nderston Quay

1 Royal Exchange Square
2 St. Vincent Street
3 Nelson Mandela Place
4 Buchanan Galleries
5 Bath Street
6 Sauchiehall Street
7 Willow Tea Rooms
8 Where the Monkey Sleeps
9 Glasgow School of Art
10 CCA
11 St. Vincent Street Free Church
12 Elmbank Street
13 Kings Theatre
14 Charing Cross

Pedestrian Zone
Church
Railway
Underground

N

0 1/5 mi
0 0.2 km

austere side of the building, the ingenuity of its design is apparent. Completed in two stages (1899 and 1909), it offers a mix of ideas promoted by the Arts and Crafts and Art Nouveau movements. Facing Renfrew Street, the wide facade offers huge studio windows. Inside, access to the public is limited (unless you're young and behave like an art student), but often the second floor museum, a large landing beneath exposed timber beams, has exhibits open to anyone. Otherwise inquire about guided tours, which include the library: a place that anyone would happily spend hours in. Nearby on Hill Street is Garnethill Synagogue, the first in Scotland. Before descending Garnethill, take in the views, particularly south.

At the west side of the Art School, turn left (south) and come down Scott Street to the:

⑨ CCA

To the right as you come down Scott Street, admire the stonework, such as acanthus leaf motifs, so typical of Alexander Thomson's buildings. Redeveloped in 2001, the home for Glasgow's Centre for Contemporary Art (CCA) is the architect's 1865 Grecian Buildings (although most of the detailing has more to do with Egypt). The structure incorporated one of the villas built previously on the hillside above Sauchiehall Street, and the interiors of the revamped CCA, with its atrium-like core, now reveal the facade of that earlier building. Stand at the corner of Sauchiehall and Scott streets and look back up the hill: This is a unique spot in Glasgow, where works by both the city's most innovative architects stand almost side by side.

Cross Sauchiehall Street and proceed south on Pitt Street to:

⑩ St. Vincent Street Free Church

Only 4 reasonably short blocks away is Thomson's most durable temple—what some have called his "magnum opus." Built originally for Presbyterians in 1859,

the stone church offers two classic Greek porticos facing north and south, aside which a clock tower rises decorated in all manner of exotic yet sympathetic Egyptian, Assyrian, and even Indian-looking motifs and designs. Recent restoration work may have actually harmed the structure, which some say is in a precarious state despite its solid appearance. Alas a similar Thomson church stands in inexcusable disrepair on Caledonian Road on the city's Southside—an indictment of Glasgow's political leaders' continuing failure to respect and maintain all of the city's richly built heritage.

Turn right (west) on St. Vincent Street to:

⑪ Elmbank Street

Looking west from the windswept corner of Elmbank and St. Vincent streets, visitors might begin to appreciate the impact of the M8 motorway, which passes noisily nearby. The feeling is a bit desolate. To the southwest, in the near but seemingly unreachable distance, the prow of St. Patrick Roman Catholic Church pokes up above the freeway's infrastructure. Going up Elmbank Street, admire the figures of Cicero, Homer, Galileo, and Watt on the facade of the old Glasgow High School. At the corner of Elmbank Crescent, offices of the Scottish Opera occupy the handsome former Institute of Engineers and Shipbuilders. If you go left here and cross the street, you'll be at an entrance to the Charing Cross station and can catch a train back one stop to Queen Street station and George Square.

Otherwise proceed up Elmbank Street to the:

⑫ Kings Theatre

Celebrating its 100th birthday in 2004, the red sandstone Kings Theatre regularly stages comedy and light drama that appeals to a range of generations. On the opposite northeast corner is the Griffin pub (originally the King's Arms) whose exterior displays some Glasgow-style Art Nouveau design.

Continue up Elmbank Street to Sauchiehall Street and:

⑬ Charing Cross

Straight ahead, facing back down Elmbank Street, is the recently restored and boldly repainted Art Deco Beresford built in the 1930s. The bit of Sauchiehall Street, from here west to the M8 underpass, is loaded with bars, nightclubs, and some late-night eateries. At the northern end of the street at St. Georges Road (technically a freeway off-ramp) comes the curving red sandstone Charing Cross Mansions by JJ Burnet in 1889. Across Sauchiehall Street, the modern Tay Building bridges the motorway with offices.

WALKING TOUR 3   THE WEST END

Start: Charing Cross.
Finish: Botanic Gardens.
Time: About 2 to 3 hours.
Best Times: Daytime.
Worst Times: Late at night.

This walk will give visitors a sense of Glasgow's salubrious and trendy West End, while hitting some of its landmarks, as well. The stroll begins in Charing Cross on Sauchiehall Street, but on the western side of the M8 motorway, which is set in a canyon. The West End's development began in the 19th century, as the booming city needed more space to house its ever-growing population, which made Glasgow the Second City of the British Empire.

Begin at:

① Cameron Fountain

From the rusty red stone fountain, built in 1896 and listing considerably eastward, one can detour briefly a few blocks south on North Street, which runs parallel to the freeway, to see the Mitchell Library, among the largest public reference libraries in Europe, with its prominent dome.

From the fountain walk up Woodside Crescent to:

② Woodside Terrace

This late Georgian row of homes (designed by George Smith in the 1830s) began an exemplary New Town development. Here you'll find Greek Doric porticos unlike any in the city. But most of the credit for the overall elegance and charm of **Woodlands Hill** goes to Charles Wilson, whose designs in the middle of the 19th century are mostly responsible for the terraces up the hillside to Park Circus.

Continue on Woodside Terrace, turning right (north) on Lynedoch Terrace to Lynedoch Street and proceed left (west) to:

③ Trinity College & Park Church Tower

The former Trinity College (now Trinity House) is a landmark whose three towers are visible from many approaches to the city. Designed by Charles Wilson, it was constructed in 1857 as the Free Church College. Most of the original interiors were lost when the complex was converted to condos in the 1980s. Across the broad triangular intersection is the cream-colored Park Church Tower. Part of JT Rochead's 1856 design, it is the other feature of the neighborhood recognizable from some distance. Alas, the church that went with the tower was razed in the late 1960s. Similar to the Tolbooth and the Tron Church at Glasgow Cross, only a steeple remains.

From here, go left (south) and follow the gentle curve (west) of Woodlands Terrace, turning right (north) at Park Street South to:

④ Park Circus

This oval of handsome and uniform three-story buildings around a small central garden is the heart of Wilson's plans, designed in 1855. No. 22 (the so-called "Marriage Suites" where the city conducts civil marriages and other registration office ceremonies) offers remarkable interiors with Corinthian columns and an Art Nouveau billiard room. Attendants are not impressed when uninvited visitors just wander in, however. Luckily, the external door is impressive enough. At the western end of Park Circus is Park Gate, leading to an entrance to Kelvingrove Park. This promontory offers excellent views towards the University and south to the Clyde.

Enter:

⑤ Kelvingrove Park

Originally West End Park, the development of this hilly and lush open space on the banks of the **River Kelvin** was commissioned to Sir Joseph Paxton in 1854, although construction apparently began a year before he produced his plans. At this elevated entrance is the statue of Lord Roberts on his steed. Down the hill to the left, the Gothic Stewart Memorial Fountain includes signs of the Zodiac and scenes that depict the source of the city's main supply of water: Loch Katrine. Crossing the river below Park Gate at the Highland Light Infantry Memorial is the faded red sandstone Prince of Wales Bridge. Across the bridge looking back at you is the head of Thomas Carlyle emerging from the roughly hewn stone.

If facing the bridge at the infantry memorial, go right (north) and follow one of the two paths that run along the river and exit the park at:

⑥ Gibson Street

Leaving the park, turn left (west) and cross the short road bridge that brings you into the Hillhead district, which

includes the main campus of the University of Glasgow on Gilmorehill, and the Western Infirmary.

TAKE A BREAK
On Gibson Street, **Stravaigin Cafe Bar** (28 Gibson St.; ② 0141/334-2665) is an ideal place to stop for a coffee, bite to eat, or wee drink. "Stravaig" means to wander in Scots. The basement restaurant is one of the most innovative and well-regarded in the city, and the same chefs prepare food on the less adventurous but still excellent cafe/bar menu. See p. 187 for full review.

Continue west on Gibson Street to Bank Street, go right (north) 1 block to Great George Street, then left (west) 1 block to Oakfield Avenue and:

⑦ Eton Terrace

Here, on the corner across from Hillhead High School, is the unmistakable hand of Alexander Thomson on an impressive (if today rather poorly kept) terrace of eight houses completed in 1864 (following his similarly designed Moray Place; see "Walking Tour 4: The Southside," below). Two temple-like facades serve as bookends—both pushing slightly forward and rising one floor higher than the rest—which have double porches fashioned after the Choragic Monument of Thrassylus in Athens. For all his admiration of Eastern design, Thomson never traveled outside the U.K.

Return to the corner of Great George Street and follow Oakfield Avenue, crossing Gibson Street to University Avenue, then turn right up the hill to the:

⑧ University of Glasgow

While aficionados rightfully bemoan the loss of the original campus east of the High Street—which may have offered the best examples of 17th-century architecture in Scotland—the university moved here in the 1860s. The city could have done worse—a lot worse. The setting high above Kelvingrove Park is befitting of a center of learning. Englishman Sir

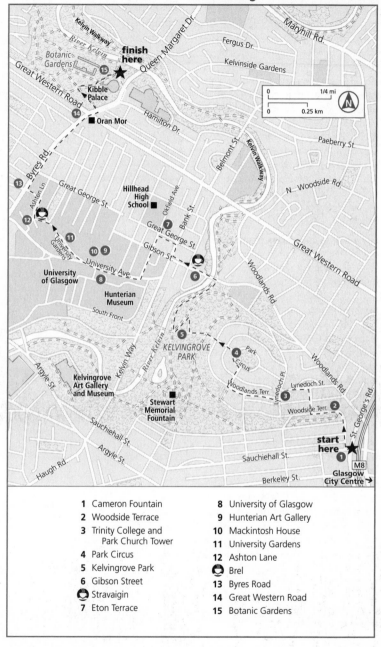

Kelvin Walkway

Kelvin

River Kelvin

Maryhill Rd.

Botanic Gardens

finish here

Queen Margaret Dr.

Fergus Dr.

Kelvinside Gardens

Great Western Road

15

Kibble Palace

14

Oran Mor

Hamilton Dr.

Paeberry St.

0   1/4 mi

0   0.25 km

N

Belmont St.

Kelvin Walkway

N.. Woodside Rd.

Byres Rd.

13

Ashton Ln.

Great George St.

Hillhead High School

Okfield Ave.

Great Western Road

12

7

Bank St.

Great George St.

11

University Gardens

10 9

Gibson St.

8

6

Woodlands Rd.

University of Glasgow

University Ave.

Hunterian Museum

South Front

River Kelvin

5

KELVINGROVE PARK

4

Park Circus

Kelvin Way

Stewart Memorial Fountain

Woodlands Terr.

Lynedoch Pl.

3

Lynedoch St.

Woodlands Rd.

Woodside Terr.

2

St. George's Rd.

Kelvingrove Art Gallery and Museum

Argyle St.

Sauchiehall St.

Argyle St.

start here

1

Haugh Rd.

Sauchiehall St.

Berkeley St.

M8

Glasgow City Centre →

1   Cameron Fountain
2   Woodside Terrace
3   Trinity College and Park Church Tower
4   Park Circus
5   Kelvingrove Park
6   Gibson Street
🍴 Stravaigin
7   Eton Terrace

8   University of Glasgow
9   Hunterian Art Gallery
10 Mackintosh House
11 University Gardens
12 Ashton Lane
🍴 Brel
13 Byres Road
14 Great Western Road
15 Botanic Gardens

George Gilbert Scott controversially won the commission and his Gothic revival is punctuated by a 30m (100-ft.) tower, which rises from the double quadrangle: a virtual beacon on the horizon of the West End. There are fragments of the original university, too, in the facade of Pearce Lodge as well as the salvaged Lion and Unicorn Stair at the chapel. The cloistered vaults and open columns under the halls between the two quads evoke a sense of meditation and reflection. From here you can enter the **Hunterian Museum,** whose exhibits include ancient coins, as well as geological and archaeological discoveries (p. 195).

Cross University Avenue north to Hillhead Street and view the:

❾ Hunterian Art Gallery

Built in the 1980s next to the university library, this gallery houses the school's permanent collection, which includes 18th- and 19th-century Scottish art as well as many works by American James McNeill Whistler. Scottish-Italian contemporary artist, the late Eduardo Paolozzi, designed the chunky, cast-aluminum internal doors to the main exhibition space.

Incorporated into the building past the gift shop is:

❿ Mackintosh House

Charles Rennie Mackintosh's and his wife, Margaret Macdonald's, West End home (originally nearby and demolished by university in the 1960s) has been replicated here, with furniture and interiors designed by the pair. Visitors enter from the side (the front door is actually several feet above the level of the plaza outside), and get to see the dining room, sitting room with study, and the couple's bedroom. At the top is a replication of a bedroom he designed for a house in England: his final commission.

Return to University Avenue, exit turning right to:

⓫ University Gardens

This fine row of houses was designed primarily by JJ Burnet in the 1880s, but it is worth stopping for—especially to admire no. 12, which was done by J. Gaff Gillespie in 1900 and exemplifies Glasgow Style and the influences of Mackintosh and Art Nouveau.

Continue down University Gardens past Queen Margaret Union and other university buildings, going left down the stairs just past the Gregory Building. At the bottom, follow the sidewalk and turn right on to:

⓬ Ashton Lane

This cobbled mews is the heart of West End nightlife, although it bustles right through the day, too, with a mix of students, University instructors, and staff as well as local residents. The host of bars, cafes, and restaurants here includes the venerable **Ubiquitous Chip,** which can be credited for starting (in 1971) the ongoing renaissance of excellent cooking of fresh Scottish produce (p. 184).

TAKE A BREAK
Especially welcome on nice days, **Brel** (39–43 Ashton Lane; ✆ **0141/ 342-4966**), a bar and bistro, provides both outdoor and conservatory seating in the back. It has a Belgian theme, serving mussels and European beers. See p. 238 for full review.

Go left past the Ubiquitous Chip down the narrow lane to Byres Road. Here is an underground station, and you can catch the train back to the city center. Otherwise, turn right on:

⓭ Byres Road

Full of bars, cafes, restaurants, and a panoply of shops, this is the proverbial Main Street of Glasgow's West End. Rarely less than buzzing, the road, for many, exemplifies the lively district. If you're not in a hurry, the streets running west from Byres Road, such as Athole or

Huntly gardens, merit a brief wander to see the proud town houses.

Proceed north up Byres Road to:

⑭ Great Western Road

It took an 1836 act of Parliament in London to create this street, then a new turnpike road into the city. Today, its four lanes remain some of the main thoroughfares in and out of Glasgow. While this particular walk has neglected Great Western Road, a stroll west for 5 or 6 blocks from this intersection will reveal the opulent terraces (including one by Thomson) along the boulevard's southern flank. Going in the opposite direction takes you to more retail and commercial shops. At this corner, the former Kelvinside Parish Church was converted in 2004 into a bar, restaurant, and center for the performing arts called Oran Mor.

Cross Great Western Road to the:

⑮ Botanic Gardens

Neither as extensive nor as grand as the Royal Botanic Gardens in Edinburgh, this hilly park is pleasant nonetheless. One main attraction, Kibble Palace, the giant, domed, cast-iron-and-glass, Victorian conservatory with exotic plants, reopened in 2006 after extensive refurbishment. Other greenhouses contain orchid collections, while the outdoor planting includes a working vegetable plot, roses and rhododendrons, and beds with lots of flowering perennials.

WALKING TOUR 4 | **THE SOUTHSIDE**

Start:	Tramway.
Finish:	Kilmarnock Road.
Time:	About 1 hour.
Best Times:	Afternoon.
Worst Times:	Late at night.

The Southside of Glasgow is mostly residential and thus presumably of less interest to visitors—although some consider it to represent the real Glasgow, and Southsiders can be very attached to their patch of the city. It encompasses a large area. This relatively short walk provides only a small sample of what the various neighborhoods south of the River Clyde are like.

Take the train one stop from Central Station upper level to the Pollokshields East station. Exit at the rear of the platform, come up the steps, and go right on Albert Drive to the:

❶ Tramway

The one-time Coplawhill Tramway Works and Depot was built in the late 1800s. After the city's fleet of electric streetcars was mothballed, the sprawling industrial building became a Museum for Transport before becoming another of the city's centers for cutting-edge art and performance. Behind the building is a recently constructed park—called the Hidden Gardens—with contributions from contemporary artists. With a mixture of structured landscaping,

wildflower meadow, and specimen planting, it is an oasis.

Exit Tramway, turing right to Pollokshaws Road, where you turn right (southwest) and:

 TAKE A BREAK
Heraghty's (708 Pollokshaws Rd.; ✆ 0141/423-0380) is an Irish pub, but not the invented type with phony atmosphere: This one's for real. Many of Glasgow's Irish immigrants settled on the city's Southside. Even if families have since moved to the outer suburbs, they often come back to this friendly, traditional pub for a pint of Guinness.

Continue southwest on Pollokshaws Road and
go right (northeast) on:

❷ Nithsdale Road

Originally Titwood Place in the old village called **Strathbungo,** this street has a
fairly long row of tenements probably
designed by Alexander "Greek" Thomson, if executed after his death by a less
than ambitious business partner. Although
the buildings are rather plain, experts see
the repetitive use of design and the manner in which the row terminates with a
single-story shop as confirming Thomson's hand. Around the corner from the
single-story shop is more evidence of
Thomson's influences with acanthus
leaves and square columns. Although tenements have a reputation as moldy, poor
places to live, many built in the 1800s
were the models of middle-class living.
Thomson's best tenement, Queens Park
Terrace on Eglinton Street north of here,
was a victim of neglect and shamelessly
demolished by the city in 1981.

To the left (west) of the roundabout at the end
of Nithsdale Road is:

❸ Moray Place

Nos. 1 to 10 Moray Place, facing the railway tracks, is the first terrace of houses
designed by Alexander "Greek" Thomson, and the first house became the great
architect's home in the 1860s. Like Eton
Terrace (see "Walking Tour 3: The West
End," above), the structure has two "tem-
ples" at either end of a row of two-story
town houses. A colonnade of some 52
square columns dominates the upper
floor's facade. The original chimney pots
were fashioned after lotus flowers, which
are repeated in urns at the front of Nos. 5
and 6. The terraces along the rest of

Moray Place to the west only attempt to
live up to Thomson's achievement.

Continue along Moray Place, go left on Queen
Square to Pollokshaws Road, and cross to:

❹ Queens Park

Although opened in 1862, this large hilly
park was not named after Queen Victoria
but rather Mary, Queen of Scots. Near
here, her disastrous battle of Langside was
fought. The Norman Gothic steeple, constructed of light stone, belongs to
William Leiper's Camphill Queen's Park
Church, finished in 1883. By walking
parallel to Pollokshaws Road, past the
upper pond with resident swans on its
island, and up a slight rise, you will come
to Camphill House. Built towards the
beginning of the 19th century with fluted
Ionic columns at the front portico, it was
once a Museum of Costume.

To the right of Camphill House, follow the tree-
lined drive past the compact soccer pitches back
to:

❺ Pollokshaws Road

One of the main thoroughfares leading to
and from the city, Pollokshaws Road
points directly at Glasgow Cathedral as it
nears the city center. At this end of the
boulevard, you'll find more of the city's
distinctive red sandstone tenements. Nos.
988 to 1004 Camphill Gate, offer some
distinctive Glasgow Style design work,
from the lettering to cupolas and the iron
railing along the roof. At the corner of the
park is Langside Halls, which originally
stood in the city center on Queen Street.
It was moved lock, stock, and barrel to
this location and rebuilt. The exterior dec-
oration is by the same man who worked
on London's Houses of Parliament.

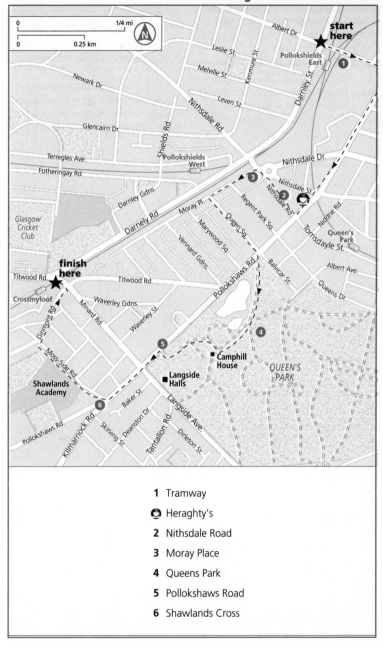

1 Tramway

🍵 Heraghty's

2 Nithsdale Road

3 Moray Place

4 Queens Park

5 Pollokshaws Road

6 Shawlands Cross

Cross Langside Avenue and continue southwest on Pollokshaws Road to the fork with Kilmarnock Road and:

6 Shawlands Cross

This is the proverbial heart of the Southside, with lots of shops, pubs, and restaurants. This is especially the case going south on Kilmarnock Road, though the west side of the street is largely occupied with the unattractive 1960s-style Shawlands Shopping Arcade. On nearby Moss-side Road, the one-time Waverley Cinema, with its Egyptian-style columns, has been converted into a sprawling bar, restaurant, and nightclub called Tusk.

Go northwest on Moss-side Road, taking a right at Dinmont Road to Crossmyloof station and catch the suburban train back to the city center.

17

Glasgow Shopping

After London, the capital of Great Britain and a city at least ten times its size, Glasgow apparently has the second most retail space in all of the U.K. It is a shopping mecca for everyone in the west of the country and, apparently, a reason for people to visit from northern England, too, as it is not as far away as the shops of London's Soho. The mainstream area for retail therapy is defined by the predominantly pedestrian zones of Argyle Street, Buchanan Street, and Sauchiehall Street, which join together and form a Z shape right in the heart of the city. But for more unique shops and fashions, it pays to venture into the Merchant City and the West End. And perhaps the city's most unique shopping experience is at the flea-market-like stalls at the weekend Barras market in the East End.

1 The Shopping Scene

For most visitors from abroad, Glasgow prices are not going to be a major selling point. In recent years, the British currency, pound sterling, has been trading strongly against other major currencies, such as the U.S. dollar or the euro (which most of Britain's partners in the European Union now use). The good news is that prices for most products in Scotland have been stable since the mid-1990s and in some cases— for example, clothes—prices have come down in real terms. Nevertheless, many items carry the same numerical price in pounds as they would in American dollars. For example, a digital camera that costs $300 in New York might well be priced £300 in Glasgow, making it 50% to 100% more expensive.

BEST BUYS

Among the few retail goods that are high quality *and* priced competitively are fine **wool knits,** particularly cashmere sweaters—or as the Scots prefer, "jumpers"—and scarves. Anything produced within the country (with the exception of whisky, which is taxed as heavily as all alcoholic products) should be less expensive than at home: from **smoked salmon** and **shortbread** to **Caithness glass,** those beguiling clear paper weights with swirling, colorful designs. Finally, given the number of artists in the country, getting an original piece of **art** to bring home might represent the most value for money.

SHOPPING COMPLEXES

Princes Square (Buchanan St.; ✆ **0141/204-1685;** www.princessquare.co.uk) is the city's most stylish and upmarket shopping center. Within a modernized and renovated Victorian building, the mall has many specialty stores, men's and women's fashion outlets as well as restaurants, cafes, and bars.

Nearby, between Argyle Street and the River Clyde is the **St. Enoch Shopping Centre** (✆ **0141/204-3900;** www.stenoch.com), whose merchandise is less expensive and

Glasgow Shopping

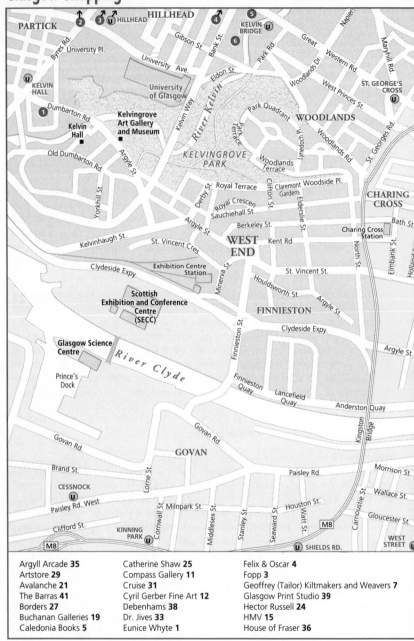

Argyll Arcade **35**	Catherine Shaw **25**	Felix & Oscar **4**
Artstore **29**	Compass Gallery **11**	Fopp **3**
Avalanche **21**	Cruise **31**	Geoffrey (Tailor) Kiltmakers and Weavers **7**
The Barras **41**	Cyril Gerber Fine Art **12**	Glasgow Print Studio **39**
Borders **27**	Debenhams **38**	Hector Russell **24**
Buchanan Galleries **19**	Dr. Jives **33**	HMV **15**
Caledonia Books **5**	Eunice Whyte **1**	House of Fraser **36**

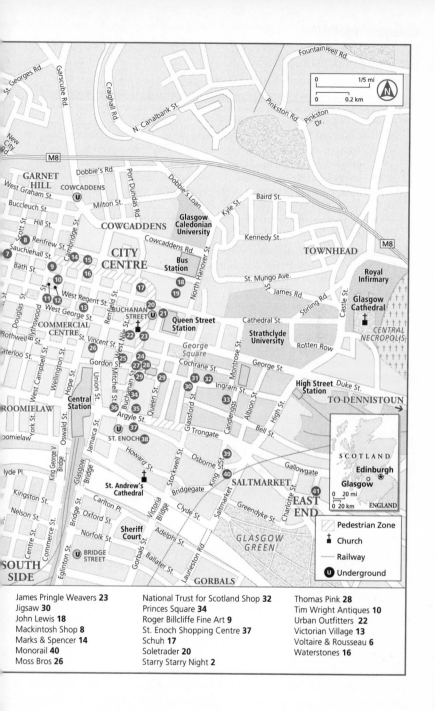

James Pringle Weavers **23**	National Trust for Scotland Shop **32**	Thomas Pink **28**
Jigsaw **30**	Princes Square **34**	Tim Wright Antiques **10**
John Lewis **18**	Roger Billcliffe Fine Art **9**	Urban Outfitters **22**
Mackintosh Shop **8**	St. Enoch Shopping Centre **37**	Victorian Village **13**
Marks & Spencer **14**	Schuh **17**	Voltaire & Rousseau **6**
Monorail **40**	Soletrader **20**	Waterstones **16**
Moss Bros **26**	Starry Starry Night **2**	

> ### *Moments* Trawling the Stalls
>
> **The Barras,** held Saturday and Sunday 9am to 5pm, takes place about .8km (½ mile) east of Glasgow's George Square. This century-old market has traders selling their wares in stalls and shops. You can not only browse for that special treasure but also become a part of Glasgow life. Alas, as the old traders have died off, younger hawkers are not replacing them. And the authorities have had their hands full with the sale of black-market goods, especially tobacco, whose proceeds fund organized crime. Still, where else can you see an auction of 4.5 kilograms (10 lb.) of chicken legs, with a pound of bacon thrown in for free? The nearby **Paddy's Market,** by the rail arches on Shipbank Lane, operates daily if you'd like to see an old-fashioned slice of Glaswegian street vending.

a lot less posh than what you'll find at Princes Square. It resembles a fairly conventional indoor mall with a couple major department stores and a food court at one end.

If you're after a fancy watch or gold ring, go to the **Argyll Arcade,** the main entrance to which is at 30 Buchanan St. Even if the year of its construction (1827) wasn't posted above the entrance, you'd still know that this collection of shops beneath a curved glass ceiling is historic. The L-shaped, Parisian style arcade contains one of the largest concentrations of retail **jewelers,** both antique and modern, in all of Europe. It's considered lucky to purchase a wedding band here.

The most recent contribution to mall shopping in the city center is the **Buchanan Galleries** (© 0141/333-9898; www.buchanangalleries.co.uk), at the top of Buchanan Street. Completed in 1999, this mammoth development is hardly groundbreaking but it does include the rightfully respected **John Lewis** department store.

On the western outskirts of town, the **Braehead Shopping Centre** (© 0141/885-1441; www.braehead.co.uk) opened most recently and somewhat controversially, as it appears to be taking people away from the city center. Its major draw is a sprawling Ikea store.

2 Shopping A to Z

In general, shops in the city center are open from 9am until 6pm. Be warned, they tend to close sharply, regardless of the number of potential shoppers that are still out on the sidewalks. But in 2006, the city was considering later opening hours for city center stores in order to compete with the shopping developments on Glasgow's periphery, which are open daily until 8pm. Thursday is the traditional evening for businesses to stay open until 8pm in the heart of town. Most established stores are now open in the afternoon on Sunday, too.

Unless otherwise indicated, the shops below are in the commercial center of Glasgow and are within walking distance of the Buchanan Street or St. Enoch underground stations.

ANTIQUES

Tim Wright Antiques   Established in the 1970s, this is the biggest antiques shop in the city with six showrooms. 147 Bath St. © 0141/221-0364. www.timwright-antiques.com.

Victorian Village   This warren of shops offers a pleasantly claustrophobic clutter of goods. Much of the merchandise isn't particularly noteworthy, but there are some worthwhile pieces if you know what you're after and are willing to go hunting. 93 W. Regent St. ℂ 0141/332-0808.

ART

Compass Gallery   Opened by Cyril Gerber (see below), this gallery has affordable pieces of contemporary art by local artists. You could find something special for as little as £20 ($37), depending on the show. The pre-Christmas sale is particularly good. 178 W. Regent St. (near Blythswood Sq.). ℂ 0141/221-6370. www.compassgallery.co.uk.

Cyril Gerber Fine Art   One of Glasgow's best small galleries, it veers away from the avant-garde, specializing in British painting of the 19th and 20th centuries. It has good Scottish landscapes and cityscapes as well as works by Colourists and the Glasgow Boys. Gerber has been the city's most respected art authority for several decades, with lots of contacts in art circles throughout Britain and Europe. 148 W. Regent St. ℂ 0141/221-3095.

Glasgow Print Studio   The shop sells limited edition etchings, wood blocks, aquatints, or screen prints by members of the prestigious collective, as well as other notable artists. Good prices and a framing facility are on the premises. 25 King St. (just below the Trongate). ℂ 0141/552-0704. www.gpsart.co.uk.

Roger Billcliffe Fine Art   Another fine art shop offers a couple floors of works, whether original contemporary paintings by Scottish and English artists or delicate ceramics. 134 Blythswood St. (just off Sauchiehall St.). ℂ 0141/332-4027. www.billcliffegallery.com.

ART SUPPLIES

Artstore   If the Glasgow's wealth of art and architecture, combined with the steely northern light, inspires you to make a wee bit of your own art, then this shop in the heart of the city will provide all the supplies you'll need. 94 Queen St. (across from the Gallery of Modern Art). ℂ 0141/221-1101.

BOOKS

Borders   The multistory U.S.-based shop at the back of Royal Exchange Square, in the heart of Glasgow, offers books, DVDs, and music CDs—with a gratifying emphasis on the culture of Scotland and plenty of places to sit and read. Borders also has the best international periodical and newspaper selection in Scotland. 98 Buchanan St. (at Gordon St.). ℂ 0141/222-7700. www.borders.com.

Caledonia Books   One of few remaining second-hand and antiquarian shops in the city of Glasgow. Charming and well-run. The stock tends to favor quality over quantity. 483 Great Western Rd., West End. ℂ 0141/334-9663. www.caledoniabooks.co.uk. Underground: Kelvin Bridge.

Waterstones   Like Borders, a giant Barnes-and-Noble-like operation with plenty of stock, a cafe, and lots of soft seats. A good Scottish section is located on the ground floor. The only downside of the place is that it has perhaps put the city's independent booksellers, such as John Smith, out of business. 174 Sauchiehall St. ℂ 0141/248-4814. www.waterstones.co.uk.

Voltaire & Rousseau   This shop in an out-of-the-way location near the River Kelvin says it is the longest running second-hand book store in the city. And if you found this place, you might as well visit nearby **Thistle Books** (61 Otago St.; ℂ 0141/ 334-8777). 18 Otago Lane (near Gibson St.), West End. ℂ 0141/339-1811. Underground: Kelvin Bridge.

CLOTHING
FASHION
Cruise   Bring your credit cards for the best selection of designer togs in town. Labels include Prada, Armani, D&G, Vivienne Westwood, and more. At the second branch nearby (223 Ingram St.), the Oki-Ni shop within the shop offers limited edition Adidas and Levi. 180 Ingram St. (at the Italian Centre), Merchant City. ✆ 0141/572-3232.

Dr. Jives   This shop began as a vintage clothing shop for men in the late 1980s but has evolved into the hippest boutique in town for cutting-edge designer looks, especially for the skatey crowds at the dance clubs. 111 Candleriggs, Merchant City. ✆ 0141/552-4551.

Urban Outfitters   Those familiar with Manhattan will recognize the stock in this popular store for youth, with a balance of metro-retro, kitsch, and chic clothing. 157 Buchanan St. (at Nelson Mandela Sq.). ✆ 0141/248-9203. www.urbn.com.

ANTIQUE & VINTAGE
Starry Starry Night   Those Victorians and Edwardians were surely tiny but they wore some pretty stunning gowns, and this shop (with a branch in the Barras) normally has a few worth dusting off. Also available are second-hand kilts and matching attire. 19 Downside Lane (off Ruthven Lane and Byres Rd.), West End. ✆ 0141/337-1837. Underground: Hillhead.

FOR MEN
Thomas Pink   This is perhaps Glasgow's closest thing to that temple of preppy sensibilities: Brooks Brothers. This is the place for the finest button-down Oxford shirts that a man could possibly hope for—and a silk tie to match. 1 Royal Bank Place (next to Borders, just off Buchanan St.). ✆ 0141/248-9661.

FOR WOMEN
Jigsaw   Recently relocated under the glorious dome of the baroque former Savings Bank of Glasgow, this is the fashionable U.K. chain of womenswear, junior, and accessories. Using its own design team in Kew, West London, Jigsaw opened its first shop in Hampsted some 30 years ago. 177 Ingram St. (at Glassford St.). ✆ 0141/552-7639. www.jigsaw-online.com.

DEPARTMENT STORES
Debenhams   Sturdy department store with mid-range prices. St. Enoch Shopping Centre, 97 Argyle St. ✆ 0844/561-6161. www.debenhams.com.

House of Fraser   This is Glasgow's modest version of Harrods. A Victorian-era glass arcade rises up four stories, and on the various levels you'll find everything from clothing to Oriental rugs, from crystal to handmade local artifacts of all kinds. 45 Buchanan St. (at Argyle St.). ✆ 0870/160-7243. www.houseoffraser.co.uk.

John Lewis   The closest equivalent of Macy's, with quality brand names, assured service, and a no-questions-asked return policy on damaged or faulty goods. Buchanan Galleries, 220 Buchanan St. ✆ 0141/353-6677. www.johnlewis.com.

Marks & Spencer   Anyone who reads international finance pages will know that M&S, despite its role as the leading department store across Great Britain, has had its share of problems with shareholders. But it carries on with clothing and a very good food hall. Two branches in Glasgow on Argyle and Sauchiehall streets. 172 Sauchiehall St. ✆ 0141/332-6097. www.marksandspencer.com.

Tips **Bring That Passport!**

Take along your passport when you go shopping in case you make a purchase that entitles you to a **VAT (value-added tax)** refund.

EDIBLES

See Picnic Fare in chapter 14, "Where to Dine in Glasgow," for a list of select food markets with Scottish specialties.

GIFTS & DESIGN

Catherine Shaw   Named after the long-deceased matriarch of the family that runs the place today, Catherine Shaw is a somewhat cramped gift shop that has cups, mugs, postcards, jewelry, and souvenirs. It's a good place for easy-to-pack gifts. Look for another branch at 31 Argyll Arcade (ⓒ **0141/221-9038**); entrances to the arcade are on both Argyll and Buchanan streets. 24 Gordon St. ⓒ **0141/204-4762.**

Felix & Oscar   This wacky and fun shop stocks off-beat cards and toys, kitsch accessories, fuzzy bags, perfumes and toiletries, as well as a selection of t-shirts that you're not likely to find anywhere else in Glasgow. In addition to the flagship shop, there is another on Cresswell Lane. 459 Great Western Rd., West End. ⓒ **0131/339-8585.** www.felixand oscar.co.uk. Underground: Kelvin Bridge.

Mackintosh Shop   This small gift shop in the Glasgow School of Art prides itself on a stock of books, cards, stationery, mugs, glassware, and sterling-and-enamel jewelry created from or inspired by the original designs of Charles Rennie Mackintosh. No cheap tatt but rather authorized Mackintosh goods. Glasgow School of Art, 167 Renfrew St. ⓒ **0141/353-4500.**

National Trust for Scotland Shop   Although the fate of this shop has been called into question, "Glasgow style" is celebrated on the ground floor in Hutcheson Hall, a historic landmark by David Hamilton that dates to 1812. Drop in here for contemporary arts and crafts, pottery, furniture, or jewelry designed exclusively by Glasgow-based artists. Hutcheson Hall, 158 Ingram St. ⓒ **0141/552-8391.**

KILTS & TARTANS

Geoffrey (Tailor) Kiltmakers and Weavers   Both a retailer and manufacturer of tartans, which means they have all the clans and have also created their own range of 21st-century-style kilts—for better or worse. 309 Sauchiehall St. (across from the CCA). ⓒ **0141/331-2388.** www.geoffreykilts.co.uk.

Hector Russell   Founded in 1881, Hector Russell is Scotland's long-established Inverness-based kiltmaker. Crystal and gift items are sold on street level, but the real heart and soul of the place is below, where impeccably crafted and reasonably priced tweed jackets, tartan-patterned accessories, waistcoats, and sweaters of top-quality wool for men and women are displayed. 110 Buchanan St. ⓒ **0141/221-0217.** www.hector-russell.com.

James Pringle Weavers   In business since 1780, this shop is known for their traditional clothing that includes well-crafted, bulky wool sweaters and a tasteful selection of ties, kilts, and tartans. Some of the merchandise is unique to this shop. Ever slept in a tartan nightshirt? 130 Buchanan St. ⓒ **0141/221-3434.**

KILT HIRE

Moss   You might just wish to don a kilt during your stay, and renting one is a heck of a lot less expensive than buying one. This clothing store has a good stock and will sometimes reduce the price of a rental for those making last-minute hires. 25 Renfield St. (near Central Station). ✆ 0141/248-7571.

MUSIC

Avalanche   The indie rock store to beat all others? Perhaps, small and cramped but possibly the best for the latest releases by everybody from White Stripes to Yo La Tengo or local stars, Franz Ferdinand, and up-and-comers like Sons and Daughters. 34 Dundas St. (near Queen St. Station). ✆ 0141/332-2099.

Fopp   Glasgow's largest independent CD outlet, offering one of the best selections, ranging from classics to hottest hits, plus a stock of DVDs, music books, and a bit of vinyl, too. Good number of re-releases priced at only £5 ($9.25). In addition to the West End flagship, there is a larger, multistory branch in the city center on Union Street (✆ **0141/222-2128**) near Central Station. 358 Byres Rd., West End ✆ **0141/357-0774.** www.fopp.co.uk. Underground: Hillhead.

HMV   Along with Virgin, HMV is Great Britain's largest purveyor of mainstream music CDs, DVDs, and videos. 154 Sauchiehall St. ✆ 0141/332-6631.

Monorail   Located within the vegan restaurant and bar called Mono, this is the most individual of independent CD and record outlets in the city. Glasgow is alight with young musicians, and this shop specializes in new music from up and coming local acts, as well as the best of cutting edge bands from elsewhere. 10 King St. ✆ 0141/553-2400.

SHOES

Schuh   Pronounced "shoe," this shop has the biggest range, from stilettos to sneakers, Converse hightops to "Doc" Martens. 9 Sauchiehall St. (near Buchanan Galleries). ✆ 0141/353-1990.

Soletrader   A more fashion-conscious selection of European designers and makers, such as Birkenstock. 164a Buchanan St. (at Dundas Lane). ✆ 0141/353-3022.

TARTANS

See "Kilts & Tartans," above.

WOOLEN KNITS

Eunice Whyte   This small, locally owned shop offers an excellent selection of wool sweaters and cardigans, scarves, and hats. 109 Dumbarton Rd., West End. ✆ 0141/339-2534. Underground: Kelvin Hall.

18

Glasgow After Dark

Some say that Glasgow today—and not Edinburgh—is the center of contemporary culture in Scotland. It is an arguable, not to say locally controversial, point of view, however.

But there is no doubt that Glasgow has seen the most progress since the middle of the 20th century, when the shipping boom went bust, giving way to an image of profound decline that began to be reversed in the 1980s. Its local arts scene was always alive, however.

Although the Scottish capital to the east is home to the country's national art galleries and museums, Glasgow is where the respected and accomplished **Scottish Opera** and **Scottish Ballet** companies—as well as the **Scottish National Orchestra**—are based. It is also the city where young talent is nurtured at the **Royal Scottish Academy of Music and Drama.** There are several theaters, including two that rank high across the U.K. for staging groundbreaking drama, the **Citizens** and the **Tron.** Even more experimental performance can be seen at the **Arches** and **Tramway.**

But for all this "high art," Glasgow has the reputation as an unsurpassed spawning ground in Scotland for pop and rock groups, such as Franz Ferdinand or Belle and Sebastian. The **Barrowland,** a former ballroom, has to be one of the best (that is, sweaty and vibrating) venues in all of Britain for seeing live contemporary music. Recently, the company that runs the well-known Brixton Academy converted an old movie house into the **Academy** on the city's Southside, while in the city center another former cinema, **ABC,** was redeveloped into a good music venue in 2005. Plus, two bars, **King Tut's Wah Wah Hut** (where the band Oasis was apparently "discovered") and **Nice 'n' Sleazy,** give Glasgow a pair of small venues with performance spaces that would rival those typical of Manhattan's East Village.

Then, of course, there are the city's many pubs and bars to consider. Most are friendly places and don't be surprised if the locals strike up a conversation. Remember, all indoor public places, including bars, are now completely nonsmoking. For a complete rundown of what is happening in Glasgow, pick up a copy of *The List,* a biweekly magazine available at all major newsstands and book shops.

1 The Performing Arts

THEATER

Although hardly competition for a drama giant such as London, Glasgow's theater scene is equal to, if not a step ahead of, Edinburgh's. Young Scottish playwrights often make their debuts here, and you're likely to see anything from Steinbeck's *The Grapes of Wrath* to Beckett's *Waiting for Godot* to *Romeo and Juliet* done in Edwardian dress.

Glasgow After Dark

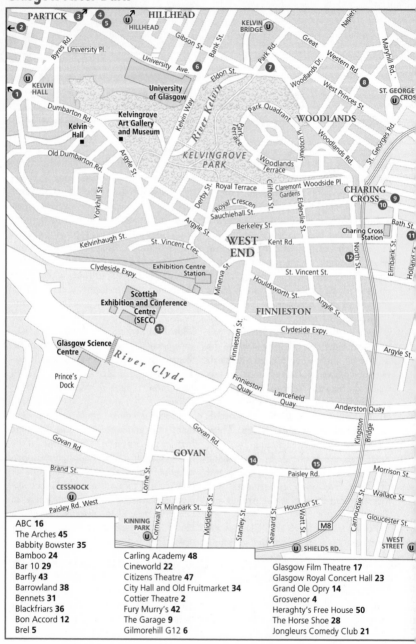

ABC **16**
The Arches **45**
Babbity Bowster **35**
Bamboo **24**
Bar 10 **29**
Barfly **43**
Barrowland **38**
Bennets **31**
Blackfriars **36**
Bon Accord **12**
Brel **5**

Carling Academy **48**
Cineworld **22**
Citizens Theatre **47**
City Hall and Old Fruitmarket **34**
Cottier Theatre **2**
Fury Murry's **42**
The Garage **9**
Gilmorehill G12 **6**

Glasgow Film Theatre **17**
Glasgow Royal Concert Hall **23**
Grand Ole Opry **14**
Grosvenor **4**
Heraghty's Free House **50**
The Horse Shoe **28**
Jongleurs Comedy Club **21**

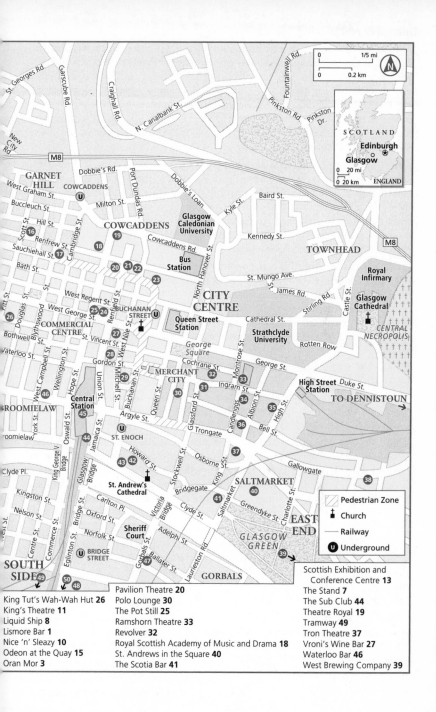

King Tut's Wah-Wah Hut **26**	Pavilion Theatre **20**	Scottish Exhibition and Conference Centre **13**
King's Theatre **11**	Polo Lounge **30**	The Stand **7**
Liquid Ship **8**	The Pot Still **25**	The Sub Club **44**
Lismore Bar **1**	Ramshorn Theatre **33**	Theatre Royal **19**
Nice 'n' Sleazy **10**	Revolver **32**	Tramway **49**
Odeon at the Quay **15**	Royal Scottish Academy of Music and Drama **18**	Tron Theatre **37**
Oran Mor **3**	St. Andrews in the Square **40**	Vroni's Wine Bar **27**
	The Scotia Bar **41**	Waterloo Bar **46**
		West Brewing Company **39**

The Arches 🟊   Located within the vaulted brick arches beneath the railway lines in and out of Central Station, the Arches offers a range of inexpensive drama and performance. That includes edgy new plays as well as Shakespeare. But the Arches also offers a fairly full schedule of live music of all description, regular dance clubs, and visual art exhibits. Although it receives grants from government arts bodies, it is an independent, not-for-profit entity. The cafe/bar at the Arches is, like at the Traverse in Edinburgh, a scene unto itself. 253 Argyle St. ℰ **0870/240-7528.** www.thearches.co.uk. Tickets £4–£10 ($7.50–$18). Underground: St. Enoch.

Citizens Theatre 🟊   Perhaps the prime symbol of Glasgow's verve and democratic approach to theater is the well-known "Citz." Located in the Gorbals, just across the River Clyde from the commercial center of Glasgow, it's home to a repertory company, and the facility has three performance spaces: a main auditorium and two smaller theaters. In 2004, new artistic director Jeremy Raison made his debut. Prices are always reasonable. 119 Gorbals St. (at Ballater St.). ℰ **0141/429-0022.** www.citz.co.uk. Tickets £5–£15 ($9–$28). Underground: Bridge St. Bus: 5, 12, 20, or 66.

Cottier Theatre   This 350-seat, nonprofit theater is housed in the former Dowanhill Parish Church in the Hyndland district of the city's West End. Small-scale productions and community theater by groups such as the local Partick Players, as well as comedy and musical events are usually staged here. The complex includes a pub with verdant beer garden and upstairs restaurant serving Latin American–influenced food. 935 Hyndland St. ℰ **0141/357-3868.** www.thecottier.com. Tickets £4–£20 ($7.40–$37). Underground: Kelvinhall.

Gilmorehill G12   Run by the University of Glasgow, and often just called G12 (the local postal code), productions by the university's drama students and other college and independent companies are staged here. The works can range from experimental to revivals. Sometimes it hosts free film festivals, too. 9 University Ave. ℰ **0141/330 5522.** www.gilmorehillg12.co.uk. Tickets £3–£12 ($5.50–$22). Underground: Kelvinbridge.

King's Theatre   The King's Theatre celebrated its centenary in 2004 with its usual offering of popular and light entertainment: whether comedies, musicals, or family-oriented plays. This magnificent, red-sandstone hall is also the place where touring Broadway and West End spectacles, such as Miss Saigon, are likely to appear. During December and January, the King's is best noted for its over-the-top pantomime presentations, often starring well-known Scottish actors. 297 Bath St. ℰ **0870/060-6648.** www.kings-glasgow.co.uk. Tickets £6–£26 ($11–$48). Suburban train: Charing Cross. Bus: 16 or 18.

Pavilion Theatre   After the King's Theatre, this equally historic theater (if less architecturally distinguished) specializes in family entertainment, variety shows, light drama, tribute acts and bands, as well as comedy. It's another prime location for pantomime around Christmas time. 121 Renfield St. ℰ **0141/332-1846.** www.paviliontheatre.co.uk. Tickets £10–£25 ($16–$40). Underground: Buchanan St. Bus: 21, 23, or 38.

Ramshorn Theatre   Another church conversion, this professional performance space is used primarily for student productions of nearby Strathclyde University and for touring companies. Ticket prices are typically low. 98 Ingram St. ℰ **0141/552-3489.** Tickets £2.50–£8 ($4.50–$15). Underground: Buchanan St.

Tron Theatre 🟊🟊   Housed in a part of the former Tron Church, which dates back to the 15th century, the Tron Theatre is one of Scotland's leading venues for new and sometimes experimental dramatic performances. The stage is often the place where contemporary local companies, such as Cryptic or Vanishing Point, debut works that go on to tour in the UK and even internationally. In addition to theater, the hall is used for music and dance. The Tron also has a modern bar/cafe as well as a beautifully restored Victorian bar/restaurant serving lunch and dinner, including vegetarian dishes, as well as a fine selection of beer and wine. 63 Trongate. ℂ 0141/552-4267. www.tron.co.uk. Tickets £3–£20 ($5.50–$37). Underground: St. Enoch. Bus: 62.

Tramway   This postindustrial, huge hangar of an arts venue is one of the only places in Glasgow able to stage sprawling performance art and modern theater, such as Peter Brook's The Mahabharata, which came here in the late 1980s. In 2004, however, the city, which owns Tramway, was controversially considering the option of renting it to the national ballet company as rehearsal space. In addition to drama, the former repair shop for the trams on the city's Southside houses art exhibits. 25 Albert Dr., Pollokshields. ℂ 0141/422-2023. www.tramway.org. Tickets £4–£12 ($7.50–$22). Suburban train: Pollokshields East. Bus: 38 or 45.

BALLET & OPERA
Theatre Royal ✿✿   This is the home theater for the ambitious, well-respected **Scottish Opera,** as well as the recently ascendant **Scottish Ballet.** The Royal also hosts visiting companies from around the world. Called somewhat exaggeratedly by the *Daily Telegraph,* "the most beautiful opera theater in the kingdom," the auditorium does offer splendid Victorian plasterwork and some glittering chandeliers. However, it's not the decor but the daunting repertoire—Wagner's *Ring* cycle, *La Bohème,* or *Don Giovanni*—that traditionally has attracted operagoers. 282 Hope St. ℂ 0870/060-6647. www.theatreroyalglasgow.com. Ballet tickets £3.50 (standby) to £55 ($6.50–$102); opera tickets £28–£180 ($52–$330); touring company tickets £10–£25 ($19–$46). Underground: Cowcaddens.

CONCERT HALLS & AUDITORIUMS
City Halls and Old Fruitmarket ✿   Emerging from £8 million ($15 million) renovations in 2006, this set of smaller halls, which date to the 1840s, is home to the **BBC's Scottish Symphony Orchestra** and the **Scottish Chamber Orchestra.** Acoustically superior to some of the city's larger auditoriums, the Merchant City venue is now a key venue in the annual Celtic Connections and the international jazz festivals, as well. Candleriggs and Albion St., Merchant City. ℂ 0141/353-8000. www.glasgowcityhalls.com. Underground: Buchanan St.

Glasgow Royal Concert Hall   Situated at the top of Buchanan Street, there is very little that's subtle about this modern music hall, which houses the most prestigious performance space in the city for everything from touring ballet companies to pop and rock acts, such as Elvis Costello or Jackson Browne. It is primarily home to the **Royal Scottish National Orchestra,** which plays its yearly Winter–Spring series and Pops

---

⌒Tips Finding Out What's On
For a complete run-down of what is happening in the city, pick up a copy of *The List,* a biweekly magazine available at all major newsstands and book shops. It reviews, previews, and gives the details of the arts and events in Glasgow and Edinburgh.

seasons in the main auditorium. The hall also produces the city's annual Celtic Connections festival every January. 2 Sauchiehall St. ✆ **0141/353-8000.** www.grch.com. Tickets £10–£35 ($19–$65). Underground: Buchanan St.

Royal Scottish Academy of Music and Drama   This mouth-full is usually shortened to its acronym: the RSAMD. The auditorium in this rather brutal red-brick structure compensates for any sins of the external architecture. 100 Renfrew St. ✆ **0141/332-4101.** www.rsamd.ac.uk. Underground: Cowcaddens.

2 The Club & Music Scene

COMEDY

Jongleurs Comedy Club   A corporate-owned entity from England, with more than a dozen venues across the U.K., Jongleurs came to Scotland a few years back dragging along its own cadre of house funny men (and women) as well as some touring comedians from overseas. The acts tend to be more mainstream. Renfield and Renfrew sts. ✆ **0870/787-0707.** Cover £12 ($22). Underground: Buchanan St.

The Stand   After starting and thriving in Edinburgh, the Stand opened a second venue in Glasgow, the city's only purpose-built comedy club. Its presence has helped to establish an annual International Comedy Festival every spring in the city. Usually Tuesday night, entitled "Red Raw," is reserved for amateurs. 333 Woodlands Rd. ✆ **0870/600-6055.** www.thestand.co.uk. Cover £2–£10 ($4–$19). Underground: Kelvinbridge.

FOLK

Oran Mor   Oran Mor is an ambitious center for the performing arts that includes a bar and restaurant as well as different spaces for live music—often in a Scottish folk vein. An afternoon drama in the popular "Play, Pie, and a Pint" series includes lunch. Contact Oran Mor for cover and ticket prices and a schedule of events. Byres and Great Western rds. ✆ **0141/357-6200.** www.oran-mor.co.uk.

St. Andrews in the Square   This sympathetically restored and converted early- to mid-18th-century church is the city's venue dedicated to folk, Celtic, and traditional Scottish music. The program includes concerts and *ceilidhs* (Scottish country dance) in the main hall upstairs. In the basement, **Café Source** serves wholesome Scottish nosh and hosts regular sessions of Scottish music, which can be rather reverentially listened to by the patrons, and jazz, too. 1 St. Andrews Sq. (off Saltmarket near Glasgow Cross). ✆ **0141/559-5902.** www.standrewsinthesquare.com. Tickets £4–£8 ($7.50–15). Underground: St. Enoch. Bus: 62.

The Scotia Bar   Along with the nearby **Clutha Vaults** and **Victoria** bars, the Scotia is one beam in a triangle of pubs that frequently offer live music, which includes a good dose of folk. 112 Stockwell St. ✆ **0141/552-8681.** No cover. Underground: Argyle St.

ROCK, POP & JAZZ

ABC ✿   Opened in 2005, this is the newest venue for bands visiting Glasgow. The main hall has room for about 1,250, making it an excellent place to get a bit closer to the musicians, themselves. The building itself dates to 1896 and reportedly screened the first film ever shown in Scotland, although it also housed a permanent circus before reverting to a film house in the 20th century. 300 Sauchiehall St. ✆ **0870/400-0818.** www.abcglasgow.com. Underground: Cowcaddens. Bus: 44.

Tips **Late-Night Eats**

Famished at 4 minutes past midnight? The options in Glasgow are fairly well focused on Sauchiehall Street. Try **Canton Express** (407 Sauchiehall St.; ☎ **0141/ 332-0145**), which looks as if it belongs on some side street in Hong Kong. It's nothing fancy—just fast Chinese food. Open daily until 4am.

Several Indian restaurants are open until 1am, but a couple trump the lot by staying open until 4am. **Charcoals** is in the city center (26 Renfield St.; ☎ **0141/ 221-9251**), while **Spice Gardens** is on the southern bank of the River Clyde (Clyde Place near Bridge St.; ☎ **0141/429-4422**).

Barfly   Part of a chain of small clubs devoted mostly to indie bands, Barfly used to be the locally owned 13th Note's club. It draws some of the best in local and national talent to the grungy space. Cover charge varies. Tickets for shows should be purchased in advance. 260 Clyde St. ☎ **0141/204-5700**. www.barflyclub.com. Underground: St. Enoch.

Barrowland 🥈🥈   No seats and generally stinking of beer, this former ballroom remains the most exciting place in the city to see visiting bands, although there is some talk of the owners selling it. The hall rocks, and groups who play here rank it among the best in the U.K. in which to perform. With room for about 2,000, it is not exactly intimate, but if you can withstand the mosh pit, you'll feel the sweat of the performers. 244 Gallowgate. ☎ **0141/552-4601**. Underground: St. Enoch. Bus: 62.

Carling Academy   A 2,500 capacity ex-cinema that opened as a live music venue in 2003, the Carling Academy was expressly designed to compete with the Barrowland. It is part of a chain, which includes the legendary Brixton Academy in London, and thus has a booking strength with touring bands. It's a pity its corporate sponsor has to be so prominent in the name. 121 Eglinton Rd. ☎ **0141/418-3000**. Underground: Bridge St. Bus: 66.

Grand Ole Opry *Finds*   Country-western music has a strong cult following in Glasgow and this club, 2.5km (1½ miles) southwest of the city center, is the largest of its type in Europe devoted to that genre. There's a bar, bingo, a "shoot-out," as well as a mildly offensive night-ending paean to the Confederacy—but mainly plenty of dancing (Texas line) plus a "chuck-wagon" eatery that serves affordable burgers and other fare. Performers are usually from the United Kingdom, but a handful of artists from the States turn up, too. 2–4 Govan Rd., Paisley Toll Rd. ☎ **0141/429-5396**. Cover £3–£10 ($5.50–$30). Bus: 9.

King Tut's Wah-Wah Hut 🥈   This sweaty, crowded rock bar has been in business for more than a decade. It's a good place to check out the Glasgow music and arts crowd, as well as local bands and the occasional international act. Successful Scottish acts such as Teenage Fan Club got their starts here. Cover is usually about £5 ($9). Open Monday to Saturday noon to midnight and Sunday 6pm to midnight. Tickets for shows should be purchased in advance. 272 St. Vincent St. ☎ **0141/221-5279**. www.king tuts.co.uk. Bus: 62.

Nice 'n' Sleazy   This bar books live acts to perform in the dark, basement space. The cover is quite reasonable, but it can get more expensive if you catch a more established act, such as ex-head Lemonhead, Evan Dando. Holding some 200 patrons, it provides a rare opportunity to catch such musicians in an intimate setting. The ground-floor bar has the city's best jukebox, and DJs spin an eclectic mix of music. Open daily 11:30am to 11:45pm. 421 Sauchiehall St. ℂ 0141/333-9637. Bus: 44. Suburban train: Charing Cross.

Scottish Exhibition & Conference Centre *(Overrated)* Incorporating the slightly more intimate Clyde Auditorium (or Armadillo because of its exterior design), the Clyde-side SECC may indeed be without charm, but it provides Scotland with the only indoor space large enough to host major touring acts, from Ozzie Ozbourne to Justin Timberlake. Finnieston Quay. ℂ 0141/275-6211. www.secc.co.uk.

DANCE CLUBS

Glasgow has one of the most active dance club scenes in Great Britain. Listed below are just a few selected venues. In local parlance, "venues" are distinct from the actual "clubs"—such as Optimo (electro-clash), Manga (drum and bass), or Pressure (house and techno)—which are associated with a specific style, DJ, or team of DJs. They can move around to different venues. It all makes perfect sense to those in the know.

Bamboo This stylish basement club has three distinct rooms, one of which is a rather posh cocktail lounge. The "Disco Badger" club, playing a mix of house and R&B, gets good reviews. It's open from 10pm to 3am. 51 West Regent St. ℂ 0141/332-1067. www.bamboo51.com. Cover £5–£8 ($9–$15); free before 10:30pm. Underground: Buchanan St.

Fury Murry's Most of the crowd here is made up of youths looking for nothing more complicated than a good, sometimes rowdy, time listening to upbeat disco. It's a short walk from the St. Enoch Shopping Centre and is open Thursday to Sunday 10:30pm to 3:30am. 96 Maxwell St. ℂ 0141/221-6511. Cover £2–£6 ($3.20–$9.60). Underground: St. Enoch.

The Garage A big student crowd tests the limits of the 1,478-person capacity here on weekends. In the downstairs area, surrounded by rough stone walls, you get the impression you're in a castle with a Brit pop and indie soundtrack. Most regulars, however, gravitate to the huge main dance floor. Open daily 11pm to 3am. 490 Sauchiehall St. ℂ 0141/332-1120. Cover £2–£7 ($3.50–$13). Underground: Buchanan St.

The Sub Club Shut for what seemed like an eternity after a fire, the city's best known "underground" club is back, with DJs such as the long-standing kings of house, Harri and Dom of Subculture. Open daily 10pm to 3am. 22 Jamaica St. ℂ 0141/248-4600. www.subclub.co.uk. Cover £3–£10. Underground: St. Enoch.

3 Bars & Pubs

COMMERCIAL CENTER

Bar 10 This is perhaps the granddaddy of the Glasgow style bar, but since opening it has mellowed into a comfortable place for drinking. The cool design is still apparent but more important is the good mix of folk and the convenient city center location just opposite the Lighthouse architecture center on tiny Mitchell Lane. Food is comforting and served from noon to about 5pm. Drinks are served Monday to Saturday from noon to midnight and Sunday from 12:30pm to midnight. DJs play on the weekend. 10 Mitchell Lane. ℂ 0141/572-1448. Underground: St Enoch.

Bon Accord This amiable pub, just west of the city center on the other side of the M8 freeway, is the best in the city for hand-pulled cask-conditioned real ale. There's an array of hand-pumps—a dozen devoted to real English and Scottish ales—while the rest of the draft and bottled beers and stouts hail from the Czech Republic, Belgium, Germany, Ireland, and Holland. The pub is likely to satisfy your taste in malt whisky as well, and offers affordable pub food. Open Monday to Saturday noon to midnight, Sunday noon to 11pm. 153 North St. © 0141/248-4427. Suburban train: Charing Cross.

The Horse Shoe ⭐ If you could only visit one pub in Glasgow, that would be a shame, but I'd advise you to pick this one. It is one of the last remaining "Palace Pubs," which opened around the turn of the 20th century. The circular, island bar is one of the longest in Europe. Drinks are relatively inexpensive (as is the upstairs buffet). Karaoke draws crowds every night of the week to a second floor lounge, but in the main bar it is conversation and sports on the many televisions that provide the entertainment. Drinks are served Monday to Saturday noon to midnight and Sunday from 12:30pm to midnight. The buffet is open until 7:30pm daily except Sunday when it closes at 5pm. 17 Drury St. (between Renfield and W. Nile sts.). © 0141/229-5711. Underground: Buchanan St.

The Pot Still Previously called the Cask & Still, this pub is the best place for sampling malt whiskies. You can taste from a selection of hundreds and hundreds of them, at a variety of styles (peaty or sweet), strengths, and maturities (that is, years spent in casks). Open Monday to Thursday noon to 11pm, Friday and Saturday noon to midnight, Sunday 12:30pm to 11pm. 154 Hope St. © 0141/333-0980. www.thepotstill.co.uk. Underground: Buchanan St.

Vroni's Wine Bar If you favor the grape over the grain, Bordeaux to brown ale, Sancerre rather than cider, then Vroni's selection of red, white, and sparkling wines, sold by the glass or the bottle, should satisfy you. The feeling of this small bar is Continental with banquette seating and candle-lit tables. Open Monday to Saturday from 10am to midnight and Sunday from 12:30pm to midnight. Food is served Monday to Thursday from noon to 7pm and until 3pm on Friday. 47 W. Nile St. © 0141/221-4677. Underground: Buchanan St.

MERCHANT CITY

Babbity Bowster A civilized place for a pint, with no pounding soundtrack of mindless pop to distract you from conversation. The wine selection is good, and the food is worth sampling, as well. Some outdoor seating, although it is rarely in full sun, is available. Every Saturday from about 4pm, folk musicians arrive for spontaneous jamming. Drinks are served daily from noon to midnight; food until about 10pm. 16 Blackfriars St. © 0141/552-5055. Underground: Buchanan St. Suburban train: High St.

Blackfriars Real ales are less plentiful in the Glasgow city center when compared to Edinburgh, but this basic pub has a decent selection of rotating beers, including some from the Continent. Jazz is often featured in the basement space, as is comedy. Drinks are served Monday to Saturday from noon to midnight and Sunday from 12:30pm to midnight. 36 Bell St. © 0141/552-5924. Underground: St. Enoch.

EAST END

West Brewing Company Opened in 2005, this bar is based on Munich beer halls. In the basement of the sprawling West is a brewery where they produce the best, freshest lager in Glasgow—perhaps in all of Scotland—following strict German laws for purity and using chemical-free processes. Don't let the name fool you, however, as West is at the east end of Glasgow Green in the former wool winding room of the Templeton Carpet Factory (near the People's Palace museum). Food leans towards Bavarian dishes, with dumplings, sauerkraut, and meaty mains, with some vegetarian options, too. Drinks are served from noon to midnight; food until about 9pm. Glasgow Green. *(C)* **0141/550-0135.** www.westbeer.com. Bus: 16 or 18.

WEST END

Brel   Ashton Lane is full of pubs and bars, but this one is possibly the best. It has a Belgian theme—with beers and cuisine favoring that French-speaking country—but it is not overplayed. The music policy is eclectic, with DJs and live acts adding atmosphere to the former stables. The bar is open daily from 10am to midnight. Food is served Monday to Friday from noon to 3pm and from 5 to 10:30pm, and on Saturday and Sunday from noon to 10:30pm. 39–43 Ashton Lane. *(C)* **0141/342-4966.** www.brel barrestaurant.com. Underground: Hillhead.

Lismore Bar   Tastefully decorated in a modern manner that still recognizes traditional Highland culture, the Lismore is a relaxed and laid-back bar. The whisky selection is excellent and the malt of the month is always a bargain. Scottish and Gaelic music is played Tuesday and Thursday nights. The bar is open Sunday to Thursday from 11am to 11pm and Friday and Saturday from 11am to midnight. No food is served. 206 Dumbarton Rd. *(C)* **0141/576-0103.** Underground: Kelvinhall.

Liquid Ship   Given its location, you're most likely to meet only locals at Liquid Ship. Owned by the same people who run Stravaigin (p. 187), it is unpretentious and smart with the main bar up a few steps and a lounge in the basement. Drinks are served Monday to Thursday from noon to 11pm, Friday and Saturday from noon to midnight, and Sunday from 12:30 to 11pm. Light fare is served daily from noon until about 8pm. 171 Great Western Rd. *(C)* **0141/331-1901.** Underground: St. George's Cross.

SOUTHSIDE

Heraghty's Free House *Finds*   The trend for Irish theme pubs has left its mark on Glasgow, but if you want the real McCoy, come to this traditional bar on the city's Southside. It serves up perfect pints of Guinness and Irish craic (banter) in almost equal portions. No food, though. Open Monday to Thursday from 11am to 11pm, Friday and Saturday from 11am to midnight, and Sunday from 12:30 to 11pm. 708 Pollokshaws Rd. *(C)* **0141/423-0380.** Bus: 38, 45, or 56.

4 Gay & Lesbian Glasgow

Glasgow and its environs are said to have the largest concentration of gays and lesbians in the U.K. outside of London. The Merchant City is the only identifiable district in the city where gay and lesbian community is particularly concentrated, dubbed the "gay triangle."

Bennets   Self-described as the city's "premier gay and lesbian night club," Bennets is the most consistently popular in the gay scene, recovering a few years back from a fire. The club extends over two levels, with cheesy chart and full on dance music. Open Tuesday to Sunday 11:30pm to 3am. 80 Glassford St. *(C)* **0141/552-5761.** Cover: £3–£6 ($5.50–$11). Underground: Buchanan St.

Cube   This gay-friendly night club has two dedicated gay nights a week: "Personality" on Monday with pop and funkier "FUN" on Tuesday nights. Open daily 11:30pm to 3:30am. 34 Queen St. ✆ **0141/226-8990**. Cover: £3 ($5.50). Underground: St. Enoch.

Polo Lounge   Gay but hetero-friendly, the Polo is often described as a cross between urbane gentleman's club and a Highland country lodge. It is both a bar and club, with dancing downstairs. Open daily from 5pm to 1am (until 3am Fri–Sat). 84 Wilson St. ✆ **0141/553-1221**. Cover after 10pm £5 ($9). Underground: St. Enoch.

Revolver   Gay-owned and operated, the Revolver bar has always tried to be a bit more grown-up and to dismiss with some of the more cheesy and stereotypical elements of the gay scene. But that doesn't mean that it is not fun or popular. Conversation generally rules and the jukebox is free. Drinks are served daily from noon to midnight. 6A John St. ✆ **0141/553-2456**. Underground: Buchanan St.

Waterloo Bar   Attracting a slightly older crowd, this place is the longest standing gay bar in town. Away from the heart of the scene in Merchant City, it's located west of Central Station. Open from noon to midnight from Monday to Saturday and from 12:30 to 11pm on Sunday. 306 Argyle St. ✆ **0141/221-7359**. Underground: St. Enoch.

5 Cinema

Glasgow Film Theatre 🎬   Two screens are used for a well-programmed daily output of independent, foreign, repertory, and art house films. The cinema was originally called the Cosmo, an Art Deco theater built in the late 1930s. Near the box office is Café Cosmo, a good place for pre- or post-movie beverages. 12 Rose St. ✆ **0141/332-8128**. www.gft.org.uk. Tickets £3–£5 ($5.50–$9). Underground: Cowcaddens.

Grosvenor   Refurbished and restored on Ashton Lane in the West End, the Grosvenor is possibly the only neighborhood cinema still operating in Glasgow, with a bar and two downstairs screening rooms with comfy big leather chairs and sofas that you can rent. The cinema screens a mix of mostly mainstream and a clutch of independent movies. Ashton Lane. ✆ **0141/339-8444**. www.grosvenorcinema.co.uk. Tickets £2.50–£6.50. ($4.50–$12). Underground: Hillhead.

Odeon at the Quay   A modern multiplex movie house on the south bank of the River Clyde, showing Hollywood films and other mainstream movies. Springfield Quay, Paisley Rd. ✆ **0141-418-0111**. Tickets £3.75–£5.50 ($7–$10).

Cineworld Renfrew Street 🎬   The towering building in the city center, the screens at the multiplex formerly known as the UGC are dominated by blockbusters and big releases, but a couple of the theaters are reserved for foreign films and independent art house features. 7 Renfrew St. ✆ **0871/200-2000**. www.ugccinemas.co.uk. Tickets £3.25–£5.35 ($6–$10).

19

Side Trips from Glasgow

One of Glasgow's attractions is its location near a diverse array of rural scenery, whether amid the hills and mountains to the north or the sea coasts to the west. A short journey in almost any direction will present visitors with open spaces and clean, fresh air.

As Sir Walter Scott dominates Lothian and the Borders, the prominence of 18th century poet **Robert Burns** is felt southwest of Glasgow in Ayrshire. The heart of "Burns Country" is there, although it extends to Dumfries, as well. Down the Clyde Coast is another popular tourist attraction: **Culzean Castle.** Pronounced approximately "cul-lane," it is more of a mansion than a castle, with extensive and picturesque gardens and woods all around.

In this region are some of the world's great links golf courses, including world-famous **Royal Troon** and **Turnberry,** with windswept coastal views and gorse-filled dunes. Although the heyday of resort towns such as Rothesay, on the isle of **Bute,** may be gone, they remain pleasant, relaxing places to visit. Or, go a bit further afield to the peninsulas west of Glasgow (where you might be lured by the scenery into spending a night). Short of that, day-trippers can easily reach Helensburgh and visit one of architect Charles Rennie Mackintosh's singular achievements: the residence known as **Hill House.**

Glasgow is also an excellent gateway to explore the southern reaches of the **Highlands.** Within an hour, you can be on the bonnie banks of **Loch Lomond,** with the mountains looming the distance. Finally, the city of **Stirling** and **Trossachs** range of mountains can be visited in a single day.

1 Ayrshire & "Burns Country"

Ayrshire and southwest Scotland is possibly best-known as "Burns Country," the region where Scotland's favorite bard, Robert (Auld Lang Syne) Burns, spent most of his life. But in addition to the historic sites of the famous poet, the region is one of the best places to golf in all of Scotland, especially on rambling links-style courses. Given its southwest exposure to the Gulf Stream influences, this is the most temperate area in Scotland. In addition to year-round golf, there is ample hiking and fishing, while the back roads and minor highways are ideal for road cycling.

The royal burgh of Ayr was once the most popular resort on Scotland's west coast. On the reasonably picturesque Firth of Clyde, it's only some 56km (35 miles) southwest of Glasgow or about an hour by train or by car. For many years it was a busy market town—with a more important and indeed larger port than Glasgow's until the 18th century. Today, it offers visitors some 4km (2½ miles) of beach, cruises, fishing, and golf—as well as the top horse racing in Scotland.

Side Trips from Glasgow

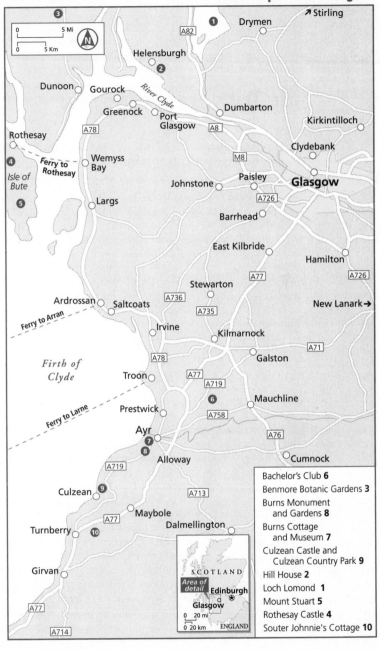

③

| | 0 | 5 Mi |
| | 0 | 5 Km |

N

①

A82

Drymen

↗ Stirling

Helensburgh

②

Dunoon

Gourock

River Clyde

Greenock

Port
Glasgow

Dumbarton

Kirkintilloch

A78

A8

Clydebank

Rothesay

Ferry to
Rothesay

Wemyss
Bay

M8

④

*Isle of
Bute*

Johnstone

Paisley

Glasgow

⑤

Largs

A726

Barrhead

East Kilbride

Hamilton

A726

Stewarton

A77

New Lanark →

Ardrossan

Saltcoats

A736

A735

Ferry to Arran

Irvine

Kilmarnock

A71

*Firth of
Clyde*

A78

Galston

Troon

A77

A719

Prestwick

⑥

Mauchline

A758

Ayr

A76

⑦

⑧

Alloway

Cumnock

A719

Culzean

⑨

A713

Maybole

Turnberry

⑩

A77

Dalmellington

Girvan

A77

A714

SCOTLAND

*Area of
detail*

Edinburgh
✱

Glasgow

| 0 | 20 mi |
| 0 | 20 km |

ENGLAND

Bachelor's Club **6**

Benmore Botanic Gardens **3**

Burns Monument
and Gardens **8**

Burns Cottage
and Museum **7**

Culzean Castle and
Culzean Country Park **9**

Hill House **2**

Loch Lomond **1**

Mount Stuart **5**

Rothesay Castle **4**

Souter Johnnie's Cottage **10**

ESSENTIALS
GETTING THERE
Trains from Glasgow's Central Station will whisk you to a variety of Ayrshire towns. The trip to Ayr takes less than 1 hour, and a standard round-trip journey, which must be made in the same day, costs £11 ($20). Stagecoach Express runs buses about twice an hour during the week from Glasgow's Buchanan Street bus terminal. Call **Travel-line Scotland** (✆ **0870/608-2608**) for specific journey times. By car, simply take the M77 south out of Glasgow, and it will take you straight to Ayr.

VISITOR INFORMATION
The Ayr **tourist information center** is at 22 Sandgate, Ayr (✆ **01292/678-100**; www.ayrshire-arran.com). It's open Monday to Saturday 10am to 5pm.

BURNS HERITAGE TRAIL
The **Burns Heritage Trail** ⊛ can be followed by car or on a bus tour. The main destinations are the national poet's places of birth and death, with a few lesser landmarks in and around Ayr thrown in for good measure. Son of a gardener and tenant farmer, Burns was born in 1759 in **Alloway,** which is now part of the suburbs of the coastal town Ayr. The **Burns Cottage and Museum** exhibits family items. Nearby are the church where his father William is buried (and where the haunted creatures of Burn's *Tam O'Shanter* come to life); the Greek revival **Burns Memorial;** and the arched bridge over the River Doon: the Brig o' Doon, which has been immortalized, for better or worse, by the Lerner and Loewe musical of the same name. Ayrshire towns of **Tarbolton** and **Kirkoswald** have other historic sites associated with the Scottish bard.

Quite a bit further afield, the town of Dumfries has the **Burns' House,** where the bard died in 1796. Here are more relics and items, the most impressive of which may be his signature, scrawled with a diamond in a window of the cottage. Twenty years after death, Burns was moved to a purpose-built mausoleum in Dumfries, where some of his pals were also interred.

AYR
Ayr is the logical place to begin any journey through Burns Country, and the town has a few associations with the bard itself.

The 15-century **Auld Brig,** according to the poet "stood flood an' tide," and it would still be standing when the "New Brig" (built in his lifetime) was reduced to a "shapeless cairn." And Burns was correct: the so-called New Brig is gone, but the Auld Brig is today one of the oldest stone bridges in Scotland. The New Brig came down and was replaced in the 19th century.

Not far away on the banks of the River Ayr is the **Auld Kirk** (old church), which dates to 1655, when it replaced the 12th-century Church of St. John, which was seized and dismantled by the invading forces of Oliver Cromwell. Robert Burns was baptized in the Auld Kirk. Its greatest curiosity, however, is a macabre series of "mort safes," metal grates which covered freshly filled graves to discourage grave-robbers or, more likely, body snatchers seeking cadavers for sale to medical colleges.

On the High Street, the **Tam O'Shanter Inn** is presumably the site of the tavern ("and ay the ale was growing better") where Tam leaves his drinking buddy Souter Johnnie and sets off riding his trusty grey mare Meg on that infamously stormy evening in Burn's epic and comic poem.

The **Wallace Tower,** also on High Street, rises some 34m (112 ft.). Constructed in 1828, it has a statue of medieval Scottish rebel William Wallace (celebrated by Mel

Gibson's film *Braveheart*) by local sculptor James Thom. Legend holds that Wallace was imprisoned here and made a daring escape.

Ayr After Dark

Rabbie's Bar   The walls are highlighted with the pithy verses of Robert Burns, and his portrait is painted directly onto the wall. However, don't come here expecting poetry readings in a quiet corner. The crowd, while not particularly literary, is talkative. There's a busy bar, crowded banquettes, and copper-topped tables. It's open Monday through Saturday from 11am to 12:30am and Sunday from noon to midnight.

23 Burns Statue Sq. (C) **01292/262-112.** Mon–Sat 11am–12:30am; Sun noon–midnight

ALLOWAY: BURNS BIRTHPLACE

Some 3km (2 miles) south of Ayr, Alloway is where Scotland's national poet was born on January 25, 1759, in the cottage—the "auld clay biggin"—that his father, gardener and farmer William Burnes (Robert dropped the "e") built by hand and to his own design in 1757.

Start your visit of the **Burns National Heritage Park** at the **Burns Cottage and Museum.** Just a 10 to 15-minute walk down the road are the simple ruins of the **Alloway Auld Kirk,** celebrated in the poem *Tam O'Shanter:* "Coffins stood round, like open presses/That shaw'd the dead in their last dresses." It stands roofless and allegedly still haunted to this day, with the poet's father buried prominently at the front of the kirkyard. The nearby stone **Brig o' Doon** still arcs elegantly over the River Doon. Admission to the cottage, museum and AV presentation in the Tam O'Shanter Experience is £5 ($9.25) for adults and £3 ($5.50) for children and seniors.

Burns Cottage and Museum ⊙   Although perennially underfunded and rather basic, this attraction remains a must visit for even the casual Burns fan. Visitors can take a self-guided tour of the cottage, built by William Burnes in 1757, and kept in the fashion of the poet's early childhood. In truth, the family only lived here for about a decade. After that, the cottage was expanded and used as a pub and inn, before the local Burns Society had it restored to the original, more compact size. An audio track explains the various uses for the rooms—one of which held both the family and their livestock. It highlights original features, such as the "box bed" in the kitchen where the poet would have been born. Outside of the cottage is the vegetable plot that the self-sufficient Burns family would have depended on.

The museum, though rather modestly housed, is a treasure trove of Burnsiana, keeping the best collection of Burn's manuscripts. The initial room has display cases with first editions of his books, signed in some cases, as well as many letters that Burns wrote and received. In the larger exhibition hall, a timeline helps place the bard in context with other historic and cultural events of his age. Cases contain various mementos and memorabilia such as the huge family Bible.

Alloway. (C) **01292/443-700.** www.burnsheritagepark.com. Admission £4 ($7.50) adults, £2.50 ($4.75) children and seniors, £10 ($19) per family. Apr–Sept daily 10am–5:30pm; Oct–Mar Mon–Sat 10am–5pm. Drive 3km (2 miles) south of Ayr on B7024.

Burns Monument and Gardens   About 1km (½ mile) from the Burns Cottage, just past the old kirk, this Grecian-classical monument, which was replicated in Edinburgh on Calton Hill, was erected in 1823 in a ceremony attended by the poet's widow, Jean Armour. The gardens overlook the River Doon and the famous arching bridge.

Alloway. (C) **01292/443-700.** Free admission. Apr–Sept daily 10am–5pm; Oct–Mar 10am–4pm.

Tam O'Shanter Experience Although the future of this attraction is in some doubt as the National Trust for Scotland takes over the Heritage Park in 2007, at writing it remains adjacent to the gardens surrounding the Burns Monument. Within the modern visitor center you can watch a video on Burns's life and poetry—as well as one that depicts the Tam O'Shanter. There's a well-stocked gift shop plus a tearoom.

Murdoch's Lane. ⓒ **01292/443-700.** Admission £2 ($3.75) adults, £1.25 ($2.30) children and seniors. Apr–Sept daily 10am–5:30pm; Oct–Mar 10am–5pm.

WHERE TO STAY & DINE

Abbotsford Hotel About a half-mile from the center of Ayr, this small hotel with a popular, civilized pub is curiously named after Sir Walter Scott's mansion rather than associating itself with Burns. The quiet residential neighborhood is less than a 10-minute walk to the shoreline and convenient to the local golf courses, too. Most of the units are smart and comfortable, with flatscreen TVs and modern bathrooms. Family-run and friendly, the Abbotsford offers sound, moderately priced accommodations.

14 Corsehill Rd., Ayr KA7 2ST. ⓒ **01292/261-506.** Fax 01292/261-606. www.abbotsfordhotel.co.uk. £85 ($160) double. Rates include breakfast. MC, V. Free parking. **Amenities:** Bar; restaurant; beer garden; concierge. In room: TV, coffeemaker.

Enterkine House MODERN SCOTTISH Dining at this highly rated country house hotel, done in Art Deco–style from the 1930s, can be a special treat. About 8.5km (5½ miles) east of Ayr in the village of Annbank, Enterkine's menus emphasize local ingredients, whether seasonal game or fish landed at nearby Troon. The rooms are 5-star quality, while the "bothy" offers a quirkier pine lodge on the woodland estate.

Coylton Rd, Annbank. ⓒ **01292/520-580.** Reservations required. £30–£40 ($55–$70) fixed-price dinner; £17–£19 ($31–$34) fixed-price lunch. Sun–Fri noon–2:30pm; daily 7–9pm. 6 units. £180 ($333) double; £185 ($345) bothy lodge. Rates include breakfast. AE, MC, V. Free parking. Off the B742. **Amenities:** Restaurant; bar/lounge; library. In room: TV, coffeemaker, hair dryer, iron/ironing board.

Fairfield House On the seafront at the edge of Ayr's Low Green, this Victorian mansion/country home was restored and converted into a 4-star hotel. The staff is attentive and, like the Abbotsford above, will help you arrange tee times at nearby golf courses. Rooms in the main building are decorated in a country-house style, while a newer wing offers more modern decor. The units are generally large and luxurious; some of the bathrooms have bidets. The hotel's **Martins Bar and Grill** was named best informal dining restaurant in 2006 by the Scottish hotel awards.

12 Fairfield Rd., Ayr, Ayrshire KA7 2AR. ⓒ **01292/267-461.** Fax 01292/261-456. www.fairfieldhotel.co.uk. 44 units. £130 ($240) double. Rates include full continental breakfast. AE, DC, MC, V. Free parking. **Amenities:** Restaurant; bar; indoor pool; health club; spa; sauna; room service; laundry service; dry cleaning. In room: A/C, TV, dataport, coffeemaker, hair dryer, trouser press.

Fouter's Bistro MODERN SCOTTISH In the heart of Ayr, this restaurant occupies the cellar of a old bank, retaining the original stone floor and a vaulted ceiling. The restaurant's name derives from the Scottish word used in the expression, "foutering about," which is equivalent to "fiddling around." But they are not goofing off here. Under new ownership since 2003, the restaurant has one of the best reputations in the region and emphasizes fresh local produce whenever possible.

2A Academy St. ⓒ **01292/261-391.** www.fouters.co.uk. Reservations recommended. Main courses £9–£16 ($17–$30). AE, MC, V. Tues–Sat noon–2:30pm and 6–9pm (till 10pm Fri–Sat).

Burns: Poet, Humanitarian & Skirt Chaser

The honest man, tho' e'er sae poor
Is king o' men for a' that
—Robert Burns, *A Man's a Man for a' That* (1795)

Robert Burns (1759–96) continues to hold a sentimental spot in the national consciousness of Scotland. When the new Scottish Parliament opened in 1999, his *A Man's a Man for a' That* (a man's a man for all that) was sung. In recent years, Ayrshire has begun to host an annual music and cultural festival, **Burns an' a' That** (www.burnsfestival.com), to help celebrate his life with contemporary Scottish culture. The only slightly surprising matter is why the country is reluctant to make *Auld Lang Syne*—surely one of the most recognized songs in the world—its national anthem.

Burns' popularity is not limited to the Scots. Every year to mark the anniversary of his birth on January 25, the poet is celebrated all over the world at ad hoc "Bachelors' Clubs," named after the debating society that Burns joined in the Ayrshire town of Tarbolton. At these "Burns Suppers," guests give readings, recite poems, and devour a traditional Scottish meal—as well as copious amounts of Scotch whisky. The first course should be a traditional cock-a-leekie soup, made with chicken and leeks. For the main course, there can be no deviation in the menu: It must be haggis, Burns' "Great Chieftain o' the Puddin' Race."

Born in Alloway on a night so gusty that part of the cottage came down, Burns was the son of a simple and pious gardener who nevertheless encouraged the boy to read and seek an education. So Burns did learn to alliterate, rhyme, and then compose lyrical poetry. He was, by trade, a hard-working if largely unsuccessful farmer and ended his life employed as tax collector. But the world knows him as the author of poetry, often set to song, such as *Auld Lang Syne*, or acclaimed narrative masterpieces, such as *Tam O'Shanter*. Of it one contemporary critic wrote that Burns displayed "a power of imagination that Shakespeare himself could not have exceeded." Other works, such as *A Man's a Man for a' That*, reveal Burns' humanitarian leanings.

But Burns was also a prodigious pursuer of women who fathered numerous children, legitimate and otherwise. In his short life, he wrote hundreds poems and songs. He died at 37 of heart disease in the southern town of Dumfries, distinguished but resolutely destitute. Almost immediately, however, contributions to his widow and family were made from across Scotland. Burns was buried with some ceremony on the very day that his wife Jean delivered their ninth child.

A WEE BIT MORE O' BURNS

Souter Johnnie's Cottage   A "souter" is a shoemaker and in Kirkoswald, some 19km (12 miles) south of Ayr, is the home of Burns' pal, cobbler John Davidson or Souter Johnnie. Davidson is name-checked in Burns's tale of Tam O'Shanter, who in real life was another friend named Douglas Graham. The cottage, which dates to 1785, contains Burnsiana, period furniture, and contemporary cobbler's tools. In the nearby kirkyard are the graves of Graham as well as Souter Johnnie and his wife Ann.

Main Rd., A77, Kirkoswald. (℃) **01655/760-603**. www.nts.org.uk. Admission £5 ($9.25) adult, £4 ($7.50) children, £14 ($26) family. Good Friday to Sept Fri–Tues 11:30am–5pm.

Bachelors' Club   Obtained in 1938 by the National Trust for Scotland, this is the infamous cottage with thatched roofing where Burns and his unmarried friends established a society—the Tarbolton Bachelors—to discuss issues of the day. The membership rules were clear: "No haughty, self-conceited person, who looks upon himself as superior to the rest of the club, and especially no mean-spirited, worldly mortal, whose only will is to heap up money, shall upon any pretence be admitted." The ground floor, previously a tavern, features period furnishings of a typical 18th-century home, while the upper floor was where Burns first came for dancing lessons and the club later debated. On Castle Street, in the nearby village of Mauchline, is the **Burns House Museum** (℃ **01290/550-045**; Tues–Sat 10am–5pm). Burns married his wife Jean Armour here in 1788, and this cottage was their home for a spell. Nearby, two locations, Mossgiel and Lochlea, are where Burns family farms were run with little success earlier in the poet's life.

Sandgate St., Tarbolton. (℃) **01292/541-940**. www.nts.org.uk. Admission £5 ($9.25) adults, £4 ($7.50) children, £14 ($26) family. Good Friday to Sept Fri–Tues 1–5pm. Off A77 south of Kilmarnock.

2 Culzean

Culzean Castle and Country Park (remember, the "z" in Culzean is silent) is situated on the cliffs above the sea about 20km (12 miles) southwest of Ayr. The attraction provides one of the more scenic and soothing stops in Ayrshire. The "castle" is of relatively recent vintage: Robert Adam designed much of the pile in between 1777 and 1792. Adam had a hand in quite a few stately houses of the period, displaying no end of Georgian symmetry and elegance. The country park (Scotland's first) stretches for more than 200 hectares (500 acres). Thanks to the influences of the mild Gulf Stream, the grounds have some exotic plants that one might not expect to find in Scotland.

Culzean Castle 🏰   This is a fine example of Adam's "castellated" style (that is, built with turrets and ramparts), which replaced an earlier castle keep as the family seat of the powerful Kennedy clan. After World War II, the castle was given to the National Trust for Scotland. Notwithstanding its architectural attributes—whether the celebrated round drawing room or the outstanding **Oval Staircase**—the pile is of special interest to many Americans because General Dwight D. Eisenhower was given an apartment for life here. He reputedly called Culzean "a place [where] I can relax." Undoubtedly Culzean's location near so many outstanding golf courses, such as Turnberry and Troon (see below), also pleased the golf-mad U.S. president. Today, tourists can rent the 6-room top-floor flat as holiday accommodations. Fans of the Scottish cult horror film, *The Wicker Man,* should know that scenes at the home of the devilish character played by Christopher Lee were filmed here, as well. Last entry is 1 hour before closing.

A719, west of Maybole. (℃) **01655/884-455**. www.culzeanexperience.org. Admission (including entrance to the Country Park) £12 ($22) adults, £8 ($15) seniors and children, £30 ($55) family. Apr–Oct daily 10:30am–5pm.

Culzean Country Park 🏰🏰 *Kids*   The property surrounding the castle became Scotland's first country park in 1969. The expansive grounds contain a formal walled

Arran: "Scotland in Miniature"

The Isle of Arran, in the Firth of Forth off the coast of Ayrshire, is often called "Scotland in Miniature'" because it combines pasture-filled lowlands with mountainous highland scenery. Indeed, the so-called Highland Boundary Fault Line bisects the island diagonally, just as it does the Scottish mainland.

In addition to the geographic and topographic mimicry, Arran offers a castle, half a dozen golf courses (including one with 12 holes), and a whisky distillery. It is a popular camping and cycling destination. Various attractions and activities range from hiking and rock climbing to pony trekking and sailing—plus good stretches of sandy, if wind swept, beaches.

For ferry information, call **CalMac** at ✆ **0870/565-0000.**

garden, an aviary, a swan pond, a camellia house, an orangery, an adventure playground, and a newly restored 19th-century pagoda. Not to mention a deer park, kilometers and kilometers of woodland paths, and a beach, too. Unless you're dead keen on historical houses, the country park is arguably the real highlight of a trip to Culzean on a fine Ayrshire day. The views over the sea to the southwest include the rounded rock of an island called Alisa Craig. Some 16km (10 miles) offshore, it's a nesting ground and sanctuary for seabirds.

On the land surrounding Culzean Castle. ✆ **01655/884-400.** Admission included in admission to Culzean Castle. Daily 9am–dusk.

3 Golfing Heavens: Troon & Turnberry

TROON

The resort town of **Troon,** 11km (7 miles) north of Ayr and about 50km (31 miles) southwest of Glasgow, looks out across the Firth of Clyde towards the Isle of Arran. Troon takes its name from the curiously hook-shaped promontory jutting out into the sea: the trone or "nose." From this port, a ferry sails March to October to Larne in Nothern Ireland.

Troon and its environs offer several sandy links courses, most prominently the **Royal Troon Golf Club** ✮, Craigends Road, Troon, Ayrshire KA10 6EP (✆ **01292/ 311-555;** www.royaltroon.co.uk). Royal Troon is a 7,150-yard seaside course that hosts the prestigious Open Championship, which was last played here in 2004. Hole 8, the famous "Postage Stamp," may be only 123 yards in distance, but depending upon the wind, pros may need a long iron or wedge to reach the green. A second course, the 6,289-yard Portland is arguably even more challenging. Visitors, with certificate of handicap (20 for men and 30 for women), can play the course from May through October on Monday, Tuesday, and Thursday. The 1-day fee to play one round on the Old Course and one on Portland is £210 ($388), which includes morning coffee and a buffet lunch. Two rounds on Portland are about half the cost.

A much less expensive and still gratifying option is to play one of the municipal courses run by the South Ayrshire Council, such as Darnley or Lochgreen, which runs parallel to Royal Troon at spots. Fees during the weekend range from £16 to £28

($30–$52). Another option is a six-round, 7-day golf pass from the council for £88 ($163). Log onto www.golfsouthayrshire.com or call the South Ayrshire Golf hot line at ⓒ **01292/616-255.**

Trains from Glasgow's Central Station stop at Troon several times daily. The trip takes about 40 minutes and the standard same-day round-trip fare is £9.40 ($18). Trains and buses also connect Ayr with Troon, which is about a 10-minute ride. Call ⓒ **0870/608-2608** for public transportation information.

WHERE TO STAY & DINE

Lochgreen House Hotel   This lovely country-house hotel is set on 12 lush hectares (30 acres) of forest and landscaped gardens. The property opens onto views of the Firth of Clyde and Ailsa Craig. The interior evokes a more elegant bygone time, with detailed cornices, antique furnishings, and elegant oak and cherry paneling. Guests meet and mingle in two luxurious sitting rooms with log fires or take long walks on the well-landscaped grounds. The spacious bedrooms have the finest mattresses.

Monktonhill Rd. Southwood, Troon, Ayrshire KA10 7EN. ⓒ **01292/313-343.** Fax 01292/318-661. www.costley-hotels. co.uk. 40 units. £150 ($277) double. Rates include breakfast. AE, MC, V. Free parking. **Amenities:** 2 restaurants; 2 bars; tennis court; room service; laundry service; dry cleaning. *In room:* TV, coffeemaker, hair dryer, trouser press.

Piersland House Hotel   Opposite Royal Troon and designed by William Leiper in 1899, this hotel was originally occupied by Sir Alexander Walker of the Johnnie Walker whisky family and remained a private residence until 1956. The importation of some 17,000 tons of topsoil transformed its marshy surface into a lush 1.6-hectare (4-acre) garden. The moderately sized guest rooms have traditional country-house styling.

15 Craigend Rd., Troon, Ayrshire KA10 6HD. ⓒ **01292/314-747.** Fax 01292/315-613. www.piersland.co.uk. 30 units. £136 ($251) double with breakfast; £178 ($330) double with dinner and breakfast. AE, MC, V. Free parking. Drive 3 min. south of the town center on B749. **Amenities:** Restaurant; bar; room service; laundry service; dry cleaning. *In room:* TV, minibar, coffeemaker, hair dryer, trouser press.

MacCallums of Troon Oyster Bar   FISH/SEAFOOD   Near the ferry terminal at the harbor, this rustic seaside bistro is adjacent to the fresh fish market, as well. Oysters, whole sardines, grilled langoustines, sole, and combination platters frequently grace the menu.

The Harbour, Troon. ⓒ **01292/319-339.** Reservations recommended. About £20–£30 ($37–$56) for dinner. AE, MC, V. Tues–Sat noon–2:30 and 7–9:30pm; Sun noon–3:30pm (May–Sept 7–9:30pm as well).

TURNBERRY

The coastal settlement of Turnberry, some 81km (50 miles) southwest of Glasgow on the A77, was once part of the Culzean Estate. It began to flourish early in the 20th century when rail service was developed, and a recognized golfing center with a first-class resort hotel was established.

From the original pair of 13-hole golf courses, the complex has developed two championship level courses, Ailsa and Kintyre, known worldwide as the **Turnberry Hotel Golf Courses.** Ailsa's 18 holes have been the scene of Open tournaments and other professional golfing events. Guests of the Westin Turnberry hotel get priority, especially on the Ailsa course. The fees vary. Hotel residents will pay between £45 and £125 ($83–$231) depending on the course and the season. If you're not staying at Turnberry, rates range from £60 to £190 ($111–$352). Log onto www.turnberry. co.uk, or call ⓒ **01655/334-032** for details.

WHERE TO STAY & DINE

Malin Court Hotel   On one of the most scenic strips of the Ayrshire coast, this well-run hotel fronts the Firth of Clyde and the Turnberry golf courses. It is not a great country house but rather a serviceable, welcoming retreat offering a blend of informality and comfort. Bedrooms are mostly medium in size. The staff can arrange hunting, fishing, riding, sailing, and golf.

Turnberry, Ayrshire KA26 9PB. © **01655/331-457.** Fax 01655/331-072. www.malincourt.co.uk. 18 units. £104 ($192) double. Rates include breakfast. AE, DC, MC, V. Free parking. **Amenities:** Restaurant; bar; room service; laundry service; dry cleaning. *In room:* TV, dataport, coffeemaker, hair dryer, iron/ironing board.

Westin Turnberry Resort ⚶   The 1908 pile is a remarkable and well-known landmark. From afar, you can see the hotel's white facade, red-tile roof, and dozens of gables. The public rooms contain Waterford crystal chandeliers, Ionic columns, molded ceilings, and oak paneling. Each guest room is furnished in unique early-1900s style and has a marble-sheathed bathroom. The units, which vary in size, open onto views of the lawns, forests, and, of course, the golf course along the Scottish coastline. Spa and health facilities are exemplary.

Maidens Rd., Turnberry, Ayrshire KA26 9LT. © **01655/331-000.** Fax 0165/533-1706. www.turnberry.co.uk. 221 units. £300 ($555) double. Rates include Scottish breakfast. AE, DC, MC, V. Free parking. **Amenities:** 3 restaurants; 3 bars; indoor pool; tennis courts; health club; spa; Jacuzzi; sauna; car-rental desk; salon; room service; babysitting; massage; laundry service; dry cleaning. *In room:* TV, dataport, minibar, coffeemaker, hair dryer, trouser press.

Glenapp Castle ⚶   This beautifully decorated castle south of Girvan offers Victorian baronial splendor with antiques, oil paintings, and elegant touches at every turn. Other accommodation in the region rather pales in comparison. The mansion was designed in the 1870s by David Bryce, a celebrated architect of his day, and it overlooks the Irish Sea. Lounges and dining rooms are elegant, while the spacious bedrooms and suites are individually furnished. Tall windows let in the afternoon and long summer evening light, making the rooms bright on many days. The hotel, open seasonally unless by special arrangement, stands on 12 hectares (30 acres) of lovely, secluded grounds, with many rare plants.

Ballantrae, Ayrshire KA26 0NZ. Some 30km (20 miles) south of Ayr. © **01465/831-212.** Fax 01465/831-000. www.glenappcastle.com. Apr–Oct. 17 units. £365–£405 ($675–$750) double. Rates include dinner and breakfast. AE, V. Free parking. **Amenities:** Restaurant; bar; tennis court; room service (8am–midnight); laundry service. *In room:* TV.

4 West Coast Highlights

Some fairly spectacular scenery can be found by heading west from Glasgow. The **Firth of Clyde** begins the display, but as you keep going, the terrain gets less populated and wilder. Depending upon your stamina and interest, it is worth doing a bit of "island hopping" from the mainland to **Bute** and then into **Argyll** and onto the **Cowal** and **Kintyre** peninsulas, finally getting as far as **Gigha,** the most southerly of Scotland's inner Hebrides. The distances are not great, and the ferry trips cut down the driving times, as well. Sunsets over the western seas rarely fail to disappoint on a good evening.

HELENSBURGH

Hill House ⚶⚶⚶   Designed by Charles Rennie Mackintosh for publisher Walter Blackie, this timeless house on the hill above the town of Helensburgh (along the north banks of the firth of Clyde) has been lovingly restored and opened to the public by the National Trust for Scotland. Inspired by Scottish Baronial style, Hill House is still pure

Mackintosh: from the asymmetrical juxtaposition of windows and clean lines that blend sharp geometry and gentle curves to the sumptuous but uncluttered interior with bespoke details by both the architect and his artist wife Margaret Macdonald, such as glass inlays, fireplace tiles, and decorative panels. Built at the beginning of the 20th century but still looking modern today, practically the entire house is open to the public. The garden, overgrown when the National Trust took over the property in the early 1980s, has been restored to its original state thanks to photography from a German design magazine published in 1905.

Upper Colquhoun St., Helensburgh. © 01436/673-900. www.nts.org.uk. Admission £8 ($15) adult, £5 ($9.25) students and seniors, £20 ($37) family. Apr–Oct daily 1:30–5:30pm. 48 km (30 miles) west of Glasgow; off the A814. Half-hourly train service from Glasgow Queen Street Station.

ISLE OF BUTE

Bute is one of the easiest Scottish islands to reach. Ferries depart from the restored Victorian railway terminal in the village of **Wemyss Bay** on the Clyde coast, about 54km (33 miles) southwest of Glasgow. Trains from Glasgow's Central Station depart hourly and the trip takes under 1 hour. The standard, same-day round-trip fare is £8.40 ($16). The ferry departs approximately every 45 minutes in the summer and the crossing to Rothesay, Bute's main port, takes 35 minutes. Single passengers pay £4 ($7.50) one-way, and cars cost an additional £15 ($28). For ferry information, call © **0870/565-0000** or go to www.calmac.co.uk. Call © **0870/608-2608** for public transportation information. By car, take the M8 west from Glasgow and then the A78 out of Greenock to Wemyss Bay.

Rothesay Castle   Located in the heart of Rothesay, only a few minutes walk from the ferry terminal and harbor, this castle is unusual in Scotland for its circular plan. It dates to the beginnings of the 13th century, with a large moat dotted by resident swans still encircling the ramparts. Interestingly, the castle plays up the connections that this part of Scotland had with Norse rulers, and King Hakon IV in particular. It is worth watching a brief video on the Scandinavian influences, Norse battles with native Scots and the latter's eventual victory over the troops from Norway in the 13th century. Although mostly a restored ruin, the castle has an impressive pigeon tower and chapel within the grassy courtyard. If you dare (and you're thin enough), you can descend from the Gatehouse into a small dungeon reserved for prisoners.

Rothesay, Isle of Bute © 01700/502-691. www.historic-scotland.gov.uk. Admission £3.50 ($6.50) adults, £2.50 ($4.60) seniors, £1.50 ($2.80) children. Apr–Sept daily 9:30am–6:30pm; Oct–Mar Sept daily 9:30am–4pm.

Mount Stuart ⊛   This mansion belongs to the Marquess of Bute's family, but it is open to the public for much of the year. Construction of the red sandstone pile began

---

Tips **Island "Hopscotch" Passes**

If you want the freedom to hop around a bit from mainland to island and from island to peninsulas west of Glasgow, then it may be worth buying an "Island Hopscotch" ticket from the ferry operator, **Caledonian MacBrayne**. For example, you can hop from Wymess Bay to the Isle of Bute, from there to Cowal peninsula, and then onwards to Kintyre. In summer the cost for that excursion is £7.30 ($14) per passenger and £29 ($53) for a car. Call © **0870/565-0000**.

Gigha: The "Good Isle"

Pronounced "*gee-*a" with a hard *g* (as in gear), this tiny island gets its name from the ancient Norse ruler King Hakon who once dominated this region of Scotland. It means the good isle. And good, indeed, it is. Tiny and placid, Gigha is best known for its Achamore gardens, with their exceptional springtime display of rhododendrons and azaleas. But as a quiet place to escape and relax, it is excellent, as well. There are plenty of rural and coastal walks. Gigha is also particularly noteworthy because on March 15, 2002, the residents established a community trust and assumed ownership of the isle. The 30-minute ferry for Gigha leaves from Tayinloan on the Kintyre peninsula. For overnight dinner, bed and breakfast accommodations contact the **Gigha Hotel** (✆ **01583/505-254;** www.gigha.org.uk).

around the early 1880s for the third Marquess and was still ongoing when he died at the turn of the century. The interiors display certain eccentricities and interests of the man, such as a ceiling in an upstairs room that is covered in stars and constellations to accommodate his interest in astrology. The garden dates back to the early decades of the 18th century, when the second earl of Bute moved the family here from the port town of Rothesay. The grounds have a woodlands park, a huge walled area—the so-called "wee garden"—and a working vegetable plot, too. The garden is open from May to mid-October.

A844 near Soulag, Isle of Bute. ✆ **01700/503-877.** www.mountstuart.com. Admission for both house and grounds £7.50 ($14) adults, £6 ($11) seniors, £3.50 ($6.50) children. May–Sept Sun–Fri 11am–5pm; Sat 10am–2:30pm. Gardens 10am–6pm. About 8km (5 miles) south of Rothesay.

COWAL & KINTYRE PENINSULAS

West of Glasgow, the Cowal and Kintyre peninsulas extend their fingers into the sea, creating long salt-water lochs that extend well north towards the Highlands. The landscape features gentle hills and forested glens. Highlights include the **Benmore Botanic Garden** (daily Mar–Oct) 11km (7 miles) north of Dunoon on Cowal. It has giant redwoods and thickets of rhododendrons. The village of **Tighnabruaich** is a mecca for sailors, set in a picturesque natural bay across from Bute. Indeed, you can get a lesson on splicing the main brace (or at least sailing a dinghy) at the local sailing school.

On Kintyre, the lovely harbor of **Tarbert** is where many local fishing boats land. Indeed, at the ferry slip you can purchase fresh scallops, as well as live crabs and lobsters. Avian populations abound in this region of Scotland and breeds include black-headed gulls, gannets, oystercatchers, razorbills, shags, and those are just a few of the seabirds. An observatory is on the island of **Sanda,** just off the tip (or mull) of Kintyre. On the peninsula itself, however, another blind is situated near the west coast village of **Machrihanish.**

WHERE TO STAY & DINE

An Lochan ✿✿ SEAFOOD   Formerly the Royal, this four-star hotel overlooking the sea in Tighnabruaich offers some luxurious rooms, but not a hint of pretension or attitude from the McKie family owners or staff. The "superior sea view" rooms fit the bill, offering huge super king-size beds and ample bathrooms (with tubs and showers), comfy leather-upholstered furnishings, and little goodies such as fresh fruit on arrival. Meals in the two conservatory dining rooms highlight locally landed seafood and fish (even the names of the scallop divers are given) as well as Argyllshire venison and beef.

Tighnabruaich, Argyll. ℭ **01700/811-236.** Fax 01700/811-300. Dinner main courses £18–£20 ($33–$37). Reservations required. Mon–Sun noon–3pm and 6–9pm. www.royalhotel.org.uk. 11 units £100–£180 double ($185–$333). Rates include breakfast. AE, MC, V. Free parking. **Amenities:** Restaurant; bar. *In room:* TV, coffeemaker, hair dryer.

Russian Tavern at the Port Royal Hotel *(Finds* RUSSIAN/SEAFOOD   You're not likely to find another place like this on your travels in Scotland. In the village of Port Bannatyne just 3km (2 miles) north of Rothesay on the Isle of Bute, the Royal is a family-run inn where the house specialties include Russian cuisine (for example blinis, spicy sausage, and pavlova), fresh fish and seafood provided by a local fisherman, and some rarely found Scottish ales served from kegs atop the bar in the small cafe/pub. All meals are cooked to order and rather generous, served with freshly baked bread while a backing soundtrack of classic jazz or a French chanteuse is played. The place is altogether charming and unique. Overnight rooms, two with en suite baths, are basic rather than luxurious.

Main St., Port Bannatyne, Bute. ℭ **01700/505-073.** www.butehotel.com. Main courses £16–£24 ($30–$44). Mar–Nov Wed–Mon 12:30–10:30pm. Closed winter. 5 units. £50 double ($93). Rates include continental breakfast. MC, V. Parking on street. **Amenities:** Restaurant/bar. *In room:* No phone.

The Seafood Cabin *Ⓐ (Finds* SEAFOOD   Open during the day, this operation south of Tarbert in Skipness (where a small summer ferry goes across to Lochranza on the isle of Arran) is worth a detour if you fancy seafood. Prepared in a converted 1950s style minitrailer set next to a stone house in the shadow of a castle ruin, the meals feature langoustines, queen scallops, mussels, smoked salmon and more. It is a completely unassuming place, with chickens and ducks freely wandering on the grass around the picnic tables. There's no better place on a sunny day to have an organic bottled of ale and chow down fresh fruits of the sea.

B8001, Skipness, Tarbert, Argyll. ℭ **01880/760-207.** Lunch £8–£16 ($15–$30). Jun–Sept Sun–Fri 11am–6pm. 20km (12 miles) south of Tarbert off the A83.

5 Loch Lomond

One of the benefits of Glasgow is its proximity to wild, open spaces. Loch Lomond is the largest inland body of water in not only Scotland but all of Great Britain. It's only about a half-hour drive or train ride from the Glasgow city limits. At the southern edge, on the outskirts of the otherwise unremarkable if pleasant town of Balloch, the **Lomond Shores** development (www.lochlomondshores.com) was opened in 2002. The complex includes a shopping mall and an information center (daily 10am–5pm; ℭ **01389/722-199**). The National Park Gateway Centre has guidance on using the adjacent national park—Scotland's first—that extends up the eastern shores of the loch.

If you're hiking, the trails up the eastern shoreline are preferable. This is the route that the West Highland Way (see below) follows. If you are a canoeing or kayaking enthusiast, the Lomond Shores' visitor center has rentals (ℭ **01389/602-576**; www. canyouexperience.com) for £15 ($28) per hour. Up the western shores, before the notoriously winding road at Tarbet, where the train from Glasgow to Oban stops, visitors

Hiking the West Highland Way

One of Scotland's best-known long-distance footpaths is the **West Highland Way** ⚐, established in the 1980s. For most people, it begins rather uneventfully northwest of Glasgow in the affluent suburb of Milngavie (pronounced "mill-*guy*"). But as the trail winds its way for some 153km (95 miles), it just gets better and better. North along the eastern shore of Loch Lomond, through the desolate and almost prehistoric looking Rannoch Moor, and along the breathtaking and historic Glen Coe, ending finally in Fort William, the trail is particularly dramatic. At the northern terminus, you're at the foot of Ben Nevis, Scotland's highest mountain.

Trains run frequently throughout the day from the Queen's Street railway station in central Glasgow to Milngavie, starting point of the walk. The 25-minute trip costs £2.35 ($4.50) one-way. In Fort William, you can catch the Scotrail train back to Glasgow. Hikers can backpack and camp along the way or stay at inns conveniently dotted along the trail. There are tour companies, as well, that will haul your luggage from stop to stop along the way. For details, www.west-highland-way.co.uk, or contact the National Park Gateway Centre at Loch Lomond Shores.

can take loch cruises. Golfers will likely be attracted to the Loch Lomond country club, which hosts the annual Scottish Open professional golf championship, near the pleasant resort village of **Luss.**

WHERE TO STAY & DINE

De Vere Cameron House ⚐ Posh, plush, and perched on the shores of Loch Lomond, the five-star Cameron House hotel offers premier lodgings. The mid-range deluxe rooms face the water, while the luxury suites are part of the original house and allow guests to have their meals in the sitting rooms. The fine-dining option is the Georgian Room, which is not deemed suitable for children under 14, and gentlemen are expected to don jackets and ties. Smollets is the casual option.

A82 north of Balloch, Dumbartonshire G83 8QZ. ℭ **01389/755-565.** Fax 01389/759-522. www.cameronhouse.co.uk. 95 units. £255–£300 ($470–$555) double. Free parking. **Amenities:** 2 restaurants; bars; tennis courts; health club; spa; Jacuzzi; sauna; car-rental desk; salon; room service; babysitting; massage; laundry service; dry cleaning. *In room:* TV, dataport, minibar, coffeemaker, hair dryer, trouser press.

Drover's Inn The stuffed, snarling, and slightly worn animals near the entrance give a pretty good hint as to the nature of this rustic tavern with restaurant and overnight rooms. The atmospheric pub usually has an open fire going, barmen in kilts, and plenty of travelers nursing their drinks. The pub food is average, but it's the ambience of the place that makes the Drovers a worthwhile stop. There are 10 overnight units in the original house built in 1705 and another 16 rooms have been added in a new building (£58/$107 for a standard double).

A82 at Inverarnan by Ardlui. ℭ **01301/704-234.** www.droversinn.co.uk. Main courses £9–£21 ($16–$38). Daily 10am–midnight.

6 Stirling & The Trossachs

North of Glasgow some 42km (26 miles) is historic Stirling, with its **castle** set dramatically on the hill above the town. During the reign of the Stuarts in the 16th century, royalty preferred Stirling to Edinburgh. As a child, Mary Queen of Scots was coronated in here. Stirling Bridge is believed to be the crucial site of a 13th-century battle between English invaders and the rag-tag band of Scots led by William Wallace (forever immortalized—if fictionalized, as well—in the movie *Braveheart*). High on a nearby hill north of the city center stands the prominent **Wallace Monument,** which is open daily, £6.50 ($12).

Just outside of the city is another famous battleground: **Bannockburn.** In these fields, a well-armed English army was nevertheless routed by Scottish troops led by King Robert the Bruce in 1314. A heritage center operated by the National Trust for Scotland is open daily March through October; admission is £5 ($9.25).

Further northwest of Stirling are the **Trossachs,** a mountain range distinct from the Highlands but appealing for its wooded forests. The main attraction here is **Loch Katerine,** popularized by Sir Walter Scott's poem, "The Lady of the Lake." Two villages that provide gateways to the more mountainous regions north are Callander and Aberfoyle. They can be over-run by bus tours in the high season but offer places to rest, eat, and shop during the day.

First Scotrail trains run frequently to Stirling from Glasgow's Queen Street Station. The same-day standard round-trip fare is £8.90 ($17), and the trip takes 30 to 45 minutes depending on the train and the number of stops it has to make in between.

Doune Castle *(Finds)*   Fans of the film *Monty Python and the Holy Grail* may recognize the exterior of Doune Castle, as it served as a location for several scenes in the movie. Because the restoration of the castle by Historic Scotland has been mostly limited to making certain the stone structure doesn't fall down, visitors (especially those with a good imagination) actually get a better idea of what living here in the 14th century may have been like. There are low doors, narrow spiral stairs, and a feeling of damp that presumably was part of medieval life.

Doune. ℂ **01786/841-742.** www.historic-scotland.gov.uk. £3.50 ($6.50) adult, £2.50 ($4.50) seniors, £1.50 ($2.80) children. Apr–Sept daily 9:30am–6:30pm; Oct–Mar daily 9:30am–4:30pm. 6.5km (10 miles) NW of Stirling off the A84.

Stirling Castle   Even if you don't bother taking a tour of the impressive castle, now run by Historic Scotland, the ramparts and grounds surrounding the well-fortified landmark are worth a stroll—particularly the cemetery and the "Back Walk" along a wall that protected the Old Town from the desires of Henry VIII. In the castle proper, there is a palace built by James V and the Chapel Royal, which was remodeled by his grandson, James VI. Recently restored, the Great Hall stands out for miles thanks to the creamy, almost yellow exterior that replicates its original color. Last entry is 45 minutes before closing.

Castle Wynd. ℂ **01786/450-000.** www.historic-scotland.gov.uk. Admission £8.50 ($16) adults, £6.50 ($12), £3.50 ($6.50) children. Apr–Sept daily 9:30am–6pm; Oct–Mar daily 9:30am–5pm (last entry at 4:15pm).

Old Town Jail *(Kids)*   Tour guides in period dress take groups through the paces of penal life, while a host of actors role-play as wardens and inmates to help enact the history of the jail. This building is a Victorian replacement for the rather less humane cells in the old Tolbooth across the street. Still when you see the crank that inmates were made to turn as punishment, one wonders if prison existence had improved all that much. On the top of the building, an observation deck offers good views of the surrounding Old Town.

St. John St. ℂ **01786/450-050**. Admission £5 ($9.25) with audio headset. Apr–Sept daily 9:30am–6pm; Oct and Mar daily 9:30am–5pm; Nov–Feb 10:30am–4:30pm.

WHERE TO STAY & DINE

The Inn at Kippen MODERN SCOTTISH   About a 10-minute drive west of Stirling on the A811, Kippen is a typical country village in the rolling hills north of Glasgow. Run by the same folk who once owned the well-regarded Olivia's in Stirling, the Inn at Kippen is a modernized version of the country tavern and small hotel. The ground floor pub and restaurant specializes in Scottish fare with contemporary twists. The four overnight rooms, starting at £60 ($111), are clean and basic.

Fore Rd., Kippen. ℂ **01786/871-010**. www.theinnatkippen.co.uk. Main courses £8–£16 ($15–$30). AE, MC, V. Daily noon–2:30pm and 6–9pm.

Creagan House ⚜ FRENCH/SCOTTISH   Cherry and Gordon Gunn run this charming inn housed in a 17th-century farmhouse north of Callander, 25km (15 miles) from Stirling. In the evenings, Gordon repairs to the kitchen where he cooks some sumptuous French-influenced meals, using mostly local ingredients. Especially welcome are the vegetables, often grown just up the road, prepared as accompaniment to the main courses. Don't be fooled by the baronial splendor of the dining room, however. It is a much, much more recent addition to the historic house, which is well-situated for country walks. A clutch of rooms, including one that has a four-poster bed, start at £110 ($203), including full breakfast.

A84, north of Strathyre. ℂ **01877/384-638**. www.creaganhouse.co.uk. Reservations required. Fixed-price dinner £22 ($40). AE, MC, V. Mar–Jan 1 seating daily 7:30–8:30pm. Closed Feb.

Monachyle Mhor ⚜ SCOTTISH   Just up the highway from Creagan House, here is another gem serving lunch and dinner in an 18th-century farmhouse. This one overlooks Loch Voil, down a ramshackle one-lane road from the village of Balquhidder. The conservatory dining room is modern and so is the cooking. Roast chicken topped with foie gras, belly of pork served with sage and onion jus, or seared fish on a bed of shredded celeriac are just some of the typical options. Dinner is expensive (albeit worth it), though lunches are less costly. The adjoining lodge has 11 units with their own bathrooms, starting at £95 ($175), which includes breakfast.

Off the A84, Balquhidder. ℂ **01877/384-622**. www.monachylemhor.com. Fixed-price dinner £44 ($81). AE, MC, V. Mid-Feb to Dec daily noon–1:45pm and 7–8:45pm. Closed Jan to mid-Feb. Turn right at Kingshouse Hotel, and drive 9.5km (6 miles).

7 The Clyde Valley

South of Glasgow, the River Clyde meanders north from its headwaters in the southern uplands of Scotland. The Clyde Valley is best-known locally for its garden nurseries and their sometimes quaint tea shops. Near the town of **Lanark,** 44km (27 miles) from Glasgow, is a bona fide bit of history and an attraction that can merit trip. Trains for Lanark leave Glasgow Central Station twice an hour and the trip takes about one hour. Standard same-day round trip fare is £8 ($15). Buses for Lanark leave Buchanan Bus Station hourly and the journey takes about 1 hour and 15 minutes. The price of a round-trip ticket is £5 ($9.25). By car, take the M74 freeway southeast from Glasgow and exit at signs for Lanark at Kirkmuirhill or via the more scenic route through the Clyde Valley on the A72.

New Lanark *(Kids)*   By the early part of the 19th century, New Lanark had become a progressive industrial mill and village under the guidance of Robert Owen, who decided that a contented work force was most likely to be a productive one. Free education was offered to employees and their children; a daycare center and social club were set up; and a co-operative store established, all along the banks of the River Clyde in the steep valley below the long-established market town of Lanark. Today New Lanark Conservation Trust runs the place (recognized by UNESCO as a World Heritage Site) as a tourist attraction. Admission includes an educational chair-lift ride that tells the story of what life here was once like, as well as self-guided tours of the principle buildings, such as the factory were cotton was spun and the old school house. A walk upstream will bring visitors to the three-tiered Falls of Clyde.

Braxfield Rd., outside Lanark. (C) **01555/661-345**. www.newlanark.org. Admission £5.95 ($11) adults, £4.95 ($9) children and seniors, £18 ($33). Daily 11am–5pm.

Appendix:
Edinburgh & Glasgow in Depth

Edinburgh and Glasgow are the principal cities in Scotland, a small nation about 443km (275 miles) long and some 242km (150 miles) wide at its broadest point. Occupying the northern half of Great Britain, the country fills about 78,761 sq. km (30,410 sq. miles). Both cities are on tributaries to the sea, and no resident in Scotland lives more than about 65km (40 miles) from salt water. Notwithstanding the size of their country, the Scots have extended their influence around the world.

Inventors Alexander Graham Bell (telephone) and John Logie Baird (television) as well as Africa explorers Mungo Park and David Livingstone came from Scotland. Philosophers David Hume (law) and Adam Smith (economics) were Scots, as were James Watt (steam engine pioneer) and John Muir (the world's first ecologist). This country gave the world entrepreneur Andrew Carnegie; poet Robert Burns; actors Sean Connery, Billy Connolly, and Ewan McGregor; and rock singers Sheena Easton, Annie Lennox, and Shirley Manson. Edinburgh spawned novelists Sir Walter Scott and Robert Louis Stevenson, while Glasgow gave the world architects Alexander "Greek" Thomson and Charles Rennie Mackintosh. But, curiously, the country's most famous offspring is neither man nor woman but the mythical Loch Ness Monster.

The border between England and Scotland is just a line on a map; you'd hardly be aware of crossing it. While the two countries have been joined constitutionally since 1707, Scotland is different from England and has its own identity. In 1999, Scotland gained greater autonomy to rule its own affairs when the **Scottish Parliament** in Edinburgh was restored. Some would prefer the country to be completely independent of its powerful partner to the south.

Although the union with England may well have saved Scotland economically in the 18th century, it also has effectively relegated the country to something little more than an administrative region within Great Britain. Although Edinburgh has long been an intellectual center and Glasgow was considered the "Second City" of the British Empire, many histories of "Britain" tend to ignore or Anglicize developments in Scotland and, in some cases, treat Scotland with condescension. Such biased accounts may in part explain why Scots sometimes act as if they have chips on their shoulders.

Still, consider this. In 1320, after decades of war against English invaders and occupiers, barons loyal to Scottish King Robert the Bruce put their names on a letter to the Pope, the **Declaration of Arbroath.** It not only clearly affirmed the country's independence but also addressed notions of freedom and liberty as Scots: abstract ideals that most nations didn't contemplate for hundreds of years.

1 History 101

Much of the history of the Scots has been shaped by their country's remote location in a corner of northwestern Europe. Amazingly, Scotland encompasses 787 islands (although only about a fourth are inhabited). Its 10,004km (6,214 miles) of coastline are deeply penetrated by the Atlantic Ocean and Irish Sea on the west and the often turbulent North Sea on the east. In fact, the sea has shaped Scotland's destiny more than any other element and bred a nation of seafarers, many of whom still earn their living on the water.

Although smaller than England, Scotland boasts considerably more open space and natural splendor: some of it easily reached from Edinburgh and Glasgow. The Scots as a people are hard to classify. They're normally generous and yet have a reputation for frugality. They can be eloquent though dour; romantic at heart but brutally realistic in their appraisals (especially of the English).

EARLY HISTORY   Scotland has long been a melting pot. As writer William McIlvanney once said with pride: it is a "mongrel nation." Its people were made stronger because of their diverse bloodlines—not weakened by inbreeding or ethnic purity.

Standing stones, brochs (circular stone towers), and burial chambers attest to Scotland's earliest occupation, but little is known about these first tribes. When the Romans invaded in A.D. 82, a people they called the **Picts** (Painted Ones) occupied the land. Despite spectacular bloodletting, the Romans were unsuccessful, and the building of Hadrian's Wall (well south of the current border) effectively marked the northern limits of their influence.

By A.D. 500, the Picts were again besieged by the Irish, called "Scots," who were successful. They established the kingdom of Dalriada in the west on the Argyll peninsulas, battling and intermarrying with the Picts. Britons emigrated from the south and Norsemen from the northeast, creating new bloodlines and migratory patterns. Languages of the era included a diverse array of Celtic (Gaelic) and Norse dialects with scatterings of Low German and Saxon English.

The role of Dalriada Scots was cemented when a pilgrim named **Columba** (later canonized) arrived from Ireland in 563. The rocky Hebridean island of Iona became his base for Christian study. Christianity, already introduced by Sts. Ninian and Mungo to Strathclyde and Galloway, became more widespread. In Glasgow, a Cathedral still stands at the spot where St. Mungo (or Kentigern) settled, established an enclave, and was later buried.

THE DARK & MIDDLE AGES   The Scots and the Picts were united in 843 under the kingship of an early chieftain named **Kenneth MacAlpin,** but it was the invasionary pressures from the south and Scandinavia that helped mold Scotland into a relatively coherent unit. Under Malcolm II (1005–34), tribes who occupied the southwest and southeast of the Scottish mainland were merged with the Scots and the Picts. Macbeth murdered Malcolm's heir, Duncan, and this event fueled the plotline of Shakespeare's famous "Scottish play."

Eventually Duncan's son Malcolm III avenged that killing and defeated Macbeth. His English-born princess wife, Margaret, drove forward church reforms that soon replaced St. Columba's Gaelic form of Christianity. She led a life of great piety, founded Edinburgh on Castle Hill, and was later canonized as St. Margaret in 1251.

However small, Scotland's terrain is full of lochs and mountains that effectively divided the territory, and the country was often preoccupied with the territorial battles of clan allegiances. **David I** (1081–1153) embarked on one of the most lavish building sprees in Scottish history, erecting many abbeys, including Jedburgh, Kelso, and Melrose, while also establishing royal burghs such as Edinburgh.

But real trouble was brewing in the south by the end of the 13th century. Certainly, Scots invaded northern England and tried to claim parts of it as Scotland.

But Edward I, ambitious Plantagenet king of England, yearned to rule over an undivided nation incorporating all of Scotland and Wales. Known as the "hammer of the Scots," Edward intervened when Scottish royal succession was under dispute, setting up **John Balliol** as a vassal king. But Balliol eventually reneged and sought assistance from France, thus beginning the **Auld Alliance.**

Some of Scotland's most legendary heroes lived during this period: particularly **William Wallace** (1270–1305), who drove the English out of Perth and Stirling. Later, **Robert the Bruce** (1274–1329), succeeded in routing English forces at Bannockburn. Crowned at Scone in 1306, he decisively defeated Edward II of England outside Stirling in 1314. In 1320, the Declaration of Arbroath was sent to the Pope. England formally recognized Scotland's sovereignty in the 1328 Treaty of Northampton, which inaugurated a heady but short-lived peace. Eventually the Scottish crown passed to the Stewarts ("Stewards"), but invariably each monarch in the family was crowned as an infant or child. Dynastic nobility and regents held real power.

THE REFORMATION The passions of the Reformation arrived on an already turbulent Scottish scene. The main protagonist was undoubtedly **John Knox,** a devoted disciple of the Geneva Protestant John Calvin and a bitter enemy of both the Catholic Church and the nascent Anglican Church of England. He had a peculiar mixture of piety, conservatism, strict morality, and intellectual independence that many still see as a pronounced feature of the Scottish character today.

In Edinburgh's Old Town, visitors can see the John Knox House, where the reformer may have lived, and St. Giles Cathedral, where he most certainly preached.

Knox helped shape the democratic form of the Scottish Church as well as establish the rather austere moral tone of Presbyterians. Foremost among his tenets were provisions for a self-governing congregation and allegiance to the word of God as contained in meticulous translations of the Old and New Testaments. Thus, he effectively encouraged people to learn to read. Later, the Church of Scotland's insistence on self-government led to endless conflicts, first with Scottish and then, after unification, with British monarchy.

MARY QUEEN OF SCOTS When Mary Stuart, Queen of Scots (1542–87), eventually took up her rule, she was a Roman Catholic Scot of French upbringing trying to govern a land (about which she knew little) in the throes of the Reformation.

Daughter of Scotland's James V and France's Mary of Guise, she technically became Queen when only 6 days old and as a child was sent to be educated in France, where, at age 15, she married the heir to the French throne. Mary only returned to Scotland after his death. Following some disastrous political and romantic alliances, she fled Scotland to be imprisoned in England, and her life was eventually ended by the executioner's axe. Her cousin, Elizabeth I, issued the death order, however reluctantly.

The subsequent cult of Mary Queen of Scots has ensured that landmarks associated with her rule and movements through Scotland, whether Stirling Castle or the Palace of Holyroodhouse, are firmly on the modern tourist trail.

Ironically, Mary's son, James VI of Scotland, succeeded the childless Elizabeth and became king of England (James I) as well in 1603. For the next 100 years or so, religious conflict between Protestants and Catholics plus the Puritan revolution and civil war occupied a fractious England and Scotland.

UNION & THE JACOBITES In 1689, the final Stuart king, the staunchly Catholic James VII (and II of England), was supplanted by his nephew William of Orange. In exile, the king and then his son James Edward—the **Old Pretender**—became focal points for Scottish (and French) ambitions to restore the Stuart dynasty. Scottish people were divided in their loyalties: The notorious Glencoe massacre of 1692 perhaps best exemplifies this split.

Scottish sovereignty was ebbing away. Economically, the country paid a huge price when its attempts to rival England with a colony in the Caribbean failed. The Darien disaster on the Isthmus of Panama and other economic pressures meant that Scotland had little choice but to merge formally with England and confirm the creation of Great Britain in 1707. After this union abolished the Scottish Parliament—and before its benefits were widely seen—the Jacobites (the name comes from Jacobus, the Latin form of James) attempted unsuccessfully in 1715 to place the Old Pretender on the throne and restore the Stuart line.

James died in exile and his son, Charles Edward (the Young Pretender), better known as **Bonnie Prince Charlie,** carried on in his stead. Charismatic but probably out of his league, he was the central figure in the 1745 Jacobite uprising. After landing near Glenfinnan in northwest Scotland and rallying sympathetic Highland clans, he began his march south. The revolt was initially promising and Jacobite troops easily reached Derby, only 125 miles from London, which flew into a panic. But they made an ill-conceived tactical retreat to Scotland and were eventually crushed at the **Battle of Culloden,** near Inverness. In an attempt to quell any further uprisings, Hanoverian loyalists ruthlessly suppressed Highland clans that supported the Jacobite cause, and Britain even banned Highland dress until the 1780s.

ECONOMIC GROWTH & THE INDUSTRIAL REVOLUTION During the 18th century, the union began to reap dividends, and the Scottish economy underwent a radical transformation. As trade with British colonies increased, the port of Glasgow flourished. Its merchants grew rich on the tobacco trade with Virginia and the Carolinas. Ships from Glasgow were making the trip back and forth to the New World much faster than competitors elsewhere in Great Britain. The **Merchant City** district of the city center is named after the tobacco and cotton barons of the day.

The infamous **Highland Clearances** (1750–1850) expelled small farmers, or crofters, from their ancestral lands to make way for sheep grazing. Similarly in the Scottish Lowlands, labor-intensive subsistence farming was deemed antiquated and, in the name of progress, people were forcibly moved on. Increased industrialization and migration into urban centers such as Glasgow changed the national demographics forever, while a massive wave of emigration to the United States, Canada, Australia, and New Zealand created a global **Scottish Diaspora.**

Rapid progress in the arts, sciences, and education in the new industrial age produced vast numbers of prominent Scots who made broad and sweeping contributions to all fields of endeavor. Victorian builders turned Glasgow into a showcase of that era's architecture. Many of the inventions that altered the history of the developing world—such as the steam engine—were either invented or installed by Scottish genius and industry.

THE 20TH & 21ST CENTURIES During this time, immigrants from Ireland and partitioned India arrived in Scotland. But like much of Great Britain, the people endured bitter privations during the Great Depression and the two world wars. In the 1960s and 1970s,

Scotland found that its industrial plants could not compete (with government subsidy) with the emerging industrial powerhouses of Asia and elsewhere. The most visible decline occurred in **shipbuilding:** The vast Glasgow yards that produced some of the world's great ocean liners were closed. Although Scottish businessmen had made fortunes out of the Empire, little was reinvested at home and when the Empire collapsed there was not much to show for it.

A glimmer of light appeared on the Scottish economic horizon in the 1970s: the discovery of **North Sea oil** lifted the British economy considerably and gave a political boost as well to the Scottish National Party, which argued that petroleum revenues should stay in Scotland.

Scots have always contributed disproportionately to the world's sciences and technology and another breakthrough occurred in the 1990s with the first cloned sheep: **Dolly.** Today the economy is primarily service-oriented, with a reasonably profitable banking and finance sector, as well as some high-tech manufacturing in what has been rather over-ambitiously called "Silicon Glen" between Edinburgh and Glasgow.

In 1997, under a newly elected Labour government in London, the Scottish electorate was allowed to vote on **devolution** again. This time the referendum passed, which allowed Scotland to have its own legislature for the first time since the 1707 union with England. Unlike the Welsh National Assembly, the **Scottish Parliament,** centered at Edinburgh, has some limited taxing powers and can enact laws regarding health, education, transportation, and public housing. Scotland, however, must bow to the greater will of the central government and Parliament in London on matters of finance, defense, immigration, and foreign policy.

Because devolution is well short of independence, critics such as Billy Connolly have dismissed the Scottish body of politicians "as a wee pretendy Parliament." Unionists who opposed devolution are equally scathing. Yet, it is proving successful despite a shaky start. Unlike members of the Westminster Parliament, members of the Scottish Parliament are elected using a system of **proportional representation.** This has enabled new, fresh-thinking parties to be elected and challenge the entrenched status quo.

2 A Portrait of the Scots

HIGHLAND GAMES & GATHERINGS Highland Gatherings or Games have their origins in the fairs organized by the tribes or clans for the exchange of goods. At these gatherings, there were often trials of strength among the men, and the strongest were selected for the chief's army.

The earliest games were probably held more than 1,000 years ago, but the formal and annual organization of them dates only to the 1820s. The same traditions are maintained today: throwing hammers, tossing tree trunks (cabers), and running in flat races and up steep hillsides. Playing the bagpipes and performing dances are part of the gatherings.

Queen Victoria, who developed a passion for Scotland (which was dramatized in the film *Mrs. Brown*), popularized the Highland Games, which for many decades had been suppressed after the failure of the 1745 rebellion. In 1848, the queen and her consort, Prince Albert, attended the Braemar Gathering and saw Duncan, her *ghillie* (originally meaning a male attendant but today referring to a fishing and hunting guide), win the race up the hill of Craig Choinnich, as she recorded in her journal. The most famous gathering is still at Braemar, held in late August or early September and patronized by the royal family.

CLANS, TARTANS & KILTS   To the outsider, Scotland's deepest traditions appear to be based on the clan system of old with the familiar paraphernalia of tartans. However, this is a romantic memory, and in any case, a good part of the Scots—the 75% of the population who live in the central Lowlands, for example—have little or no connection with the clansmen of earlier times. Clan tradition dates from the tribal units of the country's earliest Celtic history. Power was organized around a series of chieftains who exacted loyalties from the inhabitants of a particular region in exchange for protection against exterior invasions.

Chieftains were absolute potentates, with life and death power over members and interlopers, although they were usually viewed as patriarchs actively engaged in the perpetuation of the clan's bloodlines, traditions, and honor. One of the country's oldest and largest is Clan Donald, whose original organization occurred during the early mists of the Christianization of Scotland and whose headquarters have traditionally been Scotland's northwestern coast and western islands. Briefly the clan head was called "Lord of the Isles" because of the size and reach of the clan. Eventually Clan Donald dissolved into subdivisions, which include the Donalds of Sleat, Glengarry, and MacAlister.

The clan system had largely broken down long before Sir Walter Scott wrote his romantic novels about them and long before Queen Victoria made Scotland socially fashionable. The clans today represent a cultural rather than a political power. The best place to see the remnants of their tradition in action is at any traditional Highland gathering, although battalions of bagpipers seem to show up at everything from weddings and funerals to political rallies, parades, and civic events throughout Scotland.

Index

See also Accommodations and Restaurant indexes, below.

GENERAL INDEX

AARP, 24
Abbotsford (Edinburgh),
  129–130
Abbotsford (Melrose), 141
ABC (Glasgow), 229, 234
Above and Beyond Tours, 23
Access-Able Travel Source, 23
Access America, 20
Accessible Journeys, 23
Accommodations. *See also*
  Accommodations Index
  Edinburgh and environs,
    54–66
    best, 7
    chain hotels, 62
    Crossford, 147
    family-friendly, 60
    Leith, 65–66
    Melrose, 143
    New Town, 55–60
    Old Town, 60–62
    reservations, 31–32
    St. Andrews, 148
    Southside, 64–65
    West End, 63–64
    what's new, 1–2
  general tips on, 31–33
  Glasgow and environs,
    163–173
    Ayrshire, 244
    best, 7–8
    chain hotels, 169
    Commercial Center,
      167–169
    Cowal and Kintyre Penin-
      sulas, 251–252
    family-friendly, 171
    Loch Lomond, 253
    Merchant City and East
      End, 163, 166
    reservations, 32, 163
    Troon, 248
    The Trossachs, 255
    Turnberry, 248–249

West End, 169–173
  what's new, 2
money-saving tips,
  17–18, 32–33
surfing for, 25
Adam, Robert, 6, 58–59,
  91–92, 95, 102, 106,
  108, 110, 163, 246
Addresses, finding
  Edinburgh, 49
  Glasgow, 156
Afternoon tea
  Edinburgh, 76
  Glasgow, 184
Airfares
  surfing for, 25
  tips for getting best,
    17, 27–28
Airlines, 27–28
  bankruptcies, 20
  long flights, 22, 28–29
Airports
  Edinburgh, 43–44
  Glasgow, 150
Alexandra Park (Glasgow), 203
Alistir Wood Tait (Edinburgh),
  122
All Bar One (Edinburgh), 130
Alloway, 243–244
Alloway Auld Kirk, 243
Alpine Bikes (Glasgow),
  160, 203
American Express, 16, 17
  Edinburgh, 51
  Glasgow, 160
Ancestry, tracing your, 122
Andrew Carnegie Birthplace
  Museum (Dunfermline), 146
Anta (Edinburgh), 121
Antiques
  Edinburgh, 117
  Glasgow, 224–225
The Arches (Glasgow),
  192, 229, 232
Argyll Arcade (Glasgow), 224
Arkangel (Edinburgh), 120

Arran, Isle of, 247
Art galleries, Glasgow, 225
Arthur's Seat (Edinburgh),
  89, 103–104
Art museums
  best, 6
  Edinburgh
    Dean Gallery, 89
    The Fruitmarket
      Gallery, 89
    Museum of Scotland,
      6, 89–90, 104
    National Gallery of Scot-
      land, 6, 85, 90
    Royal Scottish Academy,
      90, 107–108
    Scottish National Gallery
      of Modern Art,
      6, 90–91
    Scottish National Portrait
      Gallery, 91
    Talbot Rice Gallery,
      94, 106
  Glasgow
    Burrell Collection, 6, 153,
      193, 196
    Centre for Contemporary
      Art (CCA), 197, 212
    Gallery of Modern Art
      (GOMA), 192–193
    Glasgow Print Studio,
      225
    Glasgow School of Art,
      7, 194, 198, 210,
      212, 227
    House for an Art Lover,
      197
    Hunterian Art Gallery,
      6, 195, 216
    Kelvingrove Art Gallery
      and Museum, 2, 6,
      193, 195–196
    The Lighthouse, 197, 198
    St. Mungo Museum of
      Religious Life and
      Art, 199

Artstore (Glasgow), 225
Art supplies, Glasgow, 225
Ashton Lane (Glasgow),
    216, 238
Assembly Rooms (Glasgow),
    128
ATMs, 16
Auditoriums. *See* Concert halls
    and auditoriums
Australian travelers,
    10, 15, 52, 161
Avalanche
    Edinburgh, 122–123
    Glasgow, 228
Avis Rent a Car, 23, 51, 160
Ayr, 242–243
Ayr Auld Brig, 242
Ayr Auld Kirk, 242
Ayrshire, 240–246

B abbity Bowster (Glasgow),
    9, 163, 166, 179, 237
The Bachelor Pad (Edinburgh),
    117
Bachelors' Club (Tarbolton),
    246
The Bailie Bar (Edinburgh),
    9, 130
Ballantrae, 249
Ballet
    Edinburgh, 125
    Glasgow, 229, 233
Balloch, 252–253
Bamboo (Glasgow), 236
Bannockburn, 254
Banqueting Hall (Glasgow),
    192
Barfly (Glasgow), 235
Barras (Glasgow), 155, 224
Barrowland (Glasgow), 235
Bars and pubs, 3–4
    Ayr, 243
    Edinburgh, 85, 124, 129–132
        best, 9
        Literary Pub Tour, 96
    Glasgow, 193, 236–238
        best, 9
Bar 10 (Glasgow), 236
Bass Rock, 137
Bath Street (Glasgow), 210
The Beehive Inn (Edinburgh),
    131
Beltane Fire Festival (Edin-
    burgh), 18
Benmore Botanic Garden, 251
Bennets (Glasgow), 238

Bernard Street (Edinburgh),
    114
Berwick Law, 137
Bicycling
    Edinburgh, 51, 98
    Glasgow, 160, 203
Big Big Country (Glasgow), 18
Bill Baber (Edinburgh), 121
Bird-watching, 137, 138, 247, 251
Black Bo's (Edinburgh), 131
Blackfriars (Glasgow), 237
Blackwells (Edinburgh), 117
BLOCK (Glasgow), 19
Blythswood Square (Glasgow),
    156, 210
Boat tours, Glasgow, 201, 202
Bon Accord (Glasgow),
    236–237
Bongo Club (Edinburgh), 129
Book Festival (Edinburgh),
    97, 124
Books, recommended, 33–34
Bookstores
    Edinburgh, 117
    Glasgow, 225
Borders (Glasgow), 225
The Borders region, 140–143
Botanic Garden, Royal (Edin-
    burgh), 85, 95–96
Botanic Gardens (Glasgow),
    200–201, 217
Bow Bar (Edinburgh), 9, 131
Braehead Shopping Centre
    (Glasgow), 224
Braid Hills Links (Edinburgh), 98
Brass Rubbing Centre
    (Edinburgh), 87
Braveheart (movie),
    40, 242–243, 254
Brel (Glasgow), 9, 238
Brig o' Doon (Alloway), 243
Britannia (royal yacht;
    Edinburgh), 93
British Tourist Authority, 10
Brodie's Close (Edinburgh),
    86, 100
Broomielaw (Glasgow),
    156–157, 202
Broughton Street (Edinburgh),
    111
    nightlife, 124, 130, 132
Bruntsfield (Edinburgh), 48
Bruntsfield Links (Edinburgh),
    4, 95, 98
Buchanan Galleries (Glasgow),
    209–210, 224
Buchanan Street Bus Station
    (Glasgow), 30, 152, 158

Bucket shops, 28
Burns, Robert, 33, 86, 96, 100,
    103, 114, 208, 240, 242–246
    biographical sketch of, 245
    Cottage and Museum
        (Alloway), 242, 243
    festivals, 18, 97, 245
    House (Dumfries), 242
    House Museum (Tarbolton),
        246
    Monument (Edinburgh),
        90, 94
    Monument and Gardens
        (Alloway), 243
Burns an' a' That (Ayrshire),
    18, 245
"Burns Country," 240–246
Burns Heritage Trail (Glasgow),
    242
Burns National Heritage Park
    (Alloway), 243
Burns Night (Edinburgh), 18, 97
Burrell Collection (Glasgow),
    6, 153, 193, 196
Buses
    Edinburgh, 44, 49–50
        tours, 96
    Glasgow, 152, 158
        tours, 201
    to Scotland, 30
Business hours
    Edinburgh, 51
    Glasgow, 160
Bute, Isle of, 249, 250–251
Bute House (Edinburgh), 110
Byres Road (Glasgow),
    153, 216–217

C abs
    Edinburgh, 50
    Glasgow, 160
Café Royal Circle Bar (Edin-
    burgh), 9, 73, 130
Caledonia Books (Glasgow),
    225
Caledonian Road Church
    (Glasgow), 200
Calendar of events, 18–20
    Edinburgh, 96–97
    Glasgow, 202
Calton Hill (Edinburgh),
    48–49, 94–95, 111
    accommodations, 58, 60
    nightlife, 132, 133
Camera Obscura (Edinburgh),
    84–85
Cameron Fountain (Glasgow),
    213

Canadian travelers, 10, 14, 15, 25, 52, 161
Canongate Church (Edinburgh), 103
Canongate Tolbooth (Edinburgh), 87–88, 103
Carling Academy (Glasgow), 235
Carnegie, Andrew, Birthplace Museum (Dunfermline), 146
Car rentals
    Edinburgh, 51
    Glasgow, 160
    surfing for, 25
Carrick Knowe Links (Edinburgh), 98
Car travel
    Edinburgh, 44, 50
    Glasgow, 152, 160
    to Scotland, 29–30
Castle Hill (Edinburgh), 100
Castles and palaces
    best, 5
    Edinburgh and environs
        Dirleton Castle, 137–138
        Dunfermline Abbey and Palace, 146
        Edinburgh Castle, 5, 84, 99
        Linlithgow Palace, 134
        Palace of Holyroodhouse, 5, 88–89, 103
        St. Andrews Castle, 144
        Tantallon Castle, 138
    Glasgow and environs
        Culzean Castle, 246
        Doune Castle, 254
        Rothesay Castle, 250
        Stirling Castle, 254
Cathedrals. See Churches and cathedrals
Catherine Shaw (Glasgow), 227
C. C. Bloom's (Edinburgh), 132
Ceilidh Culture (Edinburgh), 18
Cellphones, 26–27
Celtic (Glasgow), 203
Celtic Connections (Glasgow), 18, 202
Centers for Disease Control and Prevention, 21
Central Necropolis (Glasgow), 205
Central Radio Taxis (Edinburgh), 50
Central Station (Glasgow), 150, 152, 158, 242
Centre for Contemporary Art (Glasgow), 197, 212

Charing Cross (Glasgow), 156, 213
Charlotte Square (Edinburgh), 108, 110
Childhood, Museum of (Edinburgh), 87
Children, families with
    Edinburgh
        hotels, 60
        restaurants, 74
    Glasgow
        hotels, 171
        restaurants, 180
    information and resources, 24
Churches and cathedrals
    best, 5
    Edinburgh and environs
        Canongate Church, 103
        Greyfriars Kirk, 92–93, 104
        St. Andrews Cathedral, 144
        St. Giles Church, 5, 86, 100, 102
        St. John's & Cuthbert's Churches, 108
        St. Michael's Parish Church (Linlithgow), 136
        South Leith Parish Church, 115
        Tron Kirk, 102
    Glasgow and environs
        Alloway Auld Kirk, 243
        Ayr Auld Kirk, 242
        Glasgow Cathedral, 5, 153, 156, 193–194, 206
        St. Vincent Street Church, 5, 194, 200, 212
Church Hill (Edinburgh), 48
Cinemas
    Edinburgh, 132–133
    Glasgow, 239
Cineworld (Edinburgh), 132
Cineworld (Glasgow), 239
Citizens Theatre (Glasgow), 229, 232
City Cabs (Edinburgh), 50
City Centre (Glasgow). See Glasgow City Centre
City Halls (Glasgow), 208, 233
CityLink, 30, 150, 152
City Observatory (Edinburgh), 94
City Sightseeing Glasgow, 201
Clan system, 265
Classical music
    Edinburgh, 125
    Glasgow, 229, 233–234

Climate, 17. See also Weather forecasts
Clydebuilt Scottish Maritime Museum (Glasgow), 200
Clyde Valley, 255–256
Cockburn Street (Edinburgh), 102
Comedy clubs
    Edinburgh, 128
    Glasgow, 234
Comedy Festival (Glasgow), 18, 234
Commercial Center (Glasgow), 153, 156
    accommodations, 167–169
    pubs and bars, 236–237
    restaurants, 180–184
    walking tour, 209–213
Compass Gallery (Glasgow), 225
Concert halls and auditoriums
    Edinburgh, 125, 128
    Glasgow, 233–234
Consolidators, 28
Constitution Street (Edinburgh), 112, 114
Consulates
    Edinburgh, 52
    Glasgow, 161
Corn Exchange (Edinburgh), 128–129
Corniche (Edinburgh), 120
Cottier Theatre (Glasgow), 232
Cowal Peninsula, 249, 251–252
Credit cards, 16–17, 20
Crosshill (Glasgow), 157
Crown Jewels (Edinburgh), 5, 84
Cruise (Edinburgh), 120
Cruise (Glasgow), 226
Cruises, in Glasgow, 201, 202
Crystal
    Edinburgh, 117
    Glasgow, 226, 227
Cube (Glasgow), 239
Cuisine, 4, 266–267
Culross, 146
Culzean, 246–247
Culzean Castle, 246
Culzean Country Park, 246–247
Cupar, 147–148
Currency and exchange, 15–16
    Edinburgh, 51
    Glasgow, 161
Customs House (Edinburgh), 114
Customs regulations, 14–15

Cybercafes. *See* Internet access

Cyril Gerber Fine Art
(Glasgow), 225

Dalry (Edinburgh), 48

Dance clubs
Edinburgh, 129
Glasgow, 236

Darvel Music Festival
(Ayrshire), 19

The Da Vinci Code (movie), 136

Deacon Brodie's Tavern
(Edinburgh), 86, 131

Dean Gallery (Edinburgh), 89

Dean Village (Edinburgh), 95

Debenhams (Glasgow), 226

Deep Sea World (North
Queensferry), 147

Deep vein thrombosis, 22

Delizique (Glasgow), 188

Dennistoun (Glasgow),
153, 155

Dentists
Edinburgh, 51
Glasgow, 161

Department stores
Edinburgh, 120
Glasgow, 226–227

DeQuincey, Thomas, 108

Design stores, in Glasgow, 227

Dining. *See* Restaurants;
Restaurant Index

Dionika (Edinburgh), 80

Dirleton, 138

Dirleton Castle, 137–138

Disabilities, travelers with, 23

Discrimination, 22

Dock Place (Edinburgh), 114

Doctors
Edinburgh, 51
Glasgow, 161

Doors Open Days, 19, 202

Dougal Stewart's Monument
(Edinburgh), 94

Doulton Fountain (Glasgow),
197, 201, 206

Doune Castle (near Dunblane),
254

Dowanhill (Glasgow), 157

Dr. Jives (Glasgow), 226

Drugstores
Edinburgh, 52
Glasgow, 162

Dumfries, 242, 245

Dunbar, 139

Dunbar's Close (Edinburgh), 88

Dundas Street (Edinburgh), 110

Dunfermline, 144, 146

Dunfermline Abbey and Palace,
146

East End (Glasgow), 154–155
accommodations, 163, 166
pubs and bars, 237–238
walking tour, 205–209

East Lothian, 137–138

East Princes Street Gardens
(Edinburgh), 112

Ecotourism, 22–23

Edibles. *See* Food stores and
markets; Picnic fare

Edinburgh, Museum of, 88

Edinburgh Bus Tours, 96

Edinburgh Castle, 5, 84, 99

Edinburgh Christmas, 19–20

Edinburgh City Art Centre, 89

Edinburgh Crystal, 117

Edinburgh Festival,
4, 19, 42, 96–97
accommodations tip, 31, 54
museums hours during, 90

Edinburgh Festival Theatre, 125

Edinburgh Information Centre,
10–11, 31–32, 44, 54

Edinburgh International
Airport, 43–44, 150
accommodations near, 54

Edinburgh International Jazz &
Blues Festival, 19

Edinburgh Literary Pub Tour, 19

Edinburgh Military Tattoo,
19, 97

Edinburgh Playhouse, 124

Edinburgh Woollen Mill Shop,
121

Edinburgh Zoo, 91

Egyptian Halls (Glasgow), 200

Elderhostel, 24

ElderTreks, 24

Elmbank Street (Glasgow), 212

Emancipation Monument
(Edinburgh), 95

Embassies
Edinburgh, 52
Glasgow, 161

Emergencies, 21
Edinburgh, 52
Glasgow, 161

Entry requirements, 14

Escorted tours, 31

Eton Terrace (Edinburgh),
200, 214

Eunice Whyte (Glasgow), 228

Euston Station (London),
30, 150, 152

Fabhatrix (Edinburgh),
120–121

Families with children
Edinburgh
hotels, 60
restaurants, 74
Glasgow
hotels, 171
restaurants, 180
information and resources, 24

Familyhostel, 24

Family Travel Network, 24

Fashion (clothing). *See also*
Kilts; Knits and woolens;
Tartans
Edinburgh, 120
Glasgow, 226

Felix & Oscar (Glasgow), 227

Ferries
Arran, 247
Bute, 250
Glasgow, 158

Festivals and special events,
18–20
Edinburgh, 96–97
Glasgow, 202

Filmhouse (Edinburgh), 133

Films set in Scotland, 34

Finlay, Ian Hamilton, 142

Finnieston (Glasgow), 157, 171

First Group (Glasgow), 158

Firth of Clyde, 240, 249

Flea markets, in Glasgow, 224

Flying Wheels Travel, 23

Folk music
Edinburgh, 9, 128
Glasgow, 234
Celtic Connections,
18, 202

Food stores and markets
Edinburgh, 80
Glasgow, 188

Football
Edinburgh, 97
Glasgow, 203

Fopp (Edinburgh), 123

Fopp (Glasgow), 228

Frequent-flier clubs, 28

Fringe Festival (Edinburgh),
4, 19, 96–97

The Fruitmarket Gallery
(Edinburgh), 89

Fury Murry's (Glasgow), 236

Gallery of Modern Art
(Edinburgh), 6, 90–91

Gallery of Modern Art (GOMA;
Glasgow), 192–193

Gallowgate (Glasgow),
154–156, 206
The Garage (Glasgow), 236
Gardens. *See* Parks and gardens; *and specific gardens*
Garnethill (Glasgow), 157
Gay and lesbian travelers
Edinburgh nightlife, 132
Glasgow nightlife, 238–239
information and resources,
23–24, 52
special events, 19
Genealogical records, 122
General Register Office
(Edinburgh), 122
Geoffrey (Tailor) Kiltmakers
Edinburgh, 121
Glasgow, 227
George Heriot's School
(Edinburgh), 107
George Square (Edinburgh),
106
George Square (Glasgow), 208
George Street (Edinburgh),
45, 108, 116
Georgian House (Edinburgh),
6, 91–92, 110
Geraldine's of Edinburgh, 121
Gibson Street (Glasgow), 214
Gift stores
Edinburgh, 121–122
Glasgow, 227
Gigha, Isle of, 249, 251
Gilmorehill G12 (Glasgow), 232
Gladstone's Land (Edinburgh),
6, 85, 100
Glasgay! (Glasgow), 19
Glasgow Art Fair, 18
Glasgow Botanic Gardens,
200–201, 217
Glasgow Cathedral, 5, 153,
156, 193–194, 206
Glasgow City Centre, 156–157
accommodations,
163, 166–169
restaurants, 178–184
sights and attractions,
192–195
walking tours, 205–213
Glasgow Comedy Festival,
18, 234
Glasgow Cross, 206
Glasgow Film Theatre, 210, 239
Glasgow Green, 153, 197–198,
201, 206
Glasgow Harbour, Tall Ship at,
199–200
Glasgow International, 18

Glasgow International Airport,
150
Glasgow International Jazz
Festival, 19, 202
Glasgow on Ice, 20
Glasgow Print Studio, 225
Glasgow River Festival, 19
Glasgow Royal Concert Hall,
189, 233–234
Glasgow School of Art, 7, 194,
198, 210, 212, 227
Glasgow Taxis Ltd., 160
Glasgow Underground, 158
Glenlee, SV, 199–200
Golf, 4
Arran, 247
Edinburgh, 98
Glasgow, 203–204
Scottish Open, 19
Muirfield, 138–139
St. Andrews, 144, 145
Troon, 247–248
Turnberry, 248
Gorbals (Glasgow), 157
Govan (Glasgow), 157
Grand Ole Opry (Glasgow), 235
Grassmarket (Edinburgh),
45, 107, 124
Greater Glasgow and Clyde
Valley Tourist Board,
11, 152–153
Great Western Road (Glasgow),
217
Grecian Buildings (Glasgow),
197, 200, 212
Greyfriars Kirk (Edinburgh),
92–93, 104
Grosvenor (Glasgow), 239
Guildford Arms (Edinburgh),
130
Gullane, 138–140
Gullane Hill, 138
Gyms
Edinburgh, 98
Glasgow, 204

Habana (Edinburgh), 132
Haggis, 72, 97, 245, 267
Hamilton & Inches (Edinburgh),
122
Hampden Park (Glasgow), 203
Hanover Street Travelshop
(Edinburgh), 50
Harvey Nichols (Edinburgh),
120
food hall, 80
restaurant, 69, 72

Hats, in Edinburgh, 120–121
Haymarket (Edinburgh), 48
Health concerns, 21–22
Health insurance, 20–21
Heart Buchanan Fine Food and
Wine (Glasgow), 188
Heart of Midlothian Football
Club (Hearts; Edinburgh), 97
Heart of Scotland Tours
(Edinburgh), 140
Hector Russell (Edinburgh), 121
Hector Russell (Glasgow), 227
Helensburgh, 249–250
Heraghty's Free House
(Glasgow), 238
Hibernian Football Club (Hibs;
Edinburgh), 97
High Kirk of St. Giles (Edinburgh), 5, 86, 100, 102
Highland Games (Gatherings),
261–262
Hiking
Southern Upland Way, 141
West Highland Way, 252, 253
Hillhead (Glasgow),
157, 195, 214
Hill House (Helensburgh),
198, 249–250
History of Scotland, 257–261
books about, 34
HMV (Glasgow), 228
Hogmanay, 20, 97
Holidays, 18
Holmwood House (Glasgow),
7, 196–197, 200
Holyroodhouse Palace (Edinburgh), 5, 88–89, 103
Holyrood Park (Edinburgh),
89, 103–104
The Honeycomb (Edinburgh),
129
Hopetoun House (South
Queensferry), 136
Horse racing, in Edinburgh, 98
The Horse Shoe (Glasgow),
9, 237
Hospital insurance, 20–21
Hospitals
Edinburgh, 51
Glasgow, 161
Hotels. *See* Accommodations;
Accommodations Index
Hot lines
Edinburgh, 52
Glasgow, 161
House for an Art Lover
(Glasgow), 197
restaurant, 187
House of Fraser (Glasgow), 226

Hunterian Art Gallery (Glasgow), 6, 195, 216
Hunterian Museum (Glasgow), 6, 195, 216
Hyndland (Glasgow), 157

J Mellis Cheesemongers
   Edinburgh, 80
   Glasgow, 188
IMAX Theatre (Glasgow), 199
Information sources. See Visitor information
Insurance, 20–21
International Association for Medical Assistance to Travelers (IAMAT), 21
International Gay and Lesbian Travel Association (IGLTA), 23
International Story Telling Festival (Edinburgh), 19
International Student Identity Card (ISIC), 24–25
Internet access, 26
   Edinburgh, 52
   Glasgow, 161
Isle of Arran, 247
Isle of Bute, 249, 250–251
Isle of Gigha, 249, 251
Italian Centre (Glasgow), 208–209
Itineraries, suggested, 35–41
   Edinburgh, 81, 84
   Glasgow, 192

James Pringle Weavers (Edinburgh), 121
James Pringle Weavers (Glasgow), 227
Jazz
   Edinburgh, 19, 128–129
   Glasgow, 234–236
      Glasgow International Jazz Festival, 19, 202
Jenners (Edinburgh), 120
Jewelry stores
   Edinburgh, 122
   Glasgow, 224
Jigsaw (Glasgow), 226
John Knox House (Edinburgh), 2, 87, 102
John Lewis (Edinburgh), 120
John Lewis (Glasgow), 224, 226
Jongleurs Comedy Club (Edinburgh), 128
Jongleurs Comedy Club (Glasgow), 234

Kelvingrove Art Gallery and Museum (Glasgow), 2, 6, 193, 195–196
Kelvingrove Park (Glasgow), 214
Kelvin Hall International Sports Arena (Glasgow), 204
Kember & Jones Fine Food Emporium (Glasgow), 188
Kilts, 262
   Edinburgh, 121
   Glasgow, 227–228
King's Cross Station (London), 30
Kings Theatre (Edinburgh), 125
Kings Theatre (Glasgow), 212, 232
King Tut's Wah Wah Hut (Glasgow), 9, 229, 235
Kintyre Peninsula, 249, 251–252
Kippen, 255
Kirkaldy, 146–147
Kirkcaldy Museum and Art Gallery, 146–147
Kirkoswald, 242, 245–246
Knightswood (Glasgow), 203
Knits and woolens
   Edinburgh, 121
   Glasgow, 221, 228
Knox, John, 86, 100, 194, 259
   House (Edinburgh), 2, 87, 102

Lady Stair's House (Edinburgh), 86, 100
Lamb's House (Edinburgh), 114
Lanark, 255–256
Laundry and dry cleaning
   Edinburgh, 52
   Glasgow, 161
Layout
   of Edinburgh, 45
   of Glasgow, 153–155
Leith (Edinburgh), 45, 49
   accommodations, 65–66
   pubs and bars, 131–132
   restaurants, 78–80
   walking tour, 112–115
Leith Links (Edinburgh), 112
Leith Walk (Edinburgh), 49, 111, 132
The Lighthouse (Glasgow), 197, 198
Lincoln (Abraham) Monument (Edinburgh), 95
Linlithgow, 134, 136
   restaurants, 137

Linlithgow Palace, 134
Linn Park (Glasgow), 203
The Liquid Room (Edinburgh), 124, 129
Liquid Ship (Glasgow), 238
Lismore Bar (Glasgow), 238
The List, 52, 67, 124, 162, 174, 229, 233
Littlehill (Glasgow), 203
Little Sparta (near Dunsyre), 142
Loch Katerine, 254
Loch Lomond, 252–253
Lost-luggage insurance, 21
Luggage storage/lockers, in Edinburgh, 52
Lupe Pintos (Edinburgh), 80
Lupe Pintos (Glasgow), 188
Luss, 253

MacBackpackers (Edinburgh), 140
Machrihanish, 251
Mackintosh, Charles Rennie, 7, 157, 168, 184, 187, 193–195, 197, 199, 210, 212, 216
   biographical sketch of, 198
   Hill House (Helensburgh), 198, 249–250
   House (Glasgow), 195, 216
Mackintosh Church at Queens Cross (Glasgow), 198
Mackintosh Shop (Glasgow), 227
Magazines
   Edinburgh, 52
   Glasgow, 162
Mail. See Post offices
Malls and shopping complexes
   Edinburgh, 116–117
   Glasgow, 221, 224
Marchmont (Edinburgh), 48, 78
Maritime Glasgow, 199–200
Markets, in Glasgow, 224
Marks & Spencer (Edinburgh), 116
Marks & Spencer (Glasgow), 226
Mary, Queen of Scots, 84, 88–89, 103, 134, 142, 254, 259
McNaughtan's Bookshop (Edinburgh), 117
Meadowbank Sports Centre (Edinburgh), 98

The Meadows (Edinburgh),
95, 106–107
Medical insurance, 20–21
Melrose, 140–143
Melrose Abbey, 141
Mercat Tours (Edinburgh), 96
Mercat Tours (Glasgow),
201–202
Merchant City (Glasgow),
153, 156, 260
accommodations, 163, 166
pubs and bars, 237
restaurants, 178–180
sights and attractions,
192–195
walking tour, 205–209
Merchant Square (Glasgow),
208
Military Tattoo (Edinburgh),
19, 97
Mitchell Library (Glasgow),
161, 213
Money matters, 15–17
Money-saving tips, 17–18
Monorail (Glasgow), 228
Moray Place (Glasgow),
200, 218
Morningside (Edinburgh), 48
Moss (Glasgow), 228
Mount Stuart (Isle of Bute),
250–251
Movies set in Scotland, 34
Movie theaters
Edinburgh, 132–133
Glasgow, 239
Muir, John, 139
Muirfield Golf Course
(Gullane), 138–139
Murrayfield Stadium (Edin-
burgh), 98, 128
Museum of Childhood
(Edinburgh), 87
Museum of Edinburgh, 88
Museum of Scotland (Edin-
burgh), 6, 89–90, 104
eating, 77
Museum of Transport
(Glasgow), 2, 196
Music. See also Classical music;
Folk music; Jazz; Rock music
Edinburgh, 125, 128–129
Glasgow, 233–236
Music stores
Edinburgh, 122–123
Glasgow, 228
Musselburgh Racecourse (near
Edinburgh), 98

Nasmyth, Alexander, 108
National Express, 30, 44, 152
National Gallery of Modern Art
(Edinburgh), 6, 90–91
National Gallery of Scotland
(Edinburgh), 6, 85, 90
National Library of Scotland
(Edinburgh), 93
National Monument
(Edinburgh), 94
National Portrait Gallery
(Edinburgh), 91
National Trust for Scotland
Shop (Glasgow), 227
The Necropolis (Glasgow), 205
Neighborhoods. See also spe-
cific neighborhoods
Edinburgh, 48–49
Glasgow, 156–157
Nelson Mandela Place
(Glasgow), 209
Nelson Monument (Edinburgh),
94, 111
Ness Scotland (Edinburgh),
121–122
Newhaven (Edinburgh), 49
New Lanark, 256
Newspapers
Edinburgh, 52
Glasgow, 162
New Territories (Glasgow), 18
New Town (Edinburgh),
42, 45, 48, 81, 85
accommodations, 55–60
pubs and bars, 129–131
restaurants, 69–74
walking tour, 107–112
New Zealand travelers,
10, 15, 52, 161
Nice 'n' Sleazy (Glasgow),
9, 229, 235–236
Nicolson Square (Edinburgh),
106
Nightlife
Edinburgh, 124–133
cinema, 132–133
club and music scene,
128–129
current listings, 124
gay and lesbian, 132
performing arts, 124–128
pubs and bars, 124,
129–132
Glasgow, 229–239
cinema, 239
club and music scene,
234–236
current listings, 229, 233

gay and lesbian, 238–239
performing arts,
229, 232–233
pubs and bars, 236–238
1901 Deli (Glasgow), 188
Nithsdale Road (Glasgow), 218
North Berwick, 137–138
North Bridge (Edinburgh), 111
North Queensferry, 147

Ocean Terminal (Edinburgh),
116
Odeon at the Quay (Glasgow),
239
Old College (Edinburgh),
94, 106
Old Course (St. Andrews), 145
Old Town (Edinburgh),
42, 45, 48, 81, 85
accommodations, 60–62
pubs and bars, 131
restaurants, 75–77
walking tours, 99–107
Old Town Jail (Stirling),
254–255
Opal Lounge (Edinburgh),
130–131
Opera
Edinburgh, 125
Glasgow, 229, 233
Oran Mor (Glasgow), 234
Organized tours
Edinburgh, 96, 140
Glasgow, 201–202
Our Dynamic Earth (Edin-
burgh), 93–94
Outdoor activities
Edinburgh, 97–98
Glasgow, 203–204
The Outhouse (Edinburgh), 131
Outlook Tower (Edinburgh),
84–85

Package tours, 30–31
Paddy's Market (Glasgow), 224
Palace of Holyroodhouse (Edin-
burgh), 5, 88–89, 103
Palaces and castles
best, 5
Edinburgh and environs
Dirleton Castle, 137–138
Dunfermline Abbey and
Palace, 146
Edinburgh Castle,
5, 84, 99
Linlithgow Palace, 134

Palace of Holyroodhouse, 5, 88–89, 103
    St. Andrews Castle, 144
    Tantallon Castle, 138
Glasgow and environs
    Culzean Castle, 246
    Doune Castle, 254
    Rothesay Castle, 250
    Stirling Castle, 254
Paolozzi, Eduardo, 89, 216
Park Church Tower (Glasgow), 213
Park Circus (Glasgow), 214
Parks and gardens, 4
    Edinburgh, 95–96
    Glasgow, 200–201
Parliament Building (Edinburgh), 88, 103
Partick (Glasgow), 157
Passports, 14, 22, 117
Pavilion Theatre (Glasgow), 232
Peckham's (Edinburgh), 80
Pekhams (Glasgow), 188
People's Palace (Glasgow), 197–198, 201, 206
The People's Story (Edinburgh), 87–88, 103
Performing arts
    Edinburgh, 124–128
    Glasgow, 229, 232–233
Pharmacies
    Edinburgh, 52
    Glasgow, 162
Picnic fare
    Edinburgh, 80
    Glasgow, 188
Piping Live! (Glasgow), 19, 202
Planet Out (Edinburgh), 132
Police
    Edinburgh, 52
    Glasgow, 162
Pollok Country Park (Glasgow), 153, 196, 201
Pollok House (Glasgow), 196
Pollokshaws (Glasgow), 157
Pollokshaws Road (Glasgow), 218, 220
Pollokshields (Glasgow), 157
Polo Lounge (Glasgow), 239
Po Na Na (Edinburgh), 129
The Pond Bar (Edinburgh), 131–132
Port Bannatyne, 252
Port Edgar Sailing Centre (near Edinburgh), 98
Post offices
    Edinburgh, 52
    Glasgow, 162
The Pot Still (Glasgow), 9, 237

Pound sterling (£), 15–16
Pre-departure checklist, 11
Prescription medications, 21–22
Prestwick International Airport (near Glasgow), 150
Princes Mall (Edinburgh), 116–117
Princes Square (Glasgow), 221
Princes Street (Edinburgh), 45, 108, 116
Princes Street Gardens (Edinburgh), 95, 112
Provand's Lordship (Glasgow), 198–199, 206
Pubs and bars, 3–4
    Ayr, 243
    Edinburgh, 85, 124, 129–132
        best, 9
        Literary Pub Tour, 96
    Glasgow, 193, 236–238
        best, 9

Queen's Gallery (Edinburgh), 89, 103
Queen's Hall (Edinburgh), 125
Queens Park (Glasgow), 153, 218
Queen Street (Edinburgh), 45, 110
Queen Street Station (Glasgow), 152, 158

Rabbie's Bar (Ayr), 243
Raeburn, Henry, 90, 91, 103
Ragamuffin (Edinburgh), 121
Rainfall, average monthly, 17
Ramsay Garden (Edinburgh), 100
Ramshorn Theatre (Glasgow), 208, 232
Rangers (Glasgow), 203
Real Mary King's Close (Edinburgh), 86–87
Rent-a-Bike Edinburgh, 51, 98
Restaurants. See also Afternoon tea; Restaurant Index
    Edinburgh and environs, 67–80
        best, 8
        by cuisine, 68
        Cupar, 147–148
        family-friendly, 74
        Gullane, 139–140
        late-night, 129
        Leith, 78–80
        Linlithgow, 137

Melrose, 143
New Town, 69–74
Old Town, 75–77
prices, 67
St. Andrews, 148
South Queensferry, 136–137
Southside, 77–78
tipping, 67
West End, 69–74
what's new, 2
Glasgow and environs, 174–188
    Ayrshire, 244
    best, 8
    Commercial Center, 180–184
    Cowal & Kintyre Peninsulas, 251–252
    by cuisine, 175, 178
    family-friendly, 180
    late-night, 235
    Loch Lomond, 253
    Merchant City, 178–180
    prices, 174
    Southside, 187–188
    tipping, 174
    Troon, 248
    The Trossachs, 255
    Turnberry, 248–249
    West End, 184–187
    what's new, 2
Restrooms
    Edinburgh, 53
    Glasgow, 162
Revolver (Glasgow), 239
Robert the Bruce, 141, 146, 254, 257, 259
Rock music
    Edinburgh, 128–129
    Glasgow, 9, 229, 234–236
Roger Billcliffe Fine Art (Glasgow), 225
Rose Street (Edinburgh), 45, 108
Roslin, 136–137
Rosslyn Chapel (Roslin), 136–137
Ross Theatre (Edinburgh), 125, 128
Rothesay Castle (Isle of Bute), 250
Rowling, J. K., 106
Royal and Ancient Golf Club (St. Andrews), 144, 145
Royal Botanic Garden (Edinburgh), 85, 95–96
Royal Commonwealth Pool (Edinburgh), 98

Royal Exchange Square (Glasgow), 208, 209
Royal Highland Show (Edinburgh), 19
Royal Lyceum Theatre (Edinburgh), 124, 125
Royal Mile (Edinburgh), 45, 48, 84
    guided tours, 96
    shopping, 116, 117, 121, 123
    sights and attractions, 81, 84–91
    walking tour, 99–104
Royal Mile Whiskies (Edinburgh), 123
Royal Museum (Edinburgh), 90, 104
The Royal Oak (Edinburgh), 9, 128
Royal Scottish Academy (Edinburgh), 90, 107–108
Royal Scottish Academy of Music and Drama (Glasgow), 229, 234
Royal Scottish National Orchestra (Glasgow), 229, 233–234
Royal Troon Golf Club, 247–248
Rugby, in Edinburgh, 98
Ryanair, 27, 150

Safety, 22
    Edinburgh, 53
    Glasgow, 162
Sailing, in Edinburgh, 98
St. Andrews, 143–145
    accommodations, 148
    golf, 144, 145
    restaurants, 148
St. Andrews Castle, 144
St. Andrews Cathedral, 144
St. Andrews in the Square (music venue; Glasgow), 234
St. Andrew Square (Edinburgh), 111–112
St. Andrew's Square (Glasgow), 206
St. Cuthbert Church (Edinburgh), 108
St. Enoch Shopping Centre (Glasgow), 221, 224
St. Giles Cathedral (Edinburgh), 5, 86, 100, 102
St. James Centre (Edinburgh), 117
St. John's Church (Edinburgh), 108
St. Kentigern (Glasgow). See Glasgow Cathedral

St. Michael's Parish Church (West Lothian), 136
St. Mungo Museum of Religious Life and Art (Glasgow), 199
St. Vincent Street (Glasgow), 209
St. Vincent Street Church (Glasgow), 5, 194, 200, 212
Sala (Edinburgh), 132
Saltmarket (Glasgow), 156
Sanda, 251
Sandy Bell's (Edinburgh), 9, 128
Sauchiehall Street (Glasgow), 210
Schuh (Edinburgh), 123
Schuh (Glasgow), 228
Science Centre (Glasgow), 199
Scotch Whisky Heritage Centre (Edinburgh), 94
The Scotia Bar (Glasgow), 234
Scotland Street School Museum (Glasgow), 198, 199
Scotstoun Leisure Centre (Glasgow), 204
Scott, Walter, 33, 86, 100, 102, 106, 141, 254
    Abbotsford (Melrose), 141
    biographical sketch of, 142
    Monument (Edinburgh), 90, 112
Scottish Ballet (Glasgow), 229, 233
Scottish Chamber Orchestra (Glasgow), 233
Scottish Cycle Safaris (Edinburgh), 51, 98
Scottish Exhibition & Conference Centre (Glasgow), 236
Scottish National Gallery of Modern Art (Edinburgh), 6, 90–91
Scottish National Orchestra (Glasgow), 229, 233–234
Scottish National Photography Centre (Edinburgh), 2
Scottish National Portrait Gallery (Edinburgh), 91
Scottish Open (Loch Lomond), 19
Scottish Opera (Glasgow), 229, 233
Scottish Parliament Building (Edinburgh), 88, 103
Scottish Seabird Centre (North Berwick), 138
Scottish Storytelling Centre (Edinburgh), 2, 87

Scottish Symphony Orchestra (Glasgow), 233
Scottish Tourist Board, 10, 32
Seasons, 17–18
Senior travelers, 24
Shawlands (Glasgow), 153, 220
    picnic fare, 188
    restaurants, 187
Shawlands Cross (Glasgow), 220
Shoe stores
    Edinburgh, 123
    Glasgow, 228
Shopping, 4
    Edinburgh, 116–123
        best buys, 116
        hours, 51
    Glasgow, 221–228
        best buys, 221
        hours, 160
    VAT refund, 117, 227
The Shore (Edinburgh), 9, 79, 114, 132
Sights and attractions. See also Walking tours; and specific sights and attractions
    Edinburgh and environs, 81–97
        favorite experiences, 3–4, 85
        suggested itineraries, 35–41, 81, 84
    Glasgow and environs, 189–202
        favorite experiences, 3–4, 193
        suggested itineraries, 37–41, 192
    what's new, 2
Silverknowes Golf Course (Edinburgh), 98
Smoking, 1, 67, 174
Soccer. See Football
Soletrader (Glasgow), 228
Souter Johnnie's Cottage (Kirkoswald), 245–246
Southern Upland Way, 141
South Leith Parish Church (Edinburgh), 115
South Queensferry, 98, 136–137
Southside (Edinburgh), 45
    accommodations, 64–65
    restaurants, 77–78
Southside (Glasgow), 153, 157, 196–197
    pubs and bars, 238
    restaurants, 187–188
    walking tour, 217–220

Special events, 18–20
Edinburgh, 96–97
Glasgow, 202
Spectator sports
Edinburgh, 97–98
Glasgow, 204
The Stand
Edinburgh, 128
Glasgow, 234
Starry Starry Night (Glasgow), 226
STA Travel, 25, 28
Stevenson, Robert Louis, 33, 66, 86, 96, 100, 106, 110, 111, 131
biographical sketch of, 92
Stewart's (Dougal) Monument (Edinburgh), 94
Stirling, 254–255
Stirling Castle, 254
Stockbridge (Edinburgh), 48, 110
accommodations, 58, 59
nightlife, 125, 130
picnic fare, 80
restaurants, 74
Story Telling Festival (Edinburgh), 19
Strathbungo (Glasgow), 218
Strathclyde Passenger Transport (Glasgow), 158
Student travelers, 24–25
The Sub Club (Glasgow), 236
Surgeons' Hall Museums (Edinburgh), 94, 106
Swimming pools
Edinburgh, 98
Glasgow, 204

Talbot Rice Gallery (Edinburgh), 94, 106
The Tall Ship at Glasgow Harbour, 199–200
Tam O'Shanter Experience (Alloway), 244
Tam O'Shanter Inn (Ayr), 242
Tantallon Castle, 138
Tarbert, 251, 252
Tarbolton, 242, 245–246
Tartan Gift Shop (Edinburgh), 122
Tartans, 262
Edinburgh, 121
Glasgow, 227
Taxes, VAT, 117, 227

Taxis
Edinburgh, 50
Glasgow, 160
Tea. See Afternoon tea
Telephones, 15
Temperatures, average monthly, 17
Tenement House (Glasgow), 194–195
Teviot Place (Edinburgh), 107
Theater
Edinburgh, 124–125
Glasgow, 229, 232–233
Theatre Royal (Glasgow), 189, 233
Theatre Workshop (Edinburgh), 125
Thistle Books (Glasgow), 225
Thomas Pink (Glasgow), 226
Thomson, Alexander "Greek," 7, 193, 194, 196, 197, 200, 210, 212, 214, 217, 218
Tighnabruaich, 251–252
Timberbush Tours (Edinburgh), 140
Tim Wright Antiques (Glasgow), 224
Tipping, 67, 174
Toilets. See Restrooms
Tollcross (Edinburgh), 48
Tollcross Park Leisure Centre (Glasgow), 204
Top of Leith Walk (Edinburgh), 49, 111, 132
Tourist information. See Visitor information
Tours. See also Walking tours
ecotourism, 22–23
escorted, 31
organized
Edinburgh, 96, 140
Glasgow, 201–202
package, 30–31
Train travel
Edinburgh, 44
Glasgow, 150, 152, 242
to Scotland, 30
Tramway (Glasgow), 217, 229, 233
Transcentre (Glasgow), 158
Transport, Museum of (Glasgow), 2, 196
Transportation
Edinburgh, 49–51
Glasgow, 158–160
Traquair House (Innerleithen), 142–143

Traveler's checks, 17
Traveling
to Edinburgh, 43–44
to Glasgow, 150, 152
to Scotland, 27–30
Travel insurance, 20–21
Travelline Scotland (Glasgow), 242
Traverse Theatre (Edinburgh), 124, 125
Trinity College (now Trinity House; Glasgow), 213
Trinity House (Edinburgh), 115
Trip-cancellation insurance, 20
Triptych, 18
Tron Kirk (Edinburgh), 102
Tron Steeple (Glasgow), 206, 208
Tron Theatre (Glasgow), 229, 232–233
Troon, 247–248
The Trossachs, 254–255
Turnberry, 248–249
Turnberry Hotel Golf Courses, 248, 249

Underground (Glasgow), 158
University Gardens (Glasgow), 216
University of Edinburgh, 94, 104, 106
University of Glasgow, 195, 214, 216, 232
University of St. Andrews, 144
Urban Outfitters (Glasgow), 226
Usher Hall (Edinburgh), 124, 128

VAT (value-added tax) refund, 117, 227
The Vaults (Edinburgh), 114
Victorian Village (Glasgow), 224–225
Virgin Megastore (Edinburgh), 123
Visitor information, 10–11
Ayrshire, 242
Edinburgh, 44
Glasgow, 152–153
Voltaire & Rousseau (Glasgow), 225
Vroni's Wine Bar (Glasgow), 237
Vue Edinburgh (Edinburgh), 133

Walker Slater (Edinburgh), 120

Walking tours
Edinburgh, 96, 99–115
Leith, 112–115
New Town, 107–112
Old Town and The Royal Mile, 99–104
south of The Royal Mile, 104–107
Glasgow, 201–202, 205–220
Commercial Center, 209–213
Merchant City and East End, 205–209
Southside, 217–220
West End, 213–217
Wallace, William, 242–243, 254, 259
Wallace Monument (Stirling), 254
Wallace Tower (Ayr), 242–243
Waterloo Bar (Glasgow), 239
Waterstones (Edinburgh), 117
Waterstones (Glasgow), 225
Waverley Bridge Travelshop (Edinburgh), 50
Waverley Excursions (Glasgow), 201, 202
Waverley Station (Edinburgh), 44, 52, 134
Weather, 17
Weather forecasts
Edinburgh, 53
Glasgow, 162
Websites, 11, 25
Wemyss Bay (Bute), 250
West Bow (Edinburgh), 104
West Brewing Company (Glasgow), 237–238
West End (Edinburgh), 45, 48
accommodations, 63–64
restaurants, 69–74
West End (Glasgow), 153, 157, 193
accommodations, 169–173
picnic fare, 188
pubs and bars, 238
restaurants, 184–187
sights and attractions, 195–196
walking tour, 213–217
West End Cycles (Glasgow), 160, 203
West End Festival (Glasgow), 19, 202
West Highland Way, 252, 253
West Lothian, 134, 136

Whisky, 247
Edinburgh, 114, 123
Scotch Whisky Heritage Centre, 94
Glasgow, 9, 237
Whistler, James McNeill, 6, 195, 216
Whuppity Scourie (Glasgow), 18
The Wicker Man (movie), 246
Willow Tea Rooms (Glasgow), 184, 198, 210
Winter Gardens (Glasgow), 197, 201
The Witchery Tours (Edinburgh), 96
Woodlands Hill (Glasgow), 157, 213
Woodside Terrace (Glasgow), 213
Woolens. *See* Knits and woolens
World Pipe Band Championships (Glasgow), 19, 202
Writers' Museum (Edinburgh), 86, 100

Zoo, Edinburgh, 91

ACCOMMODATIONS— EDINBURGH AND ENVIRONS

A-Haven Townhouse, 60, 66
Aonach Mor, 65
Ardmor House, 66
Balmoral Hotel, 7, 55, 69, 76
The Bank Hotel, 62
The Bonham, 7, 63
Borough, 65
Burt's Hotel (Melrose), 143
Caledonian Hilton Edinburgh, 55
The Carlton Hotel, 60–61
Channings, 58
Chester Residence, 2, 63
Edinburgh Marriott, 54
The Edinburgh Residence, 63
George Hotel, 1, 58
The Glasshouse, 58
Greenside Hotel, 60
Holyrood Hotel, 61–62
The Howard, 7, 55
Ibis, 62
Keavil House Hotel (Crossford), 147
Macdonald Roxburghe Hotel, 58–59

Malmaison, 7, 65–66
Old Course Hotel (St. Andrews), 148
Old Waverley Hotel, 59
Pilrig House Apartment, 66
Point Hotel, 64
Premier Travel Inn, 62
Prestonfield, 64–65
Radisson SAS Hotel, 62
Ramada Mount Royal, 59
The Scotsman, 61
Seven Danube Street, 59
Sheraton Grand Hotel, 7, 63–64
16 Lynedoch Place, 64
Thrums Hotel, 60, 65
Tigerlily, 1–2, 131
The Walton, 59–60
The Witchery by the Castle, 7, 61, 75

ACCOMMODATIONS— GLASGOW AND ENVIRONS

Abbotsford Hotel (Ayr), 244
ABode, 167, 181
Albion Hotel, 170
Ambassador Hotel, 170
Argyll Hotel, 170, 171
Babbity Bowster, 9, 163, 166, 179, 237
Bewleys Hotel, 168
Brunswick Hotel, 7, 166
Carlton George Hotel, 183
City Inn, 170–171
Corus Hotel, 169
De Vere Cameron House (near Balloch), 253
Devoncove Hotel, 171
Drover's Inn (Inverarnan), 253
Fairfield House (Ayr), 244
Glasgow Loft Apartments, 2, 167
Glenapp Castle (Ballantrae), 249
Hilton Glasgow Hotel, 167
Ibis, 169
Kelvingrove Hotel, 171
Kirkland House, 172–173
Kirklee Hotel, 171, 172
Langs, 167–168
Lochgreen House Hotel (Troon), 248
Malin Court Hotel (Turnberry), 249
Malmaison, 7, 168
Manor Park Hotel, 172
Merchant Lodge Hotel, 166

Millennium Hotel Glasgow, 168
One Devonshire Gardens,
    7, 169–171
Piersland House Hotel (Troon),
    248
Premier Lodge, 169
Quality Hotel Glasgow, 169
Rab Ha's, 166
Radisson SAS, 169
The Town House, 8, 172
Travel Inn, 166
Tulip Inn, 169
Westin Turnberry Resort, 249
The Wickets Hotel, 172

RESTAURANTS—
EDINBURGH AND
ENVIRONS

Atrium, 8, 69
The Baked Potato Shop, 74
Barioja, 75
Bell's Diner, 74
blue bar café, 73
The Boat House (South
    Queensferry), 136–137
Burt's Hotel (Melrose), 143
Café Royal Oyster Bar, 73
Calistoga, 2, 78
Champany Inn (Champany
    Corner), 137
Chapters Bistro (Melrose), 143
Clarinda's Tearoom, 76
Creel Restaurant (Dunbar), 139
David Bann's Vegetarian
    Restaurant, 8, 75–76
Dome Grill Room and Bar, 69
Dusit, 73
Favorit, 129
Fishers Bistro, 79
Forth Floor Restaurant,
    8, 69, 72
Gordon's Trattoria, 129
The Grain Store, 75
Greywalls (Gullane), 139–140
Halcyon (Peebles), 143
Haldanes Restaurant, 72
Henderson's Salad Table, 74
Howies, 76
Kebab Mahal, 8, 78
La Garrigue, 76
La Potiniere (Gullane), 140

Lazio, 129
Le Café St. Honoré, 73
Livingston's (Linlithgow), 137
Macsween of Edinburgh, 72
The Marque Central, 73
Namaste, 76–77
Number One, 69
Off the Wall, 75
Oloroso, 8, 72
Ostlers Close (Cupar), 147
Peat Inn (Cupar), 147–148
Plaisir du Chocolat, 76
Restaurant Martin Wishart,
    8, 78–79
Rhubarb, 77–78
Santini, 72
The Seafood Restaurant
    (St. Andrews), 148
The Shore Bar & Restaurant,
    9, 79, 114, 132
Spoon, 8, 77
Sweet Melindas, 78
Time 4 Thai, 2, 74
The Tower, 77
Valvona and Crolla Caffe Bar,
    74, 80
The Vintners Rooms, 79
Wannaburger, 77
Zinc Bar & Grill, 79–80

RESTAURANTS—
GLASGOW AND
ENVIRONS

An Lochan (Tighnabruaich),
    251–252
Art Lover's Café, 187
Balbir's, 185
Bar Gandolfi, 179
Bella Napoli, 187
Bistro du Sud, 180
Brian Maule at Chardon d'Or,
    180
The Buttery, 184
Café Cossachok, 178
Cafe Gandolfi, 8, 179
Café Mao, 178
Canton Express, 235
Charcoals, 235
China Buffet King, 180
City Merchant, 178

Corinthian, 179
Creagan House (Strathyre), 255
The Dhabba, 8, 179
Dragon-i, 182
Enterkine House (Annbank),
    244
Étain, 180–181
Fouter's Bistro (Ayr), 244
Fratelli Sarti, 183
Gamba, 8, 181
Grassroots Café, 186
Harry Ramsden's, 187–188
Ho Wong, 181
The Inn at Kippen, 255
Konaki, 186–187
La Parmigiana, 186
MacCallums of Troon Oyster
    Bar (Troon), 248
Malmaison Brasserie, 182
Michael Caines @ ABode,
    2, 8, 167, 181
Monachyle Mhor (Balquhidder),
    255
Mono, 179–180
Mother India, 185
Mussel Inn, 182
No. Sixteen, 185–186
Papingo, 182–183
Rogano, 181–182
Russian Tavern at the Port
    Royal Hotel (Port Ban-
    natyne), 252
Schottische, 179
The Seafood Cabin (Tarbert),
    252
Spice Gardens, 235
Stravaigin Café Bar, 187
Tchai Ovna, 184
Two Fat Ladies, 186
Ubiquitous Chip, 184–185
University Café, 180
Urban Bar and Brasserie, 2
Urban Grill, 2, 188
Wagamama, 2, 183
Wee Curry Shop, 8, 183
Where the Monkey Sleeps,
    183–184
The Wild Bergamot, 8, 185
Willow Tea Rooms,
    184, 198, 210
Windows Restaurant, 183

FROMMER'S® CRUISE GUIDES

Alaska Cruises & Ports of Call

Cruises & Ports of Call

European Cruises & Ports of Call

FROMMER'S® NATIONAL PARK GUIDES

Algonquin Provincial Park
Banff & Jasper
Grand Canyon

National Parks of the American West
Rocky Mountain
Yellowstone & Grand Teton

Yosemite and Sequoia & Kings
  Canyon
Zion & Bryce Canyon

FROMMER'S® MEMORABLE WALKS

London
New York

Paris
Rome

San Francisco

FROMMER'S® WITH KIDS GUIDES

Chicago
Hawaii
Las Vegas
London

National Parks
New York City
San Francisco

Toronto
Walt Disney World® & Orlando
Washington, D.C.

SUZY GERSHMAN'S BORN TO SHOP GUIDES

France
Hong Kong, Shanghai & Beijing
Italy

London
New York

Paris
San Francisco

FROMMER'S® IRREVERENT GUIDES

Amsterdam
Boston
Chicago
Las Vegas

London
Los Angeles
Manhattan
Paris

Rome
San Francisco
Walt Disney World®
Washington, D.C.

FROMMER'S® BEST-LOVED DRIVING TOURS

Austria
Britain
California
France

Germany
Ireland
Italy
New England

Northern Italy
Scotland
Spain
Tuscany & Umbria

THE UNOFFICIAL GUIDES®

Adventure Travel in Alaska
Beyond Disney
California with Kids
Central Italy
Chicago
Cruises
Disneyland®
England
Florida
Florida with Kids

Hawaii
Ireland
Las Vegas
London
Maui
Mexico's Best Beach Resorts
Mini Mickey
New Orleans
New York City

Paris
San Francisco
South Florida including Miami &
  the Keys
Walt Disney World®
Walt Disney World® for
  Grown-ups
Walt Disney World® with Kids
Washington, D.C.

SPECIAL-INTEREST TITLES

Athens Past & Present
Best Places to Raise Your Family
Cities Ranked & Rated
500 Places to Take Your Kids Before They Grow Up
Frommer's Best Day Trips from London
Frommer's Best RV & Tent Campgrounds
  in the U.S.A.

Frommer's Exploring America by RV
Frommer's NYC Free & Dirt Cheap
Frommer's Road Atlas Europe
Frommer's Road Atlas Ireland
Great Escapes From NYC Without Wheels
Retirement Places Rated

FROMMER'S® PHRASEFINDER DICTIONARY GUIDES

French

Italian

Spanish

THE NEW TRAVELOCITY GUARANTEE

EVERYTHING YOU BOOK WILL BE RIGHT, OR WE'LL WORK WITH OUR TRAVEL PARTNERS TO MAKE IT RIGHT, RIGHT AWAY.

*To drive home the point,
we're going to use the word "right" in every single sentence.*

Let's get right to it. Right to the meat! Only Travelocity guarantees everything about your booking will be right, or we'll work with our travel partners to make it right, right away. Right on!

Here's a picture taken smack dab right in the middle of Antigua, where the guarantee also covers you.

The guarantee covers all but one of the items pictured to the right.

For example, what if the ocean view you booked actually looks out at a downright ugly parking lot? You'd be right to call – we're there for you. And no one in their right mind would be pleased to learn the rental car place has closed and left them stranded. Call Travelocity and we'll help get you back on the right track.

Now, you may be thinking, "Yeah, right, I'm so sure." That's OK; you have the right to remain skeptical. That is until we mention help is always right around the corner. Call us right off the bat, knowing that our customer service reps are there for you 24/7. Righting wrongs. Left and right.

Now if you're guessing there are some things we can't control, like the weather, well you're right. But we can help you with most things – to get all the details in righting,* visit **travelocity.com/guarantee**.

*Sorry, spelling things right is one of the few things not covered under the guarantee.

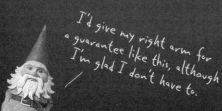

I'd give my right arm for a guarantee like this, although I'm glad I don't have to.

travelocity
You'll never roam alone.

IF YOU BOOK IT, IT SHOULD BE THERE.

Only Travelocity guarantees it will be, or we'll work with our travel partners to make it right, right away. So if you're missing a balcony or anything else you booked, just call us 24/7. **1**-888-TRAVELOCITY.

travelocity

You'll never roam alone.